HOW
ONE MAN
TRANSFORMED
A TOWN

Winslow 1640–1770
and William Lowndes

The Buckinghamshire Archaeological Society

has members throughout the historic county of Buckinghamshire and beyond, including the new city of Milton Keynes. Their interests, despite the society's name, range across the spectrum of history, archaeology, natural history and historic buildings.

The society supports the research, understanding and preservation of the county's historic assets, publishes the annual journal *Records of Buckinghamshire* and regular books and papers, and runs a variety of lectures and outings on historic subjects.

To learn more about the society's activities, see our website at **https://bas1.org.uk** or visit our Library in the County Museum in Aylesbury. Details of our other recent publications are in the back of this book.

• **If you would like to join the society**, membership details are also inside the back of this book, or go on-line to **https://bas1.org.uk/membership-2**

How one man transformed a town

Winslow 1640–1770 and William Lowndes

DAVID NOY

COVER: A view of the town around 1900
with Winslow Hall on the right
– from a photograph by J H Turnham
and, right, the portrait of William Lowndes
by Sir Godfrey Kneller.
(Crown Copyright ©
UK Government Art Collection (GAC 0/223).)

Buckinghamshire Archaeological Society

Published November 2020
Buckinghamshire Archaeological Society
County Museum, Church Street, Aylesbury,
Buckinghamshire HP20 2QP, UK
Website: https://bas1.org.uk

ISBN 978-0-9957177-6-3

First published in 2020.

Edited, designed and typeset by Peter Marsden
Printed and bound by BookPrintingUK, Peterborough, England.

Contents

Illustrations

Author's Preface

It is easy for anyone who is familiar with Winslow to take its present appearance for granted: a mixture of brick and timber-framed houses dominated by a Grade I listed mansion; a main road running through from north-west to south-east; farmhouses out of sight in the fields; well-preserved grass-covered ridge and furrow (where it has not yet been built over); shops and offices providing a wide range of services; a variety of schools and places of worship including Buckinghamshire's oldest nonconformist meeting-house; a large open space in the middle of the town giving a clear view from Winslow Hall to Granborough.

Most of these features would have surprised anyone who was alive in 1640, and they are all due to changes in the following 130 years. Many were directly or indirectly the work of one extraordinary man, William Lowndes (1652–1724), who transformed the town he left when he was 15.

This book covers the period from the English Civil War to enclosure of the common fields. The former loomed over Lowndes' life as the Second World War does for those born in the 1950s, and the latter was the inevitable conclusion of his land purchases. At the same time Winslow was in many respects a typical small market town whose development reflects broader trends and national events, and its fairly well-documented history is of much more than local interest.

The chapters of this book which deal with the main themes of Winslow's history and the role played by William Lowndes have been interspersed with case-studies of individual families which illustrate how people's lives were affected and the causes of their failures and successes.

The Author

David Noy is a native of Winslow, where his great-grandfather Arthur Midgley arrived in 1867.

He runs the Winslow History website (www.winslow-history.org.uk) and is also author of *Winslow in 1556: The survey of the manor*, published by the Buckinghamshire Archaeological Society in 2013. He is also the editor of the Buckinghamshire Record Society.

By profession he is a Lecturer in Classics who has also published widely on Roman history

Acknowledgements

I am grateful to Peter Marsden and the Buckinghamshire Archaeological Society for taking on this book and preparing it for publication, and to John Broad for reading the draft and making many suggestions. I would also like to thank Julian Hunt and the late Norman Saving for much discussion and information, Terry Foley for providing photographs, and everyone who has transcribed documents for the Winslow History website, particularly Lyn Robinson, Vin Kenny, Nick Abraham, Christine Dodds and Sue Stainthorpe. I am grateful to many other people for their help, including Ian Beckett, Jill Borrow, David Critchley, Jill Elliott, Paul Goring, Ed Grimsdale, Ken Harris, Andrew Kemp, Diana Kemp, the late Geoff Kirk, Mary Munro-Hill, Clive Rodgers, Peter and Rose Scott, Austin Walker, Anne Watson, Sue Webb and the staff of the Centre for Buckinghamshire Studies.

Sources and their handling

Sources are noted at the foot of each page and in the Bibliography. Transcriptions or summaries of many of the documents referred to can be found on the Winslow History website, www.winslow-history.org.uk, and many official documents can be found through British History Online, www.british-history.ac.uk.

Quotations of English text follow the original spellings but capitalisation has been regularised and some punctuation added. For sums of **money**, shillings and pence have usually been omitted. For most people mentioned, **years of birth and death** are those of their recorded baptism and burial in the parish registers.

Dates: Until 1751 the new year began not on 1 January but on 25 March. The Gregorian calendar was adopted in September 1751 after the omission of eleven days, and the year 1752 began on 1 January. However dates in this book have been rendered as 'new style' as if the new year always started on 1 January; for example a date written as 20 February 1750 in the original document is given as 20 February 1751. William Lowndes, among others of his time, was aware of the discrepancy, and often wrote dates in the form '1st January 1710/11', indicating both old and new styles.

Glossary

Admission	Owners of copyhold property had to be admitted to it at the manor court.
Advowson	The right to appoint a vicar, which in Winslow belonged to the Crown.
Alehouse recognizances	Pledges for the good conduct of alehouses, which provide lists of all licensed premises from 1753.
Allotment	Land allotted to someone at enclosure.
Amercement	Payment to the lord of the manor for an offence; the offender was said to be 'in mercy'.
Annuity	An annual income for life, often bequeathed in a will.
Archdeacon	The church official responsible for proving wills and controlling morals. For Winslow this was the Archdeacon of St Albans.
Assizes	Court held twice a year at Aylesbury or Buckingham with power to impose capital punishment.
Association Roll	Record of an oath of loyalty to William III in 1696.
Brazier	A worker in brass.
Buttery	A room or building for storing barrels.
Chaise	A light, horse-drawn carriage, smaller than a coach.

Chapman	An itinerant seller of general goods
Chirurgeon	Surgeon.
Close Rolls	Chancery records containing conveyances of property.
Collection	Alternative name for poor relief.
Common recovery	*see* Procedure of Common Recovery.
Copyhold	Property held from the lord of the manor by copy of court roll.
Cordwainer	A maker and repairer of shoes.
Cottesloe Hundred	The administrative unit to which Winslow belonged for many purposes.
Currier	Someone who dresses tanned leather.
Delinquent	The term used for Royalist supporters in the Civil War after their defeat.
Demesne	Land farmed or managed directly by the lord of the manor.
Desperate debts	Bad debts.
Dissenter	A Protestant not conforming to the Church of England.
Dower	A widow's claim to a third of her husband's property for the rest of her life, even if she remarried.
Entail	An arrangement which governed the future inheritance of property, for example providing for it only to go to male heirs.
Execution	The enforcement of a court judgment.
Farmer	Someone who made a fixed payment ('farm') for the right to run a property or service; also used in its modern sense.
Feet of Fines	Official record of transfers of property ownership.

Fine	Payment to the lord of the manor when copyhold property was transferred.
Frankpledge	*see* View of frankpledge.
Glebe	Land belonging to the church which was farmed or rented out by the vicar.
Goody	Short for goodwife. 'Mrs' was only used for women of high status; Goody was the prefix for others.
Hayward	Overseer of the common fields.
Heriot	Payment to the lord of the manor when the owner of copyhold property died or gave up all his/her property. It could be the most valuable individual possession or a cash sum.
Husbandman	A small-scale farmer.
Jointure	Property to provide an income for a widow, usually fixed in a marriage settlement.
JPs	Justices of the Peace, magistrates.
Levellers	Prominent radical movement in the 1640s and 1650s.
Mantua-maker	A dressmaker.
Marriage settlement	Property arrangement which usually provided a home and income for a married couple and/or made arrangements for younger children.
Mercer	Dealer in textiles and haberdashery.
Messuage	A substantial house with associated land.
Milkhouse	A dairy.
Nuncupative will	An oral will made before witnesses shortly before death.
Oath of Allegiance	An oath of loyalty to the Hanoverian dynasty taken in 1723.

Overseer (of will)	Someone appointed to help an executor or (usually) executrix.
Overseer of the poor	Parish official responsible for collecting and spending the poor rate.
Peruke	A wig.
Plump, to	To cast only one vote in an election where the voter had two.
Posse Comitatus	A survey of able-bodied adult males that was carried out in 1798[1]
Primogeniture	Inheritance by the eldest son. This was the 'custom of the manor' for copyhold property in Winslow.
Probate inventory	An inventory of the deceased's personal estate, taken and valued by two or more 'appraisers'.
Procedure of Common Recovery	An elaborate legal fiction which was used to break an entail or clear other anomalies: the owner surrendered the property to a third party who, after various 'warrants', transferred it to the intended recipient. William Lowndes insisted that vendors should 'suffer a recovery' if there was any doubt about their right to sell.
Quarter Sessions	Meeting of the county's JPs held four times a year.
Quit-rent	Payment to the lord of the manor for copyhold property. By the period studied here it was usually a nominal amount which bore no relation to the market rent (sometimes called rack-rent).
Rack-rent	Market rent as opposed to quit-rent.

---

[1] Ian Beckett (editor), *The Buckinghamshire Posse Comitatus 1798* (Aylesbury: Buckinghamshire Records Society 1985).

Rectory	The right to collect the great tithes, which in Winslow in this period did not belong to the church.
Regicide	One of the men who signed Charles I's death warrant.
Reversion	The ownership of property after someone's life-interest or other temporary tenure has expired.
Rubbing brick	High-quality brick with a smooth surface.
Sheriff	The county officer whose duties included executing court judgments and organising elections.
Standards	Potentially moveable items treated as fixtures of a house.
Tallow Chandler	Candlemaker.
Tithes	A tenth of agricultural produce and profits, payable to the vicar (small tithes) or owner of the rectory (great tithes).
Tithingman	Manorial official.
Vestry	A meeting of ratepayers for parish business.
View of frankpledge	A meeting of the manor court which appointed officers for the following year and dealt with minor offences; held annually at Winslow during this period.
Virgate	Medieval land measurement, about 30 acres.
Visitation of Bucks	An inspection by heralds of coats of arms and pedigrees.
Whitesmith	A worker in tin, pewter or similar metal.
Yeoman	A substantial farmer, on a larger scale than a husbandman. In Winslow the term did not have any specific meaning.

Abbreviations

BAS	Buckinghamshire Archaeological Society
BL	British Library
BQS	Buckinghamshire Quarter Sessions[2]
BRS	Buckinghamshire Record Society
CBS	Centre for Buckinghamshire Studies
f.	folio
HALS	Hertfordshire Archives and Local Studies
JP	Justice of the Peace
LMA	London Metropolitan Archives
m.	membrane (in a roll)
ODNB	*Oxford Dictionary of National Biography*
OED	*Oxford English Dictionary*
p.a.	per annum, once a year
TNA	The National Archives
VCH	*Victoria County History*
WMC	Winslow manor court
WMCB	*Winslow Manor Court Books 1327–1377 and 1423–1460,* edited by David Noy (BRS volumes 35 and 36, 2011)

---

[2] Printed calendars for the Quarter Sessions up to 1733 are available at www.bucksrecsoc.org.uk/quartersessions.html. References given in this book are by date rather than page.

MAP 1: **Winslow and its surrounding settlements**

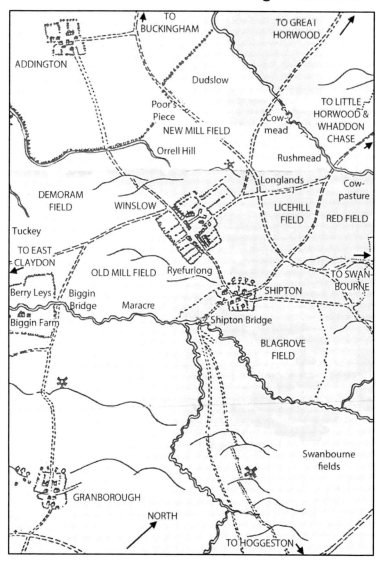

TO BUCKINGHAM

TO GREAT HORWOOD

ADDINGTON

Dudslow

Poor's Piece

NEW MILL FIELD

Cow-mead

TO LITTLE HORWOOD & WHADDON CHASE

Orrell Hill

Rushmead

Longlands

Cow-pasture

DEMORAM FIELD

WINSLOW

LICEHILL FIELD

RED FIELD

Tuckey

TO EAST CLAYDON

OLD MILL FIELD

Ryefurlong

SHIPTON

TO SWAN-BOURNE

Berry Leys

Biggin Bridge

Maracre

Shipton Bridge

Biggin Farm

BLAGROVE FIELD

Swanbourne fields

GRANBOROUGH

NORTH

TO HOGGESTON

MAP 2: The town of Winslow

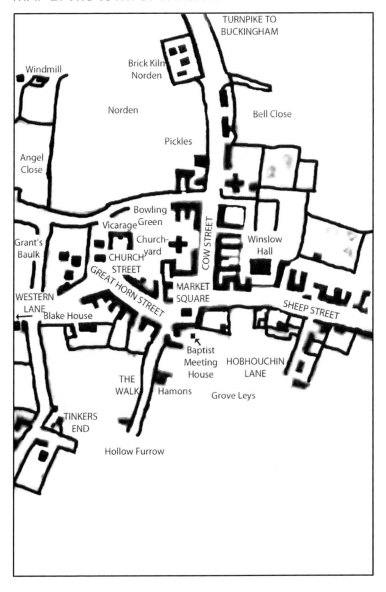

TURNPIKE TO
BUCKINGHAM

Windmill

Brick Kiln
Norden

Norden

Bell Close

Pickles

Angel
Close

Bowling
Green

Vicarage

Church-
yard

Grant's
Baulk

CHURCH
STREET

Winslow
Hall

COW STREET

GREAT HORN STREET

MARKET
SQUARE

WESTERN
LANE

SHEEP STREET

Blake House

Baptist
Meeting
House

HOBHOUCHIN
LANE

THE
WALK

Hamons

Grove Leys

TINKERS
END

Hollow Furrow

MAP 3: **Buildings around the Market Square**

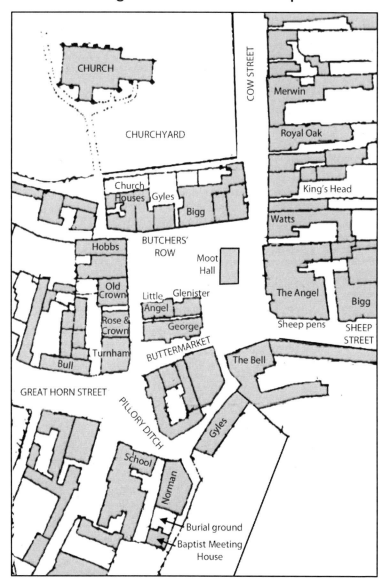

Chapter 1:
Winslow in 1640

Winslow in 1640 was a commercial centre providing a weekly market and services for surrounding villages, but it was also an agricultural community with a system of farming based on open fields. It was centred on the Market Square (more often referred to as Market Place) and three main streets with significant names: Great Horn Street, Sheep Street and Cow Street. Even the vicarage was basically a farmhouse. Most tradesmen also farmed: the draper Silvester Stutsbury owned twenty acres and had 'a hovell with some hey and beanes', and the glover Nicholas Mason kept cattle, sheep and pigs.[1]

Winslow was not on a major road, and anyone travelling from Aylesbury to Buckingham went through East Claydon instead. Nicholas Mitchell who kept The Bull used to 'ride to Buckingham market which was five miles & to Leighton which was seaven miles distant'.[2] It is now nearly thirteen miles from Winslow to Leighton Buzzard, but in the seventeenth century it was considered to be a nearer place than Aylesbury even if the miles were longer than later statute miles. The Leighton road also took people to St Albans, where they had to travel to prove their wills or attend the Archdeacon's court.

To the north-east of Winslow was Whaddon Chase, still at this time heavily wooded and not easy to travel through: there is a story (probably apocryphal) of a man losing his way there and only finding it again by hearing the church bells of Winslow, so that he left a bequest for an annual payment to the ringers.[3]

---

[1] Hertfordshire Archives (HALS), A25/3025 (1629) and A25/2914 (1626).
[2] The National Archives (TNA), C8/182/185 (1664).
[3] *Northampton Mercury*, 4 April 1902 (written by A J Clear, son of the Winslow historian Arthur Clear).

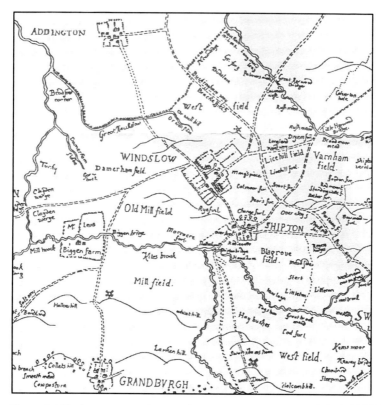

Figure 1: Winslow, surrounding settlements and fields on the map of the estates of Sir John Fortescue drawn in 1599.[4]

Ownership of the manor

After being an estate of St Albans Abbey for more than seven centuries, the ownership of the manor of Winslow remained with the Crown from 1539 until it was sold to Sir John Fortescue of Salden near Mursley in 1599. Fortescue's son sold it to James I's favourite, George Villiers, in 1619. Villiers, then Marquess (later

---

[4] This is a tracing of the original made by Barbara Hurman, Brendan Murphy and John Small for R A Croft and D C Mynard, *The Changing Landscape of Milton* Keynes (Buckinghamshire Archaeological Society (BAS) 1993).

Duke) of Buckingham, already owned the confiscated estates of Lord Grey of Wilton around Whaddon and Bletchley, but did not go much further as a serious landowner in Buckinghamshire.

Whaddon Chase would have attracted him for hunting purposes, but there is no reason to suppose that he ever visited Winslow. Winslow had never had a resident lord of the manor, and, after a brief period in which Fortescue took a close interest, it returned to being a source of income for an absentee owner.

Villiers was assassinated in 1628, so in 1640 the manor of Winslow was in the hands of his widow Catherine and her second husband Randall MacDonnell, second Earl of Antrim, as part of her dower. In 1635 they handed it over to trustees who then made a ten-year agreement which put it under the management of a Winslow resident, Peter Fige the elder.[5] He took the tithes of hay, corn and grain, and held the office of bailiff or steward. His headquarters was 'the stewards seate and chamber thereupon builded called the Mote [Moot] Hall scituate in the Markett Place', and he took the tolls of all fairs and markets.[6]

The Figes were Winslow's leading family, but they were of little significance within the Buckinghamshire gentry, and in fact Peter had led the tenantry in a long dispute with the Fortescues at the beginning of the century.

The manor court

Much of the evidence for the whole period of this book comes from the records of the manor court, so a brief explanation of its functions is necessary. The manor court worked in much the same way as it had in the Middle Ages.[7] It normally met twice a year, but there were sometimes extra sessions for specific business. One of the meetings was the view of frankpledge,[8] which appointed the

---

[5] British Library (BL) Add..Ch 53940. For details of the Fige family and their family tree see pages 26-30.
[6] Centre for Buckinghamshire Studies (CBS) D/LO/4/1 m.11.
[7] See *Winslow Manor Court Books (WMCB)* for the medieval texts and their background.
[8] For definitions of this and other terms see the Glossary on pages xii-xvi.

manorial officers, including the constables who were in charge of maintaining order.

Most business was performed by the jury of between twelve and twenty-four men whose work became slightly more rewarding in 1701 (if not earlier) when William Lowndes started providing them with money for drink.[9] They represented Winslow and the 'members': Shipton (a hamlet within the parish of Winslow), Little Horwood and Granborough. All the manor's tenants were expected to attend the court and all adult male residents had to attend the view of frankpledge, and as a result each court roll contains a list of people who were amerced (fined) for non-attendance.

Almost all property in Winslow in 1640 was copyhold: it was held by copy of court roll from the lord of the manor, to whom a yearly quit-rent was payable, usually about 3d per acre for land and a few pence for a house. Technically all copyholders were tenants, but the system effectively gave them security as long as they made the appropriate payments, so for the rest of this book they will be referred to as owners. Under an agreement made with the Fortescues in 1613 after many years of wrangling, the payments were fixed at 2s per acre when land was sold or inherited and 5s for a house without land. The sums remained unchanged for the rest of Winslow's manorial history, which lasted until 1923.

Heriot was payable when someone died or surrendered their entire holding. This payment was the most valuable individual possession of the tenant, which was usually an animal but could be a household item or even a tree. It is likely that the heriots were often bought back at the value recorded, and in many cases the heriot was only expressed as a sum of money, but even as late as 1799 a cow valued at £14 was taken for the lord of the manor's own use.[10] The only freehold apart from Biggin Farm was 60 acres in the hands of the Paxton family. In the period 1640–1770 there was very little creation of new freehold tenures, something in

---

[9] Folger Shakespeare Library, W.a.147 f.63: account book of William Lowndes.
[10] Arthur Clear, *The King's Village in Demesne* (Winslow, 1894), 11.

which Winslow differed from the general trend.[11]

The main business of the manor court was transfers of property by sale or inheritance. The procedure for selling copyhold property involved a surrender into the lord's hands followed by a grant by the lord to the purchaser. The court was not interested in the payment made by purchaser to vendor, which is almost never recorded, but only in what was due to the lord. It was also possible to mortgage property by a conditional surrender which was cancelled when the loan was repaid.

The court was also responsible for the management of the common fields. It dealt with anti-social offences such as blocking the highway or causing a fire hazard, but rarely with matters of a criminal nature or serious disputes since it could not award damages above £2.

Biggin Farm

There was a medieval building of some sort at Biggin, adjacent to the brook between Winslow and Granborough, which was used by St Albans Abbey and its agents.[12] There was probably a chapel for the use of monastic visitors, but contrary to popular belief it is unlikely that any monks ever lived there. It seems to have been separated from the rest of the estate before the Dissolution of the monasteries, and came into the hands of the Lee family.

The 1599 estate map (*figure 1*) shows Biggin as a clearly defined block of land consisting of 180 freehold acres in Winslow and about 100 acres in Granborough. It was bought in 1628 by Emanuel Scrope, Earl of Sunderland.[13]

Scrope died in 1630, having given Biggin to Martha Janes, his mistress and the mother of his children, for her life.[14] It had been

---

[11] Christopher Clay, 'Landlords and estate management in England', in Joan Thirsk (editor), *The Agrarian History of England and Wales volume 2 1640–1750: Agrarian Change* (Cambridge: Cambridge University Press, 1985), 119–297, 208.

[12] See for example *WMCB*, 14 May 1431.

[13] TNA, CP25/2/397/4CHASITRIN.

[14] For the background to this story see David Noy, 'Martha Janes (1601–1687), An earl's mistress: from Turville via Winslow and Granborough to the siege of Bolton Castle', *Records of Buckinghamshire* 60 (2020).

Martha's main residence until 1630, and she appears to have been occasionally resident in 1640, but she also had the use of a manor house in Nottinghamshire and of Bolton Castle in Yorkshire. The earthworks which survive must be the remains of the building in which Martha lived, but part of it was occupied by her brother Stephen Janes, a yeoman.[15] His inventory shows that he had a hall, kitchen and two chambers as well as various farm buildings.[16] In 1640 the occupants were Stephen's widow and son.

The population in 1640

Browne Willis, the antiquarian of Whaddon, believed that Winslow's population was about 1,100 around 1735, which agrees with later figures.[17] Before that it can only be estimated on the basis of information compiled for very different purposes. A population of 700 or slightly more is a reasonable estimate for 1640, for reasons which will be explained below. Up to a quarter of these people lived not in Winslow itself but in the physically separate hamlet of Shipton.

The parish registers seem to have been kept carefully up to and including the 1640s, although there was no doubt some under-reporting.[18] There were 24 or 25 baptisms per year in the 1640s.[19] On the basis of a crude birth rate of about 32 per thousand this suggests a population of around 750.[20] There were usually between 15 and 17 burials per year over the same period, so the population was on a clear upward trend, which would make its actual size rather less than 750.

This population growth is confirmed by the manor court, where in the 1630s and 1640s people were punished for accepting

---

[15] HALS, 80AW24 (1638).
[16] HALS, A25/3381 (1638).
[17] BL, Add.Ms. 5840, ff.177v–181r: transcription of Willis' notes by Reverend William Cole.
[18] Christopher Hill, *People and Ideas in 17th-Century England* (Brighton: Harvester, 1986), 210–14.
[19] Nine-year moving average; annual totals varied only between 20 and 28.
[20] E A Wrigley and R S Schofield, *The Population History of England 1541-1871* (Cambridge: Cambridge University Press, 1989), where Table A3.1 has a crude birth rate for 1636 of 31.64, for 1641 of 32.42, for 1646 of 30.68.

incomers into their houses and for building unauthorised houses. In 1656–57 plots of land were sold for which a fine of 5s was paid, the normal fine for transferring a house. They must have been building plots: one was 57ft x 21ft and the other a 'backyard' measuring 84ft x 24ft.[21] All this suggests a growing population needing more housing.

The Protestation Return of 1642, an oath of support for Parliament and a Protestant Church of England, listed 296 people.[22] This included both men (180) and women (216). With the normal multiplier of 1.66 to allow for those under eighteen who did not take part,[23] this would indicate a total population of 656. The return does not mention non-participants, but twenty were listed at Wing and even a lower rate of absenteeism at Winslow would still be consistent with a population of 700. The Hearth Tax return for 1662/3 lists 94 households which paid, and certificates for 1670–73 list an average of 65 households which were exempt.[24] With a multiplier of 4.75[25] this represents about 755 people, fairly close to the figure suggested by the parish registers of the 1640s.

Winslow in 1640 was a town with no great disparity in wealth among the leading inhabitants and no-one lived in a house substantially bigger than anyone else's, but a significant number of people had an income well above subsistence level. This aspect of the social structure is illustrated by the Poll Tax return of 1641 which lists 57 people with an annual income of £5 or more:[26]

---

[21] Winslow Manor Court (WMC) 18 April 1656,
see www.winslow-history.org.uk/winslow_court1656.shtm.
[22] Transcribed at www.winslow-history.org.uk/winslow_protestation.shtm.
[23] Nigel Goose and Andrew Hinde, 'Estimating local population sizes at fixed points in time: Part II–specific sources', *Local Population Studies* 78 (Spring 2007), 74–88, 83.
[24] TNA, E179/80/352 (reconstructed at
www.winslow-history.org.uk/winslow_hearth_tax2.shtm); and E179/80/362.
[25] John S Moore, *Counting People* (Oxford: Oxbow, 2013), 29; Keith Wrightson and David Levine, *Poverty and Piety in an English Village: Terling, 1525–1700* (New York: Academic Press, 1979), 41. Others prefer a multiplier of 4.25.
[26] *Buckinghamshire 1641 Poll Tax* (Buckinghamshire Family History Society CD-ROM, 2009).

- 2 men paid £5 tax, representing income of £100: the vicar and William Lowndes, the biggest farmer;
- 1 man paid the £3 fixed rate for an attorney: Richard Edmunds;
- 5 men paid £2 for an income of £50: this included both Peter Figes, father and son;
- 16 people paid 5s for an income of £20;
- 21 people paid 2s for an income of £10;
- 12 people paid 1s for an income of £5.

Everyone else over sixteen was supposed to pay 6d but no list of these payments has survived. According to estimates made in 1688, £15 was the family income of a labourer and £6 10s of a cottager or pauper,[27] but family income would be greater than assessed income due to casual earnings of wives and children.

Winslow can be compared to the other villages in Cottesloe Hundred for which returns survive:[28]

Poll tax rate	Number in Winslow	Winslow percentage	Number in rest of Cottesloe	Cottesloe percentage
£10+	0		4	2
£2–£5	8	14	17	7
5s	16	28	50	20
2s	21	37	87	35
1s	12	21	89	36

Table 1: Poll Tax return for Cottesloe Hundred, 1641[29]

There was no-one in the highest category except Catholics, who automatically paid the top rate. Winslow had a higher proportion than the villages of people in the next two brackets, consisting of yeomen and tradesmen such as Henry Pym, who kept The Bell, and William Wyatt, a butcher with land in Winslow and Shipton and property at Leighton Buzzard. This was due to

---

[27] Gregory King, *Two Tracts*, edited by G E Barnett (Baltimore: Johns Hopkins Press, 1936).
[28] Drayton Parslow, Great and Little Horwood, Mursley, Nash, Swanbourne, Shenley and Whaddon.
[29] *Buckinghamshire 1641 Poll Tax* (BFHS CD-ROM 2009).

the fact that they could combine agricultural and commercial income at Winslow in a way which was not available in the villages. They were people who made comfortable livings.

The lack of rich inhabitants was clear when 60 people in Winslow made voluntary contributions towards suppressing the rebellion in Ireland in 1642.[30] The highest contributor was Robert Mainwaring the vicar (10s), followed by William Lowndes (5s), while nine people gave between 4s and 2s 6d, and 49 gave 2s or less. In comparison, Francis Dodsworth of Whaddon gave £1 10s, Mr Busby of Addington £2 and John Duncombe of East Claydon £4. Winslow was not less enthusiastic or meaner, but lacked any individuals with the resources of those members of the gentry.

The market

Winslow's distinctive feature was the weekly market which it had held since 1235. The clearest evidence for how it worked in the seventeenth century is from a dispute between the Duke of Buckingham's trustees and William Gyles in 1673–77.[31]

The legal issue was whether Gyles had the right to set up stalls in front of his house, but some of the witnesses recorded what had been happening for fifty years or more. It should be noted that his house was also his draper's shop, and most of the buildings around the Market Square were shops if they were not inns, for example an ironmonger's at what is now 6 High Street and a mercer's at 14 Market Square.

The market was held on Thursdays and was normally run by the bailiff, who collected rents and arranged the stalls. For most of the first half of the seventeenth century this was Peter Fige senior, eventually succeeded by his son. It was agreed that inhabitants of Winslow could have one stall each if they paid 4d a year.

---

[30] J Wilson (editor), *Buckinghamshire Contributions for Ireland, 1642, and Richard Grenville's Military Accounts, 1642–1645* (BRS volume 21, 1983).

[31] For information about the market in this and the following two paragraphs see the Court of the Exchequer's records of the dispute at TNA, E112/364/118; E134/29Chas2/Mich22 .

Figure 2: Market Square looking east in about 1900.

Outsiders could have a stall if they paid the bailiff 1d each market day, or 2d for the annual fair on St Laurence's Day (10 August).

Gyles reported an old tradition that his house was given special privileges when the market was moved to the Market Square from its original location in Horn Street. This seems unlikely but there was clearly some permanent encroachment into the south side of the open area before the seventeenth century (this is now The George and adjacent buildings).

Sometimes the running of the market was leased at a set rate. The lessee paid the bailiff £30 a year and took all the profits. Several people referred to times when the market was heavily used and other times when it was not. It was well enough attended for there to be an area designated as Butchers' Row in the north-west corner. A witness said that Gyles set up between two and eleven stalls in front of his house 'according as the number of butchers did come into the said markett'. At least one of these butchers came from Stony Stratford. The Verneys of Claydon House also used the market: when Sir Ralph wanted to buy roses in 1655, he wrote: 'I will appoint my man Roades to take care of it there, hee seldome misses a market day'.[32]

---

[32] Frances and Margaret Verney, *Memoirs of the Verney Family* (London, 1894), 3.250.

People who lived around the Market Square could set up only temporary stalls and were not allowed to extend their shops. Some stalls were freestanding, but it is likely that some were physically attached to the shops, boards folding up and down as required. Wooden stalls of this type are still preserved at Lavenham in Suffolk. They could display goods from a shop in front of an open or unglazed window.[33] Trestle tables or more substantial wooden 'bulks' might also be erected.[34] Failure to remove stalls at the end of market day was an offence often punished at the manor court, and may refer to displays of this sort.[35]

Some people claimed the right to set up sheep pens in front of their houses 'as the same are now paved with stone or gravell'; these pens are mentioned when a property was sold, and were around the junction of the Market Square and Sheep Street. William Lowndes let the sheep pens at The Angel, probably the longest frontage (*see Figure 5 on page 54*), for £3 a year.[36] An area on the Horn Street side of the Market Square came to be known as the Buttermarket, but this name is not documented until the eighteenth century.

Inns and alehouses

One consequence of the market and annual fair was that Winslow for many centuries supported more drinking establishments than its resident population would have justified: 25 were listed in 1753.[37] A list from 1577 includes five inns, six alehouses and a vintner.[38] Around 1640 the manor court tried to enforce the medieval assize of ale, which was in effect a charge for permission to sell this. Twenty people are listed as 'common innkeepers and

---

[33] Andrew Hann and Jon Stobart, 'Sites of consumption: The display of goods in provincial shops in eighteenth-century England', *Cultural and Social History* 2:2 (2005), 165–87, 170.

[34] Claire Walsh, 'Stalls, bulks, shops and long-term change in seventeenth- and eighteenth-century England ', J H Furnée and C Lesger (editors), *The Language of Consumption* (Basingstoke: Palgrave Macmillan 2014), 37–56, 38.

[35] For example. WMC 18 May 1666,
see www.winslow-history.org.uk/winslow_court1666.shtm.

[36] TNA, E134/29Chas2/Mich22: evidence of Mary Gearle née Lowndes.

[37] CBS, Q/RLV1 (alehouse recognizances).

[38] CBS, D/X 423 (certificate of alehouses).

tipplers of beer and ale in Winslow, and sold ale and beer by illegal measures and broke the assize'. Their amercements were between 8d (The Bell, Angel and Bull) and 2d, which presumably reflects the relative sizes.[39]

The Mitchells, who ran The Bull in Horn Street, were also bakers. Henry Pym of The Bell called himself an innholder but also made bread.[40] Abel Sear must have done the same as in 1636 he confessed to the Archdeacon that he sold bread on Sundays and had people drinking in his house during the time of divine service.[41] Henry Wyatt of the Rose and Crown (7–9 Market Square) was a butcher.[42]

At the Michaelmas Quarter Sessions in 1678, Dorothy Pitkins was 'suppressed' for three years from keeping an alehouse, on conviction for 'suffering divers lewd, dangerous and suspicious persons for severally dayes together to drink and tipple in her house.'[43] Her goods were valued at £6 when she died in 1690: her customers must have been entertained with 'brass and pewter vessells' in the 'first lower room' where there was a table and stools.[44] Evidently the alehouse gave her only a very basic living, and for most people it was part of an income derived from a range of different sources.

Housing

Probate inventories provide some evidence of housing arrangements, biased towards the most prosperous inhabitants whose goods were worth recording when they died. There are sixteen surviving from the period 1630–50.[45] Two do not mention individual rooms, probably because the deceased only occupied part of a house. Of the other fourteen, every house had a hall, which was used for eating but never for sleeping. There was a

[39] WMC 6 Oct 1641, see www.winslow-history.org.uk/winslow_court1641.shtm.
[40] HALS, 9AR80 (1666).
[41] HALS, ASA 7/31.
[42] TNA, PROB 11/335/112 (will made in 1670).
[43] BQS, 10 October 1678.
[44] HALS, 126AW16.
[45] Listed at www.winslow-history.org.uk/winslow_wills.shtm.

separate kitchen in eight cases, in two of which it was mentioned after the upstairs rooms as if it was a separate building.

The smallest houses had only one room apart from the hall: a chamber in one case and a parlour in another. Both were used for sleeping, and presumably the difference was that the parlour was downstairs. The occupants of these were a gardener and a labourer.

Four houses had three rooms, which always included a hall and a loft (used for sleeping). The third room could be kitchen, parlour or chamber. The occupants were two yeomen (one had a loft big enough for three beds, four coffers and a table), the parish clerk and a widow. In at least one case there seems to have been an outbuilding too.

The occupants of larger houses were all farmers, usually described as yeomen. Three of them had a cellar. All had at least two rooms upstairs, described as chamber, loft or upper room. Three houses had an upstairs room which was used for storage rather than sleeping. Three farmhouses had three upstairs rooms each. All these houses had at least four domestic rooms, usually with the addition of a brewhouse, milkhouse, buttery or stable, any of which could have a chamber over it.

The largest house for which there is an inventory in the period is the vicarage. This had all the features of a substantial farmhouse: dairy house, buttery, barn, woodhouse. It also had the usual domestic features: hall, parlour (with bed), kitchen, four upper rooms. In addition, there was a study and a closet, unique for Winslow.[46]

The vicarage was not significantly better furnished than the other houses: there were court cupboards, two tables, eight chairs, many stools and forms, five bedsteads and two truckle-beds. The most luxurious items were a spice cupboard and a glass cupboard, a crystal jug, and £10 worth of apparently silver items such as two mazers (goblets). The contents of the study, mainly the books, were valued at £20.

---

[46] HALS, A25/3573 (1650).

Documentary evidence for a wider range of housing comes from the first Hearth Tax return.[47] Tax was paid on 214 hearths, and the number of hearths per house in 1662/3 breaks down as follows:

1 hearth	32 houses
2	26
3	24
4	6
5	3
6	2
7	1

Table 2: Hearth Tax return, 1662/3.[48]

The striking thing about Winslow is the rarity of large houses (with 5–7 hearths) and the complete absence of any very large ones. For comparison Valentine Fige, a native of Winslow, was living in Fleet Street in London in 1666 in a house with thirteen hearths.[49] In towns of comparable size in Bedfordshire, Biggleswade had a house with fifteen hearths, Woburn one with twelve, and Dunstable five with twelve or more.[50] Winslow's lack of gentry and gentry-style housing is clearly illustrated.

Two of the three largest houses (with six hearths each) were inns: The Bell and The Angel. The Bell may in reality have been slightly larger, as two other households with one hearth each were probably part of it. The largest private house belonged to Wendover Lowndes and had seven hearths.[51] It can last be

---

[47] TNA, E179/80/352 (reconstructed at www.winslow-history.org.uk/winslow_hearth_tax2.shtm); and E179/80/362.

[48] The figures are not entirely reliable as some are damaged or illegible.

[49] www.british-history.ac.uk/london-hearth-tax/london-mddx/1666/st-bride-fleet-street-fleet-street-south [accessed 20 January 2020].

[50] Lynda M Marshall, *The Rural Population of Bedfordshire* (Bedfordshire Historical Record Society 16, 1934), 74–75, 101–02, 111–12.

[51] The entries for this house and The Angel (owned by Robert Lowndes) are very fragmentary and it is possible that they should be the other way round.

identified in the manor court records in 1747 when it was 'one ancient messuage divided into five tenements in Winslow adjoining the Bell Inn'.[52]

A house known as the Brick House, later demolished to build Winslow Hall, seems to be recorded as two households with five and two hearths respectively. The Brick House is first mentioned in a document of 1661, and may not yet have been built in 1640.[53] All other houses at that date were timber-framed, some with stone-lined cellars which still survive.

One house which has retained much of its 1640 form is Old Crown House in the Market Square, an inn until 1895.[54] The

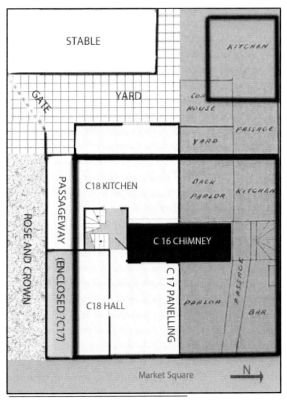

Figure 3: The Old Crown, based on a plan made in 1843 before its northern part (later the Punch House) was rebuilt. The heavy black lines show the extent of the building in 1640.

[52] WMC 27 October 1747, see www.winslow-history.org.uk/winslow_court1747.shtm.
[53] CBS, BAS 376/22/1.
[54] See www.winslow-history.org.uk/winslow_crown.shtm for full documentation.

current building (white on the plan in *Figure 3*) is only about 60 per cent of the original, but shows clear signs of being a medieval hall-house with a massive chimney and stone fireplaces inserted in the centre. It retains much of its timber frame and some internal walls of wattle and daub, although most were replaced with brick. There was a separate kitchen at the rear, and a stone-lined cellar. During the seventeenth century it was divided into two, and the northern part was largely rebuilt in 1860, but the surviving southern section has seventeenth-century wooden panelling in the largest downstairs room.[55] There was a passage from the Market Square to the yard and buildings at the back, partly built over and later completely enclosed when a new access was created from Horn Street.

Agriculture

The vicar's inventory taken in 1650[56] shows that he was involved in almost the full range of Winslow's farming activities, if only on a small scale: he owned a cow, pigs, poultry including turkeys, hay, straw and oats. He had wheat, barley and beans growing, and a manure-heap in the yard. Only sheep were missing.

The glebe land which the vicar farmed lay in strips in the three open fields of Winslow, by this date known as Demoram Field, New Mill Field and Old Mill Field (sometimes called Hollow Furrow) (*see the map on page xvii*). Apart from the creation of the enclosed farm at Biggin, the system was still that which had been in use in the Middle Ages. Shipton had its own three fields: Red, Lice Hill and Blagrove. An area had been converted in the late sixteenth or early seventeenth century into the Cowpasture where there was permanent grazing.

Farmers had holdings distributed around the three open fields, usually in either Winslow or Shipton and rarely in both. The fields were designated annually as the wheat field, bean field and fallow field but there was more diversity in crops than this suggests:

---

[55] There is an unidentified five-hearth house in the Hearth Tax return which might be the Old Crown, if so the division was later than 1663.
[56] HALS, A25/3573.

inventories which included growing or harvested crops normally listed barley too. Individual strips were referred to by the furlong in which they lay, a smaller area where all strips ran in the same direction. The furlong was probably the principal cropping unit.[57]

Although there was no extensive enclosure, by 1640 there had been some consolidation of holdings to create closes immediately around the town. The Lowndes family owned Albons Close, which later took the name of their inn and became Angel Close. The Figes had a five-acre close called Rose Close, and there was a three-acre pasture 'once called Mill Close and now called the Bell Close'.[58] There had also been some apparently haphazard conversion of arable land into semi-permanent pasture called leys.

There is a schedule of holdings of land in Winslow from 1610 which shows how much each individual owned[59]:

Size of holding	Number of owners	Notes
90+ acres	3	
60 acres	3	
40–55 acres	3	
30–35 acres	2	
20–28 acres	6	
10–19 acres	8	
6–9 acres	5	
4 acres	4	Supposedly the minimum amount of land to support a cottage.
1–3 acres	12	
<1 acre	5	Excluding people with an unquantified 'plot of ground' etc.

Table 3: Landholdings in Winslow in 1610.

[57] Robert C Allen, Enclosure and the Yeoman: The Agricultural Development of the South Midlands 1450–1850 (Oxford: Clarendon, 1992), 26.
[58] WMC 7 October 1670, see www.winslow-history.org.uk/winslow_court1670.shtm.
[59] CBS, WF538/44.

In Winslow, the largest holdings were 120 acres (Henry Wendover), 94 acres (William Lowndes) and 90 acres (Peter Fige). The first of these was broken up through lack of a male heir, and the other two gradually disappeared because of financial problems, so they were all gone by 1680.

In 1610 the larger holdings in Shipton[60] (*Table 4*) were still recorded in yardlands (roughly 30 acres, the same as the medieval virgate). There was one holding of three yardlands (Thomas Bowden by his wife's right) and five others of two yardlands or more; these were yeomen's farms. The Elliott, Glenister and Snow families still held three of them by the late seventeenth century.

Size of holding	Number of owners	Notes
60–90 acres	6	Assuming that a yardland = 30 acres.
30–50 acres	2	
½ yardland	1	
6–9 acres	2	
4 acres	1	
1–3½ acres	6	
<1 acre	1	

Table 4: Landholdings in Shipton in 1610.

People who lived in Shipton were mainly full-time farmers, but in Winslow they were likely to combine farming with another trade. This meant that in Winslow there had been a much more active land market, with holdings being built up and then broken up, and individual half-acres being more worthwhile purchases. This explains why the yardland system was no longer in use there.

Winslow, like the rest of the Vale of Aylesbury, was characterised by small, mixed farms producing wheat and barley,

---

[60] CBS, WF538/44.

cattle and sheep for meat, and some dairying. No-one had enough land for a big herd or flock: Thomas Grant alias Miller in 1636 had twelve 'kine and bullocks' and 144 sheep, which were probably as much as any holding could support.[61]

Most yeomen had a cheese press and Richard Glenister of Shipton had a cheese chamber with twenty small cheeses produced from the milk of his three cows, but this was as far as production extended.[62]

The system worked successfully enough for there to be no great pressure for enclosure or other 'improvements'. There was little permanent meadow or pasture, except the closes near the farmhouses and some meadows such as Rushmead by the brooks at the parish boundaries, so a high proportion of people relied on common rights for grazing when the open fields were not sown with crops. This was also a disincentive to change.[63]

The court rolls give some indication of the issues which were of particular concern, in terms of rules being made and broken: grazing was the main problem. Officials called the overseers of the orders (plural) or hayward (when there was only one) were appointed for several years at a time. In 1710 Roger West the overseer was amerced the substantial sum of £4 for not reporting people who broke the rules, so there was still expected to be sufficient spirit of cooperation (or mutual denunciation) to maintain a system which relied on people working together.[64]

Families

Wills are an important source of evidence for family life around 1640. They survive at the rate of about one a year, and were mainly but not exclusively made by yeomen and their widows. They give some insight into the priorities of individuals but they were not entirely a personal matter: between 1610 and 1641 nearly

---

[61] HALS, A25/3321.

[62] HALS, 97AW15 (1658).

[63] J R Wordie, 'The South', in Joan Thirsk (editor), *The Agrarian History of England and Wales volume 1, 1640–1750: Regional Farming Systems*, 317–57, 326.

[64] WMC 18 Oct 1710,
see www.winslow-history.org.uk/winslow_court1710.shtm.

all Winslow wills are in the handwriting of the vicar, Robert Mainwaring, who provided standard introductory formulae about the testator's soul and body.

People made wills if they were not satisfied with the consequences of intestate inheritance, under which all copyhold property went to the eldest son and the widow had dower for her lifetime on a third of it (even if she remarried). Wills were mainly used to enhance provisions for younger children and widows, and some of the consequences of this can be seen in the studies of individual families. People without children could make special arrangements: John Chinnall left bequests to his nieces and nephews, godchildren, servants, friends and the poor of Winslow, and his widow Margaret left all her goods to her servant who was also her niece by marriage.[65]

In principle copyhold property could not be bequeathed. The ways around this were to give it away during one's lifetime or to make a deathbed surrender. Clearly both of these had their disadvantages, and at the end of the seventeenth century the procedure of 'surrender to the use of one's will' started to be employed in Winslow, effectively meaning that property so surrendered through the manor court could be left in a will. The family studies in this book show that people with property did not usually leave it to 'the custom of the manor' to determine who should inherit but made their own arrangements.

At Terling in Essex it was found that property rarely remained in the hands of the same family for more than two generations. Villagers set up their children independently, often elsewhere, so the heirs were already established by the time they got their inheritance and were happy to sell it.[66]

At Winslow, in contrast, there are many examples where the descendants of property owners in the 1640s still owned it, or at least some of it, in the eighteenth century: The Bell remained partly in the hands of the descendants of Henry Pym although they

---

[65] HALS, 8AR95 (1619); 83AW3 (1641).
[66] Keith Wrightson and David Levine, *Poverty and Piety in an English Village: Terling 1525-1700* (New York: Academic Press, 1989) 30–31.

did not live in Winslow, 6 High Street, which belonged to John Watts probably from the 1640s, remained in the family for four generations until it was sold in 1750; William Lowndes even bought back the family land which his father had lost.

It is true, however, that inheritances sometimes fell to people who had already moved away or set up a new household on marriage. Thomas Blake bought a freehold house in Horn Street with 100 acres of land in 1683,[67] and it still belonged to his descendant Robert Williatt Jones who died in 1889, but the Blake/Jones family did not always live in the house because the heirs had sometimes set up their own household before inheriting. William Wyatt's 'cottage recently built' in 1647 (32 High Street) was sold by his great-granddaughter, who lived at Soulbury, in 1730.[68]

There is no indication of whether marriage in Winslow around 1640 tended to be based on romance or arrangement, but for people with property it usually involved a financial settlement between the spouses and their families. This trend was also noted in a study of the manor of Preston in Sussex, where property was transferred more by settlements made in the owners' lifetimes than by will.[69]

At Winslow Henry Pym entailed The Bell to his son Henry who got married in 1641.[70] Henry Wyatt's marriage in the same year was followed by his father giving him a messuage and 9 acres of land, which explains why he did not benefit under his father's will.[71]

Twenty-one weddings are recorded in Winslow parish register between 1639 and 1641.[72] Two were second marriages which have

---

[67] See www.winslow-history.org.uk/winslow_blake-house.shtm.
[68] WMC 23 Oct 1730, see www.winslow-history.org.uk/winslow_court1730.shtm.
[69] Lloyd Bonfield, 'Normative rules and property transmission: Reflections on the link between marriage and inheritance in early modern England', in L Bonfield, R M Smith and K Wrightson (editors), *The World We Have Gained* (Oxford: Blackwell, 1986), 155–76, 171–75.
[70] WMC 6 October 1641, see www.winslow-history.org.uk/winslow_court1641.shtm.
[71] TNA, PROB/11/281/503 (1658).
[72] CBS, PR237/1: Winslow parish registers.

not been included here (there may have been more than two in reality). Of the other nineteen:

Bride and groom baptised at Winslow or Granborough	2
Bride only	8
Groom only	5
Neither	4

Table 5: Origins of people married at Winslow, 1639–41.

Weddings tended to be celebrated in the bride's home parish, but that was not always the case. The two marriages where both parties were baptised at Winslow took place at unusually young ages: Henry Pym of The Bell, aged 21, married draper's daughter Joan Stutsbury aged 16; Thomas Pitkins aged 18 or 22 married Mary Lowndes aged 18, both from yeoman families.

The known ages of the other grooms are between 25 and 34, and the other brides between 16 and 28. There is not enough evidence to calculate the typical age difference, but the overall pattern seems to be women in their early twenties marrying men in their late twenties.

Even allowing for under-recording of baptisms and for people moving as children, the rarity of marriages between two natives of Winslow is striking. There was probably a different tendency for people with property: William Lowndes (1586–1654) married the heiress of the Wendover family of Winslow, and their son Wendover Lowndes married a Fige, while the two daughters of Richard Snow of Shipton, a yeoman who died in 1636 without a son, married men from Winslow yeoman families, Phipps and Glenister.

For others, the market probably made Winslow into the centre of social networks which led to marriages beyond the immediate locality.

Literacy

The extent of literacy in Winslow at any point was not entirely related to educational opportunities available in the town itself, since a significant proportion of the population had always in this period grown up elsewhere.[73] It has been estimated that in Essex between 30 and 40 per cent of adult men were literate in the 1640s, with the rate rising to 45–50 per cent by the 1690s.[74]

In the letter of 1603 which empowered Peter Fige and others to negotiate on behalf of the tenants of the manor of Winslow, 54 made their mark and 14 men (21 per cent) signed.[75] In 1696, 49 of the 133 men who signed the Association Roll made their mark, meaning that about 63 per cent were literate enough to sign their names.[76] So by some means male literacy levels trebled during the seventeenth century.

Someone named Edward Bennett may have been licensed as a schoolmaster in 1609,[77] and there appears to have been a school of some sort in Winslow in 1642 when 'Roger Fyles school-master' signed the Protestation Return.[78] Families such as the Figes and the Lowndeses probably sent their sons to the Royal Latin School at Buckingham, if not further afield. The development of other schools in Winslow will be discussed later.

The only evidence for female literacy in the seventeenth century is from women who made or witnessed wills. Since people known to be literate sometimes made a mark on wills because they were too weak to sign, this is not necessarily conclusive.[79] The only women between 1630 and 1670 who clearly signed their own wills were Margaret Holiman and Rebecca Gerard née Fige, both women from wealthy backgrounds. Emma Bletchley, another outsider with gentry connections, signed as witness to the will of Elizabeth Foster in 1667. Of the eight other testatrixes in the period, five made a mark and three wills had no mark or signature.

The impression is that female literacy in Winslow even at

---

[73] Wrightson and Levine, *Poverty and Piety*, 145.

[74] Wrightson and Levine, *Poverty and Piety*, 146.

[75] CBS, D/BASM/84/12. This includes men from Granborough and Little Horwood.

[76] TNA, C213/16. About thirty men seem not to have signed or made a mark.

[77] Clergy of the Church of England Database (https://theclergydatabase.org.uk/), Person ID: 67610 [accessed 16 October 2019]. There is some doubt about whether the place name actually is Winslow, but an Edward Bennett is recorded as an absentee at the manor court of 1619.

[78] Transcribed at www.winslow-history.org.uk/winslow_protestation.

[79] Wrightson and Levine, *Poverty and Piety*, 147.

yeoman level was unusual. The rise of the Baptists (*see Chapter 4*) was one factor that led this to change, and the 1723 Oath of Allegiance shows that at least 33 per cent of women and 59 per cent of men could sign their names then.[80]

Piety

Robert Mainwaring's standard opening to wills made in the 1630s was:

> 'First I bequeth my soule unto allmightie God, who created me and redeemed me by his sone Jesus Christ, by whose merites onely I trust to obtaine remission of my sinnes, and consequently eternal life in the kingdom of heaven.'[81]

His own will began with the same wording. This wording does not, therefore, say much about the personal beliefs of the testators, only that they did not differ from their vicar strongly enough to reject it.

Some other will-writers were much briefer, for example Thomas Stevens of Shipton, yeoman, 1641: 'First I commend my Soule unto Almighty God that gave it'. William Norman of Shipton, who appears to have written his own will in 1658, did not mention his soul at all.[82] After that date, putting one's soul 'into the hands of Almighty god my creator' became the usual formula.

On the other hand Thomas Fige, a former Parliamentarian soldier, used a lengthy Calvinistic form of expression which he probably composed himself, referring to 'eternall life in ye kingdome of heaven amongst the elect children of God'.[83] This is the only example from Winslow around this time of a 'strikingly individual will' with 'complex, essentially personal clauses' of the sort which was common among pious Puritans at Terling.[84]

The Archdeacon's court in the 1630s dealt with various people who were clearly not Puritans for sabbath-breaking offences and

---

[80] Information provided by Professor John Broad.
[81] HALS, 78AW22 (will of Richard Snow of Shipton, yeoman, 1636).
[82] HALS, 97AW24.
[83] TNA, PROB 11/240/373 (1654).
[84] Wrightson and Levine, *Poverty and Piety*, 158.

unruly conduct in church.[85] There was no reason to record pious behaviour, so it is impossible to say how much Puritan influence there was in Winslow around 1640. Mainwaring's name was carved into the chancel wall (where it still remains) on 14 October 1641, by which time he had been vicar for 44 years. The significance of the date is unknown, and so is the identity and purpose of the carver. Mainwaring was undoubtedly a very influential figure in Winslow but how far he succeeded in developing his flock's piety, or even whether he tried to do so, is unknown.

Winslow in 1640 was a place of commerce and agriculture with a growing population, no particularly wealthy inhabitants and a substantial population of farmers, shopkeepers and tradesmen. It was about to change due to the national calamity of the Civil War and a purely local factor: the life and career of William Lowndes.

---

[85] HALS, ASA 7/31–32.

The Fige family tree

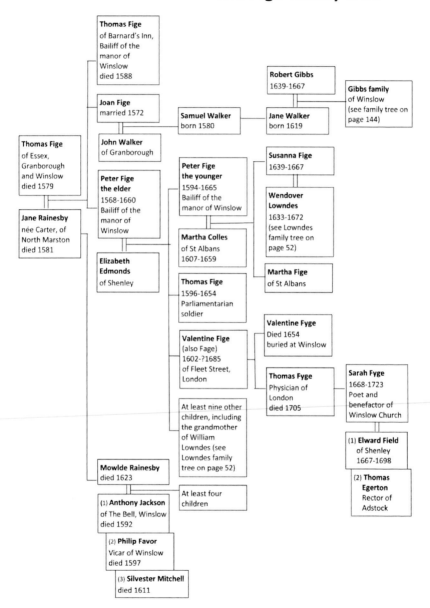

Thomas Fige
of Barnard's Inn,
Bailiff of the
manor of
Winslow
died 1588

Joan Fige
married 1572

John Walker
of Granborough

Samuel Walker
born 1580

Robert Gibbs
1639-1667

Jane Walker
born 1619

Gibbs family
of Winslow
(see family tree on
page 144)

Thomas Fige
of Essex,
Granborough
and Winslow
died 1579

Jane Rainesby
née Carter, of
North Marston
died 1581

**Peter Fige
the elder**
1568-1660
Bailiff of the
manor of
Winslow

**Elizabeth
Edmonds**
of Shenley

**Peter Fige
the younger**
1594-1665
Bailiff of the
manor of Winslow

Martha Colles
of St Albans
1607-1659

Thomas Fige
1596-1654
Parliamentarian
soldier

Valentine Fige
(also Fage)
1602-?1685
of Fleet Street,
London

At least nine other
children, including
the grandmother
of William
Lowndes (see
Lowndes family
tree on page 52)

Susanna Fige
1639-1667

**Wendover
Lowndes**
1633-1672
(see Lowndes
family tree on
page 52)

Martha Fige
of St Albans

Valentine Fyge
Died 1654
buried at Winslow

Thomas Fyge
Physician of
London
died 1705

Sarah Fyge
1668-1723
Poet and
benefactor of
Winslow Church

(1) **Elward Field**
of Shenley
1667-1698

(2) **Thomas
Egerton**
Rector of
Adstock

Mowlde Rainesby
died 1623

At least four
children

(1) **Anthony Jackson**
of The Bell, Winslow
died 1592

(2) **Philip Favor**
Vicar of Winslow
died 1597

(3) **Silvester Mitchell**
died 1611

Winslow families
1: **The Fige Family**

The Figes (or Fyges) were a dominant force in Winslow for almost exactly a century, from the arrival of the elder Thomas to the death of the younger Peter in 1665, then briefly revived by Sarah Fyge Egerton (1668–1723).

Thomas Fige (died 1579) came from Essex, but arrived in Granborough around 1558 and later moved to Shipton. Presumably this was connected to his marriage to Jane Carter of North Marston. Jane already had a daughter, Mowlde, from her first marriage to Ralph Rainesby of Herefordshire.[1] Both her husbands were styled 'gentleman'. She died in 1582.

Thomas' will left his extensive property in Essex to his elder son Thomas.[2] His younger son Peter was to have his property in Winslow, Granborough and Whitchurch, and he left some land he had bought at Botolph Claydon to his daughter Joan, married to John Walker.

There is a probate inventory for his widow Jane, which shows that although she had some luxuries (a silver spoon, two gold rings, some expensive clothes), her house was effectively a farmhouse, with stores of wheat, barley, rye, oats, beans, peas and malt, and fifteen pigs.[3]

Thomas Fige (died 1588), the elder son, was a lawyer at Barnard's Inn in London. He was also bailiff of the manor of Winslow, an office which he sub-contracted to his brother-in-law John Walker and bequeathed to his brother Peter. He had a house

---

[1] There is a family tree in W Harry Rylands (editor), *The Visitation of the County of Buckingham made in 1634* (Harleian Society volume 58, 1909).

[2] TNA, PROB 11/62/158.

[3] HALS, 22AW8.

in Olney as well as the estate in Essex, but the witnesses show that he made his will at Winslow a few days before his death, and he left money for casting the fore-bell of Winslow church.[4]

Mowlde Rainesby (died 1623), stepdaughter of the first Thomas Fige, married Anthony Jackson in 1569. He kept The Bell, and was also given a lease on the farm in Essex for a time. By his death in 1592 The Bell was a substantial inn catering for travellers, with 27 beds of various sorts, and 35 pairs of sheets.[5]

He left his wife Mowlde the use of the inn for four years but she continued to run it for much longer. Her second husband Philip Favor was the vicar of Winslow, and she probably lived with him at the vicarage since the rather sorry list of belongings in his probate inventory were apparently not at The Bell.[6] According to Mowlde's accounts his debts heavily outweighed his assets.[7] She then married Silvester Mitchell, whose inventory of 1611 must have been taken at The Bell.[8]

Peter Fige the elder (1568–1660) became the most influential figure in Winslow, as well as the longest-lived. He must have received some legal training, which was probably curtailed when his brother Thomas' death obliged him to take over all the family affairs. He married Elizabeth Edmunds, daughter of the rector of Shenley and previously curate at Winslow, and they had at least twelve children. Her sisters married Robert Mainwaring the vicar and Henry Wendover, one of the most substantial yeomen.

Peter Fige took over the office of bailiff of the manor and he eventually claimed to have been bailiff for 60 years.[9] In 1603 he was at the head of the list of men appointed to negotiate with Sir John Fortescue about his rights as lord of the manor.[10] Peter's name is also mentioned first in the agreement drawn up in 1611

---

[4] TNA, PROB 11/72/502.
[5] HALS, A25/1351.
[6] HALS, A25/1610 (1598).
[7] HALS, A25/1755 (1600).
[8] HALS, A25/2181.
[9] TNA, E134/29Chas2/Mich22 (evidence of Robert Lowndes).
[10] CBS, D/BASM/84/12.

and eventually ratified in 1613.[11] He was clearly the inhabitants' champion, but also their intermediary with the lord of the manor, and later became bailiff and contractor for the tithes. Apparently he was not universally popular: in 1634 he was abused by Samuel Rawlins 'as he was coming to make proof of his gentry'.[12]

Peter Fige the younger (1594–1665) studied at Oxford, but it is not known what else he was doing before he got married in 1638 (surprisingly late in life) to Martha Colles of St Albans. He then returned to Winslow, took over half his parents' house, which seems to have been on the south side of Sheep Street, and entered an agreement to replace his father as bailiff and farmer of the tithes – but then returned the offices to his father for ten years.[13]

By 1647 he was in financial trouble: he sold some of his land, and used some of it as security for the tithes contract.[14] He continued to sell and mortgage land during the 1650s, but he was often the foreman of the jury at the manor court and may have become a JP.[15] His wife died in 1659 and perhaps he moved to St Albans before his own death; his unmarried daughter was living there when she was granted administration of his estate in 1665 after he died intestate.[16] His other daughter Susanna (1639–67) married her cousin Wendover Lowndes.

Valentine Fige (1602–?1685): One of the strategies used by wealthy Winslow families was to have a younger son apprenticed in London, and that is what happened to Peter the elder's third son Valentine Fige. He was apprenticed as an apothecary in 1618, became an apothecary in his own right in 1626, and was a citizen of London and a friend of Samuel Pepys (who refers to him as 'Mr Fage'). Valentine lived in Fleet Street, and prospered during the

---

[11] CBS, D/BASM/84/15.

[12] *Calendar of State Papers Domestic 1634–35*, 187.

[13] BL, Add.Ch. 53941; CBS, D97/104/1/3.

[14] WMC 23 April 1647,
see www.winslow-history.org.uk/winslow_court1647.shtm.

[15] He is mentioned as 'justice of Winslow' in an agreement between the vicar and churchwardens of Swanbourne from 1659 recorded in Swanbourne parish register.

[16] HALS, 101AW24.

1650s. He was a Common-Councilman and a leading Presbyterian.[17] He reported to Pepys on how General Monck was received in London in 1660. He retained property interests in Winslow, and his son, also Valentine and a Cambridge student, was buried there in 1654.

Sarah Fyge Egerton (1668–1723), Valentine's granddaughter, lived in Winslow at the end of her life.[18] She was a poet and advocate of women's rights who was sent to live with relatives at Shenley after publishing a poem titled 'The Female Advocate', making her a significant figure in the history of feminist literature.

Sarah married a Shenley lawyer named Elward [*sic*] Field, and after his death she married the rector of Adstock, who was also descended from Peter Fige the elder. They had a stormy marriage which included an attempted divorce. She published a collection of verse titled *Poems upon Several Occasions*, installed a memorial tablet to her father in Winslow church, and left the church a silver salver which is still in use. She wrote her name as 'Fyge' although previously the spelling 'Fige' was more common.

There were no Figes in Winslow after 1663 when Peter the elder's daughter Rebecca Gerard died. However, their descendants remained: Thomas Fige's daughter, Joan Walker, was the ancestor of the Gibbs family, while William Lowndes the builder of Winslow Hall recorded that 'my owne mother was the daughter of Anne one of the daughters of Mr Peter Fige'.[19]

---

[17] Margaret Pelling and Frances White, 'FIGH, Valentine', in *Physicians and Irregular Medical Practitioners in London 1550-1640 Database* (London, 2004), www.british-history.ac.uk/no-series/london-physicians/1550-1640/figh-valentine [accessed 17 October 2019]; J R Woodhead, 'Fabian–Fyge', in *The Rulers of London 1660–1689: A Biographical Record of the Aldermen and Common Councilmen of the City of London* (London, 1966), www.british-history.ac.uk/no-series/london-rulers/1660-89/pp67-74 [accessed 17 October 2019].

[18] Richard Greene, 'Egerton [née Fyge; other married name Field], Sarah (1670–1723), poet', *ODNB*, www.oxforddnb.com/view/article/37390 [accessed 5 February 2020].

[19] CBS, D/LO/4/3 page13 (William Lowndes' notebook). For the Gibbs family see pages 144-149 and the Lowndes family pages 52-60.

Chapter 2:
Winslow in the Civil War and Commonwealth

On 17 June 1642 the Trained Bands of Buckinghamshire and nearly a thousand volunteers assembled at Aylesbury and petitioned Parliament to appoint a new Lord Lieutenant.[1] This is the point at which Winslow Parliamentarians would have signed up to fight, but no list of names is preserved. The Civil War technically began two months later when Charles I raised his standard at Nottingham.

The important question for the inhabitants of a small town such as Winslow was not which side was right but which side was closest. With Parliamentarian garrisons eventually established at Aylesbury and Newport Pagnell and Royalists at various times at Brill, Boarstall and Hillesden, north Buckinghamshire lay open to raiding by forces which became increasingly desperate for supplies as the conflict dragged on until early 1646.

There were no large-scale battles but a number of skirmishes between roaming bands. The inhabitants of Addington lamented what they had to contribute to both sides, 'our poor village lyinge betweene the two armies', and Winslow was in the same position.[2] Without the protection of a substantial river, steep hill or dense woodland it was not a site which could be defended readily. It was at least not on the main route from Aylesbury to the north of the county, and did not have a big house to attract plunderers or a permanent garrison to feed, but it still felt the war's full effects: temporary quartering of troops, raiding, excessive taxation, complete disruption of normal commerce.

---

[1] *Humble Petition of Captains, Officers, and Souldiers of the Trained Bands, Voluntiers of the County of Buckingham* (BL, 190g12 no.36).
[2] TNA, SP 28/151.

There are vivid retrospective comments in evidence given in a Chancery case from 1661 about property in Little Horwood: Robert Grange took the profits of his land as far 'as the extreamity of the then rageing warres would permit him', out of which 'the taxes & billeting of souldiers were paid & defrayd'. He would have been glad if the mortgagor Richard Edmunds had repaid him £150 'in the height of the rage of the late unhappy civill wars when itt was much better to have had money then land'.[3]

Events in which Winslow was involved are documented mainly in a claim for reimbursement of the costs of quartering Parliamentarian troops and in the writings of Sir Samuel Luke, commander of the Newport Pagnell garrison.

Raids and counter-raids

In February 1643, Winslow was already of interest to the Parliamentarian army as Colonel Thomas Tyrrell paid 'a guide to Winsloe with Sir Robert Pye'; Pye was John Hampden's son-in-law.[4] The first serious fighting is recorded in a pamphlet entitled *The Insolency and Cruelty of the Cavaliers*, printed on 19 May 1643.[5] It is described as:

'A true and exact relation of the plundering and pillaging of Winslow, and Swanborne ... with the manner of their coming to the said towns, the number of their forces, what opposition they found, how they fired Swanborne, and forced the townsmen into the church...'

This reports that on 16 May four hundred men of the King's army quartered at Bicester 'marcht towards Winslow, a fair market town about 8 miles from Aylsbury in Buckinghamshire, (it being no garrison-town, and unprovided of arms and ammunition)'. They plundered whatever they could, 'making no difference betweene friends and foes'. They were welcomed by an inhabitant named Jackson who promised 'that he would do them

[3] TNA, C8/189/41, Richard Edmunds v John Grainge.
[4] TNA, SP28/127 f.67v.
[5] Anon, *The Insolency and Cruelty of the Cavaliers* (London, printed by Robert Wood, 1643), BL, E.102.(16.).

the best offices he could both in discovering to them the wealth of the towne, and also the persons that were enemies to them'. They found that he was rich and plundered his house along with the rest, taking £20 in money and all his linen, pewter and brass. They stole corn, cattle and 40 horses, and spoiled whatever they could not take away. They then moved on to Swanbourne, which was defended by 30 or 40 musketeers who were eventually besieged in the church, and a significant part of the village was burned.[6]

Some details of the account can be questioned (there is no trace of a rich man called Jackson living in Winslow in the 1640s) but the raid clearly happened. Sir Samuel Luke recorded in his journal for 1 July 1643 an event which sounds similar but cannot be the same one so this illustrates that such raids became regular:[7]

'Robert Cox saith that there came 2000 of the King's forces this afternoon through Winslowe to Swanburne, and heareing of a party of ours coming from Aylesbury that way they retreated to Winslow, and he heares that they intend this night either to quarter there or else at Buckingham.'

Control of the area switched rapidly from one side to the other, and around midsummer 1643 'his excellence the Earle of Essex laye in the towne with his army'.[8] Essex was Captain-General of Parliament's forces. No numbers are given but it was said to have cost Winslow £200, the biggest single expense for quartering troops during the war. Presumably this was in the aftermath of the Battle of Chalgrove on 18 June, when John Hampden was fatally wounded. Essex was taking control of the area between London and the King's headquarters at Oxford. His army was quartered around Aylesbury at the time.[9]

Sir Samuel Luke's informants saw 30 of the King's scouts on

---

[6] Clive Rodgers, 'Swanbourne in the English Civil War', www.swanbournehistory.co.uk /swanbourne-in-the-english-civil-war/ [accessed 22 January 2020].

[7] Journals of Sir Samuel Luke, edited L G Philip (3 volumes, Oxford: Oxfordshire Record Society, 1947–53), 110.

[8] TNA, SP28/151: answer from Winslow to 29 Articles, September 1646.

[9] Ian F W Beckett, Wanton Troopers: Buckinghamshire in the Civil Wars 1640–1660 (Barnsley: Pen and Sword, 2015), 68.

6 August who had travelled from Winslow to beyond Thame, and went on to Bicester, and 'took onely one horse'; meanwhile 60 of the King's horse were at Buckingham.[10] On 29 October he heard that 'six or seven troopes of horse' (a troop would contain sixty or seventy men) were quartered at Winslow,[11] while there were 2,000 Royalist horse at Brackley and 2,000 foot at Buckingham.

Winslow was suffering from regular Royalist impositions and requisitions. On 2 November, Luke heard that Winslow 'hath raised money for the Kinge and doth daily looke for another tax to be layd upon them.'[12] On 2 December he was told that his agent John Appleby had been captured at Winslow the previous Wednesday and taken to Buckingham, but escaped in the night.[13] On 7 December, Luke recorded that Colonel Smith had plundered Winslow and 'pilledged one Seyer and Pym there'.[14] Henry Pym kept the Bell and Abel Sear was a grocer.

More Cavaliers were recorded on 30 December as being at Winslow 'Thursday last' when there was an exchange of fire with Parliamentarians and both sides retreated 'no hurt done'.[15] On 10 February 1644, the Royalists at Hillesden were threatening to levy £200 on Winslow and other places in order to raise 300 horse.[16]

On 11 January 1644 the Parliamentarian commander, Jecamiah Abercromby from Newport Pagnell garrison, temporarily based at Addington, was told that the enemy were at Winslow: 'ten within the town drinking, dancing, and sinking themselves, and some fortie-foure with their cullers at the towns end'.[17] They retreated by Padbury bridge to Hillesden and 200 mounted Parliamentarian soldiers in pursuit stayed overnight in Winslow on 13 January.[18]

An alternative version of (presumably) the same incident was printed in the Royalist newspaper *Mercurius Aulicus* for

---

[10] *Journals of Sir Samuel Luke*, 129.

[11] *Journals of Sir Samuel Luke*, 177.

[12] *Journals of Sir Samuel Luke*, 188.

[13] *Journals of Sir Samuel Luke*, 205.

[14] *Journals of Sir Samuel Luke*, 208.

[15] *Journals of Sir Samuel Luke*, 226.

[16] *Journals of Sir Samuel Luke*, 255.

[17] Letter of Abercromby to Earl of Essex, 15 Jan 1644, quoted by Clear, *King's Village*, 77.

[18] TNA, SP28/151.

10 February 1644. Colonel William Smith's party, under the command of the German Lieutenant-Colonel Johan Philip Hirtter:

> 'met with another [party] of the Rebels about a mile from *Wenslow*, in a faire field, where they fought handsomely a good while, till the Rebels being put to flight, ranne into a house in *Wenslow*, whither the Lieutenant Colonell very eagerly pursued them, and (notwithstanding they got a house and shot out of the windowes) the Lieutenant Colonell forced his way in, killed some, and took all the rest, *viz* their Captaine (*Thomas Shilborn*) with all his officers and company, which were this day brought Prisoners into *Oxford*.'

Luke confirms the last part of this. He recorded that on 15 February Captain Shilborne and twelve men were captured at Winslow and taken to Oxford.[19] Immediately afterwards, at Shrovetide (18 February), 'Cromwell had five troops three dayes and nights' – in total 1,100 soldiers – quartered at Winslow.[20] Oliver Cromwell, still an officer in the Eastern Association Army at this stage, was on his way to the assault on the Royalist stronghold at Hillesden, which was taken on 4 March.[21] His whereabouts in February are otherwise largely unrecorded.[22]

According to Arthur Clear, while Charles I was staying at Buckingham in June 1644 his forces temporarily held Winslow.[23] He had between nine and ten thousand men with him, whose quarters must have extended well beyond Buckingham itself.[24]

The King's army had moved on to Cropredy Bridge by the time a Parliamentarian force of 4,500 reached Buckingham on 29 June; they too would have needed quartering, but Winslow only

---

[19] *Journals of Sir Samuel Luke*, 255. Also in *The Letter Books of Sir Samuel Luke 1644–45* (Historic Manuscripts Commission JP4, HMSO 1963), Scout Report 1, 19 February(?) 1644, which refers to Shilborne and 22 soldiers being taken to Oxford, and Scout Report 3, which makes it 20 men.

[20] TNA, SP28/151.

[21] Beckett, *Wanton Troopers*, 75.

[22] Peter Gaunt, *The Cromwellian Gazetteer* (Gloucester: Alan Sutton and The Cromwell Association, 1987), 224.

[23] Clear, *King's Village*, 78.

[24] Beckett, *Wanton Troopers*, 103; *Letter Books*, Scout Report 169, 22 June 1644 refers to 9,000 foot and 3,000 horse at Buckingham.

seems to have suffered a horse being taken for the use of the Earl of Manchester.[25] Cromwell was back for two days and nights around Michaelmas with about 300 soldiers, at a time when he was based at Banbury where Parliament held the town but the castle was still in Royalist hands.[26]

On 16 November 1644 Luke wrote to Major Lydcot at Leighton Buzzard that he was 'sorry you missed your prize at Winslow', apparently referring to a raiding party from Boarstall.[27]

By 8 December Winslow and surrounding villages were considered suitable for a Parliamentarian force to base itself there for action against Royalists at Thame, Bicester and Brackley.[28] Thirty horse from Newport were waiting at Winslow for reinforcements on 9 December before launching an assault on Boarstall, intending 'to drive away all their oxen and fat cattle which will be very useful to this garrison'.[29] Royalists were reported to have mustered at Preston Bissett and elsewhere to prevent this.[30] The livestock really belonged to the local population of course, and this was the equivalent of the Royalist raids which Winslow had suffered previously.

On 3 January 1645 the *Weekly Account* reported that Royalists were quartered at Winslow and Buckingham while Parliamentarians were at Wing and Waddesdon, and commented that 'that fertile country, which though heretofore hath been esteemed the Garden of England, is now much wasted, by being burthened with finding provision for two armies'.[31]

The market at Fenny Stratford ceased to function because there was nothing left to sell,[32] and the same had probably happened at Winslow. The manor court had also stopped meeting, which had

---

[25] TNA, SP28/151; this is said to have happened at 'midsomer'.

[26] Gaunt, *Cromwellian Gazetteer*, 225.

[27] *Letter Books*, no.125.

[28] *Letter Books*, no.202, Sir Samuel Luke to Colonel B Vermuyden.

[29] *Letter Books*, no.1536, Cokayn to Vermuyden; no.1537, Cokayn to Quartermaster William Crane.

[30] *Letter Books*, Scout Report 207, 10 December 1644, Buckingham.

[31] *The Weekly Account*, 3 January 1645, BL, Burney Newspapers Collection.

[32] Sir Frank Markham, *History of Milton Keynes and District* (Luton: White Crescent, 1973), 214.

not even happened during the Black Death three centuries earlier. There are no more claims for reimbursement of free quarter of Parliamentarian forces until Easter, suggesting that Winslow was under Royalist control for several months.

There was a large concentration of Parliamentarian troops at Winslow around Easter (6 April): in total 1,720 stayed overnight that day or the next. Most were under the command of Major-General Lawrence Crawford who was notorious for his depredations in friendly territory to the extent that he was denounced by the County Committee as 'plunderer and oppressor'.[33] A manor court was held on 29 April, but the town was not yet clear of trouble.

On 6 May Luke was trying to arrange a rendezvous at Winslow between horse and foot forces from Newport Pagnell and Northampton on their way to reinforce Aylesbury.[34] The foot soldiers quartered at Winslow that night.[35] Along with the horse, they were waiting for the Northampton troops the next day, who were coming from Stony Stratford.[36] Free quarter was taken by 360 men from Newport and 680 from Northampton.

On 27 August, Charles I spent the night at the Earl of Carnarvon's house at Wing, and led his forces towards Boarstall the next day.[37] They must have passed through Winslow as they would have had to avoid Aylesbury. In November Winslow was one of the places affected by a major Royalist raid from Oxford and Boarstall.[38] Colonel Ireton, later Cromwell's son-in-law, stayed for two nights in December 1645 and troop movements through Winslow continued in significant numbers until January.

Fighting in Buckinghamshire ended with the surrender of Boarstall in June 1646, but troops continued to require quartering.

---

[33] Beckett, *Wanton Troopers*, 126.
[34] *Letter Books*, no.587, Luke to Northants Committee, 6 May 1645; no.1274, Major Anthony Buller to Luke, 6 May 1645.
[35] *Letter Books*, no.589, Luke to [?], 7 May 1645.
[36] *Letter Books*, no.590, Luke to Marmaduke Tuckington (commander of the Northampton forces) at Stony Stratford, 7 May 1645; no.1276, reply from Tuckington, same date.
[37] Charles Edward Long (editor), *Diary of the Marches of the Royal Army during the Great Civil War, kept by Richard Symonds* (Camden Society LXXIV, 1859).
[38] Beckett, *Wanton Troopers*, 140.

In all, Winslow claimed £960 for the provision of free quarter to Parliamentarian forces between mid-1643 and September 1646. This is not much less than the £1,286 lost by the much more strategically located Beaconsfield.[39] Perhaps most significant is the lament at the end of the claim submitted to the County Committee:

> 'The charges and losses which we have suffered by the Kings soldiers will be above double this here specified in this answere. If it please this honorable Comittee to take this into conscideration and desire the particulars we shall endevour to give them satisfaction.'[40]

Even after fighting stopped locally, people still had to pay for the Parliamentarian army. Winslow was assessed to pay a weekly tax of £2 1s 3d between June 1645 and August 1646.[41] The collectors invariably failed to collect the amount due and there were arrears of £77 by the end of the period as well as a shortfall of at least £1 in each four-weekly payment.

Arrears were still being paid off in January 1649 when £49 was collected.[42] In comparison, the total paid by Winslow for the six subsidies in 1640–41, the main parliamentary tax, was about £34,[43] the 1641 Poll Tax raised £37, and the assessment for the first part of the £400,000 voted by Parliament in 1642 was £18, making a total of £89.

Over the next four years the economy of Winslow, with no rich inhabitants, probably lost £3,000 to emergency taxation, raids and quartering troops. In proportion to the size of the town this was in the same order as the £8,500 worth of goods lost in the fire of Buckingham in 1725.

---

[39] Beckett, *Wanton Troopers*, 129.
[40] TNA, SP28/151.
[41] TNA, SP28/150 f.619.
[42] TNA, SP28/150 f.490.
[43] TNA, E179/80/300 is the return for 1641; TNA, SP28/151 states that about £24 was paid for the four Subsidies of 1640.

Divided loyalties

At the 1645 manor court two men were amerced £5 for refusing to serve as constables or take the oath and two were amerced 30s for refusing to serve as tithingmen.[44] Refusals to serve recur throughout the court rolls, but four together suggest that national issues were somehow involved. Otherwise, once the court resumed after a two-year gap, its records do not show any direct effects of the war, although some absences, sales and mortgages may have been at least indirect consequences. Two large landholdings in Shipton changed hands in 1646–47: John Henley bought 55 acres from John Burt, and William Townsend bought 33 acres from Richard Edmunds.[45]

There are records from 1697 of two men who had fought for the King during the war. William Burrell, butcher of Winslow, produced a certificate that he had served Charles II under Prince Rupert, presumably in 1651.[46] He was granted a county pension of £2, later increased to £3. Geoffrey Savage of Winslow, aged 86, had a certificate that he had served under the Earls of Northampton, and was granted a pension of £2.[47] Neither man owned property in Winslow; they were perhaps soldiers of fortune in the King's army rather than politically motivated supporters.

In 1642, Robert Lowndes, eldest son of one of Winslow's main yeoman farmers,[48] left for America where he had relatives, perhaps because of the Royalist sympathies later expressed by his son William, although he had returned to Winslow by 1650.[49]

On the Parliamentarian side was Thomas Fige.[50] When he made his will in 1652 he still had money owing to him from his army pay.[51] He described himself as gentleman, perhaps because

---

[44] WMC 29 April 1645, see www.winslow-history.org.uk/winslow_court1645.shtm.

[45] WMC 11 December 1646 and 26 February 1647, see www.winslow-history.org.uk/winslow_court1646.shtm;

[46] BQS, 16 January 1697.

[47] BQS, 15 April 1697.

[48] For the Lowndes family see pages 52–60.

[49] Jennifer Moss, *Ways and Means: A study of the life and career of William Lowndes, Secretary to the Treasury and his descendants* (Chesham, 2014), 5.

[50] For the Fige family see pages 26–30.

[51] TNA, PROB 11/240/373.

he was a lawyer, but he shows the humble place of Winslow in Buckinghamshire's Parliamentarian hierarchy because although he was a member of the leading family he served only as corporal and quartermaster under a captain who served under Colonel Arthur Goodwin.

Presumably no-one who made a will after the restoration of Charles II in 1660 would have mentioned their service to Parliament, while the record of the Royalist soldiers only concerns those who were still alive 40 years later. More men from Winslow must have fought on both sides.

The manor of Winslow was part of the dower of the widowed Duchess of Buckingham until she died in 1649, and so was in the hands of her second husband the Earl of Antrim. Their property was sequestrated by the Buckinghamshire County Committee in 1646 as a delinquent and a Papist respectively.[52]

The others who had their property sequestrated were Martha Janes, the now absentee owner of Biggin Farm, and Richard Snow of Shipton. Martha had retreated to Bolton Castle in Yorkshire where her son became an active Royalist. The 1645 manor court shows that John Snow, Richard's father, on his deathbed entailed his property to his wife, then to Richard's wife and Richard's son – but not to Richard himself.[53] This was probably a way of avoiding imminent sequestration, although John might have disinherited his son for political reasons.

A new lord of the manor

George Villiers, second Duke of Buckingham, inherited the manor of Winslow on his mother's death but was proscribed as an enemy and traitor to the Commonwealth in March 1649.[54] He stayed in exile and missed any chance to buy back his confiscated lands as many other Royalists did.[55]

---

[52] TNA, SP 28/151; Beckett, *Wanton Troopers*, 81.

[53] BL, Add.Ch. 53944.

[54] *Journal of the House of Commons, 14 March 1649*.

[55] Joan Thirsk, 'The sales of Royalist land during the Interregnum', *Economic History Review* n.s.5 (1952), 188–207, 193.

In September 1650 Parliament ordered the Buckinghamshire Committee and the tenants and occupiers of the manors of Whaddon, Water Eaton and Winslow not to fell any trees 'until the Parliament take further order.' This may be connected to the intended grant to Major-General Philip Skippon, which was discussed the same day.[56] Skippon was an important commander in the Parliamentarian army, formerly leader of the London Trained Bands. He had no previous Buckinghamshire connections, although he had been involved in military actions in the county.[57] He was granted land worth £1,000 a year. which probably reflected money due to him for his services to the state.[58]

'An Act to settle Manors, Lands, and Tenements upon Major General Philip Skippon' was passed in Parliament on 8 July 1651.[59] He appears as lord of the manor of Winslow in the court roll of 3 October 1651. It is not clear if he took a personal interest in the town, but in his will of 1660 he referred to an annual payment of £3 6s 8d to the poor of Winslow forever.[60] Skippon's steward was Oliver Lawrence, who held manor courts much more often than the traditional cycle of twice a year. Jurors were now sworn 'for the Common Wealth' instead of 'for the lord King', with records kept in English instead of Latin, but otherwise proceedings continued as always, with the usual fines and heriots.

Winslow's Commonwealth?

Skippon's time as a north Buckinghamshire landlord was brief, and from early 1655 he began a policy of dismembering his estate.[61] By Christmas 1657 he had sold twenty parcels around Bletchley and Whaddon to 27 mainly local buyers.[62] Only three

---

[56] *Journal of the House of Commons*, 26 September 1650.

[57] Ian J Gentles, 'Skippon, Philip, appointed Lord Skippon under the protectorate (*d.* 1660)', *ODNB*, www.oxforddnb.com/view/article/25693 [accessed 19 October 2017].

[58] Thirsk, 'Sales of Royalist land', 202.

[59] *Journal of the House of Commons*, 8 July 1651.

[60] TNA, PROB 11/300/257, made on 21 February 1660.

[61] Thirsk, 'Sales of Royalist land', 201–02; Beckett, *Wanton Troopers*, 98.

[62] Full details are given by Joan Thirsk, 'The sale of delinquents' estates during the Interregnum, and the land settlement at the Restoration' (University of London PhD thesis, 1950), App. IV. The figure of twenty which she used in later work includes some large sales such as that of the manor of Winslow.

were gentry, including Francis Dodsworth of Whaddon Park who was co-purchaser of the manor of Whaddon.[63] Dodsworth and the London haberdasher John Hatch made further sales of their new acquisitions to local people.[64]

Skippon received £12,075 from his sales, as well as income from rents, manorial payments and issuing new leases. He profited considerably, but the historian Joan Thirsk raises the possibility that he was responding to appeals by his tenants (since other comparable vendors did not sell to locals) or was even influenced by Leveller thinking. Frank Markham simply believes that he 'preferred cash in hand', a view also suggested by Melanie Harrington for sales by initial purchasers of sequestrated estates.[65] He might have wanted to cash in estates which were of no particular interest to him and had not cost him anything.[66] Skippon was fairly radical in politics, although he was attacked by an anti-radical contemporary for his 'fat belly and full purse'.[67]

Levellers hoped to use the sale of Royalists' lands to convert copyholds to freeholds.[68] This ambition must have been shared by many farmers who did not otherwise have radical opinions. People who purchased confiscated land did not have great faith in their purchases being permanent.[69] Skippon was probably more willing to part with his acquisitions than if he had thought his title was secure, but the redistributive effects of his sales at Whaddon and Water Eaton were exceptional in the 1650s.

Unlike the other manors, Winslow did not have a large demesne which could be sold off in small parcels.[70] Instead Winslow manor was bought from Skippon in 1656 by a local

---

[63] *VCH* Buckinghamshire, 3.435–42: Whaddon with Nash.

[64] Thirsk, 'Sales of Royalist land', 202.

[65] Markham, *History of Milton Keynes*, 218; Melanie Harrington, 'The earl of Derby and his tenants', *Economic History Review* 64 (2011), 1195–1217, 1212.

[66] Professor Ian Beckett, personal.communication.

[67] Theodorus Verax [Clement Walker], *Anarchia Anglicana or The History of Independency* (1649), 119–20.

[68] Thirsk, 'Sales of Royalist land', 189. Compare Christopher Hill, *The World Turned Upside Down* (London: Penguin, reprinted 1991), 121.

[69] Thirsk, 'Sales of Royalist land', 191.

[70] Thirsk, who had no reason to be interested in precise local details, did not realise that Skippon treated Winslow differently from his other manors.

consortium [71] The entry in the Feet of Fines states that in May Michael Norman, John Bowden and William Coleman paid Skippon £260 for the manor and 640 acres of land.[72]

An apparently separate sale appears in the Close Rolls: on 3 March Skippon sold the manor, moot-hall, quit-rents and manor courts (but not the tithes) to the same Norman, Bowden and Coleman (of Winslow, Granborough and Twyford respectively) but in trust for Richard Hodgkins of Winslow, Robert Bowden of Granborough and Francis Woodcock of Great Horwood, all yeomen, for £1,500.[73]

Melanie Harrington has shown that yeoman farmers formed a significant group of potential purchasers of Royalists' land, and sometimes several acted together.[74] Dispossessed owners might also move behind the scenes: the Earl of Derby approached his former tenants to buy up his family's confiscated land on his behalf. Some were willing to cooperate with him, but others who were strong Parliamentarians worked against him.[75]

In other words tenants might buy up confiscated estates for diametrically opposed reasons. They also had the negative motivation of not wanting their manors to fall into the hands of outsiders who would be more interested in maximising revenue than respecting local traditions.[76]

There are two possible explanations for the way in which the manor of Winslow was sold in 1656: either the purchasers were acting in their own interests and that of their neighbours by making a cheap purchase (a third of what had been paid for the manor in 1619) when they had the opportunity, or they were acting on behalf of the Duke of Buckingham. A third possibility can be ruled out, as they do not seem to have had any Leveller-type ideological motivation.

---

[71] Thirsk, 'The sale of delinquents' estates', 365.

[72] TNA, CP25/2/537/1656EASTER:BUCKINGHAMSHIRE.

[73] TNA, C54/3888/37.

[74] Harrington, 'The earl of Derby and his tenants', 1202–04.

[75] Harrington, 'The earl of Derby and his tenants', 1206.

[76] Harrington, 'The earl of Derby and his tenants', 1212–13.

The manor courts for 1656–57, after the sale, do not show any unusual activities apart from the appointment of a new steward. Building on the waste of the manor was prohibited, and the new owners clearly did not share the Levellers' desire to settle wastes and commons on the poor forever.[77] In April 1657 proceedings were recorded as usual, with the lords of the manor acting out of their 'special favour'.[78] Fines and heriots were carefully noted. They were still going to Skippon until Michaelmas 1657 under arrangements made in the sale. That may explain why the court rolls after April 1657 are not preserved: they would have been kept somewhere different as Skippon was no longer involved at all. It is therefore possible that the new lords pursued different policies after Michaelmas 1657, but there is no evidence for this.

The Duke of Buckingham returned to England from exile in France in 1657, and rapidly married Mary, daughter of Thomas, Lord Fairfax, the man who had acquired most of his property apart from his Buckinghamshire estates.[79] In 1659, after temporary imprisonment in the Tower of London, he claimed the manor of Whaddon from Francis Dodsworth, on the grounds that when he bought it Dodsworth was acting as his agent (as he had been in the 1640s). The Court of Chancery decided that Buckingham should recover the land except what Dodsworth had sold off, paying compensation for any expenditure not covered by Dodsworth's profits.[80]

In his bill of complaint Buckingham explained what he claimed had happened: when Dodsworth heard that Skippon was going to sell Whaddon, he proposed to buy it on Buckingham's behalf, and Buckingham then asked him to buy, or find someone to buy, Skippon's other estates on condition that Buckingham 'might have them upon the same termes they were bought', which Dodsworth refused.[81]

---

[77] Hill, *World Turned Upside Down*, 345–46.

[78] WMC 10 April 1657, see www.winslow-history.org.uk/winslow_court1657.shtm.

[79] Bruce Yardley, 'Villiers, George, second duke of Buckingham (1628–1687)', *ODNB*, www.oxforddnb.com/view/article/28294 [accessed 20 Oct 2017].

[80] Thirsk, 'The sale of delinquents' estates', 278, 282–83.

[81] TNA, C8/136/22.

Figure 4: George Villiers, second Duke of Buckingham, a line engraving by Robert White in 1679. Copyright © National Portrait Gallery, London, D26513, reproduced with their permission.

There is no reference to the sale of the manor of Winslow, since Dodsworth was not directly involved, but it is possible that he found purchasers with the expectation that Buckingham would eventually reimburse them. According to Buckingham, Dodsworth had the sale of Whaddon 'clogg[ed] ... with incumbrances' in order to disguise the trust, and the very complicated arrangements about the manor at Winslow, with three men holding it in trust for three others, could have had the same purpose.

Two of the three purchasers of the manor of Winslow had had to use credit. Robert Bowden in February 1656 borrowed £500 from Robert Lovett of Elstow, which must have been for his share of the purchase money. He was going to pay it off over seven years, and by 1661 £150 of the principal was outstanding.[82] He also had creditors in London who brought a suit against him in 1662 for a debt of unspecified size.[83]

Bowden clearly did not get full reimbursement from a grateful Duke if that was what he had expected, but was going to pay off the loan from his share of manorial income. In 1662 he also sold some land in Granborough to his brother William for about £180, 'being indebted to divers persons in divers greate sommes of money'.[84] He seems to have moved to Addington by 1674, when he brought a counter-suit against William. Bowden's role in purchasing the manor brought him financial trouble, but it did not drive him from the area when the old order was restored.

Richard Hodgkins also got himself into debt, presumably to fund his share of the purchase of the manor. He had been baptised at Granborough in 1604, married there in 1629, and was living in Winslow by 1642. From about 1651–54 he was tenant of some land in Middle Claydon which brought him into a dispute about tithes with the rector, who told various people rather mysteriously 'that there was other businesse between Hodskins and him'.[85]

---

[82] TNA, C9/24/45: a case brought against Bowden in 1661.

[83] TNA, C8/145/24.

[84] TNA, C7/502/29; C 5/451/4.

[85] TNA, E134/1653-54/Hil1: John Aris v Richard Hodgkins concerning a close in Middle Claydon called Mardich. Only the writ and the statements of deponents have been preserved.

Hodgkins also farmed land at Lillingstone Dayrell where he had another dispute over tithes.[86] In 1653 he bought twenty acres of land in Winslow from Peter Fige the younger,[87] and he had a small quantity of freehold land at Tuckey Mead.[88]

Hodgkins was evidently expanding his activities at the time when the manor came up for sale in 1656. He borrowed £500 from various people, with Robert Bowden acting as his guarantor, according to a later case which Bowden brought against him and others in 1664.[89] In 1658 he had also borrowed £15 from Nicholas Brinsall, shoemaker and moneylender of Winslow, secured on 'all his parte of the baylywick of Winslowe then in the occupacion of Michael Norman', that is, his third of the office of bailiff of the manor.[90]

Then, according to Bowden, Hodgkins 'fallinge into greate poverty and necessity and not knowinge how to free and discharge the debts' made over all his property to his son-in-law William Grassum. So the speculation of buying the manor did not pay off for Hodgkins either, but he and his descendants remained in Winslow and Swanbourne.

Francis Woodcock of Great Horwood, the third co-purchaser, seems to have been a rather different sort of man. He is described as gentleman in his will which shows that he owned property all over north Buckinghamshire.[91] At the time of his death in 1683 he held some land in Winslow which he had bought recently, but he was already buying property there in 1649, and he is found later as a mortgagee.[92] Woodcock would not have needed to go into debt to raise his share of the £1,500.

The most likely explanation for the actions of Bowden, Hodgkins and Woodcock is that it was a speculation with two

---

[86] TNA, E134/1654/MICH4 (1654).

[87] CBS, BAS 376/22/3.

[88] CBS, D/LO/4/1 m.11; the land later came into the possession of William Lowndes.

[89] TNA, C 8/154/112, ff. 1 and 3.

[90] TNA, PROB 11/309/231 (1662).

[91] TNA, PROB 11/372/519 (1683).

[92] WMC 24 October 1649, see www.winslow-history.org.uk/winslow_court1648.shtm; 21 Oct 1662, see www.winslow-history.org.uk/winslow_court1662.shtm.

possible outcomes: they would keep the manor long enough to make a profit from it, or the Duke of Buckingham would buy it back from them. As it turned out, neither of these materialised and they suffered financially, but they were not hounded out as extremists after the Duke's return.

It has been claimed that the chancels of Winslow, Addington, East Claydon and Granborough churches were destroyed by Cornelius Holland in the 1650s.[93] Holland was MP for New Windsor, was regarded as one of the regicides although he did not actually sign the warrant for Charles I's execution, and was a prominent figure in the Commonwealth who had to flee the country in 1660.

Holland had been lessee of Creslow Pastures at Whitchurch from the Crown since 1635, and was comptroller of the Prince of Wales' household before the civil war broke out.[94] Banns for the marriage of his daughter Rebecca to Daniel son of Colonel Axtell of Berkhamsted were read at Winslow in 1659, and Axtell senior was executed as a regicide in 1660. But Cornelius does not seem to have been related to the Holland family of Granborough as was thought by William Cole, who spread the story about the destruction of the chancel; his father was a merchant taylor and had a post in the royal household.[95]

Moreover the chancel of Winslow church was clearly not destroyed, as it still has a graffito of 1641 today. The story might have arisen because of issues arising from the sequestration of the Duke of Buckingham's estates. As holder of the rectory the Duke was responsible for the chancel, which he later did repair in 1679. This was apparently not effective, because according to Reverend John Croft when William Lowndes became lord of the manor in 1697 he 'found this chancell in the same pickle Cornelius Holland

---

[93] Raymond South, *Royal Castle, Rebel Town: Puritan Windsor in Civil War and Commonwealth* (Buckingham: Barracuda, 1981), 78. The story was transmitted by Rev. William Cole of Bletchley, quoted by W. Hastings Kelke, 'Creslow Pastures', *Records of Buckinghamshire* 1 (1858), 255–67, 262, and George Lipscomb, *History and Antiquities of the County of Buckingham*, 1.250–51, but Kelke does not include Winslow in the list.

[94] TNA, S03/11; *VCH Buckinghamshire*, 3.335–38: Creslow.

[95] J T Peacey, 'Holland, Cornelius (1600–1671?)', *ODBN*, www.oxforddnb.com/view/article/13517 [accessed 29 Oct 2017].

left it: the ground of it level & arable, the roof a colender'.[96]

In 1652 the Committee for Plundered Ministers (with which Holland had some dealings) had awarded the vicar of Winslow a £50 augmentation, and the Committee for Compounding ordered a half-year's share to be paid to Frances, widow of the recently deceased vicar John Bishop.[97] The Merchant Taylors also had a rent charge on the rectory of £14 for the poor, which they stated in 1653 had been in arrears for nine years.[98] Perhaps Holland was responsible for making the payments and despoiled the chancel in the process, although the other churches allegedly involved were not connected to the Duke.

The restoration of the Duke of Buckingham

The future Charles II had various contradictory policies about the return of confiscated land before he arrived in England, and in the Declaration of Breda he undertook to leave the question to Parliament.[99] As with matters of religion, this led to harsher and more partisan measures than appeared to have been promised.

In 1660 Buckingham petitioned for full recovery of his estates, and despite Charles' suspicions about his loyalties, the House of Lords ruled in his favour on 14 June.[100] He would have recovered them anyway in due course, as major-generals in the Parliamentary army such as Skippon were among those whose acquisitions of confiscated land were not protected by the eventual land settlement.[101]

The men who had purchased the Duke's land from Francis Dodsworth in Bletchley protested to the House of Commons, claiming that they had bought the land to stop it going to strangers, and that they had paid fourteen or sixteen years'

[96] BL, Add.Ms. 5840 f.202r: William Cole's transcription of a letter from Croft to Browne Willis.

[97] Calendar of the Committee for Compounding, 2191.

[98] Calendar of the Committee for Compounding, 2191.

[99] Joan Thirsk, 'The Restoration land settlement', Journal of Modern History 26 (1954), 315–28, 315–16.

[100] Journal of the House of Lords, 14 June 1660.

[101] John Habakkuk, 'The land settlement and the restoration of Charles II', Transactions of the Royal Historical Society, 28 (1978), 201–22, 213.

purchase to the value of £13,000, borrowing money or selling other land.[102]

In general, profits made in the 1650s were considered to remove the need for any compensation. Joan Thirsk concludes that 'purchasers of delinquents' land, although not guaranteed compensation, were often dealt with benevolently by re-instated owners.'[103] She suggests that purchasers in Water Eaton, Whaddon and Winslow may have extracted new leases from the Duke which provided a sort of compensation when their land was returned to him.[104] However this was not the case in Winslow where it was manorial rights which had been sold, not land, and as has been seen at least two of the three purchasers were left badly out of pocket.

Traces of events in the 1650s were excluded from later documents, and abstracts of title never mention the change of ownership under the Commonwealth.[105] Buckingham sent round a questionnaire to all his recovered manors, and the responses for Winslow were recorded on 8 October 1660.[106] This record provides a little information which is not available from the regular court rolls of the 1650s. The jurors, when asked about manorial officers for the past twelve years, reported that Peter Fige was bailiff until 1655, then 'Richard Hodgkins Robert Bowden and Francis Woodcock, the then reputed lords of the said mannor' acted as their own bailiffs until Lady Day 1660. The Moot Hall was said to be in the occupation of William Norman, and Hugh Seaton had a lease of the malt mill from the 'former lords of the mannor' for hundreds of years. The jurors itemised all fines, heriots and tolls payable to the lord. Their attitude to the Duke's return does not emerge.

If Bowden, Hodgkins and Woodcock were regarded as speculators or were believed to have acted primarily to prevent the

[102] Thirsk, 'The sale of delinquents' estates', 277–78; Thirsk, 'Sales of Royalist land', 202; BL, Add.Ms. 5821, ff.190–91 (copy of the petition made by Reverend William Cole).
[103] Thirsk, 'Restoration land settlement', 328.
[104] Thirsk, 'The sale of delinquents' estates', 284.
[105] Thirsk, 'Sales of Royalist land', 205.
[106] CBS, D/BASM 84/16.

manor from falling into the hands of a different and more profit-orientated purchaser, people might not have objected to Buckingham's restoration, expecting him to be a fairly mild absentee landlord like his father.

The Lowndes family tree

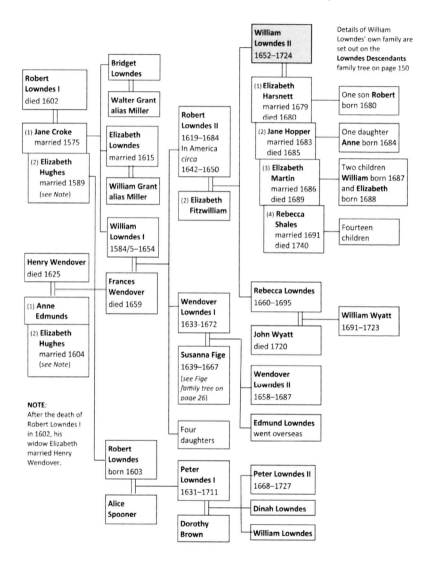

William Lowndes II
1652–1724

Details of William Lowndes' own family are set out on the **Lowndes Descendants** family tree on page 150

Robert Lowndes I
died 1602

Bridget Lowndes

Walter Grant alias Miller

(1) **Jane Croke** married 1575

Elizabeth Lowndes married 1615

William Grant alias Miller

(2) **Elizabeth Hughes** married 1589 (see Note)

Robert Lowndes II
1619–1684
In America circa 1642–1650

(1) **Elizabeth Harsnett** married 1679 died 1680

One son **Robert** born 1680

(2) **Jane Hopper** married 1683 died 1685

One daughter **Anne** born 1684

(3) **Elizabeth Martin** married 1686 died 1689

Two children **William** born 1687 and **Elizabeth** born 1688

(4) **Rebecca Shales** married 1691 died 1740

Fourteen children

(2) **Elizabeth Fitzwilliam**

William Lowndes I
1584/5–1654

Henry Wendover
died 1625

Frances Wendover
died 1659

(1) **Anne Edmunds**

Wendover Lowndes I
1633-1672

Rebecca Lowndes
1660–1695

William Wyatt
1691–1723

(2) **Elizabeth Hughes** married 1604 (see Note)

John Wyatt
died 1720

Susanna Fige
1639–1667
(see Fige family tree on page 26)

Wendover Lowndes II
1658–1687

NOTE:
After the death of Robert Lowndes I in 1602, his widow Elizabeth married Henry Wendover.

Edmund Lowndes
went overseas

Four daughters

Robert Lowndes
born 1603

Peter Lowndes I
1631–1711

Peter Lowndes II
1668–1727

Alice Spooner

Dinah Lowndes

Dorothy Brown

William Lowndes

Winslow families

2: **The Lowndes family**

The arrival of the Lowndes[1] family in Winslow can be dated fairly precisely. They were not recorded in the Survey of the Manor of 1556, but in 1565 Geoffrey Lowndes became vicar of Swanbourne[2] and in 1575 **Robert Lowndes I** (died 1602) married Jane Croke at Winslow.[3] It is likely that they were brothers but there is no direct evidence for this.

The family came from Overton in Cheshire, but Robert's mother (according to a pedigree compiled in 1862, though this is of doubtful reliability[4]) was Margaret Tyrrell of Thornton. The family were not of sufficient status to be listed in the Visitation of Bucks in 1634, but through purchase or inheritance Robert's eldest surviving son **William Lowndes I** (1586–1654) owned an inn called The Angel and 94 acres of land in 1610.[5] This made him the second largest landholder in Winslow.

In 1612 William married Frances, daughter and co-heiress of Henry Wendover, the largest landholder in Winslow with 120 acres (William's stepmother, Elizabeth Lowndes, had become Henry Wendover's second wife in 1604). William was styled 'gentleman' in some documents, but seems to have remained a working farmer: his will refers to 'all my working tools in the shopp, and all the plough timber in the chamber over the shopp'.[6] He served regularly as foreman of the jury at the manor court. He

---

[1] The spelling of the name was very variable until the late seventeenth century, including Lounds and Lowns.

[2] Swanbourne History website: www.swanbournehistory.co.uk/swanbournes-anglican-clergy/ (accessed 2 July 2020).

[3] CBS, PR237/1: Winslow parish registers.

[4] CBS, D-LO/5/12.

[5] CBS, WF538/44: schedule of tenants.

[6] TNA, PROB 11/265/438 (1657).

Figure 5: This photograph from around 1900 shows the full extent of The Angel, the Lowndes family's home until 1670, on the south-east corner of the Market Square with Sheep Street to the right. The Angel occupied the whole frontage shown here, though by 1900 there had been subdivision into four properties and some rebuilding.

was also high constable of Cottesloe Hundred when he had to make a Ship Money return in 1637.[7]

When Henry Wendover died intestate in 1625 he seems to have been in rather embarrassed circumstances according to the accounts presented by his daughter Frances, who had less than £5 left from his goods and chattels after paying his debts and expenses.[8] Nevertheless, most of his land must have passed to her, as she held 80 acres in 1654.

In 1651 William Lowndes handed over The Angel, the family property on the Market Square, and 93 acres to his elder son Robert Lowndes II and Robert's wife Elizabeth.[9] His wife Frances

---

[7] TNA, E179/244/2.
[8] HALS, A25/4852.
[9] WMC 14 November 1651 see www.winslow-history.org.uk/winslow_court1651.shtml.

made provisions for four daughters in 1654, and left most of her land to the younger son Wendover Lowndes I. This is the largest example in Winslow of a strategy often used when two people with property married: the husband's estate was passed on more or less intact to the eldest son and the wife's property went to the other children.

Robert Lowndes II (1619–84), their elder son, should have been set for a comfortable life as one of Winslow's leading citizens. However, around 1642 he left for America.[10] He married there and had two daughters and apparently a son Thomas, who is only known from a reference to him by his half-brother William in 1680, when, if still alive, he was in the West Indies.[11] After one daughter and his wife died in 1649, Robert returned to England, which was normal behaviour for ex-Royalists after the Commonwealth was established, leaving his other children in America.

In 1651 he married Elizabeth Fitzwilliam, granddaughter of Peter Fige the elder.[12] This was the occasion when his father handed over most of his property, a tradition which was followed by his descendants on the eldest son's marriage.

Robert and Elizabeth had five children baptised between 1652 and 1663, of whom three died young. Their daughter Rebecca married John Wyatt of Shipton, from a comparable yeoman family, and died in 1695. Her husband acted as a general agent for his brother-in-law William Lowndes II during the building of Winslow Hall.[13]

Their son **William Wyatt** (1691–1723) seems to have been a protégé of his uncle: there is an entry in William Lowndes' accounts for a payment of £5 for his nephew's education, and when William Wyatt died he was described as gentleman at the manor court.[14]

---

[10] Moss, *Ways and Means*, 5.

[11] CBS, D/LO/4/1 m.1. William called him 'my brother in law'.

[12] For the Fige family see pages 26-30.

[13] G Eland, 'The building of Winslow Hall', *Records of Buckinghamshire* 11 (1926), 406–29. This article is based on building accounts which are now in the CBS.

[14] Folger Shakespeare Library, W.a.147 f.59.

On Robert's return from America he soon started raising money from his property. He must have brought financial problems back to Winslow with him, or run into them quickly. He mortgaged everything between 1652 and 1668, including The Angel for £100 in 1664 and again in 1666.[15] The mortgages turned into sales: eighteen acres in 1656; 60½ acres in 1668; The Angel in 1670.[16] He was involved in a speculation buying sheep in Cheshire in 1664, investing £40, which led him to bring a lawsuit to claim his share of the alleged profits.[17]

Some of the background emerges from another suit brought by Robert and his wife in 1669.[18] According to this The Angel was run by Elizabeth. She had wine brought from London by a carrier who took her payments back with him. When her supplier died in the 1665 plague, she owed him nothing according to Robert – but £57 according to the supplier's heirs.

The agreed facts seem to be that when first taken to court for the debt in 1667, Robert did not enter a plea (which he said was due to his attorney's incompetence) and a judgment was entered against him for £62, leading to the sheriff sending a bailiff to seize his goods. Robert and Elizabeth, helped by the pleading of their neighbours, seeing him 'plunged into greate misery', came to an agreement which only led to the debt multiplying.

Elizabeth was sent to London and made a new agreement to pay in instalments, but the payments were not made. The sheriff's bailiff seized Robert's 'houschold goods, cattell, corne & hay' which were sold to Edward Palmer of London for £42 because Robert 'was & is very poore & not able to pay the debt'.

It was Palmer who bought The Angel in 1670.

---

[15] WMC 19 April 1664,
see www.winslow-history.org.uk/winslow_court1664.shtm; and 18 May 1666, see www.winslow-history.org.uk/winslow_court1666.shtm.
[16] WMC, 18 April 1656,
see www.winslow-history.org.uk/winslow_court1656.shtm; 16 March 1668, see www.winslow-history.org.uk/winslow_court1668.shtm; and
7 October 1670, see www.winslow-history.org.uk/winslow_court1670.shtm.
[17] TNA, C7/215/77.
[18] TNA, C7/582/96.

By 1669 Robert had also given a hill for £60 to Richard Shreive of Shipton Lee, who had apparently lent him some money towards an earlier payment. This was all to Robert's 'wife & childrens utter undoeing and destruccion', and coincided with his son being sent to work in London.[19]

This represents a remarkable decline of a previously prosperous family. Robert lived long enough to see his son **William Lowndes II** (1652–1724) rebuild the family fortunes, but not long enough to see him take them beyond anything of which previous generations could have dreamed.

The careers of William Lowndes II, who was the builder of Winslow Hall, and his eldest son **Robert Lowndes III** (1680–1727) are the focus of the following chapters and will not be discussed further here: William amassed a huge fortune in London and invested some of it in Winslow property (*chapter 3*), built Winslow Hall and handed it over in 1703 to his son (*chapter 5*) and was ancestor of a long line of squires of Winslow (*chapter 6*).

There is some indirect evidence that Robert Lowndes II and his son William Lowndes II remained on reasonable terms, and William II chose to name his eldest son Robert after his father, but there is nothing to show how he felt about his father's financial collapse, only some later pride in having recovered the lost land.

There is a document of 1681 in which Henry Hughes, ironmonger of Winslow, renounces all claims against Robert Lowndes II 'from the beginning of the world', which sounds as if William had made a settlement to pay off his father's debts.[20] It is endorsed 'Mr Hughes his relese no.10' as if there might have been nine similar documents. Perhaps the fact that William did not buy back The Angel gives us a hint about where his father's problems lay. In fact The Angel, having been one of Winslow's foremost inns, soon disappeared altogether.

Wendover Lowndes I (1633–72), Robert II's much younger brother, does not seem to have been any more of a financial success despite the arrangements made for him by his mother. In

---

[19] TNA, C10/103/104.
[20] CBS, D/BASM/375/22/26.

1654 she gave him a house called Hamons and 80 acres of land.[21] In 1657 he married Susanna Fige.[22] He mortgaged his house in 1660 for £100 and failed to make the repayments.[23] He also mortgaged some land and gradually sold it off in small parcels. The house is probably the one with seven hearths recorded in the Hearth Tax return, making it the biggest in Winslow.

Wendover Lowndes I made his will in 1672, describing himself as a gentleman.[24] This was evidently done on his deathbed, as his inventory was taken six days later. He had already sold two messuages and 60 acres of land to William Gyles.[25] He made two friends executors, and did not mention his brother Robert, who would have been the natural person to take charge of his very young children. He left his son Edmund only £2 because 'I am in hopes that my and his good uncle Coles will please to consider him'. This was his wife Susanna's maternal uncle Edmund Colles who did what was hoped when he died seven years later in 1679: he left £50 to bind his nephew Edmund as apprentice, £500 to set him up in trade, and a house in St Albans.[26]

According to a note made by William Lowndes II years later in 1703, Edmund 'went beyond sea and is supposed to be dead as is his son which he left in England'.[27]

The rest of Wendover Lowndes I's own estate was to be divided between his other son, also named Wendover, and two daughters, but his inventory shows that he was in very reduced circumstances: it came to £80, of which £62 was in 'money' but not cash as he only had eight shillings in his purse.[28] William Gyles had undoubtedly paid him far more than that for the two messuages and 60 acres, and presumably the rest had gone in paying off debts. The inventory only mentions two rooms (parlour and chamber) so he had moved out of the seven-hearth house.

---

[21] WMC 18 Oct 1654, see www.winslow-history.org.uk/winslow_court1654.shtm.
[22] For the Fige family see pages 26-30.
[23] WMC 8 Oct 1661, see www.winslow-history.org.uk/winslow_court1661.shtm.
[24] HALS, 109 AW17.
[25] WMC 18 April 1672, see www.winslow-history.org.uk/winslow_court1672.shtm.
[26] TNA, PROB 11/360/615.
[27] CBS, D/LO/4/1 m.1.
[28] HALS, A25/3918.

A document of 1683 refers to his son **Wendover Lowndes II** (1658–87) as a citizen of London, and he was described as gentleman of Westminster in 1687.[29] He was buried at Winslow that year, as he requested in his will.[30]

The younger Wendover Lowndes went some way towards restoring the fortunes of his branch of the family, apparently thanks to his cousin William's influence. In June 1680 William seems to have proposed Wendover for the post of 'King's waiter, London port', a sort of customs inspector, and he certainly had a civil service function as he is recorded several times receiving or disbursing official funds.[31] Wendover must also have worked as a law writer: in December 1680 he received a payment from secret services funds for 'making copies of several commissions', and another in 1685 for 'engrossing a list of severall baronets'.[32] He left £100 to his brother-in-law Robert Mountague, 2s 6d a week to his sister Frances Coates, and to his brother Edmund his lease of a house in Dulwich and several mortgages, including two at Winslow.

The other member of the Lowndes family who played a significant role in Winslow was Robert II's cousin **Peter Lowndes I** (1631–1711). His parents were another Robert, the younger half-brother of William Lowndes I, and Alice Spooner, a member of a well-established Winslow family. Both his parents were younger children so there cannot have been much inheritance, but he was established as a farmer by 1667 when he was fined for overburdening the common with 40 sheep.[33] He is first recorded as a juror in 1668, and regularly after that, and he was churchwarden in 1676 and 1685. He bought a house in what is now Church Street, Winslow, in 1685.[34] He was a trustee of the Lowndes marriage settlement of 1703.

---

[29] CBS, D/BASM/375/22/43/6; D175/21 f.2.

[30] TNA, PROB 11/389/237.

[31] *Calendar of Treasury Books, Volume 6, 1679–1680*, 588.

[32] *Moneys Received and Paid for Secret Services of Charles II and James* 2.22, 122.

[33] WMC 21 October 1667, see www.winslow-history.org.uk/winslow_court1667.shtm.

[34] CBS, D/97/104/2/3.

His will shows fairly limited resources: he left £60 to his daughter Dinah and £50 to his son William.[35] His widow received an annuity of £4 10s through a deathbed surrender. By the time of his death he owned a messuage, twenty acres of land, a cottage and four acres of pasture.[36] The name of Peter Lowndes Close was attached to the field between his house and Vicarage Road until the end of the eighteenth century. Some of it later became part of the churchyard.

His son **Peter Lowndes II** (1668–1727) continued to represent the interests of his second cousin William Lowndes II and was named as a trustee in his will. He regularly served as overseer of the poor,[37] and often appeared at the manor court to represent people who could not attend, which suggests that he was a lawyer of sorts although still described as a yeoman. He was also highways surveyor in 1716 but neglected his duties, according to the manor court. He sold his house to George Barrett in 1724, and also disposed of his remaining land.[38] With his brother William and sister Dinah he seems to have moved to Ramsey, near Harwich in Essex, before he died unmarried.[39]

---

[35] HALS, 149AW14.
[36] WMC 21 April 1712, see www.winslow-history.org.uk/winslow_court1712.shtm.
[37] CBS, PR 237/12/1.
[38] WMC 6 April 1716, see www.winslow-history.org.uk/winslow_court1716.shtm.
[39] TNA, PROB 11/617/391.

Chapter 3:
From bankrupt duke to bankrupt's son: the lords of the manor 1660–1703

George Villiers, second Duke of Buckingham, had his estates restored in 1660, and was gradually reinstated in Charles II's favour. He was helped by his relative, the King's mistress Barbara Villiers, Duchess of Cleveland, although he was briefly arrested on suspicion of treason in 1667 and was held in the Tower of London again in 1677. He tried unsuccessfully to introduce legislation on behalf of religious dissenters in 1668 and 1675.[1]

Although the Duke inherited a vast fortune, he died in allegedly impoverished and squalid circumstances in 1687, making a nice morality tale for people such as Alexander Pope, who wrote:

'In the worst inn's worst room … Great Villiers lies …'[2]

The Duke's finances and his political and personal life were usually in turmoil. His lavish lifestyle and unrestricted spending were paid for by borrowing and the debts piled up. In 1668 he had an annual rental income of £19,306, including £1,507 from Bletchley, Whaddon and Winslow.[3] Yet in 1671 his debts were £123,140, with annual interest of £9,097 due. He had already mortgaged Winslow and Biddlesden in 1662 to Edward Watson, second Baron Rockingham, for £4,000.[4] In 1671 he created a

---

[1] Yardley, 'Villiers, George', *ODNB*; David C Hanrahan, *Charles II and the Duke of Buckingham* (Stroud: Sutton, 2006).
[2] Frank T Melton, 'A rake refinanced: The fortune of George Villiers, Second Duke of Buckingham, 1671-1685', *Huntington Library Quarterly* 51 (1988), 297–318, 297–98, quoting Alexander Pope, *Moral Essays*, Epistle III verses 299-305.
[3] BL, Add.Ms. 5821, ff.222v–223v.
[4] CBS, D/LO/4/1 m.11. The mortgage was discharged in 1684 following the sale of Biddlesden.

freehold trust to administer the estate in return for an allowance of £5,000 a year – a very substantial income, if modest compared to his father's £13,000, or to the £30,000 which he claimed that his estates had produced as a gross yield in 1650.[5]

Frank Melton suggests that this trust was partly a device to protect his estate if he was prosecuted for treason, since he could have achieved the better management which ensued simply by taking his bankers' advice.[6] Buckingham could override the trust in order to sell any of the estates, and sometimes received income above the regular allowance.

The manor court held at Winslow on 8 January 1672 lists the trustees as lords of the manor.[7] William Gyles was able to claim in 1673 that he had never heard of them, so the people who attended the manor courts thought they were still dealing with the Duke.[8] The trustees changed several times. John Wildman, a former Leveller who had plotted against Cromwell and who tried with Buckingham to forge an alliance between Levellers, Baptists and Royalists after Cromwell's death,[9] was appointed a trustee in 1674. When he was not in prison or exile he worked for Buckingham, and he became the active manager of the Duke's affairs.

Buckingham was interested in his Whaddon property for hunting, and his expenditure in the area was largely related to keeping Whaddon Chase in good order. He kept a pack of hounds in a kennel at Shucklow, Little Horwood, until shortly before his death,[10] and the Chase was 'driven' (hunted across) once or twice a year.[11] In contrast, he was not usually interested in Winslow except as a source of income. From 1671 the Whaddon and Winslow manors were managed at a local level by the bailiff

---

[5] Melton, 'A rake refinanced', 299–300.

[6] Melton, 'A rake refinanced', 309.

[7] www.winslow-history.org.uk/winslow_court1672.shtm.

[8] TNA, E112/364/118 f.2.

[9] Richard L Greaves, 'Wildman, Sir John (1622/3–1693)', ODNB, www.oxforddnb.com/view/article/29405 [accessed 25 October 2017]; Hanrahan, Charles II, 167–68.

[10] TNA, C11/1403/25 (Selby v Lowndes); C11/1919/6 (Selby v Lowndes) ff.3–4.

[11] TNA, C11/1919/6 (Selby v Lowndes) f.6 (evidence of Francis Coy).

Richard Bodlly, at a salary of £20.[12] while Edmund West was steward of both.

The Duke was in the area in 1679 when he spent £109 at Buckingham in an unsuccessful attempt to influence the borough election there.[13] He was also involved in the county election, which was to be held at Aylesbury on 21 August that year.[14] At the last minute the sheriff moved it to Buckingham. The Duke led a procession of 'four thousand horse, with drums beating, and trumpets sounding', which spent the night at Winslow where they 'were well satisfied with the mean accommodation'. They set off for Buckingham at 5 am, determined to spend no money there. In the end there was no poll, but a riot broke out all the same.

The elections probably led the Duke to a prolonged stay at Whaddon, the only one mentioned in the accounts. Buckingham also seems to have found that the infrastructure for which he was responsible at Winslow needed smartening up.[15] His regular glazier Francis Bradford, who probably came from Bletchley or Fenny Stratford, was paid for glazing work in the chancel of Winslow church and for mending the leads.

Thomas Deely, a Winslow brickmaker, mended the chancel walls, and Francis Dorsett, grocer and churchwarden, was paid for a lock and bolt for the chancel door. In the same year Thomas Smallbones was paid for repairing the Moot Hall.

There is also an entry in Buckingham's accounts for £35 'for charges att Winslow by his Graces order'. This might refer to treating the inhabitants for election purposes, but Winslow had very few voters. The accounts for 1678 include £7 'for ye comision keept against Mr Giles of Winslow', so perhaps the Duke felt the need to improve his image. In 1680 Francis Bradford came back to glaze the Moot Hall and mend the chancel leads

---

[12] Melton, 'A rake refinanced', 306.
[13] History of Parliament, www.historyofparliamentonline.org/volume/1660-1690/constituencies/buckingham [accessed 22 January 2020].
[14] Samuel Johnson (1649–1703), *A Letter from a Freeholder of Buckinghamshire* (1679). There was an anonymous reply, *A True Account of What Past at the Election of Knights of the Shire for the County of Buckinghamshire*.
[15] Details from CBS, D135/A2/1 and TNA, C101/1555: accounts books 1677–80.

again. Stephen Bigg, the Winslow blacksmith, whose name was given as Briggs, was paid for ironwork in Winslow chancel, and 17s was spend on weights for the market.

Cliveden and Winslow

The Duke's real interest in Buckinghamshire became his new house at Cliveden overlooking the Thames, which he began building in the 1670s as a home for his lover the Countess of Shrewsbury, whose husband had died as the result a duel with Buckingham in 1668.[16] They were separated by order of the House of Lords but Buckingham went on with the building project regardless of expense, and lived there with his wife from the late 1670s.[17]

He sold the manors of Water Eaton, Bletchley and Fenny Stratford to Thomas Willis, the historian Browne Willis' grandfather, in 1675, presumably to raise funds for Cliveden.[18] After that, his strategy for carrying out a project which he could not afford was simple: he avoided paying the contractors who did the work.[19] A decade after his death in 1687 some of them were still trying to get their money from his estate.

This had unexpected consequences for Winslow. One of the tradesmen was Stephen Bigg, the Winslow blacksmith. In 1694 he joined in a lawsuit against the Duke's estate.[20] Bigg 'did provide greate quantity of iron' between 1676 and 1682, and was owed £908 for his work, of which £441 still remained due. According to a case brought against him by Mary Mortimer of Burnham in 1684, her late husband James had worked for Bigg as a smith at Cliveden but Bigg could not pay him until he was paid himself.[21] Bigg later did ironwork for Winslow Hall but at the same time

---

[16] Natalie Livingstone, *The Mistresses of Cliveden* (London: Arrow, 2015), 62, believes that work only started in 1676, ten years later than previously thought.

[17] Livingstone, *Mistresses of Cliveden*, 79–80.

[18] *VCH* Buckinghamshire, 4.274–83: Bletchley. Melton incorrectly includes Whaddon and Nash in this sale.

[19] Frank T Melton, *Sir Robert Clayton and the Origins of English Deposit Banking 1658–1685* (Cambridge: Cambridge University Press, 1986), 203, calls this 'long-term credit from artisans'.

[20] TNA, C7/140/6.

[21] TNA, C7/240/94 (complaint and answer).

developed a separate business as a postmaster. The patronage of the Duke or his trustees might have set him on this path.

Nicholas Goodwin

A bigger creditor was Nicholas Goodwin or Gooding, brickmaker of Hammersmith. He was another complainant in 1694. Between 1676 and 1682 he had provided bricks and lime and did work to the value of £9,748. The Duke cleared part of this in 1679 by granting him the manor of Winslow for £4,600, £100 more than his father paid for it 59 years earlier. The sale specifically excluded the right of hunting and hawking in Whaddon Chase.[22]

The valuation of £4,600 seems to have been fixed at about twenty years' purchase (twenty years' net income), because in 1661 Buckingham had leased the Winslow rectory, manor and market to Charles Tyrrell of Whaddon for one year for a payment of £220.[23] Goodwin agreed to allow the Duke to buy back the manor if he wished, at twenty years' purchase.[24] He also bought the rectory of Winslow (the right to collect the tithes), which according to William Lowndes was worth much more than the manor.[25]

Goodwin does not appear to have been a man with any local connections. His will of 1728, in which he styles himself 'esquire', refers only to property in Hammersmith, although he left a bequest to the poor of Bray, close to Cliveden.[26] Presumably he accepted the manor of Winslow as the best way of getting back some of what was owed to him, and continued the tradition of absentee lords.

He evidently used local agents: during his ownership Stephen Bigg, whom he knew from Cliveden, 'rented the fines quitt rents harriotts & other profits' of the manor of Winslow.[27]

---

[22] TNA, C11/1403/25 (Selby v Lowndes) f.1 (name written as Gooding), f.2 (Goodwin).

[23] CBS, BAS 377/22/1.

[24] CBS, D/LO/4/1 m.12.

[25] TNA, C11/1403/25 f.4.

[26] TNA, PROB 11/621/243.

[27] TNA, C11/1919/6 (Selby v Lowndes) f.9, evidence given by Robert Bigg his son in 1717.

The transfer of the manor to Goodwin was complicated because of the trust in which the Duke's property was held, and there were several changes of trusteeship and nominal ownership of the manor and rectory in 1680–82.[28] Buckingham still included Winslow among the estates which he used as security for debts in 1683.[29] After he died in 1687 the Duchess was able to claim dower on the manor, a right she sold to Goodwin in 1692 for £300.[30]

A private Act of Parliament (no doubt arranged by William Lowndes II) was passed in early 1697 authorising Goodwin and his eldest son Nicholas to sell the manor of Winslow and reinvest the proceeds.[31] By 29 May 1697 the manor court was held in the name of William Lowndes' trustees.[32] Various indentures between May and November 1697 transferred the manor from Goodwin and Buckingham's trustees to Lowndes, ending with a court order on 11 November to the surviving trustees to sell the manor to Goodwin for £4,280 'discounted out of the mony due to the said Goodwin from the Duke'.[33] They had been reluctant to make the conveyance before without a court order to indemnify them.

This nominal sale was to enable Goodwin to complete the transfer to Lowndes, which is dated 25 November 1697, just two weeks later.[34] Lowndes paid £4,900 for two acres and a barn in the Parsonage Close, eight acres lying dispersedly in Winslow fields, the manor of Winslow, the rectory of Winslow and the town of Winslow with the fairs and markets.[35] They were all let to Robert Gibbs 'at an old rent of £220 per annum'. According to Lowndes' son Robert, the sum of £4,900 paid was 23 years' purchase.[36]

---

[28] John Rylands Library, GB 133 RYCH/181; TNA, C11/1403/25, ff.1, 2; TNA, C6/310/9 f.2; CBS, D/LO/4/1 mm.11–12.
[29] TNA, C6/418/50 f.3.
[30] CBS, D/LO/4/1 m.13.
[31] Parliamentary Archives, HL/PO/JO/10/1/488/1103, HL/PO/PB/1/1696/8&9W3n25; *Journal of the House of Lords*, 26 January, 28 January, 1 February, 3 February 1697; *Journal of the House of Commons*, 22–23 February 1697.
[32] www.winslow-history.org.uk/winslow_court1697.shtm.
[33] TNA, C11/1403/25 f.1; CBS, D/BASM/375/22/43/10.
[34] TNA, C54/4825 no.10 (Close Rolls).
[35] CBS, D/LO/4/1 m.2; TNA, C11/1403/25 f.1. Lowndes said that the Moot Hall was excluded.
[36] TNA, C11/1403/25 f.2.

William Lowndes II

When William Lowndes[37] was born on 1 November 1652 he would have appeared destined to continue a lifestyle which was recovering from the Civil War: a role among the larger-scale yeoman families farming around 100 acres; marriage connections with other families of similar local status such as the Spooners and Wyatts; a relationship to the current bailiff of the manor, Peter Fige the younger, who was his mother's first cousin. He was probably educated at the Royal Latin School in Buckingham, where he must have received a good grounding in Latin because the philosopher John Locke later complimented him on his erudition.[38] However, his prospects changed when he was fourteen or fifteen: 'I (who in the year 1667 came from Winslow the place of my birth to the Citty to abide there)...'[39] he wrote later.

It was not unusual for the leading Winslow families to send a younger son to London, usually for an apprenticeship, and there were recent success stories. For example Valentine Fige[40] became an apothecary and when Peter Jackson, from the family which owned The Bell, died in London in 1644 his will, which described him as a skinner, shows that he had an estate of more than £2,500.[41] Both were members of their London livery companies, and that sum would have bought Peter Jackson nearly three times as much land in Winslow as anyone else owned at the time, if he had chosen to invest it in that way. Walter Tomlin, third son of a Winslow family, became a mariner in London and the mortgagee of the family property which descended to his eldest brother.[42]

However William Lowndes' departure for London was not the strategy of a prosperous family but a desperate measure taken for someone whose inheritance was rapidly disappearing. As we have

---

[37] He is William Lowndes II in Family 2 (see pages 52–60, though the 'II' will be omitted in future references to him).

[38] Moss, *Ways and Means*, 6–7; A Hanham, 'Lowndes, William (1652–1724), Treasury official', *ODNB*, www.oxforddnb.com/view/article/17099 [accessed 10 December 2017].

[39] CBS, D/LO/4/2 m.22.

[40] See the Fige family on pages 26-30.

[41] LMA, Archdeaconry Court of London, Register 29 f.355v.

[42] www.winslow-history.org.uk/winslow_will_tomlyn1645.shtm.

seen, 1667, the year he went to London, was the year his father had a court judgement against him for debt and the bailiff came to seize his goods.

Eight years later at the age of 23 Lowndes was an under-clerk of the Treasury at Whitehall, but records are incomplete so it is not known if he began working there earlier or had some other sort of employment first. Achieving a position at the Treasury would have required patronage, which is how numerous members of the Lowndes family found work there later, but the identity of William's patron is unknown.[43] A Thomas Lowndes who was already an excise clerk in the Treasury may be significant.[44] Fige connections are a possibility, although the Winslow Figes would not have had the necessary influence. Another is that he somehow became a protégé of the Duke of Buckingham or his agents. The Earl of Danby, previously Sir Thomas Osborne, who became one of Buckingham's trustees in 1671, helped to advance Lowndes in the 1670s and in 1679 gave him various sinecures.[45]

Lowndes recorded in his notebook the New Year gifts which he made for 1679.[46] They totalled just over £22, of which the biggest was £5 for 'Mr Kingdon' – which must be Lemuel Kingdon, Deputy Paymaster of the Forces at the time.[47] Nell Gwynn received £1 and the Duchess of Portsmouth £2 10s. These could also be people who had helped him.

Lowndes' remarkable career in London will be summarised only briefly here, as background to his impact on Winslow. Full details can be found in his entries in the *Oxford Dictionary of National Biography* and the *History of Parliament*, and Jennifer Moss has looked closely at his life in the Treasury. His portrait by Godfrey Kneller, when at the height of his power, is on the cover.

---

[43] Moss, *Ways and Means*, 7–9.

[44] History of Parliament, www.historyofparliamentonline.org/volume/1690-1715/member/lowndes-william-1652-1724 [accessed 22 January 2020]; Pete Smith, 'Winslow Hall', in M Airs and G Tyack (editors), *The Renaissance Villa in Britain, 1500–1700* (Reading: Spire, 2007), 223–46, 229.

[45] History of Parliament, Lowndes.

[46] CBS, D/X/1435.

[47] History of Parliament, www.historyofparliamentonline.org/volume/1660-1690/member/kingdon-lemuel-1654-86 [accessed 22 January 2020].

As under-clerk in 1675 he received a salary of £50, later raised to £100 as he became more senior, with additional fees of £30–300.[48] He came to the attention of Charles II in 1676 through an investigation into the handling of coffee duties, and in 1677 received from him a reward of £100.[49] Henry Guy of Tring Park, who became Secretary to the Treasury in 1679, made Lowndes in effect his deputy, and in 1686 chief clerk, with annual income from salary and fees of up to £700.[50]

Lowndes became an expert on the workings of the Treasury and Exchequer. In 1685 he also became agent for taxes, with a salary of £200. He stood in as acting Secretary to the Treasury in 1691 and 1695 when Guy was removed on charges of corruption. Guy was godfather to Lowndes' son Edward and left Lowndes £500 and a fulsome commendation in his will:[51]

'He hath behaved himself with that extraordinary justice and gratitude towards me that it may be there has not been so great (I am sure not greater) example and I do pray to God from my heart that he may never want as true a friend as he hath been to me.'

Guy was allowed to nominate his successor, and Lowndes became Secretary in April 1695, but shared the profits of the office with him, taking a salary of £1,000, later increased to £1,200.[52] He held the post for 29 years, the rest of his life.

Lowndes became Member of Parliament for Seaford in Sussex in November 1695 and transferred to St Mawes in Cornwall in 1715. Throughout his parliamentary career he avoided being labelled as a clear Tory or Whig, although he was linked most closely with the Tory Earl of Godolphin. He became associated with the Committee of Ways and Means, to which he proposed the Treasury's financial measures each year, and 'Old Ways and Means' was his nickname. He also served on many non-legislative

---

[48] Moss, *Ways and Means*, 13.
[49] Moss, *Ways and Means*, 12; *Calendar of Treasury Books, Volume 5, 1676–1679*, 651 (7 June 1677).
[50] Moss, *Ways and Means*, 14.
[51] TNA, PROB 11/520/25 (proved 1711).
[52] Moss, *Ways and Means*, 14.

committees. His desire to enforce high standards in public finance was attributed to his devout Anglicanism.

In 1722 he again stood unsuccessfully for Parliament, but regained his seat in the House of Commons through a by-election for East Looe later in the year. His last appearance in the House was four days before he died on 20 January 1724. He was credited, perhaps incorrectly, with inventing the expression 'take care of the pennies and the pounds will take care of themselves', and the financial records which he kept show that he lived up to it.

William Lowndes as a Winslow landowner

Lowndes' first purchase of land in Winslow was in 1676–77. In two instalments, he bought from William Retchford, rector of Addington, 29 acres of copyhold land for which he paid £296.[53] In 1678 Lowndes, described as 'scrivener' (clerk) of the parish of St Martin-in-the Fields in Westminster, bought from Edward Palmer the 72 acres of land which his father had mortgaged to Palmer in 1668.[54] He paid £513.[55] In two years he acquired as much land as his grandfather had ever owned. The price he paid (just over £8 per acre overall) was rather but not excessively more than the £6 per acre which William Illing paid Robert Williatt for 40 acres in Little Horwood in 1670.[56]

Palmer himself provided some of the finance: on 25 April 1678 Lowndes mortgaged the land bought from Retchford to him for £210.[57] Palmer acknowledged receipt of the last instalment of purchase and mortgage money ahead of schedule on 31 December 1678. Lowndes was by then described as gentleman. The mortgage provided only part of the purchase money, for which he must have used the £100 reward he received from Charles II in 1677 and virtually everything he had earned since going to London.

[53] CBS, BAS 376/22/32 & 40, D/LO/4/1 m.1.
[54] CBS, BAS 376/22/42.
[55] CBS, D/LO/4/1 m.1.
[56] TNA, E112/364/96–97.
[57] CBS, D/BASM/375/22/43/4. Lowndes was due to pay Palmer £109 on 31 January 1679 and £112 on 31 July 1679.

On 26 October 1679 Lowndes married Elizabeth, daughter of Sir Roger Harsnett of Dulwich, at the church of St Martin-in-the-Fields in London. Much later when he made his will he referred with untypical emotion to the 'memory of the true love' between him and Elizabeth. His father-in-law was serjeant-at-arms to the House of Lords from 1660, was knighted by Charles II for service to Charles I,[58] and was buried in Westminster Abbey in 1692.

Lowndes was evidently a staunch Royalist in retrospect; in recording the earlier history of one of his properties he wrote:[59]

'This purchase was within few days [in 1649] after the execrable murther of the best of kings wherein (according to common fame) John Norbury contracted a guilt by giving some advice or assistance in the hellish prosecution & though he is remembered to have had a very mean understanding in the laws he was afterwards made one of the judges for Wales by the usurper Cromwell.'

Lowndes was involved in the management of his father-in-law's property in Dulwich.[60] Harsnett made Lowndes executor of his will (even though Elizabeth had died in 1680), and left him and Robert, his son by Elizabeth, £10 each.[61] This was a distinct social advance for a man from a farming family in Winslow, and shows what a different world Lowndes moved in when in London, but his ownership of land offered security. Dr Robert Harsnett, presumably Elizabeth's brother, was later trustee for the marriage settlement of Anne, Lowndes' daughter by his second marriage.[62]

Lowndes' contribution to his own first marriage settlement was made on 2 January 1680 when he surrendered his 101 acres to Elizabeth for her life in lieu of dower if she survived him, then to their joint heirs male.[63] His father-in-law probably contributed money too, which is almost certainly (directly or indirectly) how Lowndes was in a position to buy more land in Winslow.

---

[58] CBS, D/LO/6/18/1: memorandum of Lowndes births, marriages and deaths.
[59] CBS, D/LO/4/2 m.6.
[60] TNA, C 8/303/123: they were co-defendants in a case brought in 1682.
[61] TNA, PROB 11/412/100.
[62] TNA, PROB 11/595/393 p.3 (proved 1724).
[63] CBS, BAS 376/22/47; D/LO/4/1 m.1.

Indentures of 3–4 February 1680 recorded the purchase by Lowndes and William Gyles together of 180 acres of freehold land in Winslow called the Berry Lands from the Duke of Buckingham's trustees. Lowndes paid £750 for his half-share, of which £375 was borrowed at interest (and repaid on 1 December 1681).[64] In 1681 Lowndes and Gyles divided up the land, which they had previously held in common, and in 1683 Lowndes put the land into the settlement for his second marriage, to Jane Hopper, assigning it to his wife's trustees in lieu of dower.

The Baptist Gyles[65] was a surprising business associate for a strong Anglican such as Lowndes, but was likely the only man in Winslow in a position to raise £750 for his share of the purchase.

At the age of 27 in 1679, Lowndes was now the largest landowner in Winslow. His purchases had been paid for with money acquired outside Winslow, but the vendors were not yet Winslow people, so the only effect felt locally was the change of one absentee landlord for another.

Lowndes' first child, Robert, was born on 25 October 1680 and his wife Elizabeth died on 6 November. She was buried at Westminster Abbey, presumably through her father's connections. There is no information about what happened to the infant Robert while his father was a widower: probably he was sent to Winslow to be looked after by relatives, or a female relative went to London where Robert was educated. A note by William about his Carnaby Street property refers to a school being 'built by Mr Lewis Maidwell who (*inter alios*) taught there my eldest son Robert'.[66]

The next stage of Lowndes' purchases is clarified by the fortunate survival of a letter sent to him on 6 December 1681 by an old acquaintance, William Spooner, representative of a long-established Winslow family and a contemporary of Lowndes' father:[67]

---

[64] CBS, D/LO/4/1 m.9.

[65] For the Gyles Family see pages 26–30.

[66] CBS, D/LO/4/2 m.22.

[67] CBS, BAS 370/22/2/53. They were distantly related (see the Lowndes family tree on page 52): William Spooner's aunt Alice had married William Lowndes' great-uncle Robert in 1627, so Peter Lowndes I was cousin to both of them.

'Mr William Lowndes my kind love to you & this is to lett you understand that I have received youre letter and according to youre desire I have sent you a perticular of those parcells of land that I have a minde to sell to you which are as followeth

[a list of strips of land follows, annotated presumably by Lowndes]

'These lands lye as they are sett downe heere in estimate according as they were sett downe when they came to mee from my father. I could sell it out in parcells but I would sell it alltogether or else I could have a many chapmen for by parcells.[68]

'Youre mind in youre letter I understand by your fathers words is to know about the prise. I shall bee upon a very modderate terme but I guess it to bee a purchasse about 5 or 6 hundred pound. There is in account six score & seven ridges of sword ground [pasture] & ariable. The whole sume is threescore & two acres soe wee common & pay taxes for itt & having noe more at presentt but desireing you to considder of it betwixt this & Christmas you do poynt to com downe I rest youre loveing friend – William Spooner'

This was not exactly the sort of letter Lowndes was used to dealing with at the Treasury. It appears that he had sent an enquiry to Spooner, and probably to other potential vendors, and was using his father as an intermediary. Spooner did not point out that the land was already mortgaged, but no doubt Lowndes knew that; it must have been why he thought Spooner would sell.

The Christmas visit and face-to-face negotiations duly ensued and a special session of the manor court was held on Boxing Day for the sale of 55 acres.[69] The purchase price was £461, which must have disappointed Spooner somewhat and was rather less per acre than Lowndes' first purchases.[70] However, he sold another ten acres to Lowndes in 1696 for £200.[71]

---

[68] Meaning that he could sell it in parcels to individual purchasers.
[69] CBS, BAS 376/22/49.
[70] CBS, D/LO/4/1 m.1.
[71] WMC 26 October 1696, see www.winslow-history.org.uk/winslow_court1696.shtml.

This was the beginning of a new policy: people in Winslow now began to receive Lowndes' London money. He brought in large amounts of cash and bought out some owner-occupiers. William Spooner and his son Robert continued to hold 60 acres as Lowndes' tenants until William Spooner's death, after which the land was transferred to other tenants who paid £24 a year rent.[72]

An agreement has survived from 1698 in which James Brittain and his wife agree to sell Lowndes a house and five acres in Shipton with common for two cows, for £110 paid to Brittain and two guineas to his wife.[73] Brittain acknowledges receipt of 2s 6d 'for earnest'. The sale duly went ahead at the manor court.[74] Presumably it was Lowndes' normal practice to make prospective vendors enter a binding agreement, but the documents would usually have been destroyed after the sale was completed. The arrangement was an attractive one for Brittain, as the land was his wife Anne's, inherited from her brother in 1696 before they were married. Land which was only Brittain's during his wife's life was thus converted to cash which was his outright.

The roll kept by Lowndes with details of all his purchases, combined with the court rolls surviving for most years, enables a full picture of his activities to be built up.[75] It has been noted that this was not a good time for buying land, with heavy taxation and rising prices. Lending money was a more profitable alternative, and the only people looking for expansion of estates were 'those who were self-consciously creating a new estate out of the profits of some non-agrarian activity'.[76] This describes Lowndes precisely. Personal satisfaction was as important as rational calculation in such cases.[77] However the nature of Lowndes' satisfaction is a subject for speculation, as his meticulous keeping of financial records did not usually extend to personal comments.

---

[72] Folger Shakespeare Library, W.a.147 p.62.

[73] CBS, BAS 375/22/43/1.

[74] WMC 25 October 1698, see www.winslow-history.org.uk/winslow_court1698.shtm.

[75] CBS, D/LO/4/1.

[76] Christopher Clay, 'Landlords and estate management in England', in Joan Thirsk (editor) *The Agrarian History of England and Wales volume 2 1640-1750: Agrarian Change* (Cambridge: Cambridge University Press 1985), 178.

[77] Clay, 'Landlords', 181.

Several strategies can be detected when looking at his purchases chronologically:

1. Recovering his father's lands. He was still doing this in 1699 when he bought five acres which were 'formerly part of my fathers land'.

2. Acquiring blocks of land which already formed closes within the open field system, or could be turned into closes. He also exchanged some land to consolidate existing holdings.

3. Buying up houses and adjacent land in Sheep Street for his new house and grounds.

4. Intensive purchases in Shipton, especially in 1698.

5. Building up the interests of his eldest son Robert. This began in 1687 when he bought 27 acres in their joint names; Robert, aged eight, duly attended the 1689 manor court.

6. In effect, re-creating the demesne (the land under the direct control of the lord of the manor), which had not existed in Winslow since the sixteenth century.

Other purchases seem to be more fortuitous as property became available, and it is likely that would-be vendors approached him, rather than the other way round, hoping for a better price than they would get locally. He bought only in Winslow and Shipton, not at all in Granborough and Little Horwood. In 1698 when Whaddon Chase and the manor of Whaddon were sold by the Duke of Buckingham's trustees it seems that Lowndes wanted to buy them:[78]

'Old Ways and Means bid £17,000 when Selby bought it, who gave £20,000 for it including the estate at Wavenden, Whaddon, etc. Lowndes would have had it then, but could not raise the money time enought, as I am told.'

His total expenditure in Winslow over 27 years (*see Table 6*) was similar to the £12,760 spent by Sir Harbottle Grimston on buying Gorhambury in Hertfordshire with 1,582 acres in 1652, but

---

[78] Margaret Maria Verney, *Verney Letters of the Eighteenth Century* (London: Benn, 1930), 2.215, Lord Fermanagh to Earl Verney, Claydon, 29 June 1746. This cannot be correct about Wavendon, which already belonged to James Selby.

1677	£296		1691	£70
1678	£513		1692	£823
1679	-		1693	-
1680	£750		1694	£525
1681	£711		1695	£2,360
1682	-		1696	£5,100
1683	£50		1697	-
1684	£390		1698	£1,532
1685	£610		1699	£447
1686	-		1700	£129
1687	£830		1701	£400
1688	£9		1702	£47
1689	£40		1703	£550
1690	£382		**Total**	**£16,564**

Table 6: William Lowndes' expenditure on buying property in Winslow and Shipton up to 1703, according to his own figures (rounded to the nearest pound).[79]

Grimston went on to spend another £39,000 on creating an estate of more than 4,000 acres. That is no doubt why the Grimstons joined the aristocracy and the Lowndeses did not.[80]

Lowndes' second marriage was on 25 November 1683 at St Clement Danes, to Jane, daughter of Simon Hopper of Richmond. He used his freehold land in Winslow as his side of the marriage settlement, along with 55 acres he had bought from William Spooner; these would be Jane's dower if she outlived him. Jane died of smallpox in 1685, leaving a daughter Anne born in 1684; a second child was born dead.[81]

---

[79] Purchases listed in CBS, D/LO/4/1 in chronological order but years of purchase are mainly from court rolls. Lowndes gave the total as £16,577 1s 11d.
[80] Clay, 'Landlords', 184.
[81] CBS, D/LO/6/18/1.

Simon Hopper made his will in 1686, although it was not proved until 1694. It refers to 'my wages or salary … for my service to his sacred Majestie'. He left Lowndes only a mourning ring, with no mention at all of his granddaughter Anne. Hopper appears to have been the King's Violinist who was given a pension of £60 in 1660 and was a colleague of the composer Henry Purcell.[82] He also had two sons who received very small legacies, and was clearly not in the same financial league as Lowndes even though he styled himself gentleman. Presumably William's marriage to Jane was a love match, so did not contribute to his buying power. He now had two motherless children.

His daughter Anne was brought up by her grandmother, Anne Hopper.[83] Lowndes' accounts for 1700–03 include £13 a year paid to Mrs Hopper for Anne's board, and another sum of £9 or £10 a year for 'her bill for Anne Lowndes' or 'necessarys & phisique'. Lowndes was also paying Mrs Hopper 6 per cent interest on £100.

His note about Anne's marriage settlement in 1703 recorded that she was to inherit the Six Bells in Richmond from her grandmother whose will was made in 1703 and proved in 1709; she left £200 and the residue of her goods to her granddaughter Anne and the remaining lease of her house in Richmond to Anne's husband, Thomas Jett, who was the executor.[84] Anne was only eighteen when she married Jett in 1703.[85] His father provided them with land at Compton Magna, Somerset, and Lowndes gave Anne a marriage portion of £1,500.

Lowndes' first purchases had been of land only. In 1681 he bought two houses with small areas of land. Abel Sear's house cannot have been very substantial as Lowndes paid only £65 for the house and 3½ acres. Dorothy Miller's house, 'in one part of which Simon Hogson now lives', had three acres and cost £185.

Between £100 and £150 seems to have been the normal range within which he bought houses, although several were much more

[82] *Calendar of State Papers Domestic: Charles II, 1660–1*, 555; *Calendar of Treasury Books, Volume 8, 1685–1689*, 130.
[83] Folger Shakespeare Library, W.a.146 p.54; W.a.147 p.40.
[84] TNA, PROB 11/511/42.
[85] CBS, D/LO/6/18/1.

Figure 6: William Lowndes bought and retained the house to the right of the horse (11 Sheep Street), and demolished other houses which stood on the left and right sides of the photograph.

expensive. Dorothy Miller's house and close in Winslow had been mortgaged by her husband Thomas in 1660 along with other property.[86] Thomas was the son of Walter Miller alias Grant and his wife Bridget, who was William Lowndes' great-aunt.[87] The house was not the Millers' residence, which was in Shipton, and Lowndes might have bought it as a favour to his relatives.

In 1685 Lowndes bought for £619 the house which is now 11 Sheep Street along with 36 acres (or 33½ in his own record) from Thomas Halfpenny, who had just inherited this from his father. The land included 'Pond Close, one of the Rose Closes and all Norden except one acre'.[88] Lowndes bought none of these houses for his own use, and when visiting Winslow must have stayed with relatives or at an inn. So he must have let Halfpenny's former house, perhaps only taking it because he wanted the land. Fifteen years later his accounts refer to the house as 'that in the tenure of

---

[86] BL, Add.Ch. 53955 (a copy which must have been preserved by Lowndes). An earlier mortgage by Thomas Miller was recorded at the 1651 court.
[87] For the connection see the Lowndes family tree on page 52 and the Grant alias Miller family tree on page 116.
[88] WMC 9 October 1685, see www.winslow-history.org.uk/winslow_court1685.shtm.

Ben. Saunders' when 'Scotts house' next door was pulled down.[89] The 'curtilages, gardens and orchards' of the house, which probably stretched back to what is now Greyhound Lane, then became part of a bigger plan, with the western pavilion of Winslow Hall built on the land – and Saunders was paid £3 for the use of his barn while the hall was being built.[90]

In 1686 Lowndes married for the third time. His wife was Elizabeth, daughter of Reverend Dr John Martin or Martyn. She and William had two children (William born 1687 and Elizabeth born 1688), but she died of smallpox in 1689.

Their son William married Margaret Leyton at St Paul's in London in 1711, when his father gave him a marriage portion of £2,000 and her father gave £1,500.[91] William had a house in Duke Street in London and inherited his father's property at Astwood in Buckinghamshire. Elizabeth married John Duncombe of Aldbury in Hertfordshire in 1706, when her father gave £2,000. She died in 1712, as her father wrote 'to ye unspeakable grief of mine and her husbands families', leaving three children alive.

From 1687 Lowndes began to buy up property elsewhere, beginning with The Bury estate in Chesham for £1,430.[92] He bought other property in Buckinghamshire, land in Romney Marsh and some London property in Carnaby Street and Knightsbridge (the latter much later became Lowndes Square). These purchases later enabled him to provide for his numerous children, though he had only three when he began buying. It was a time of rising land prices, and twenty to twenty-two years' purchase was typical.[93]

By 1687 Lowndes was living with his family in Princes Court, near St James's Park in Westminster, with The Bury as their country house in Chesham. He bought a permanent base for himself in Winslow in 1692, and moved to a large house in Broad Sanctuary, outside Westminster Abbey, in 1695 or 1696.[94]

---

[89] Eland, 'Building of Winslow Hall', 411.
[90] Eland, 'Building of Winslow Hall', 429
[91] CBS, D/LO/6/18/1.
[92] Moss, *Ways and Means*, 16
[93] Clay, 'Landlords', 173 Table 14.1, 177–78, 181.
[94] Moss, *Ways and Means*, 67.

Lowndes married for the fourth time in 1691. This brought some distinguished connections. His bride Rebecca Shales came from a prominent banking family, and could also claim descent from the Duke of Clarence, brother of Edward IV. Her brother Charles, who became a trustee and executor for Lowndes, was appointed Royal Goldsmith in 1694.[95] His daughter Anne later married William and Rebecca's son Charles, and two other daughters married William's grandchildren, the sons of his eldest son Robert Lowndes III.

Lowndes' and Rebecca's first child was a daughter, Rebecca, born in 1692. She died in 1715, when her father wrote: 'Her loss is extreamly lamented, for the sake not only of her beautifull person, but also of her piety and all other vertues, which endeared her to all her relations.'[96] A son John born in 1697 died aged four and was 'a good child in every respect'. In all Rebecca produced fourteen children between 1693 and 1710 including one set of twins. Three were baptised at Edmonton, presumably because of Shales connections there, and the others at Westminster.

William Lowndes as lord of the manor

It was probably in 1692 and as a result of his fourth marriage that Lowndes started to develop a bigger scheme for Winslow, which led him to buy the manor itself. The various arrangements took most of 1697 to finalise and previous negotiations could have taken several years. The £4,900 which Lowndes paid for the manor was less than he had so far spent on buying land in Winslow[97] and slightly more than its valuation when the Duke of Buckingham transferred it to Nicholas Goodwin. Goodwin was no doubt a willing seller, but Lowndes did not pay an excessive price. It was the last time the manor was sold as a meaningful entity.

In practical terms, becoming lord of the manor was less significant for Lowndes than becoming Winslow's biggest property owner. The Lowndes family used their economic power rather than the lordship to transform Winslow. The manor courts

---

[95] Moss, *Ways and Means*, 17–18.
[96] CBS, D/LO/6/18/1.
[97] See *Table 6* on page 76.

were held in the names of his trustees, and he was even fined on three occasions for failing to attend his own court. However the manor was important symbolically. The building of Winslow Hall would have been anomalous if it had not become the manor house, and there would have been a risk of Goodwin selling to someone else who might have been a local rival.

As the lord of the manor, Lowndes followed the practice of leasing his rights to a farmer who paid a fixed rent and kept any profits. This was Robert Gibbs, who was a distant relative since they were both descended from the Figes.[98] Lowndes' accounts record that Gibbs was due to make his annual payment of £220 at Michaelmas 1699 for the manor and rectory.[99] In fact most of it was paid not to Lowndes but to others on his behalf or was offset against work done for him, but £55 was still due in April 1700. Gibbs continued to provide carriage and some goods such as wheat straw for thatching, and £10 was 'forgiven for a bad crop anno 1699', so the balance was cleared in April 1701.

Gibbs collected the tithes and the fines at the manor court, including the fines which Lowndes himself paid when buying land (£1 at the May 1699 court). The arrangement was still in place in 1703 when Lowndes recorded it as an 'old rent'.[100]

Lowndes also repaired the church. According to Reverend John Croft he found the chancel, now his responsibility as owner of the tithes, was still as left after the Civil War. He replaced the lead in the roof, 'pav'd it with Bister stones rubb'd & broad: at the east end sunk a vault for a dormitory, o're which he raisd the altar-place, 2 handsom steeps compast it with a neat rail, pav'd with Danish marble; gave a new elegant communion table'.[101]

The family vault was a crucial part of his vision, and many of his children and grandchildren who died in infancy were buried in it before his own burial, although it did not have the intended long-term effect as there is now no visible trace of it in the church.

---

[98] See the Fige and Gibbs family trees on pages 26 and 146.
[99] Folger Shakespeare Library, W.a.146 pp.37, 50.
[100]   CBS, D/LO/4/1 m.2.
[101] BL, Add.Ms. 5840 f.202r.

He also replaced the glass, inserting the Lowndes arms in the east window. A bill dated 5 December 1702 includes a mason working for a day and a half 'to let in ye barrs to fasten glass coat of armes in ye chancel window'.[102]

Lowndes transferred the lordship of the manor to his son Robert in 1703, but retained an interest in Winslow. On 31 December 1709 he paid 13s 4d for 'charges of a journey to Winslow' and 14s for 'horse hire to Winslow' in addition to his usual expenses of keeping a coach and coachman.[103] He probably made only an annual visit by this time, but continued to buy more property which he kept under his own control, and paid for more repairs to the chancel.[104] He was still paying for repair and maintenance of 'ye new house at Winslow' even though he had handed it over to his son Robert.[105] He also had expenses 'for making a farmyard at Winslow', including stone from Oving and Thornborough and tiles from Stewkley: £11 in all.[106] Most of these expenses were directly or indirectly for Robert's benefit.

Lowndes' made his will in 1721 three years before his death. It was a massive document.[107] Having passed the Winslow estate to Robert in the 1703 marriage settlement, in his will he distributed his other Buckinghamshire estates among his sons and confirmed settlements already made. The executors were Charles Shales, brother of his fourth wife Rebecca, John Duncombe, who had married his daughter Elizabeth, and Richard Hill, the uncle of his eldest son Robert's wife Margaret.[108]

His second son, William, already had a house and manor at Astwood Bury near Newport Pagnell. Charles, the eldest son by his fourth wife Rebecca, inherited The Bury and extensive property at Chesham, where his descendants remained until the twentieth century.[109] Two younger sons, Richard and Joseph,

---

[102] Wren Society, *Seventeenth Volume* (Oxford, 1940), 59.

[103] CBS, D/X/1435 p.23: 1709 notebook.

[104] CBS, D/X/1435 p.25.

[105] CBS, D/X/1435 p.26.

[106] CBS, D/X/1435 p.27.

[107] TNA, PROB 11/595/393 (William Lowndes' will).

[108] For William Lowndes' descendants see the family tree on page 152.

[109] Moss, *Ways and Means*, 91–100.

received estates at Pitchcott and Barton Hartshorn respectively, both of which passed to Charles after they died unmarried. An estate around North Crawley known as Crawley Grange was entailed to Lowndes' eldest grandson, Robert's son Richard, and his descendants, and the advowson of North Crawley was reserved for members of the Lowndes family.

Lowndes' remaining property in London was to be used to pay various legacies, including marriage portions for his unmarried daughters, and was to be sold if necessary. This led to litigation within the family and the site of his house was sold, then later under other ownership was developed into Lowndes Square in Belgravia.

Lowndes died on 20 January 1724.

The *Reading Mercury* reported that his body was carried from London 'to lye in state at his seat at Chesham', and to proceed to Winslow the next day, 'there to lye also in state till late in the evening, and then to be interr'd in the parish church there.'[110] The parish register records the burial of 'William Lowndes esq' on 29 January. His will required the funeral to 'be performed with as little charge as may be', but bread to the value of £20 was to be distributed to the poor.[111] That was the gesture of someone who wanted a good send-off, rather than a serious attempt to help the poor, who would have benefited more from land left to the parish to bring an annual income for distribution to the poor.

Eighteenth-century custom among the gentry and aristocracy was to leave something to all one's servants, usually a year's wages. Lowndes did not do that, perhaps a sign of his self-made origins. The man who had gone away from Winslow to make his fortune left people in no doubt that he had succeeded.

---

[110] Quoted by Moss, *Ways and Means*, 71.
[111] TNA, PROB 11/595/393.

The Gyles family tree

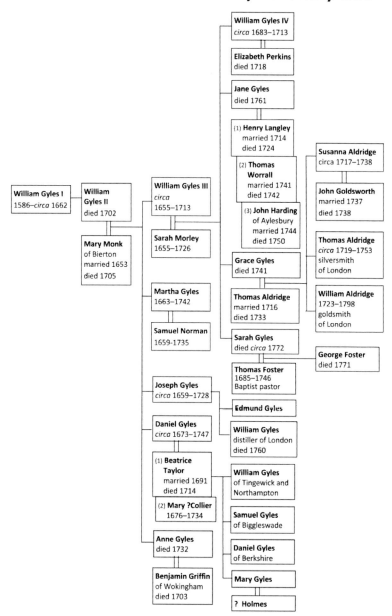

Winslow families
3: **The Gyles Family**

The Gyles family was established in Winslow by 1547.[1] The surname first appears in the parish register in 1571 with the baptism of Joan, daughter of William Gyles. A succession of men named William Gyles continued in Winslow for nearly two centuries. By about 1595 they lived in a house on the north side of the Market Square where the Bank now stands.[2]

William Gyles I (born 1586) was the son of William and Margaret. His mother, who died in 1625, probably shared his house as most of her inventoried goods were in two rooms, a great chamber and a little chamber.[3] It is not known if this William was already a draper as his descendants were. His son, also William and probably born in the 1620s, is not recorded as having an Anglican baptism so the family may already have become dissenters. In 1638 William Gyles I and his second wife Anne sold 'a cottage in Winslow called the Crowne Corner', probably adjacent to the house in which they lived.[4] In 1662 they gave a house and piece of pasture to their son William and daughter-in-law Mary[5] – and they probably died soon afterwards. The burial records for the 1660s have many gaps.

Their son **William Gyles II** (died 1702) was fully integrated in local society, even while he was liable to discrimination for his

---

[1] HALS, A25/162 (inventory of John Wenylborowe).

[2] In the dispute with the Duke of Buckingham about market stalls (*see following page*), Mary Rawlins née Gyles, aged 82, said she had been born in the house. It is marked on the map on page xx.

[3] HALS, A25/2831.

[4] WMC 12 September 1683, see www.winslow-history.org.uk/winslow_court1638.shtm. The occupant was Abel Sear, who in the evidence for the dispute is said to have at one time occupied part of the Gyles house.

[5] WMC 21 April 1662, see www.winslow-history.org.uk/winslow_court1662.shtm.

Baptist faith. In 1682 he served as high constable for Cottesloe Hundred.[6] He was at various times overseer of the poor in Winslow, foreman of the manor court jury and overseer of the orders for the common fields. He was a draper by trade but was described as gentleman by 1692.[7]

He was a regular buyer of property, and in 1690–91 he sold off building plots to the west of what is now the High Street, on land called the Pickles extending Winslow to the north.[8] At Epiphany 1696 Quarter Sessions he was indicted 'for obstructing the road to Adstock, at a place called The Pickles, by making a ditch and a hedge', presumably in connection with the new housing.[9]

He also did a little farming: in 1682, a labourer named Thomas Smallbones stole from him a turkey hen, value 6d, and a duck, value 4d, and was ordered to be whipped in the gaol 'until his body be bloody'.[10] It has been suggested that dissenters were at the forefront of commerce during this period, partly because of their exclusion from public life,[11] and William Gyles certainly seems to have been Winslow's most successful businessman.

The only land which Gyles inherited was the pasture which he received from his father. In 1679 he and William Lowndes bought 180 acres which they later divided between them. Their co-operation continued to the next generation: William Gyles III was a trustee for the marriage settlement which William Lowndes made for his son Robert in 1703. Ninety-three acres of freehold land were still held by descendants of William Gyles II in 1766.

Gyles' dispute with the Duke of Buckingham's trustees, which began in 1673 and led to evidence being taken in 1677, has left a large amount of documentation, although most of it is about the market rather than the Gyles family.[12] The dispute was about

---

[6] BQS, 27 April 1682.
[7] TNA, E134/4WandM/Mich41.
[8] WMC 22 April 1690, see www.winslow-history.org.uk/winslow_court1690.shtm; 15 April 1691, see www.winslow-history.org.uk/winslow_court1691.shtm.
[9] BQS, 16 January 1696.
[10] BQS, 5 October 1682.
[11] John Richetti, *The Life of Daniel Defoe* (Chichester: Blackwell-Wiley 2005), 4.
[12] TNA, E112/364/118; E134/29Chas2/Mich22.

whether Gyles had the right to set up market stalls in front of his house on the north side of the Market Square and charge traders rent for them. The case had already gone to law in around 1656 when it went to the assizes at Aylesbury, apparently because 'the then pretended lords of the manor' had confiscated some cloth as part of the dispute; the verdict at that time went to Gyles.

The outcome of the case is not recorded in the Court of Exchequer records but when Gyles handed over the house to his son in 1682 it was described as 'a messuage with the stalls', so it appears that he won. At the 1703 manor court a number of people were amerced 10s for leaving their stalls standing on a Sunday 'in or near the road leading to the church'.[13] They included Gyles's son and seven butchers, so these were the occupants of the stalls in front of Gyles' house, known as Butchers' Row.

George Shaw, clearly no friend to the Gyles family, claimed that six years earlier he was summoned to see the steward who was apparently trying to sort out the issue, and Gyles told him: 'George if you will not speake what you doe know I will be a friend to you as long as you live'. The Gyles version was that Shaw had 'been an idle loose and debauched liver & greatly guilty of drunkennesse and prophane sweareing', and had previously given false evidence.

The entry for Gyles' death in the 1702 manor court roll states that he held two messuages and 48 acres of copyhold land.[14] This land he had bought from Wendover Lowndes I in 1672 along with the house where he lived from 1682 after his son William got married and took over the house in the Market Square, and it included the home close on which he would build the Baptist meeting-house.

The family house was probably the largest in Winslow, with seven hearths, but appears to have been subdivided for Gyles to share with his son Daniel. When his freehold land is added, William Gyles II was the largest landowner in Winslow apart from

[13] WMC 1 October 1703, see www.winslow-history.org.uk/winslow_court1703.shtm.
[14] WMC 22 April 1702, see www.winslow-history.org.uk/winslow_court1702.shtm.

William Lowndes II, even after he had handed over some property to his other children before he died.

Mary Gyles (died 1705), William Gyles II's wife, came from the Baptist family of Monk in Bierton. She was a medical practitioner in her own right. The Archdeacon's visitation in October 1684 recorded that 'Mary Gyles wife of William Gyles was found to have introduced a letter to exercise the art of surgery'.[15] She would have been required to present testimonials from other practitioners and satisfied patients, and probably to restrict herself to medical activities which were not of interest to male doctors.[16]

In fact as a Baptist she can have had no chance of receiving a licence, and probably applied only because someone had complained that she was acting without one. In the following month, November, the strongly anti-Baptist vicar John Croft was installed. This was probably connected. She apparently continued to practise: in the will she made in 1704 she bequeathed to her daughter-in-law 'my still and the frame belonging to the same and my stone mortarr and all my surrupp glasses surrupp and stilld waters in and belonging to the same and my saves and oyles'.[17]

After her husband's death, Mary continued to live in their part of the same house, apparently with her unmarried daughter Mary (died 1722). Her will mentions the best room, parlour and least chamber, and the inventory also refers to the hall.[18] Among the possessions she bequeathed were her 'biggest gold ring', 'silver taster', 'best black silck gown' and 'redd bedd'. The inventory includes a clock, which was a rare item in Winslow at the time. She evidently lived in some style, but also owned five cows, so presumably did some small-scale dairying.

William and Mary Gyles had six children. Their son Joseph (*circa* 1659–1728) stayed in Winslow and is variously referred to as hatter, draper and gentleman; he must have left the Baptists,

---

[15] HALS, ASA 7/36.
[16] Doreen Evenden, 'Gender differences in the licensing and practice of female and male surgeons in early modern England', *Medical History* 42 (1998), 194–216.
[17] HALS, 142AW10.
[18] HALS, A25/4562.

because his son Edmund had an Anglican baptism in 1708. Their daughter Anne (died 1732) married Benjamin Griffin, a leading Baptist of Wokingham, but returned to Winslow as a widow. Their daughter Martha (1663–1742) married Samuel Norman, grocer and Baptist of Winslow.

William Gyles III (*circa* 1655–1713) was the eldest son of William and Mary, and took over the property in Market Square and the running of the drapery business in 1682, probably when he married Sarah Morley (1655–1726). Her father Benjamin was a Baptist minister from Ravensthorpe in Northamptonshire, who came to live in Winslow and was buried in the meeting-house.

William expanded the business, no doubt a strategy to help his growing extended family: his will refers to shops and warehouses in Winslow, Buckingham and Leighton Buzzard and freehold property at Great Horwood.[19] He described himself as a woollen draper, and there was evidently a division between the woollen and linen parts of the business, with his brother Daniel being a linen draper. He often served as foreman of the manor court jury, and he had mortgages on a number of properties in Winslow. He prospered enough to leave legacies of £480 to three of his daughters and an annuity of £20 to the fourth. Two of his daughters were to have parts of his house.

Daniel Gyles (1673–1747) inherited his father's dwelling-house near The Bell and, as he outlived his brother William by 34 years, inherited his role as effective leader of the Winslow Baptists. He was also a significant figure in the parish, serving as overseer of the poor and foreman of the jury. He is described as a linen draper, but it is not clear if he had a separate shop or shared the one in the Market Square. In 1715 he was able to buy 43 acres of land from his nieces Jane, Grace, Sarah and Martha after they inherited when their brother William Gyles IV died childless, and he was often a mortgagee of copyhold property.[20]

He made other purchases of small pieces of land, so that in a list drawn up around 1743 he owned 56 acres, farmed by Richard

---

[19] TNA, PROB 11/533/209.
[20] WMC 30 September 1715, see www.winslow-history.org.uk/winslow_court1715.shtm.

Gibbs, which made him Winslow's fourth biggest landowner.[21] In all members of the extended Gyles family owned 199 acres.

Daniel's first marriage was very different from the rest of his family. In 1691, when he was aged 18[22] he married Beatrice Taylor of Woburn, a member of an Anglican gentry family. The marriage settlement included half of his father's house for them and their heirs.[23] Their eldest son William seems to have benefited from his mother's family's property, and moved away from Winslow. He lived at Tingewick and Northampton. Daniel was buried in the meeting-house with his second wife Mary.

The marriage-settlement property also led to a dispute, brought in the name of Daniel and Beatrice's daughter Mary when she was aged about eleven by her 'next friend', her uncle Samuel Norman, the husband of Daniel's sister Martha.[24] According to this law suit Daniel administered his mother-in-law's estate but had failed to pay Mary the interest on a mortgage as had been requested. Whatever the outcome of this case, relations between Daniel and his brother-in-law must have been very bad despite their positions as Winslow's leading Baptists.

When Daniel died, his house was described at the 1747 manor court as 'one ancient messuage divided into 5 tenements in Winslow adjoining the Bell Inn, now in the several occupations of Samuel Gyles, Dorothy Haynes, Catherine Snow, Richard Gibbs and Mary Holmes'.[25] Samuel Gyles and Mary Holmes were Daniel's son and daughter. Samuel seems to have run the business with his father but by 1750 he had moved to Biggleswade. The house went to William, Daniel's eldest son, under the 1692 marriage settlement. In 1753 he sold it to Robert Lowndes of Great Brickhill, younger brother of Richard Lowndes of Winslow Hall.[26] Part of it seems to have survived today as the Old George Inn, now part of The Bell.

---

[21] CBS, BAS 375/22/41/7.

[22] According to his age at death given on his memorial.

[23] WMC 20 April 1692, see www.winslow-history.org.uk/winslow_court1692.shtm.

[24] TNA, E112/779/10 (Easter Term 1703).

[25] WMC 27 October 1747, see www.winslow-history.org.uk/winslow_court1747.shtm.

[26] BL, Add.Ch. 53998.

Daniel's son Samuel was the last representative of the family with the Gyles surname to live in Winslow, although the Fosters descended from William Gyles III's daughter Sarah remained until the early nineteenth century.

William Gyles IV (*circa* 1683–1713) was the only son of William Gyles III and Sarah, and his early death within a few months of his father completely undermined the strategy for the family business. His will mentions goods at Stony Stratford, where he was apparently running a shop in 1711,[27] shops at Winslow and Leighton Buzzard and land at Buckingham.[28] He made provision for his wife Elizabeth, who seems to have been from another Baptist family, but she outlived him by only five years and moved to London before she died.[29] They had no children, so William's heirs were his four sisters.

The family business in the Market Square was carried on by William's widowed mother Sarah, along with her daughter Grace (died 1741) and Grace's husband Thomas Aldridge (died 1733) who is described as woollen draper in Sarah's will.[30] Sarah and Grace both seem to have been effective businesswomen. Grace's probate inventory shows the business was still flourishing.

Grace had two sons but they were apprenticed as a goldsmith and a silversmith in London, and, although they continued to own property in Winslow and one became a trustee of the meeting-house, they were not available to continue the business. The building later came into the hands of Grace's cousin William Gyles, son of Joseph, who was a distiller in London, and was occupied by and bequeathed to his brother-in-law Francis Collins, a grocer, who eventually left it to his maidservant.[31] It later became a gentleman's residence for the lawyer James Burnham.

Jane Gyles (died 1761) was another of the four sisters of William Gyles IV, and the one with the most unusual life. In 1714 she acquired her mother's and sisters' interest in 9 acres of land

---

[27] BQS, 12 April 1711: prosecution of a theft from the shop.
[28] TNA, PROB 11/542/101.
[29] TNA, PROB 11/565/38.
[30] HALS, 163AW5.
[31] TNA, PROB 11/860/439 (1760); PROB 11/965/112 (1771).

which they had jointly inherited from their brother William.[32] This was the beginning of her acquisitions, which reached 53 acres of land by the time of her death.

Her first marriage in 1714 was to the lawyer Henry Langley (died 1724). He came from Leighton Buzzard and had been working in Winslow, but they were married at Northampton and Jane's residence was given as Old Stratford. Perhaps this was connected to the business interests at Stony Stratford of her brother William, who had died the previous year. They lived at Leighton Buzzard, and had a son named William Gyles Langley who died as an infant and three daughters who all died fairly

Figure.7: The Gyles family's house in the Market Square was refronted, probably by James Burnham, before it was demolished in 1891 to build the Bank

---

[32] WMC 29 March 1714, see www.winslow-history.org.uk/winslow_court1714.shtm.

young – although one married a London map-seller and left a daughter who was brought up in London.

In 1725 Jane brought a case in Chancery against John Woodward of Little Horwood concerning property there which Woodward had mortgaged to her husband Henry Langley, who had died the previous year, and she won the case, although Woodward was alleged to have 'confederated' with Robert Lowndes, who was then lord of the manor.[33]

Jane must have returned to Winslow because in 1741 she married Thomas Worrall, a butcher and 53-year-old bachelor who died within three months. The arrangements for the marriage included Worrall's purchase of The Bull, referred to as the Red Bull, which Jane would hold for her life if she survived him.[34] They do not appear to have lived there themselves.

In 1744 Jane made her third marriage, to John Harding of Aylesbury, a bachelor aged 50. They rebuilt The Bull after a fire, having purchased full ownership from Worrall's niece Mary

Figure 8: The Bull in Horn Street was one of Winslow's largest inns, rebuilt by Jane Gyles and her husband in the 1740s.

---

[33] TNA, C11/2172/25.
[34] BL, Add.Ch. 53989 f.2v.

Seaton,[35] who held the reversion after Jane's death.[36] Harding is described as gentleman, which could mean that he was a lawyer. He had extensive property in and around Aylesbury which he left to his sisters and nephews, but Jane remained in Aylesbury after his death, presumably in his house.[37]

Jane made her will in 1755, although it was not proved until 1761.[38] She left all her property in Winslow to her nephew William Aldridge, goldsmith of London. He was a trustee of the meeting-house and Jane had remained a Baptist, because she left £2 a year for 99 years 'unto Mr James Hall the present minister of the Protestant dissenting congregation called Baptists at Winslow aforesaid and to his successors'.

---

[35] For the Seaton family see pages 206–218.
[36] BL, Add.Ch. 53994.
[37] CBS, MsWillsPec 26/1/31.
[38] CBS, MsWillsPec 26/1/41.

Chapter 4:
The Fall and Rise of the Baptists

In the 1650s people in Winslow and the rest of England enjoyed unprecedented religious liberty – as long as they were not Catholics. This makes it difficult to trace the activities of dissenting religious groups such as the Baptists, who could meet, discuss and preach without falling foul of the Archdeacon's court or the civil authorities. Their fundamental difference from other dissenters was their rejection of infant baptism, which also means that they did not produce the baptismal registers which are so useful for Anglican genealogy.

The early Baptist movement in Winslow

The Baptists left a record only when they reached a wider stage. *The Humble Representation and Vindication* of 1654, a manifesto of the General Baptists[1] which disavowed the radical Fifth Monarchist movement, was produced by a meeting in London and signed by 25 local leaders known as messengers and elders. The messengers included Benjamin Morley, Thomas Monk and John Hartnoll.[2] They also signed *Ye Gennarel Agrement* (London, July 1656) and *A Brief Confession or Declaration of Faith* (London, March 1660).[3]

Thomas Monk, from Bierton, was probably the uncle of Mary Monk, who married William Gyles II of Winslow, and Benjamin Morley's daughter Sarah married Gyles' son, William Gyles III.[4]

---

[1] There was a difference between the General Baptists who believed in general salvation and the group referred to as Calvinistic or Particular Baptists who believed in salvation of the elect. Their opponents in the 1660s often referred to them all as Anabaptists.

[2] W T Whitley (editor), *Minutes of the General Assembly of the General Baptist Churches in England, voume 1 1654–1728* (London: Baptist Historical Society, 1908), 5.

[3] *Minutes of the General Assembly*, 9, 21.

[4] See the Gyles family tree on page 84.

Figure 9: A William Gyles halfpenny. The initials WMG, for William and Mary Gyles, are also on the porch of Winslow's Baptist meeting-house.

Morley was a well-known figure in London, but lived at Winslow later in life; in 1698 he was messenger of the Winslow church.[5] Hartnoll was the messenger for Winslow. He was a thatcher from North Marston, probably the son of Francis Hartnoll who held some property in the manor of Winslow.

At the election for Buckinghamshire held at Buckingham in January 1659, the rector of Middle Claydon feared that 'the Anabaptist party were like to carry it on the other side', but in the event the 'gentlemen' won.[6] Baptists were not necessarily radical in politics, as they tried to convince Charles II in 1660: 'We and all men are obliged by gospel rules to be subject to the higher powers, to obey magistrates, and to submit to every ordinance of man, for the Lords sake', except in matters of religious conscience.[7] On the whole they were pacifist and (unlike the Quakers) non-political 'but not all, and not immediately.'[8]

---

[5] *Minutes of the General Assembly*, 57; Ruth Butterfield, "The royal commission of King Jesus': General Baptist expansion and growth, 1640–1660', *Baptist Quarterly* 35.2 (April 1993), 56–80, 75; Adam Taylor, *The History of the English General Baptists: Part First* (London, 1818), 321, 327.

[6] *Memoirs of the Verney Family* 3.444; Christopher Hill, *A Tinker and a Poor Man* (London: Norton, 1988), 112.

[7] *Minutes of the General Assembly*, 20.

[8] Hill, *A Tinker and a Poor Man*, 106.

The early Winslow Baptists seem largely to have been shopkeepers and artisans. Their secular leader and sponsor, one of the most influential figures in seventeenth-century Winslow, was William Gyles II, whose life has already been outlined.[9] Along with other Winslow shopkeepers he produced his own trade tokens, for use as small change, in 1666.

The attitude of the Winslow Baptists, or anyone else in Winslow, to the collapse of the Protectorate and the restoration of the monarchy in 1660 is unknown. If they believed Charles II's promises of religious liberty, they were to be disappointed. Winslow at least had some advantages for dissenters: it was under the ecclesiastical authority of the Archdeacon of St Albans, physically more remote than the Archdeacon of Buckingham, and the lord of the manor, the Duke of Buckingham, was a supporter of religious toleration.

Benjamin Keach

On 31 May 1660, two days after Charles II's arrival in London, Benjamin Keach, a tailor from Stoke Hammond, married Jane Grove at Winslow.[10] Keach, who had had an Anglican baptism in 1640, was baptised into the General Baptist faith in 1655, and began operating as an unlicensed preacher in Winslow in 1658.[11] His association with the Winslow Baptists seems to have been a fairly loose one. He was not their official pastor, and his children were born between 1663 and 1667 at Tingewick and Aylesbury.[12]

Keach's name appears at the manor court for 1661 as one of the tithingmen, but this could be a mistake for Benjamin Leach, a well-documented contemporary.[13] Alternatively, it might have been an attempt to embarrass Keach by making him take a manorial office. He was certainly living in Winslow in 1662/3 when he paid Hearth Tax on a two-hearth house,[14] and in 1664. He

---

[9] For the Gyles family, see pages 84-94.

[10] Austin Walker, *The Excellent Benjamin Keach* (Dundas: Joshua Press, 2004), 77.

[11] Walker, *The Excellent Benjamin Keach*, 41, 44.

[12] Walker, *The Excellent Benjamin Keach*, 77–79.

[13] WMC 8 October 1664, see www.winslow-history.org.uk/winslow_court1661.shtm.

[14] TNA, E179/80/352.

must have associated with the Gyles family, who as drapers as well as Baptists would have been in a position to put work his way. He probably moved around to avoid detection, and his brother Henry Keach, of Stapleford Mill in the parish of Soulbury, tried to operate a safe house for dissenters.

Baptists were not the primary target of the extreme Anglicans who dominated the new Cavalier Parliament of 1661, but were gradually caught up in measures to enforce religious and political conformity. Some of their problems were created by the Licensing Act of 1662 which required all books to be registered with the Stationers' Company and was intended to end the publication of 'heretical, schismatical, blasphemous, seditious and treasonable' books.[15] Thomas Monk of Bierton was called to appear at the Summer 1662 assizes to answer charges of printing a pamphlet titled *Syons groanes for her distressed* (possibly an early version of a work of the same name by Keach) and denying the King's supremacy in religion.[16] In all 189 Buckinghamshire dissenters were indicted at those assizes for failure to attend their parish churches for four Sundays.[17]

The most dramatic event in Buckinghamshire took place in April 1663,[18] when another purge of dissenters by Aylesbury magistrates filled the gaol and two other houses. Ten men and two women (including Monk, as well as a bookseller, a mercer and a tallow-chandler[19]) were held in prison for three months, and then brought to the Quarter Sessions where, under an Elizabethan Act against conventicles, they were required to take the oaths of allegiance and supremacy or abjure (that is, to leave) the realm,

---

[15] John Raithby (editor), *Statutes of the Realm: Volume 5, 1628–80* (1819), 428–35.

[16] TNA, ASSI 16/4/4: recognizance of £100 at the Lent assizes to appear at the next session.

[17] Larry J Kreitzer, *William Kiffen and His World (Part 4)* (Oxford: Regent's Park College, 2015) has a transcription of the list of names from ASSI 16/5/1 m.34. None of them were from Winslow.

[18] Thomas Crosby, *The History of the English Baptists* (London, 1739), 2.180–85. Ronald Hutton, *The Restoration* (Oxford: Oxford University Press, 1995), 201, points out that Crosby misdated the event to 1664.

[19] Kreitzer, *William Kiffen*, 245, proposes that William Monk was the father and among the Twelve, and Thomas was the son who rode to London. Both were among the people indicted in 1662.

being told 'that if they refused to do either of these, sentence of death should be passed against them.' They threw themselves on the mercy of the court, and they were convicted of felony, their goods confiscated and the death sentence passed.

Thomas Monk's son (probably Mary Gyles' cousin) rode immediately to London, managed with the help of the prominent Baptist William Kiffen to bring the matter to the attention of the Lord Chancellor, the Earl of Clarendon, and secured a reprieve from the King.[20] The outcome is recorded in the Privy Council register: the petition of the twelve was read with the King present, it was decided that all proceedings should be suspended, and the Solicitor-General and Attorney-General should look into the matter.[21] The prisoners were released at the next Quarter Sessions.

Part of the Buckinghamshire Militia was always on duty to arrest suspects and harass dissenters.[22] The passing of the Conventicle Act in 1664 (it expired in 1668) led to a wave of prosecutions: at least 98 people nationally were sentenced to transportation in 1664 and 111 in 1665.[23] This was the background to the events which brought Keach into trouble in May 1664. He was denounced by Thomas Disney, rector of Stoke Hammond, for printing 1,500 copies of a 'primer' which should 'be seized before it is dispersed to the poisoning of the people, as it contains much schismatic and heretical matter'.[24]

Disney's letter is preserved in the State Papers.[25] The Primer 'owned [acknowledged] by Benjamin Keach as the authore' was bought by Disney's man George Chilton for 5d from Henry Keach of Stapleford Mill, who told him 1,500 were printed. 'This Benjamin Keach is a taylor, & one that is a teacher in their new fangled way, & lives at Winslow a market towne in Buckinghamshire.' Some had been distributed at Stoke Hammond

---

[20] Kreitzer, *William Kiffen*, 225–38.
[21] TNA, P/C 2/56 p.402, 13 May 1663.
[22] Ian F W Beckett, *Call to Arms: The Story of Buckinghamshire' Citizen Soldiers* (Buckingham: Barracuda, 1985), 16.
[23] Hutton, *Restoration*, 263.
[24] *Calendar of State Papers Domestic: Charles II, 1663–4*, 595 (26 May 1644).
[25] TNA, SP29/98 f.116.

by Keach's sister and 'some others of his gang'. Thomas Strafford JP of Tattenhoe visited Keach's house with a constable and seized 30 copies.[26] They first tried to buy it at 'Moody's stall', probably at Winslow market.[27] Keach was bound over to the next assizes on two recognizances of £50 each, and was tried at Aylesbury on 8–9 October by Clarendon's brother Sir Robert Hyde.[28]

Keach was presented at the assizes as a man 'badly disposed to the religion established within this kingdom' who had 'made a certain poisonous, seditious & schismatical book' which contained 'many various positions insalubrious & dangerous against the liturgy of our Church of England' including the rejection of infant baptism and of the Anglican clergy. [29]

An account of the trial was first published in 1712 by Benjamin Stinton, Keach's son-in-law, taken from a manuscript found among Keach's papers after his death, which Keach had told Stinton was a record made by someone who was present at the trial.[30] This was the basis of the account later given by Thomas Crosby, which also includes a description of how, at another of his numerous arrests (not necessarily at Winslow), four mounted troopers threatened to trample him to death until an officer intervened.[31]

Crosby, the Baptist historian, married Keach's daughter from his second marriage, but probably did not know Keach himself.[32] He describes how Keach argued with the judge, who objected to someone of Keach's class writing books on divinity. Keach at first refused to plead unless he could read the full indictment, but when the judge said he would take this as a confession, Keach pleaded not guilty. The judge then gave a theology lesson, and in the

---

[26] Crosby, *English Baptists*, 2.195.
[27] In 1669, William and Anne Moody sold a messuage in Winslow to William Gyles. It was stated by the judge that Moody had six copies of the book.
[28] Walker, *The Excellent Benjamin Keach*, 65–66.
[29] TNA, ASSI 16/9/2 (translated from Latin). Details of the sentence were added later.
[30] Benjamin Stinton, *A Repository of Divers Historical Matters Relating to the English Antipaedobaptists* (Oxford, 1712), no.21
[31] Crosby, *English Baptists*, 2.185–209.
[32] B R White, 'Thomas Crosby, Baptist Historian (I)', *Baptist Quarterly* 21.4 (October 1965), 154–68, 155–56.

argument which ensued, he said that Keach was 'a Fifth Monarchy man' and he would not let him preach in court.[33] The Jury tried to find Keach 'guilty in part' because the indictment misquoted a statement in the book, but under pressure from the judge returned a guilty verdict.

His sentence was to be taken to gaol for a fortnight without bail, then to stand in the pillory at Aylesbury market the next Saturday from eleven to one with a paper on his head 'for writing, printing and publishing a schismatical book'. The following Thursday he would stand in the pillory at Winslow market for two hours and have his book burned before his face by the common hangman. He was fined £20, and must find sureties for his good behaviour and appearance at the next assizes to renounce his doctrines.

The spell in gaol could have been fatal in itself, as conditions were notoriously bad at this time due to the overcrowding as dissenters were rounded up. Keach survived, and took the opportunity of being in the pillory at Aylesbury to justify himself to the onlookers, assisted by his wife, until the sheriff threatened to gag him. A clergyman who argued with him was derided for being found drunk in a ditch. The eye-witness who gave this account was not present at Winslow when the rest of the sentence was carried out, so added no further details. The burning of the book seems to have been effective enough for no copy of the original edition to survive.

Keach's wife Jane died on 7 October 1670 aged 30. Keach paid tribute to her in a poem entitled *A Piller Set Up*:

'… I in the Pillory sometimes did stand,
The Cause is known to thousands in the Land:
Whilst I in pain did suffer in that place,
She did rejoice, and count it no disgrace,
When I was forced to silence, and by pain,
For to give o're, then she would speak again,
And vindicate the Cause for which I stood

---

[33] This misrepresentation has stuck well enough for Christopher Hill to refer to 'the Fifth-Monarchist Benjamin Keach' (*A Tinker and a Poor Man*, 137).

(A gazing-stock for Christ) then in the Wood.
Goals [*sic*], Fines, Bridewel, Scourgings and Pillory,
Did not her Soul amaze or terrify.
She zealous was for Truth, very sincere,
To God, by her some Souls converted were …'

By this time they were living in London, having left Winslow in 1668. According to Crosby, Keach converted all his property to cash but was robbed by highwaymen on the journey.[34] He went on to a distinguished career in London among the Particular Baptists. His London writings may have influenced John Bunyan.[35] It is possible that he remained in touch with his Winslow contacts, and was later involved in setting up the meeting-house, as at other places in London and Essex,[36] but there is no evidence for this.

Continued persecution

Keach had thus left Winslow by the time the Return of Conventicles was made in 1669, a nationwide attempt to count dissenters. This is the first direct evidence for the number of Baptists in and around Winslow. Winslow then had 40 'Anabaptists' meeting at the houses of Eliot a carpenter, Foster a baker, John Holland of Granborough and at North Marston, with John Hartnoll as their preacher.[37] Hartnoll and 'William Gyles, a shopkeeper at Winslow' were 'chiefe speakers' for the twenty people meeting at Swanbourne.[38]

As the returns were made by the Anglican clergy, the numbers were probably understated. The man who provided the meeting place was probably a member of the Elliott family of Shipton.[39] Foster the baker has not been identified but Thomas Foster

---

[34] Crosby, *English Baptists* 3.144.

[35] Hill, *A Tinker and a Poor Man*, 142.

[36] Beth Lynch, 'Keach, Benjamin (1640–1704), Particular Baptist minister', *ODNB*, www.oxforddnb.com/view/article/15202 [accessed 11 Dec. 2017].

[37] Clear, *King's Village*, 93–94.

[38] John Broad (editor), *Buckinghamshire Dissent and Parish Life 1669–1712* (BRS volume 28, 1993), 58.

[39] Arnold Baines (*Baptist Quarterly* 17 (1957), 42) identified him as Nathaniel Elliot, carpenter of Aylesbury, one of the Twelve, but that is hardly likely. For the Elliott family see pages 278–286.

(1685 1746), who married William Gyles III's daughter Sarah, was later the Winslow pastor.

The Orthodox Creed of General Baptists was signed on 30 January 1679 by 54 men from Buckinghamshire, Hertfordshire, Bedfordshire and Oxfordshire. The names were analysed by Arnold Baines in 1957.[40] Some definitely belonged to the Winslow church, including William Gyles II and III and William Norman of Steeple Claydon who was originally from Winslow and the father-in-law of William Gyles II's daughter Martha. John Hendly is probably the John Henley of Shipton who had his house registered for public worship in January 1693.[41]

The signatories also included John Holan, presumably the John Holland of Granborough who was providing a meeting-place in 1669, and John Hobbs of Great Horwood. Robert Goodson was later recorded as an elder of the Winslow Baptists but lived at Long Crendon in 1702, and Leonard Wilkins of Shipton Lee also represented the Winslow church as messenger at the General Association of Baptists. Others not identified by Baines as being connected with Winslow were Angel Mantell (Mantill) who had property at Granborough, and various Glenisters: two Williams, a Hugh and a John. The surname was very common in Winslow.

The Conventicle Acts of 1664 and 1670 prohibited meetings for religious purposes unless they used the official Prayer Book, and Parliament forced Charles II to withdraw a Declaration of Indulgence in 1672, which left dissenters liable to denunciation by people with personal grudges as well as religious motivation.[42] At the Christmas 1682 Quarter Sessions, a long list of people were presented for being absent from their parish church.[43] The list for Winslow is: William Giles II, William Giles III, Thomas Ellyott, Thomas Deely senior, Thomas Deely junior, John Stevens, William Firth, John Glenester, Thomas Gabins (Gubbins) and Daniel Coleway (Coley).

---

[40] 'The signatories of the Orthodox Confession of 1679', *Baptist Quarterly* 17 (1957), 35–42, 74–86, 122–28, 170–78; also published as a booklet (Carey Kingsgate, 1960).
[41] BQS, 12 January 1693.
[42] Richetti, *Daniel Defoe*, 3.
[43] BQS, 11 January 1683.

Similar lists were recorded regularly in the 1680s until Easter 1687, but this is the only time when Winslow was included. The presentments were made by the parish constables, who in Winslow were sometimes Baptists themselves. This was actually the case in 1682, when Thomas Deely was one of the constables appointed in October, so presumably he and the other Baptists were denounced by his colleague Simon Hogson, who served as churchwarden at least four times.[44]

Between 1684 and 1686 failure to attend church was also recorded by the Archdeaconry Court.[45] The court's list includes all the same people except Ellyott and Firth, who was known later as a Quaker, and contains eight members of the extended Gyles family including William Gyles II's daughter Martha and her husband Samuel Norman – who was said to be a 'reputed Anabaptist and keepe frequent conventicles'.

This all amounted to harassment rather than the serious persecution of the 1660s. It shows that the Baptists tended to be tradesmen: the Deelys were brickmakers, William Norman was a grocer, Thomas Gubbins was a wheelwright. From the 1650s, General Baptists in south-east England drew support from a cross-section of the community.[46] People such as Keach could be supported by the wealthier members. William Gyles II evidently expected the Winslow church to include the poor, leaving money in his will for their support, so their absence from the lists of non-attenders might be because they were of less interest to the authorities as long as they did not start preaching.

Freedom of worship

The overthrow of James II and accession of William III and Mary II led to freedom of worship for dissenters, even if it did not give them full civil rights. At the first opportunity, the Midsummer 1689 Quarter Sessions, William Gyles II registered his house as a

---

[44] WMC 10 October 1682, see www.winslow-history.org.uk/winslow_court1682.shtm. For the Hogson family see pages 178-182.
[45] HALS, ASA 7/35–36a.
[46] Butterfield, "The Royal Commission of King Jesus", 65.

public meeting-house for religious worship.[47] He was now living in the house to the south of The Bell which he had bought from Wendover Lowndes I. Houses were also registered as public meeting-houses at Granborough (Widow Holland), North Marston (Ralph Stevens) and Great Horwood (John Hobbs).

Three other houses were registered later for nonconformist worship: those of Robert Udding of Winslow in 1690, John Henley of Shipton in 1693, and William George of Shipton in 1719.[48] Henley appears to have been a Baptist but the allegiance of the others is unknown. There is also some evidence for Quakers: in 1695 the vicar baptised Elizabeth, daughter of Joseph and Mary Collins, and in 1697 Joan, daughter of William Firth, who had been presented for not attending church in 1682. In each case he wrote *tremuli* at the end of the entry in the register, apparently indicating that the father was a Quaker. There is no direct evidence for an organised Quaker presence in Winslow, but it is possible that this was the reason Udding registered his house.

The meeting-house

William Gyles' house had a home close on which he decided to build a meeting-house. A recurrent idea in Winslow that the meeting-house was built in 1625[49] derives from a mistaken restoration of one of the date-stones, possibly by someone who wanted to associate it with Benjamin Keach. The date of 1695 is clear on the stone above the porch, with the initials WMG. The site was dictated by the availability of land: it was on the western edge of the close, with access from the road which came to be known as Pillory or Pillows Ditch. The site had the advantage of being secluded, in keeping with the modest nature of the building.

At the same time that the meeting-house was built, Samuel Norman, William Gyles II's son-in-law, acquired the adjacent piece of land (out of sight to the right in *Figure 10*).[50] Norman built a barn or warehouse on the site, and its successor building

---

[47] BQS, 18–31 July 1689.
[48] BQS, 9 October 1690, 12 January 1693, 25 January 1719.
[49] Clear, *King's Village*, 88.
[50] WMC 29 April 1696, see www.winslow-history.org.uk/winslow_court1696.shtm.

when it was replaced in the 1960s using the original bricks now obscures the view of the meeting-house from the road. It is not clear if the earlier buildings would have left the meeting-house more or less visible, but Norman's purchase of the land ensured that the access from the road had a friendly neighbour. The meeting-house is now approached by a narrow path which must have been reserved when the rest of Gyles' land was sold.

The land on which it was built was copyhold, so any change of ownership was recorded at the manor court. Records for the October 1695 court are missing, but it is likely that no formal transfer took place then. There is a trust deed of 1696 giving the building to charitable uses but it does not appear to have been enrolled at the court then. The trustees named were William Gyles III, Joseph Harding, Samuel Norman and Thomas Deely.[51]

William Gyles II had already, in 1692, given the reversion of his house and the home close to his son Daniel after he and his wife Mary died. At the 1722 manor court, Daniel surrendered:[52]

'a piece of land in Winslowe, formerly parcel of a close belonging to him called the home close, which was divided from the other part of the close by Daniel's father William Gyles deceased to build a house or structure called the Meeting House, with the structure lately erected there extending from the ground of Mr Samuel Norman 43½ feet to the south and from the garden late Joseph Harding's 25 feet to the east, and liberty of ingress at all times to the Meeting House or parcel of land in and through the backyards, yards and 'gatewayes' belonging to Daniel, leading from the said house to the street near the 'poole' called Pillers Ditch.

A procedure of common recovery followed because William Gyles II had entailed the land to Daniel and his heirs. The building was described in English as:

[51] Clear, *King's Village*, 95; Kenneth Dix, *Benjamin Keach and a Monument to Liberty* (Dunstable: Fauconberg, 1985), 22; Norman Saving, *Glimpses of Past Days: Being a Historical Survey of the Town and Parish of Winslow cum Shipton* (Winslow, 1973), 13.
[52] WMC 26 October 1722, see www.winslow-history.org.uk/winslow_court1722.shtm. Original text in Latin apart from the words in inverted commas.

the Meeting House for such people who are or shalbe called or distinguished by the name or names of Baptists dissenting from the way and comunion of the Church of England and presbitery to meet in for to worshipp and serve God'

and was vested in trustees. This appears to have been a new arrangement, so until 1722 the meeting-house was technically the private property of the Gyles family.

The meeting-house has been generally known since the late nineteenth century as 'Keach's Meeting-House', although it was built nearly 30 years after Benjamin Keach left Winslow. The building has undergone some alteration, with changes to windows and doors, and a gallery added in 1827, but it retains most of its original appearance, internally and externally. It was clearly intended to be an unostentatious building designed primarily for preaching, and without provision for adult baptism, which was done (at least in the nineteenth century) in the brook between Winslow and Great Horwood.

Figure 10: The Baptist meeting-house in the early twentieth century. The door on the left has since been blocked, probably restoring the original design. Access was originally through William Gyles' home close.

William Gyles II made his will in March 1702, although he had already provided for his children.[53] It was drawn up by the lawyers Nicholas Merwin and John Markham, and largely concerned his property, and provisions for his widow and unmarried daughter. There is no direct reference to the Baptist cause, perhaps a consequence of the pre-1688 situation when it could have created legal difficulties, but he left an annuity of 13s to be paid monthly by his eldest son William to two prominent Baptists, Robert Goodson of Long Crendon and Clement Hunt of Westlington, 'to be given and disposed of unto such poor people as they ... together with my said son William Gyles ... shall think meet'. This was clearly a counterpart to the bequests to the poor sometimes made by Anglicans and was intended for local Baptists. No clear arrangements were made for its continuation after the death of the younger William, which followed unexpectedly.

William and Mary Gyles must have been buried in the meeting-house: their wills left arrangements to their executors' discretion but their burials are not recorded in the parish register. There are slabs in the floor commemorating some of their children and grandchildren, but not the founders themselves. The Gyles family seemed well-established in Winslow when William and Mary died: their sons William and Daniel carried on the drapery business, and remained the leaders of the Winslow Baptists with their son-in-law Samuel Norman. His widow Martha, in her will of 1742,[54] left £10 each to three Baptists including James Hall of Tingewick who was closely involved with the Winslow church.

William Gyles III was very active in the Baptist movement, which was flourishing in the county to the extent that a traveller wrote in November 1702 that Buckinghamshire 'is lookt upon to be ye most fanatic county in England'.[55] He or his father represented Winslow along with Robert Goodson at the Assembly at Goodman's Fields in 1692.[56] As elder, he attended the General

---

[53] HALS, 139AW6.
[54] TNA, PROB 11/723/119.
[55] CBS, D192/25/32 p.4.
[56] Minutes of the General Assembly, 36.

Association in 1702.[57] He took part in a theological debate at Upton in Buckinghamshire in 1707, and preached at Risborough in 1708 and Ford in 1709.[58]

In 1711, in a dispute within the Baptist Church of Ford which covered central Buckinghamshire, it was claimed that Brother John Begent said 'he had a profer of too years board from Winslow', and 'Bro. Gyles and Bro. Norman had each of them proferred him a years board if he would come to Winslow'.[59] Whether or not there was anything in the story, it was evidently understood by other congregations that the Gyles family subsidised the Winslow Baptists. In 1713 William and a business partner purchased the tithes of Padbury, an unusual although according to Baines not entirely unprecedented reversal of the usual ecclesiastical precedence.[60]

William Gyles III left one son and four daughters, of whom two married Baptists, one from Chesham, one with Berkhamsted connections. One son-in-law, Thomas Foster, was pastor at Winslow until 1728.[61]

Marriage to a non-Baptist was ruled to be a sin in 1704, but did not necessarily limit the Gyles family: Jane Gyles married three times, apparently never to a Baptist, but left an annuity to the Winslow Baptists.[62] William's son, another William, died later in 1713 leaving an annuity of 20s to 'the Generall Baptist Church in Winslow' and other legacies totalling £90 to men who were apparently fellow-Baptists.[63]

---

[57] *Minutes of the General Assembly*, 73.

[58] Baines, 'The signatories of the Orthodox Confession of 1679', 83.

[59] W T Whitley (editor), *The Church Books of Ford or Cuddington and Amersham in the County of Buckinghamshire* (London: Baptist Historical Society, 1912), 76–77.

[60] *VCH* Buckinghamshire, 4.214.

[61] Strict Baptist Historical Society, 'Baptist Pastors and Chapels', www.sbhs.org.uk/pastorchapels/ [accessed 23 January 2020]. Presumably he was the Thomas Foster who was ordained elder at Chesham, where he still lived, in 1714 according to G Reid Doster, 'Discipline and ordination at Berkhamsted General Baptist Church, 1712–1718', *Baptist Quarterly* 27.3 (July 1977), 128–38, 132.

[62] For Jane Gyles' marriages, see the Gyles family on pages 84 and 91–94.

[63] TNA, PROB 11/542/101. According to Clear, *King's Village*, 96, there was 'a small ancient endowment, consisting of a rent charge in Oxfordshire … until comparatively recently'; perhaps this was to pay William Gyles' legacy.

The trust created for the meeting-house by Daniel Gyles in 1722 had nine trustees: his son Daniel Gyles, described as draper of Winslow; Matthew and Daniel Deely, bricklayers of Winslow; James Brittain, yeoman of Winslow; Thomas Mountague, yeoman of Granborough; Elias Clarke, gentleman of Quainton; William Foster, gentleman of Oving; Thomas Wootton junior, tailor of Whitchurch; Robert Bell, yeoman of Swanbourne. Although the Baptist faith did not have much impact on farming families in Winslow, it clearly did in the nearby villages. Brittain and Leonard Wilkins of Shipton Lee represented Winslow at the General Baptist Association for Buckinghamshire in the 1720s.[64]

Influential Baptists

In 1717, evidence given in a legal case stated that four men held keys to a chest containing manorial documents.[65] Two of them, Thomas Mountague of Granborough and Daniel Gyles, were Baptists, and this demonstrates the influence they had acquired in Winslow. Poll books for Buckinghamshire elections between 1705 and 1722 show that thanks to William Gyles II's acquisition of freehold land up to four members of the Gyles family cast a vote, and no more than three other Winslow residents.

In 1710 William Gyles III, his brother Daniel, son William and brother-in-law Samuel Norman all voted for the Whig candidates. The only other voters, the lord of the manor Robert Lowndes III and the vicar John Croft, voted Tory.

Lord Fermanagh of Claydon House was one of the two Tory candidates in 1710, and had set about purchasing the freeholders' debts – who could therefore be made to vote for him. He wrote:[66]

'The shopkeepers of Winslow who are most Whiggs have bought in (as I am told) severall of these debts, and doubtless the [Stony] Stratford dealars and those of other townes have done the like, for which they have given in return wares at high rates. Now it shoud bee look't into that these shopkeepers are

---

[64] *Baptist Quarterly 4.2*, 84–87; 4.3, 173–184.
[65] TNA, C11/1919/6 f.8, evidence of Thomas Mountague, 1717.
[66] *Verney Letters*, 1.301–02, Lord Fermanagh to Barnaby Blackwell, 23 September 1710.

not paid with our money by giving out their notes to their friends for that purpose.'

That is, he did not want his business going to the Gyles family.

The only exception to this pattern of the Baptists voting Whig or independent Whig and the Anglicans voting Tory was in 1722 when the vicar, James Edmunds, himself voted for the independent Whig candidate.

John Croft, vicar of Winslow from 1684 until his death in 1716, clearly did not adjust well to the rise of the Baptists during his period in office. An annual return of burials in the parish had to be made under the Burials in Woollen Act.[67] The writing varies, but it is in Croft's own hand in 1703, where a separate entry for the burial of Mary Baldwin is headed 'Buryd of the Roundheads'. For 1704 there are three entries (Benjamin Morley, Alice and Mary Gyles) headed 'By regester of the Round-heads'.

These people must have been buried at the meeting-house as they are not in the parish register, but by 1713 Baptists were again being buried at the church, leading Croft to record the burial of 'Daniel Coley Antichristian' on 6 January, 'William Gyles Antichristian Bishop' on 21 April, and 'William Gyles Antichristian Baptist' on 2 November. These were William Gyles III and IV, father and son who died in the same year. In 1713, the parish baptismal register records that he baptised Sarah and John 'filii Johannis & Mariae Ashfield cacabatistorum', thus putting his Latin and Greek to good use to create a word for 'evil Baptists'.

Despite Croft's hostility to the Baptists, when witnesses were required for Robert Lowndes III's marriage settlement in 1703 of which William Gyles III was one of the trustees, the signatures of Gyles and Peter Lowndes were witnessed by John Croft, Nicholas Merwin the lawyer and Daniel Gyles (*see Figure 11*). In his will, which suggests he was a man of limited means, Croft bequeathed some books as 'my poor tribute towards a parochiall library to be contained in the vestry belonging to the parish church of Winslowe aforesaid forever for the use of such persons who shall

---

[67] CBS, PR/237/21/1.

resort thither to consult the meaneing of the holy scriptures'.[68] He evidently wanted a theological debate with the Baptists as well as a continuation of the Civil War.

In 1747, probably as a consequence of the death of Daniel Gyles senior, new trustees were appointed.[69] In addition to the two surviving trustees, who were Daniel Gyles junior, now of Abbotsfield in Berkshire, and Matthew Deely, the five new trustees were to be the other two sons of Daniel senior: Samuel Gyles, linen draper of Winslow, who moved to Biggleswade soon afterwards, and William Gyles, gentleman of Tingewick, with James Hall, gentleman of Tingewick, who became pastor, and his son John Hall, Edward Howlett, gentleman of Long Crendon, and William Coates, yeoman of Bow Brickhill. A note was added that they were admitted as copyhold tenants 'by favour of the lord [of the manor] for this time only'.

In April 1759, Winslow was the only church represented at the General Baptist Association for Buckinghamshire, a sign of the decline of the General Baptist cause in the area.[70] That in turn was a symptom of a perceived decline in dissent nationally, which

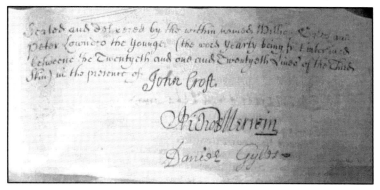

Figure 11: The signatures of John Croft, Nicholas Merwin and Daniel Gyles witnessing William Gyles III's sealing of Robert Lowndes' marriage settlement in 1703.

---

[68] HALS, 154AW8.
[69] BL, Add.Ch. 53992.
[70] 'The G.B. Association in Buckinghamshire (continued)', *Transactions of the Baptist Historical Society* 4.4 (1914), 214–18.

some contemporaries attributed to the fact that it was no longer persecuted.[71] In 1760, the Association was wound up with only Berkhamsted appearing, 'the other sister churches being entirely decay'd & broke off from us because they were too stiff in their mode of faith'. A note dated 1775 records: 'But Jas. Hall of Winslow and his church is dead & gone – & hes turn'd Calvine &c', meaning that he had gone over to the Particular Baptists. Hall gave up his office about 1777, and for some years there was no preacher for six or eight weeks, until the church was dissolved.[72] Hall is thought to have lived in the building next to the meeting house which had previously been Samuel Norman's warehouse.[73]

James and John Hall surrendered the building at the 1774 manor court to new trustees, none of whom lived in Winslow.[74] Two of them were descended from William Gyles II, the founder: his great-grandson Samuel Norman esquire of Henley-on-Thames, who was not a Baptist, and his great-great-grandson William Aldridge the younger, goldsmith of Holborn. William Brittain, tallow-chandler of the City of London was probably descended from an earlier trustee.

The others seem to have come from two Buckinghamshire Baptist families not known to have previous connections with Winslow. There were two Shenstones, John, silk-dyer of the City of London and Samuel, tallow-chandler of Stony Stratford, and three Coxes, all dairymen: Francis of Waddesdon, Richard of Shenley and William of Tattenhoe.

This at least had the effect of retaining the meeting-house for future use, and it was revived in 1799 by the Particular Baptists of Leighton Buzzard.[75] Its demise in the 1770s was decades before there was any religious alternative in Winslow (the Independents were only established in 1816), and is a symptom of the decline of nonconformity and radicalism of all sorts in Winslow.

---

[71] W A Speck, *Stability and Strife: England, 1714–1760* (London: Arnold, 1977), 100–02.
[72] Dix, *Benjamin Keach*, 22–23.
[73] Clear, *King's Village*, 95.
[74] CBS, D82/1 p.175.
[75] Dix, *Benjamin Keach*, 23.

The Grant alias Miller family tree

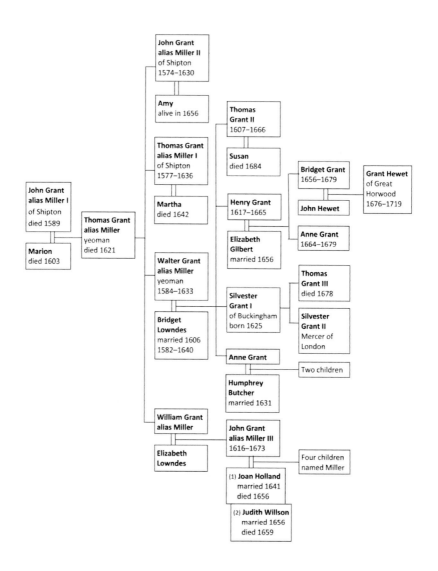

Winslow families
4: **Grant alias Miller**

Members of this family sometimes used one surname or the other, or both in either order, at different points of their lives, making them difficult to trace. They were one of the main yeoman families in Winslow up to the seventeenth century but declined rapidly as their relatives the Lowndes family rose. Some of their descendants were, however, tenacious in preserving the name Grant.

John Grant (or Graunt) alias Miller I, of Shipton, was a substantial property owner in Winslow in 1556.[1] If he was the man of the same name who died in 1589 he left a son, Thomas, and four grandsons.[2] In 1610 five men named Grant between them owned five houses and 111 acres of land, and **John Grant alias Miller II**, who died in 1630, had a messuage and two yardlands (about 60 acres) mainly in Shipton.[3]

John apparently died without children, so his lands, which are not mentioned in his will, must have gone to his brother Thomas. John's two other brothers married two sisters from the Lowndes family: Walter married Bridget Lowndes and William married Elizabeth Lowndes, the daughters of Robert Lowndes I.

Thomas Grant alias Miller I, yeoman of Shipton, was a wealthy man whose land in Winslow was called Grant's Baulk, west of what is now Burleys Road. When he died, only six years after his brother in 1636, he did leave a will, with an inventory

---

[1] David Noy, *Winslow in 1556* (Aylesbury: BAS, 2013), 35–37.
[2] HALS, 7AR134.
[3] CBS, WF538/44.

valued at £263.[4] His house had a hall, three chambers and a separate kitchen, and his livestock included cows, horses, pigs and 144 sheep. He had stocks of wheat, barley and oats so it must have been a mixed farm.

His main beneficiary was his nephew **Thomas Grant II** (1607–66), the son of his brother Walter and wife Bridget, who received his uncle's messuage and land in Shipton and 16 acres in Winslow under a deathbed surrender, while 5 acres went to another nephew.[5]

This younger Thomas made very complicated arrangements about his house and adjacent land, apparently at Grants Baulk, which are known because they were later recorded by William Lowndes II.[6] He was married but childless, like the uncle from whom he had inherited. After the death of his wife Susan, the house was to go to his nieces Bridget Hewet and Anne Grant, his brother Henry's children, on condition that they paid £100 to their cousin Silvester Grant II, who was the son of his other brother, Silvester Grant I. He also left £5 each to two other cousins, the children of his sister Anne Butcher.

Bridget and Anne's father, **Henry Grant** (1617–65) had died just one year before his brother Thomas. Henry had left goods worth £114 but no will.[7] He must have kept an inn as he had a large quantity of beer and malt and some brewing vessels, and stables but no livestock except pigs. As a second son he had apparently been set up in business but did not inherit any of the family's land.

The third brother, **Silvester Grant I**, who was born in 1625, had moved to Buckingham. It was normal for a yeoman family like this to apprentice a younger son elsewhere.

The family's land in Shipton, however, passed in unknown circumstances to the three brothers' cousin, **John Grant alias Miller III**, who was the son of William and Elizabeth. John had

[4] HALS, A25/3321.
[5] HALS, 77AW9.
[6] CBS, D/LO/4/3 pp.10–11.
[7] HALS, A25/3763.

also inherited some land in Winslow from his father William, but had exchanged this with Nicholas Spooner in 1647 for land in Shipton.[8] He began to mortgage his property in 1658, and in 1662 he sold a messuage and 73½ acres in Shipton to William Bignell of Chesham; this later came into the hands of the Bowler family.[9]

John died in 1673 in very reduced circumstances: with only furniture to leave to his children and goods valued at £26.[10] He may have overstretched himself if he had to buy the land from his cousin, or have suffered from a prolonged illness as he was 'ill in body' when he made his will. He had married twice and had been left with young children after his second wife died, which cannot have helped. His economic decline was of similar scale and abruptness to that of Robert Lowndes II at about the same time.[11]

A family dispute developed which led to a Chancery case in 1698.[12] Bridget and Anne, the daughters of Henry Grant, had both died before Thomas Grant's widow Susan, which meant that when Susan died in 1684 the property descended to Bridget's son Grant Hewet (1676–1719), who was only eight. It then emerged that the £100 condition in Thomas's will had never been paid to Silvester Grant II. So Grant Hewet's father had to pay him off by mortgaging the property.

Then Silvester's son, Silvester Grant III, a mercer of St Martin-in-the-Fields in London, claimed in 1698 that the property had been entailed in the male line to continue it in the family name. He does not seem to have been well informed because he gave his great-grandfather's name incorrectly, saying he was Thomas when in fact he was Walter.

Grant Hewet claimed that he had never heard of his cousin Silvester, and produced evidence of all the transactions at the manor court. He won the case, but mortgaged the property to his distant relative William Lowndes II in 1715 and sold it to him in

---

[8] WMC 19 October 1647, see www.winslow-history.org.uk/winslow_court1647.shtm.
[9] WMC 9 July 1662, see www.winslow-history.org.uk/winslow_court1662.shtm.
[10] HALS, 109AW18, A25/3919.
[11] For Robert Lowndes II's economic decline see the Lowndes family on pages 52-60.
[12] TNA, C6/310/9.

1716 for £340, by which time the messuage came with 6½ acres.[13]

The Miller branch of the family went from substantial landowners to landless within a few years, for reasons which cannot now be recovered, but some Miller descendants remained in Winslow.

The Grant surname died out by genealogical accident. In three cases in succession the main heir was childless, and the only other descendants in the male line had already left Winslow, as younger sons of yeoman families usually did. By the time Grant Hewet inherited, the property was encumbered with a mortgage, and there was not enough land left for a viable farm anyway. He provided some tiles for Winslow Hall which were probably from a dismantled building. He was a yeoman of Great Horwood when he made his will in 1719.[14] His main legacy was his name. He had a son, Grant Hewiet, maltster of Great Horwood (1702–60), and grandsons including Grant Harris and two Grant Hewietts. One Grant Hewiett (1730–98) became a wealthy merchant in London with a country home at Great Horwood.[15] His sister Anne was the grandmother of Grant King, draper and former postmaster of Winslow who died in 1892.

It is not known if this last bearer of the family name in Winslow realised how far back it went.

[13] WMC 20 April 1715, see www.winslow-history.org.uk/winslow_court1715.shtm; 10 October 1716, see www.winslow-history.org.uk/winslow_court1716.shtm.

[14] CBS, D/A/We/56/155.

[15] TNA, PROB 11/1281/252.

Chapter 5:
Winslow Hall

In eight hundred years of recorded history, Winslow had never had a resident lord, or a manor house, or any dwelling which was out of proportion to all the others. Visitors from St Albans Abbey had probably stayed at Biggin, but it was not in the town and is unlikely to have had a permanent resident other than servants until it became a farmhouse after the Dissolution of the Monasteries. Within the town of Winslow, the largest houses such as the Figes' or The Bell only differed from the others in having one or two extra bays, more outbuildings, and a home close.

The development of an idea

Thanks to William Lowndes' extremely careful record-keeping, precise details are known of who worked on building Winslow Hall and how much he paid them, but nothing survives to show the thinking behind it. He owned plenty of land in the fields, and could have used a block of it on Dene Hill or at Shipton for a true country residence, as happened on the other side of Winslow when Redfield was built nearly two centuries later. He may even have thought of doing this while he accumulated the land, but instead he chose a site next to the main road out of Winslow, which was to become a turnpike route within three decades.[1] When his house was built it faced other houses across the road, even though it had extensive private grounds behind it.

Perhaps William Lowndes placed the house as he did because that was the part of the site which he acquired first, but it was also an effective way of reminding the people he had grown up among that he, the product of a family which had nearly lost everything,

---

[1] Peter Gulland, *The Toll Roads of Buckinghamshire 1706–1881* (Aylesbury: BAS, 2017), 101.

Figure 12: This view of the south and east sides of Winslow Hall shows how it was intended to dominate the rest of the town.

was rich beyond anything they had seen and that he could put himself and his descendants in a position where his legacy was always in everyone's view.

For someone with Lowndes' excessive workload at the Treasury, building a home more than 50 miles away from London is a surprising choice. People with active careers did not want to bury themselves in the countryside.[2] He was not an aristocrat who could leave London for the summer. However he did not know that he would be in post at the Treasury for another two decades, and it is possible that he was preparing for an enforced retirement. Alternatively he might always have envisaged the house as a home for his son Robert and future descendants, as it actually became in 1703, by which time William had decided to remain in his existing country residence at The Bury in Chesham.

It was probably in 1692 and as a result of his fourth marriage that Lowndes started to develop a bigger scheme for Winslow, including becoming lord of the manor and building a 'great house'. The court roll records his acquisition of a property known as the Brick House.[3] Lowndes paid £400, by far the most he paid

[2] Clay, 'Landlords', 183.
[3] WMC 16 October 1692, see www.winslow-history.org.uk/winslow_court1692.shtm.

for any house in Winslow, and noted:[4]

> 'This was a brickhouse standing near the street, puld downe to build my new house more backward, its orchard with another that belonged to Halfpenny make the first garden that lyes next behind my new house.'

The size of the Brick House is also indicated in the Winslow Hall building accounts with an entry for

> 'taking down cleaning & stacking 60000 bricks & 12 thousand tiles of my old house ... pulling down the ceilings & particions &c ... carpenters work in taking down the roof'.[5]

It must have been the most impressive house in Winslow in 1692 when any building in brick was still locally unusual – though it was barely a twentieth of the size of its replacement. Lowndes probably made it his temporary base for his occasional visits to Winslow. In 1694, when he subscribed £1,000 to the newly formed Bank of England, he described himself as William Lowndes of Winslow.[6]

Lowndes adopted a policy of intensive purchases in Sheep Street in 1694–95, and started planting his garden in 1695. By now he was clearly not waiting for property to come on the market but proactively extending the block of land he held in order to redevelop it. Most of the houses he bought were not occupied by their owners but let to tenants. Three purchases in Sheep Street were recorded at the April 1695 manor court:[7]

1. A house owned by John Seaton, in the occupation of Robert Grainger, for which Lowndes paid £50. This was on the east side of the Brick House (as described in 1692).

2. A house owned by Dorothy Norman and her son William. It came with yard, orchard and backyard, 64 feet by 161 feet. Lowndes paid £123. This was a sub-division of a larger house: Dorothy and her husband John Norman had bought the western

---

[4] CBS, D/LO/4/1 m.2.
[5] Folger Shakespeare Library, W.a.146 f.38.
[6] Moss, *Ways and Means*, 32.
[7] www.winslow-history.org.uk/winslow_court1695.shtm.

two bays of a messuage from Mary Shelton in 1682, with the ground as it was later described in 1695.[8] Presumably this was on the east side of John Seaton's house.

3. The unsold part of the same house, now owned by William Shelton who had inherited from his mother Mary in 1692. The court roll describes in detail the yard and garden, 170 feet long and varying in width between 21 feet and 48 feet, at one point adjoining a lane called Astons Lane. The sale to Lowndes included an adjoining piece called the Upper Orchard measuring 109 feet by 89 feet. Lowndes paid £156.

There was another purchase later in 1695, known only from Lowndes' records[9] because the court roll does not survive. Lowndes paid Benjamin Scott, a butcher, and his mother Anne £280 for a house in Sheep Street 'now demolishd to build my new house'. This was west of the other houses, adjoining 11 Sheep Street (*see Figure 6*).

Astons Lane is only mentioned by name in the 1690s in connection with properties bought by William Lowndes, and apparently disappeared when he demolished them. It seems to have been parallel to and north of Sheep Street, to the east of the Winslow Hall site, presumably giving rear access to properties in Sheep Street and entry to the land to the north. This might explain why there appear to be two rows of houses on the north side of Sheep Street on the 1599 map (*see Figure 1*).

Lowndes now had the site of four substantial houses (Scott's, Brick House, Seaton's, and the house divided between the Normans and Shelton). He evidently did not feel the need to demolish 11 Sheep Street, which he had bought in 1685 from Thomas Halfpenny, although he took the land behind it for the future Winslow Hall site. In 1698 he completed his acquisition of the site by adding some small plots on the north side of the grounds, including at least two house sites.[10] In addition he bought from Henry Hughes a house in Sheep Street 'at ye corner of

[8] CBS, BAS 376/22/54.
[9] CBS, D/LO/4/1 m.2.
[10] BL, Add.Ch. 53986; CBS, BAS 376/22/44.

Astons Lane' with a half-acre of land for £85. Three more pieces of orchard were added in 1698, each two-thirds of an acre, for which he paid £170 in all. These were high prices when Lowndes normally paid between £10 and £30 for an acre of farmland. The vendors did well through knowing how much he wanted the land.

Later in 1699 he extended the holding further to the north, so that it included all the land north of Winslow Hall and west of the road to Little Horwood as far as the parish boundary with Great and Little Horwood. The 1699 purchases probably filled in a block as far as an old road to the north of Winslow (now a cycle path). He also extended the site in Sheep Street with some small parcels of land adjoining Astons Lane. The vendors were allowed to remove their timber-framed houses. William Shelton, who had already sold one house, received a particularly good price of £91 for a quarter-acre: 'On this ground a house doth or did stand fronting to Sheep Street'.[11]

In all, nine houses or sites of houses disappeared to make way for Winslow Hall and its grounds. Most of the vendors who were owner-occupiers remained in Winslow, for example Benjamin Scott bought another house in 1696 and Dorothy Norman was living in 1697 in part of the house which became Brook Hall, at 9 Sheep Street.[12] Of the tenants who are recorded in the sales, only William Daniel and Thomas Crofts do not appear again in manor court records; Robert Grainger is still listed as a resident in 1700 and 1701; Thomas Wainwright was living in Winslow when he died in 1714; Christopher Bigg was tenant of a house on the other side of Sheep Street in 1704. The building of Winslow Hall did not lead to an exodus of dispossessed people from Winslow.

The money which Lowndes brought into the town must have caused temporary inflation in the property market as the people who had sold to him made new arrangements. It is possible that they in turn displaced other people who were not able to compete with them financially, but it seems more likely that new houses

---

[11] CBS, D/LO/4/1 m.6.
[12] WMC 29 April 1696, see www.winslow-history.org.uk/winslow_court1696.shtm; 2 August 1697, see www.winslow-history.org.uk/winslow_court1697.shtm.

were built to replace what was lost, perhaps using building materials from the old ones. Lowndes, who noted the salvaging of 60,000 bricks from the Brick House, would not have been the only one to recycle. The timber frames removed from the land adjoining Astons Lane would most likely have been reassembled elsewhere.

Winslow in the late 1690s was prospering thanks to the money Lowndes brought in and the work he was creating.

Designing the house

When building started the suppliers and workmen for the Hall were given exceptionally detailed instructions in individual contracts. Lowndes' cousins Peter Lowndes senior and junior and brother-in-law John Wyatt[13] acted as local agents, making payments in Winslow on William's behalf. William Gyles and the lawyer Nicholas Merwin also seem to have had a supervisory role as some payments were made through them. A surveyor named Mr Churchill is mentioned in the accounts; he was John Churchill, son-in-law of the King's Carpenter Matthew Banks and a carpenter himself who worked on royal palaces and Marlborough House.[14]

The accounts do not, however, show who was in charge of the overall design and issued the instructions. It is clear that Sir Christopher Wren looked over the accounts and suggested some places where Lowndes was being overcharged, for example £80 was 'abated by judgment of Sir Christopher Wren' from the joiner's bill.[15] The attribution of the design of Winslow Hall to Wren was considered strong enough for the Wren Society to include the Winslow Hall accounts, then in the possession of the McCorquodale family, in a volume published in 1940, and for many architectural historians to be convinced. Peter Smith regards it as 'the closest [Wren] ever came to designing a country house

---

[13] See the Lowndes family tree on page 52.
[14] Nicholas Pevsner and Elizabeth Williamson, *The Buildings of England: Buckinghamshire* (second edition, London: Penguin, 1994), 756; Smith, 'Winslow Hall', 240.
[15] Wren Society, *Seventeenth Volume*, 71.

on the villa scale'.[16] Nikolaus Pevsner says the Hall is probably by Wren, and 'the design's structural ingenuity and economy of plan certainly seem to suggest the involvement of a first-rate mind.'[17] Howard Colvin also thinks that Wren 'probably' designed it.[18]

However no direct evidence is provided that Wren was involved in the original design. Colvin admits that examining the bills, which Wren also did for Blenheim Palace, does not prove that Wren was the architect. If he was, he must have done it as a favour to Lowndes, because there is no record of a payment to him (or any other architect), which there surely would be when everything else was recorded so carefully.[19] Even so according to the Wren Society this 'fact … has no importance.'[20]

Wren and Lowndes were colleagues and friends: Wren was Surveyor-General of the King's Works, and they were both closely involved in planning the recoinage in the 1690s. Lowndes was a commissioner for the Royal Hospital at Greenwich when Wren was surveyor there.[21] Wren had designed Tring Park for Henry Guy, Lowndes' superior at the Treasury, in the 1680s. Tring in the form created by Wren was similar to Winslow Hall in its pedimented central front, but the arrangement of the chimneys and the internal layout and decoration were completely different.[22]

According to the entry for Wren in the *Oxford Dictionary of National Biography* Tring and Winslow were his only private house commissions.[23] Smith suggests that Wren did private work for Guy and Lowndes because their position at the Treasury gave

---

[16] Smith, 'Winslow Hall', 223.

[17] Pevsner and Williamson, *Buckinghamshire*, 754.

[18] Howard Colvin, *Biographical Dictionary of British Architects* (3rd ed., London & New Haven: Yale UP, 1995), 1092.

[19] Eland, 'Building of Winslow Hall', 407.

[20] Wren Society, *Seventeenth Volume*, 54.

[21] Smith, 'Winslow Hall', 228.

[22] The house has been much altered but there is an engraving of the Wren house on display in Tring Local History Museum and reproduced by Smith, 'Winslow Hall', 224. According to Smith the houses are 'completely different' because of the different requirements of Guy and Lowndes: Guy was a courtier with grand designs.

[23] K Downes, 'Wren, Sir Christopher (1632–1723), architect, mathematician, and astronomer', *ODNB*, www.oxforddnb.com/view/article/30019 [accessed 18 December 2017].

them power over spending on his major public works.[24] Adrian Tinniswood is only certain about Tring but he 'can give Winslow the benefit of the doubt' and believes the Office of Works provided the craftsmen.[25] He writes:

'This isn't to say that he necessarily provided the design, of course, and stylistically, Winslow is hardly at the cutting edge of Baroque architecture. A double-pile dolls' house of a building with hipped roof, slightly projecting pedimented centre and four tall panelled chimneystacks, it could easily have been built in the 1660s by Pratt, May or William Winde. But it wasn't. And there is an austere restraint about it that fits well with Wren's character.'

The house shows similarities to the Royal Hospital at Chelsea, designed by Wren and built 1682–92,[26] and to buildings by Wren in the Inns of Court.[27]

There is no indication that anyone other than Wren worked as architect for the building. Lowndes himself was a polymath but it seems unlikely that he would have had the skill or time to design a house from scratch. It seems likely that Wren provided some designs which Lowndes or someone on his behalf put into effect, and Lowndes employed the various contractors directly and gave the overall instructions himself.

Wren would surely not have approved of the position in which the house was placed if he had ever visited the site. If the designs did not take account of the site where they were actually used, that would explain the Hall's incongruous appearance in the surroundings of Sheep Street. Pevsner describes it as 'stately, very restrained, and very urban'.[28] As he says, it is 'overlooking open country' now but not when it was built, or only if one looked

---

[24] Smith, 'Winslow Hall', 225.

[25] Adrian Tinniswood, *His Invention So Fertile: A Life of Christopher Wren* (London: Jonathan Cape, 2001), 289.

[26] This was pointed out to me by Mrs Diana Kemp. Smith, 'Winslow Hall', 233, notes similarities to Chelsea in the use of coloured brick and rubbed-brick staff-mouldings around the windows.

[27] Moss, *Ways and Means*, 63.

[28] Pevsner and Williamson, *Buckinghamshire*, 756.

beyond the houses and yards immediately opposite. Joyce Godber, discussing houses of similar date in Bedfordshire, writes: 'The gentleman took a personal part in the building of his house, chose the general style, and discussed details with a local builder.'[29] That is likely to be what Lowndes did, with some sporadic help from Wren and with the use of craftsmen who were often not local but found through his London connections in the King's service.

The contractors

Most of the main tradesmen used were not from Winslow. For example Richard Mapletoft the stonecutter, who had the contract for the masonry dated 18 January 1700 and still referring to 'a house to be erected'.[30] He was a mason from Taplow who did work for the Duke of Buckingham at Cliveden in 1680–84.[31] Winslow Hall was the first building in the town apart from the church to use stone in significant quantities. Mapletoft obtained most of it from Cosgrove in Northamptonshire, but some was already in Lowndes' possession. Stone from Denton, Helmdon, Reigate and Bedfordshire is also mentioned, and Bicester and Ketton stone was used for paving, flooring and steps. Loads arrived from Hornton, Wollaston and Dinton.[32] Lowndes allowed Mapletoft a bonus of £40 in a total payment of £398 'because of the dearness of his stone and great trouble in getting it, and because he performed his work well'.[33]

Another stonecutter called Mr Franks is also mentioned, whose work had to be transported from Brentford, and some stone and chimney-pieces were supplied by Edward Chapman of London.[34] Lowndes employed a glazier named Robert Adams from London and the royal locksmith Robert Greenway.[35] These were occupations which were only in a rudimentary form in Winslow at

---

[29] Joyce Godber, *History of Bedfordshire* (Bedford: Bedfordshire County Council, 1984), 305.
[30] Wren Society, *Seventeenth Volume*, 57.
[31] TNA, C7/140/6.
[32] Wren Society, *Seventeenth Volume*, 60.
[33] Eland, 'Building of Winslow Hall', 418.
[34] Eland, 'Building of Winslow Hall', 425; Wren Society, *Seventeenth Volume*, 62.
[35] Eland, 'Building of Winslow Hall', 422; Wren Society, *Seventeenth Volume*, 71.

the time. The brass locks on the internal doors, which cost £52, have survived.[36]

Lowndes' governmental connections or his association with Wren enabled him to use the King's Joiner Charles Hopson, who was paid £1,268 after Wren deducted £100, the King's Plumber Matthew Roberts and the King's Carpenter, Matthew Banks who was paid £651 while the work appears to have been done by his foreman John Wright.[37] Hopson worked on wainscoting, cornices and mouldings, and sash windows.

Banks (or Banckes) was Master of the Carpenters' Company in 1698, did carpentry work at some of Wren's London churches, and acted as Wren's executant surveyor at Trinity College Library, Cambridge, and Eton College.[38] He contracted with the Earl of Rochester to rebuild his house at Petersham (1692–93), was consulted by the Duke of Hamilton about Hamilton Palace (1693) and was the architect for refitting the choir of Eton College Chapel (1699). He would have been an appropriate person to interpret designs provided by Wren. He was also the father-in-law of Henry Wise the gardener. An agreement with him was dated to 23 November 1699.[39]

Another principal contrator was the bricklayer John Yeomans. Colvin describes him as a master bricklayer of Hampton on Thames, and his other work included the central tower of Kingston upon Thames church, and Trumpeters' House at Richmond.[40] He styled himself gentleman when he made his will in 1726.[41] If he is the same person as 'John Yeomans of Westminster brickmaker' who loaned £100 on mortgage to Grant Hewet in 1684, his association with Winslow began much earlier, presumably due to Lowndes.[42] He is certainly the bricklayer of Hampton Wick who was mortgagee of the King's Head in Winslow between 1701 and

---

[36] Smith, 'Winslow Hall', 240.
[37] Eland, 'Building of Winslow Hall', 421, 419.
[38] Colvin, *Biographical Dictionary*, 98.
[39] CBS, D/LO/6/10/3 f.2.
[40] Colvin, *Biographical Dictionary*, 1134.
[41] TNA, PROB 11/614/39.
[42] CBS, D/LO/4/3, pp.10–11; TNA, C6/310/9, ff.2–3.

1707 His contract with Lowndes is dated 1 February 1700 and the work was to be finished by 1 October, though in fact his final bill covered a period ending 27 December 1701.[43]

Yeomans received extremely detailed instructions, for example about the construction of the cellars, the building of the chimneys and the preparation of the mortar.[44] He was in overall charge of building the shell of the house, and was expected to erect the scaffolding and lay the roof. He was paid £570 in all.[45] Any instructions for extra work were to come from Lowndes himself. This indicates that, whoever actually designed the house, Lowndes directly oversaw the implementation.

An account book for Yeomans (or Yemans as he signed himself) survives covering the period 1699–1710, but it has some pages missing and only includes relatively small jobs, so does not mention Winslow.[46] He charged for his own work at a rate of 2s 6d a day although sometimes his bricklayers were paid 3s, and his labourers normally received 1s 8d.

Local brickmakers were employed too. A total of 1,040,850 bricks were burned in kilns, largely in Winslow, at between 14s and 18s per thousand.[47] John Stutsbury was given a £20 subsidy 'for building ye middle kilne in Norden', and £10 for filling pits there; the field was later known as Brick Kiln Norden.[48] He also made bricks on site at Astons Lane and this must be the land with a brick kiln which William Lowndes bought from him in 1699.[49] He was the main supplier of new bricks, producing 778,700.[50] John Spratley's kiln is also mentioned, producing 163,850 at a greater cost per thousand (17s 8½d against 14s). Margaret Deely, whose brickyard was near the churchyard, provided 51,300 at 17s 6½d per thousand.

---

[43] Wren Society, *Seventeenth Volume*, 62–65.
[44] Eland, 'Building of Winslow Hall', 413.
[45] Eland, 'Building of Winslow Hall', 415.
[46] Kingston History Centre, KP6/27/4.
[47] Eland, 'Building of Winslow Hall', 412.
[48] Eland, 'Building of Winslow Hall', 412.
[49] Wren Society, *Seventeenth Volume*, 66; CBS, D/BASM 376/22/106.
[50] Wren Society, *Seventeenth Volume*, 66.

Stutsbury made 46,200 rubbing bricks at Norden and Astons Lane and 99,450 rubbing bricks were purchased at much higher prices (up to £1 11s 11d per thousand) from Stony Stratford, Bletchley, Tattenhoe and Deanshanger, and 49,110 tiles came mainly from Brill, but Margaret Deely made 5,500 and Grant Hewet sold Lowndes 1,000.[51] Lime was burned, mainly by Stutsbury, using stone from Whitchurch and Thornborough.[52]

Stephen Bigg, the Winslow blacksmith, was the main contractor for metalwork, including basic door hinges, pot hangers and the 'ornament on ye front gate' weighing 75lb. His total charges came to £257 (after £7 had been abated by Wren in five separate reductions).[53] He too had worked for the Duke of Buckingham at Cliveden.

Carriage formed a substantial part of the building costs, totalling £619.[54] Most of the people listed were Lowndes tenants who provided transport for building materials over short distances and offset their charges against rent. Three Winslow carriers are mentioned: Nicholas Plested, Thomas Tomlin and William Kirby, as well as many who were not from Winslow. Tomlin and Kirby provided transport from London to Winslow at 2s per foot for timber. Plested (or Plestoe), who also worked for the Verneys, was paid £110 in all for the period 25 May 1700 to 7 August 1701, transporting Portland stone, glass, lead and joiner's goods among much else.[55]

Many local tradesmen were also used for smaller jobs. Joseph Bigg, bricklayer, seems to have worked mainly on walling the garden.[56] Robert Eden alias Udding, carpenter, was paid £26.[57] Charles Coates or Coutts, painter, was paid £56;[58] he was the husband of Lowndes' first cousin Frances. Local people did some of the less skilled work, at a rate of 10d or 1s a day. In June 1700

[51] Wren Society, *Seventeenth Volume*, 66.
[52] Eland, 'Building of Winslow Hall', 413.
[53] Wren Society, *Seventeenth Volume*, 72.
[54] Eland, 'Building of Winslow Hall', 423–24.
[55] Wren Society, *Seventeenth Volume*, 74.
[56] Eland, 'Building of Winslow Hall', 426.
[57] Eland, 'Building of Winslow Hall', 426.
[58] Eland, 'Building of Winslow Hall', 427.

there was a payment of £1 'given to ye man that broke his leg'. This was not particularly generous but there was no obligation to give anything.[59]

Despite the detail of the accounts, exact dates are not usually given for when the work was done. The first stage must have been the demolition of the four houses which made way for the Hall itself, for example 3s was 'paid for work in pulling downe Scotts house'.[60] Robert Grainger lived in the house belonging to John Seaton which Lowndes bought in 1695; he paid £2 4s rent at Michaelmas 1699, and Lowndes recorded 11s 7d 'given him to leave his tenement'.[61] He also noted 'his tenement is now demolisht'. Some of the demolition work is dated precisely to 22 January and 6 April 1700.[62] Work on digging the new foundations was under way by April.[63]

The task of demolishing the Brick House was given to the bricklayer Thomas Deely, brother-in-law of Margaret: he took down, stacked and cleaned 60,000 bricks and 12,000 tiles, pulled down the ceilings and partitions and took down the roof;[64] 35,000 bricks were actually reused. Deely was also paid for making two wells and coping a wall, and for 'workmanship in pitching', meaning surfacing the new courtyards.[65]

Work was going on across the whole site, not only the house. Lowndes was able to use the eminent garden design and supply partnership of George London and Henry Wise; London was the royal gardener at the time and Wise succeeded him.[66] The planting of the garden began in 1695.[67] They provided fruit trees and other 'greens … to plant the largest garden, ye kitchen garden and the platt before ye house' at a total cost of £46.[68] They recommended

---

[59] Folger Shakespeare Library, W.a.146 p.45.
[60] Eland, 'Building of Winslow Hall', 411.
[61] Folger Shakespeare Library, W.a.146 p.47.
[62] CBS, D/LO/6/10/3 p.1.
[63] CBS, D/LO/6/10/2 p.6.
[64] Eland, 'Building of Winslow Hall', 412.
[65] Eland, 'Building of Winslow Hall', 425, 428.
[66] Bucks Gardens Trust, *Winslow Hall* (2015), 11.
[67] Bucks Gardens Trust, *Winslow Hall*, 5.
[68] Eland, 'Building of Winslow Hall', 423.

a gardener, Michael Bough, who was working throughout 1702. Some intensive labour must have been required: £94 was spent on labourers.[69] Enough orchard remained for £1 to be spent on 'making an engine to break apples & a press to presse them.'[70]

Work completed

Although the date 1700 is inscribed over the south door in Roman numerals beneath William Lowndes' name, work continued on doorways, sash windows and chimneys in 1701.[71] Sash windows must have been another new feature in Winslow. The 5s charge for the inscription over the door was only included in the bill for work done before 30 August 1703, so it was intended to record when the building of the house started, as the contracts indicate.[72]

Smith reproduces a painting of Winslow Hall done very soon after its completion.[73] The appearance of the central building has not changed since then, but the painting shows the two service blocks as completely separate, symmetrical two-storey pavilions reached across rectangular courtyards walled off from the garden. The painter's bill includes 'outer dores at the end of the great house',[74] which were presumably used for access to the other buildings and led off the staircases. One pavilion was the kitchen and the other the laundry and brewhouse.

The coach house and stables were in a separate, adjoining building to the east which was not part of the symmetrical design but this has since been altered less than the service blocks and it is now two private houses. There was also a separate privy house.[75] The bill of Mapletoft the stonemason refers to the kitchen building with 600 feet of paving, which was the west pavilion, and 'brewhouse laundery stables coach house and milkhouse'.[76]

---

[69] Eland, 'Building of Winslow Hall', 428.
[70] Eland, 'Building of Winslow Hall', 420.
[71] Eland, 'Building of Winslow Hall', 414–15.
[72] Wren Society, *Seventeenth Volume*, 61.
[73] Smith, 'Winslow Hall', 233.
[74] Wren Society, *Seventeenth Volume*, 74.
[75] Wren Society, *Seventeenth Volume*, 67.
[76] Wren Society, *Seventeenth Volume*, 58–59.

The main house also has a basement with partial windows at ground level; there were four large and four small vaulted rooms. Mapletoft was contracted to provide 'the pavements of the cellars' as part of the preparatory work at 5d per square foot, as well as 'the pavement in the hall' at 8d per foot.[77] He charged for 2,021 feet of paving in the cellars. The bricklayer's contract stated that the cellars were to be 'nine foot high in the clear'.[78] They were fitted out with a five-tier bottle rack 15 feet long.[79] This probably held more wine than could previously be found in the whole of Winslow, but no doubt the wine was brought directly from London and did not benefit any local dealers, although William Lowndes must have known the trouble his parents created for themselves by having wine sent from London.

A charge is listed under payments made to Peter Lowndes the elder for a contribution to 'a raysing dinner'.[80] The *Oxford English Dictionary* records this only as a North American expression, with the first example dated 1702. Perhaps it was brought back to Winslow by Robert Lowndes, even if it was more applicable to setting up a timber-framed house than a brick mansion. The dinner was apparently held before April 1702, and £6 13s was also 'given several workmen to drink'.[81]

Lowndes recorded his total expenditure on the building work up to 29 August 1705 as £6,585 10s 2¼d. He also paid more than £1,800 for the various pieces of land making up the site of the Hall and grounds. Little of this money originated in Winslow: local rents only represented a tenth of Lowndes' total rental income in 1709, and much less than 1 per cent of his total income.[82] Allowing for what was paid to contractors who were not local, this represents an injection of between £4,000 and £5,000 into the local economy. To put this in context, the highest values of personal estates in Winslow for which inventories survive in the

---

[77] Wren Society, *Seventeenth Volume*, 58.
[78] Wren Society, *Seventeenth Volume*, 62.
[79] Eland, 'Building of Winslow Hall', 420.
[80] Folger Shakespeare Library, W.a.146 f.34.
[81] Eland, 'Building of Winslow Hall', 429.
[82] Calculated from Moss, *Ways and Means*, 56–57.

same period were £149 for William Short, baker, and £86 for William Spooner, yeoman.[83]

M W Barley has listed other costs of building large houses in the period, noting that different owners included different costs so comparison cannot be taken too far.[84] Winslow Hall cost more than houses for the gentry such as Ven House in Somerset £2,895, or Belton House in Lincolnshire £5,000. The estimate for demolishing and rebuilding Stanford Hall in Leicestershire for Sir Roger Cave was £2,137; the new house was of a similar size to Winslow Hall and became the home of Margaret Verney of Claydon when she married Sir Thomas Cave in 1703.[85]

The aristocracy spent much more: £14,000 for the Duke of Newcastle at Nottingham, £30,657 for the Earl of Nottingham at Burley-on-the-Hill in Rutland. According to Barley 'the typical Caroline double pile … was of modest dimensions', and he gives Winslow Hall as an example of a small length of front, which was 68 feet, though the pavilions would have made it much longer.[86] Kirtlington in Oxfordshire was 300 feet wide and Moor Park in Hertfordshire was 500 feet.

The Wren Society produced a detailed floor plan of the four storeys of the original main house (*see Figure 13*). On the ground and first floors and in the basement there were four rectangular principal rooms arranged around the chimney stack, two rather larger than the other two, and four small rooms or closets about nine feet square in the corners. On the second floor, where the ceilings were much lower, two of the rectangles were combined to form one long room. According to Smith this was a gallery or saloon for social gatherings, and could also have been a 'prospect room' for admiring the view – although these were no longer fashionable.[87]

---

[83] These only exist for wills proved at St Albans rather than London, and therefore exclude the wealthiest people.

[84] M W Barley, 'Rural building in England', in Joan Thirsk (editor), *The Agrarian History of England and Wales Volume 2, 1640–1750: Agrarian Change*, 590–685, 601–03.

[85] *Stanford Hall* (2018 guidebook), 6.

[86] Barley, 'Rural building', 607.

[87] Smith, 'Winslow Hall', 238, 244.

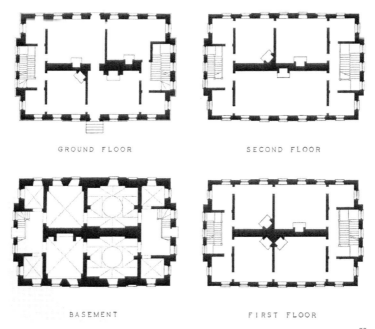

GROUND FLOOR

SECOND FLOOR

BASEMENT

FIRST FLOOR

Figure 13: A reconstruction of the original floor plan of Winslow Hall.[88]

There were no corridors, but each principal room could be reached directly from one of the staircases. The eastern staircase was rather larger than the western, which must have been for the servants, although neither was at all grand. The basic layout remains today although some closets have been altered or removed. An inventory taken in 1727 after the death of William Lowndes' son Robert shows how the rooms were actually used.[89]

It appears that Winslow Hall was largely finished but standing empty in 1702. Thomas George was paid 'for looking to ye yard & house 22 weeks to 22 May 1702'.[90] In early 1703 there was a small payment to Peter Lowndes for 'tending fires to ayre ye house'. This was before the building took on what had become its intended role, which may or may not have been the original

[88] Wren Society, *Seventeenth Volume*, plate LVIII, drawn in 1940.
[89] TNA, PROB 3/26/181.
[90] Folger Shakespeare Library, W.a.147 f.59.

intention, as the marital home of Robert Lowndes.

A traveller through Buckinghamshire who began his journey from Uxbridge on 26 November 1702 left the first description of Winslow Hall, as it was not yet called:[91]

'Winslow is a town about 40 miles north west of London, & about 6 miles direct north of Aylesbury & in the County of Bucks, the town stands on a rising ground, & is a small town. The cheif officer there is a constable, it is a post town, & hath a market every Thursday for provisions & some corn, as also for cattle & sheep; the buildings of it are timber & but indifferent, but the best houses are about the market place, where also are 2 or 3 tolerable inns; herein also is one church.

'In this town towards the south end of it, in the year 1702 Wm Lowndes Esq Secretary of the Treasury (& whose father formerly kept an inn in this town) was building a good house, which was near finished then; it was a handsome brick building of about 6 rooms on a floor, & outhouses convenient, standing on a rising ground, in which he had laid out about £5 or 6000 but the house standing too near the road, hath the dust of it in summer & the dirt of it in winter which then is very miry.'

The marriage settlement

On 24 June 1703 at the church of St Stephen Walbrook in the City of London, William Lowndes' eldest son Robert married Margaret Atcherley. She was the daughter of Richard Atcherley of Shropshire and Margaret Hill, who had married in 1680, and the niece of Richard Hill, a diplomat who was deputy paymaster of William III's army in Flanders and a substantial landowner in Shropshire.[92] He was acting as British envoy to Savoy in 1703, was also one of the executors of William Lowndes' will, and they must have been friends since the 1690s.

Margaret Atcherley and her mother are mentioned in Richard Gough's *History of Myddle* of 1701, one of the landmarks of local

---

[91] CBS, D192/25/32.
[92] Randolph Vigne, 'Hill, Richard (1655/6–1727), diplomat and public servant', *ODNB*, www.oxforddnb.com/view/article/13289 [accessed 25 Oct 2017].

hlstoiy writing. He describes how Margaret's father Richard Acherley, third son of a tanner and dealer in tlmbei, had married the daughter of Mr Rowland Hill of Hawkstone:[93]

> 'Richard Acherley died, and left his wife priviment insent of [pregnant with] a daughter, which was borne after the father's decease, and is yet liveing (1701). The widow married Mr. Thomas Harwood, a rich groser in Shrewsbury… Mr. Harwood, in right of his wife, and as gardian to Margaret, daughter of Richard Acherley, has the tithes and lands in Weston Lullingfeild, Onslow's tenement in Marton, and a lease of a small tenement in Marton, called Edge's tenement.'

It is likely that Margaret's marriage was arranged by the older generation, like that for her half-sister, about which Richard Hill wrote to his sister in 1706 in similar terms to those he might have used about Robert Lowndes:[94]

> 'I have had a proposal from Sir Henry Goff for your daughter and I have promised to give £4000 with her, on condition that Sir Henry does settle £500 per annum in present upon his son, & £700 per annum more in reversion after his death. Sir Henry is in town but his son is in ye country in Staffordshire, & they do desire that your daughter may go down to you, where ye young gentleman will come to wait on her. If they like each other, I will pay ye £4000 to Sir Henry upon his signing & sealing ye marriage settlements. I have promised that your daughter shall go down to Terne, ye end of next month. Sir Henry is a parliament man,[95] a man of buisiness, his son is by his inclinations a sober country gentleman, & loves ye country.'

However Hill does not seem to have been fully aware of developments between his niece and Robert Lowndes. On 26 May 1703, less than a month before they married, he wrote from London to Margaret's stepfather Thomas Harwood at Tern Hall

[93] Richard Gough, *The History of Myddle*, edited by David Hey (Harmondsworth: Penguin, 1981), 90.

[94] Shropshire Archives, X112/12/6/1/Box 93 no.58.

[95] Sir Henry Gough (1650–1725) of Perry Hall, Staffordshire, was MP for Lichfield at the time. Martha Harwood the niece married his son Walter.

about the difficulty of sorting out Margaret's affairs:[96]

'If my neice Atcherley comes to be marryed here, I must pay her portion down in ready mony, & I would therefore secure what is to be her own, both from her husband if she has one, & lives to have children, & likewise from her fathers relations, in case she should dye without children. This will not be easy to doe, especially as she is not at age; and not possible to be don unless we knew exactly ye nature and title by which she holds her portion, & ye quantum of it.'

The marriage settlement (*see Figure 11*) is actually dated 12 June 1703, so things moved remarkably quickly after this letter. Using his own resources and Margaret's inheritance, Hill provided a marriage portion of £4,000 which was used to purchase land in Winslow, Broughton and Stoke Mandeville.[97]

This sum was in the normal range for the marriage of a 'county magnate' according to Clay, and comparable to the £3,500 provided by the London haberdasher father of John Verney's third wife in 1697,[98] but because the Lowndes estate was a new one it could be used for expansion rather than clearing existing incumbrances.[99] John Verney of Claydon gave portions of £3,000 with his daughters, but the eldest of the three, Elizabeth, did not marry.[100] William Lowndes also left £3,000 each as a portion to his unmarried daughters. Margaret would therefore have been seen as a good catch for Robert.

Hill did not mention Margaret or Robert in his own will made in 1726, so he gave them everything he intended when they married.[101] William Lowndes' contribution to the marriage settlement was the manor of Winslow, nearly 600 acres of land, the market and tithes, 'the Parsonage Close and barn' and

---

[96] Shropshire Archives, X112/12/6/1/Box 93 no.55.

[97] Details are given in William Lowndes' will: TNA PROB 11/595/393..

[98] Susan Whyman, *Sociability and Power in Late Stuart England: The Cultural Worlds of the Verneys, 1660–1720* (Oxford: Clarendon, 1999), 122.

[99] Clay, 'Landlords', 193.

[100] Whyman, *Sociability and Power*, 129–32. Her younger sisters married in 1702 and 1703; was Elizabeth a potential bride for Robert Lowndes?

[101] TNA, PROB 11/615/473.

Winslow Hall ('a capitall messuage or mansion house with outhouses and other conveniencys thereunto belonging').[102]

According to Moss the value of the property was £23,462.[103] This settlement put the property in the hands of four trustees: Richard Martin, who was the brother of William Lowndes' third wife Elizabeth Martin, Charles Shales, who was his brother-in-law from his fourth marriage, William Gyles III, the son of his old business partner, and Peter Lowndes the elder. In 1716 Lowndes added another 286 acres of land in Winslow and Shipton to the trust.[104]

In his will, Lowndes described the settlement like this:

'all which I have freely and heartily done in a full sense of that particular affection which I bear towards my said eldest son (the only issue which I had by my first wife Elizabeth ...) and with regard to his primogeniture and in memory of the true love that was between me and his dear mother whom it pleased God to take from me soon after his birth.'

This is not a ringing endorsement of Robert himself. He is recorded as a student at Gloucester Hall, Oxford, aged 14 in 1695, and then at the Inner Temple. He may be the Robert Lowndes who was one of the commissioners for wine licences from about 1701 to 1717 with a salary of £200, and/or the Robert Lowndes recorded as a supernumerary clerk at the Treasury 1704–07. On 24 July 1714 Robert Lowndes of Winslow and his brother William, of Westminster, became two of the seven auditors of the Exchequer Court for Crown Land Revenues.[105] This was clearly the result of their father's patronage.

The manor court of October 1703 was held in the name of Robert Lowndes.[106] In 1708 the parish register records the baptism of the son of Robert Lowndes 'the squire'. This was new: Winslow had never had a squire before.

---

[102] CBS, D/LO/4/3.

[103] Moss, *Ways and Means*, 77.

[104] TNA, PROB 11/595/393: William Lowndes' will, p.2.

[105] *Queen's Warrant Book XXVI*, pp. 156–57

[106] www.winslow-history.org.uk/winslow_court1703.shtm.

To the south of Sheep Street

The author of the Buckinghamshire Gardens Trust report on Winslow Hall believes that the land to the south of Sheep Street, now known as Home Close, was an integral part of William Lowndes' original design.[107] However Lowndes only acquired this land in a piecemeal fashion after the Hall had been completed and handed over to his son. He continued to add to his Winslow estate after Robert's marriage settlement, but mainly in Shipton. His own records have survived for 1715–20, with his comments.[108]

In 1709 Lowndes bought from Thomas Foster 'a messuage in Sheepstreet now in the occupation of Richard Benboe, the messuage of Thomas Deely east and the messuage late Benjamin Bigg's west, and the common street north', and a newly built cottage behind it occupied by Widow Hodgkins.[109] Earlier transactions show that Benboe's house had a shared gateway with Bigg's and that Bigg's was next to The Bell, which was on the edge of the Market Square. Then in 1710 Lowndes' trustees bought four acres called Grove Leys.[110] Both of these purchases were in the area south of Sheep Street (*see Figure 14*).

Thomas Deely's house was sold to Lowndes in 1714 by Deely's widow and his sons. Two years later in 1716 it was described as 'A piece of land on part of which a messuage stood in or near the Sheep Street, lately demolished.[111]

Four years later in 1720 Lowndes purchased for £800 from Jane Glenister and her daughter Anne:[112]

> 'One house in Sheepstreet conteyning four bays of buildings with a little room and porch thereto adjoining. One barn thereunto likewise adjoining conteyning two bays with a leanto, an old barn and a stable conteyning five little bays, a yard an orchard and a garden and the home close thereto

---

[107] Bucks Gardens Trust, *Winslow Hall*, 4, 8.

[108] CBS, D/LO/4/3.

[109] WMC 9 May 1709, see www.winslow-history.org.uk/winslow_court1709.shtm.

[110] WMC 28 August 1710, see www.winslow-history.org.uk/winslow_court1710.shtm.

[111] WMC 1 October 1714, see www.winslow-history.org.uk/winslow_court1714.shtm;
WMC 10 October 1726, see www.winslow-history.org.uk/winslow_court1716.shtm

[112] CBS, D/LO/4/3 p.13b.

adjoining by estimation five acres divided into two closes by a quick sett hedg … the common street north part of the said house & orchard.'

This 'home close' of five acres had been that of the Fige family, which suggests that the house called Glenisters was the remains of their house. In the same year, 1720, Lowndes also bought two cottages in Sheep Street from Robert Udden alias Eden and his mother, paying £160.[113]

These purchases on Sheep Street opposite Winslow Hall can be set in their geographical order in 1720, when Lowndes stopped buying there. As the street heads east from the corner of Market Square outside The Bell it passes first Bigg's house, then Benboe's, with Widow Hodgkins' newly-built cottage behind it, then Deely's, then Glenisters, which is a larger house with four bays, a barn and stables, and finally Udden's two cottages. Jackmans, on the right, was not purchased at the time.

To the south behind these houses were the four acres of Grove Leys and the Glenisters' 'home close' of five acres, which was probably of more interest to Lowndes than the house. It seems likely that these two closes together formed what is now known as Home Close opposite Winslow Hall.

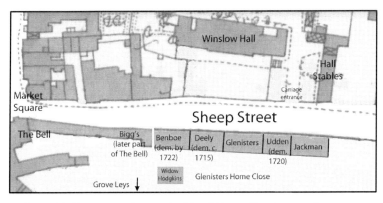

Figure 14: Houses on the south side of Sheep Street opposite Winslow Hall, showing those demolished by Lowndes and the dates.

---

[113] CBS, D/LO/4/3 p.13c.

Figure 15: A view of Winslow from the Home Close with the Hall on the right. The open vista in front of the hall was partly achieved when William Lowndes demolished some houses, but was completed only in the nineteenth century.

In 1721 and 1722 some more of these were demolished. After purchasing Robert Udden's cottages Lowndes allowed Udden to 'take off the buildings and have ye materials thereof to his owne use' before Lady Day 1721.[114] He later recorded that these were 'since demolished to open the veiw from my sons house toward Granborow'.[115] These cottages are also mentioned in his will as 'two small tenements since demolished.'

Two more demolished houses are recorded in 1722: 'ground on which Benbows house ~~stands~~ stood / ditto Hodgbyis house stood'. These had been bought 13 years earlier in 1709 and had been still standing in 1716.[116]

Bigg's house, however, was not demolished, later becoming an alehouse called The Cock, then being absorbed into The Bell after 1755.[117] Nor was the house known as Glenisters, which was still there in 1722 when Lowndes recorded that he was allowing Robert to receive £14 rent for 'part of Glenisters house and close', and it is mentioned again in the 1767 Enclosure Award.[118] The

---

[114] CBS, D/LO/4/3 p.13c.
[115] CBS, D/LO/4/3 p.53.
[116] WMC 10 October 1726, see www.winslow-history.org.uk/winslow_court1716.shtm
[117] www.winslow-history.org.uk/winslow_cock.shtm
[118] CBS, D/LO/4/39/1.

1051 Census records a building called Johnsons Farm between Hobhouchin Lane and The Bell which could be the same house, though this had disappeared by 1861.

And Lowndes did not acquire the whole south side of Sheep Street opposite Winslow Hall. It was only in 1793, more than 70 years later, that the Lowndes estate bought the blacksmith's shop of William Jackman, and the Jackmans continued to occupy it until at least 1841. It is said to have been 'in the field immediately opposite the Hall gates … a very antique house'.[119]

In total five houses were demolished on the south side of Sheep Street in the 20 years after the completion of the hall, while three others probably remained standing until the nineteenth century.

The houses probably did not affect the view of Winslow Hall from a distance, but they must have been very apparent to anyone standing at the south door and looking out through the gates. From first-floor level one could probably overlook the houses, but the land behind them was in a variety of uses, including orchards and farmyards. It was not until 1720 that Lowndes had the chance to turn it into genuine parkland, but the 1722 list shows that he was receiving a significant rent for Glenisters, suggesting that it was still being farmed seriously. Home Close as part of the unified Winslow Hall landscape is a development of later in the eighteenth century.

Nevertheless, building the Hall completely changed the appearance of Winslow: a massive brick house of unprecedented design now towered over the timber-framed and thatched houses of the rest of the population.

---

[119] Clear, *King's Village*, 117.

The Gibbs family tree

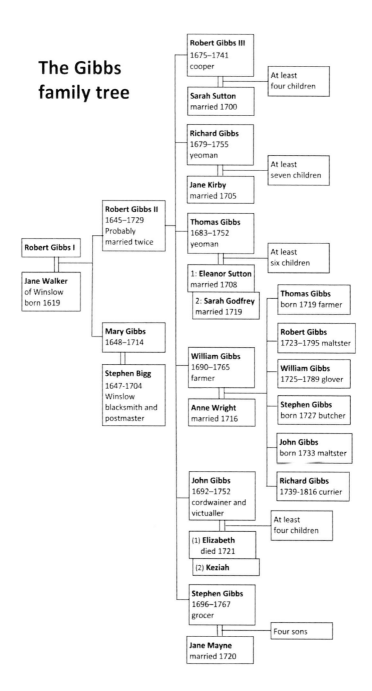

Winslow families
5: **The Gibbs Family**

The surname Gibbs first appears in Winslow parish registers in 1633, when an Elizabeth Gibbs married Edmund Brown. The name is found earlier at Granborough and Gibbs became the most common surname in Winslow during the eighteenth century. But only four people named Gibbs were recorded in the 1911 Census.

One generation of the family which achieved brief national fame will be the focus here:

> 'Robert Gibbs, of Winslow in the county of Bucks, had six sons, Robert, Richard, William, Thomas, John, and Stephen, which said sons rang the bells of Winslow Church on New-year's-day, for forty years successively: The senior son rang the tenor, and every son had his bell in right of seniority; and they were every New-year's-day, for a great number of years, entertained at a dinner by the worthy family of the Lowndess at Winslow. Richard, William, and Stephen are now living at Winslow aforesaid.'[1]

This seems to be the first occurrence of a story which was repeated many times with various embellishments. The biographical details below have been reconstructed as accurately as possible bearing in mind how frequently the surname is found and the limited range of forenames associated with it.

Robert Gibbs II was baptised in 1645, the son of Robert Gibbs I and Jane Walker, a descendant of the Fige family[2] in Winslow. He lived at 22 High Street and died in 1729. His sister Mary (1648–1714) married Stephen Bigg, the Winslow blacksmith and postmaster.

---

[1] *Whitehall Evening Post*, 19 November 1754.
[2] See the Fige family tree on page 26.

Robert Gibbs II became the bailiff and farmer of the manor under his very distant relative William Lowndes, which implies that he had enough capital to take on a rent of £220 a year. He also rented some land for himself at £4 10s a year. He passed on 12 acres of land in two blocks, previously mortgaged, to his son William before his death, but does not appear to have owned other property when he died.[3] He had already given the reversion of his house to William in 1716 and an adjacent house to another son Richard in 1706, the latter probably as a marriage settlement.[4] It is likely that he set up his other sons in business too.[5]

Robert Gibbs III (1675–1741), the eldest son, was a regular juror at the manor court from 1701, and served as constable in 1706 and overseer in 1709. He married Sarah Sutton in 1700, and his father provided them with a house near his own. He is referred to in the 1717 manor court records as a cooper, presumably set up in business by his father.[6] The court did not record what property he held when he died, but his heir was his eldest son Robert. He made a mark for the 1723 Oath of Allegiance whereas his father and brothers signed.[7]

Richard Gibbs (1679–1755) was described as a yeoman from 1709, but also a corn chandler in 1710. Dealing in corn does not seem to have been a full-time occupation in Winslow, but corn merchants must have attended the market; either they were all outsiders or, as in Richard's case, farming was their main occupation. He married Jane Kirby in 1705. He served as a juror from 1706, constable in 1710, overseer in 1715 and churchwarden in 1724. In 1730 he gave the reversion of a house which he owned but did not live in to his son William.[8] In about 1743 he was the tenant of 109 acres of land belonging to Daniel Gyles and Jane Worrall (née Gyles). This explains how he could be called a yeoman apparently without owning any land.

[3] WMC 20 October 1729, see www.winslow-history.org.uk/winslow_court1729.shtm.

[4] WMC 6 April 1716, see www.winslow-history.org.uk/winslow_court1716.shtm; 21 June 1706, see www.winslow-history.org.uk/winslow_court1706.shtm.

[5] Thanks to Sue Webb for some of the information used here and in the family tree.

[6] WMC 26 April 1717, see www.winslow-history.org.uk/winslow_court1717.shtm.

[7] See www.winslow-history.org.uk/winslow_oath1723.shtm.

[8] WMC 23 October 1720, see www.winslow-history.org.uk/winslow_court1730.shtm.

Thomas Gibbs (1683–1752) was a baker. He had a wife named Eleanor by 1709 who died in 1715. He then married Sarah Godfrey at Addington in 1719. He was constable in 1712 and again in 1742. He was, at least in 1712–15, a tenant of the Gyles family at the house called the Little Angel, at 12 Market Square. He was a juror for the first time in 1724, and fairly regularly after that. In 1713 he became a mortgagee for £100, which suggests that his father had provided money as well as setting him up in business. He made two purchases of small pieces of land which he sold in 1733.[9]

William Gibbs (1690–1765) was a husbandman, as he described himself in his will, and the father of the second generation of bellringers, most of whom he started off in business as his father had done for him. His will mentions three messuages in Cow Street (now 20–22 High Street), one in Great Horwood, and the land which he had received from his father.[10] He married Anne Wright, daughter of a Winslow wheelwright, in 1716.

His farming activities were mainly as the biggest tenant of the Lowndes estate and as farmer of the glebe land: in about 1743 he was farming 167 acres for Richard Lowndes, who was by then lord of the manor, 60 acres for the vicar, 17 acres for Benjamin Saunders and 9 acres of his own.[11] Tenants could now be farmers on a much bigger scale than owner-occupiers had been, and being a fourth son was no disadvantage. He was also bailiff of the manor court in succession to his father. He was able to vote in 1734 due to property at Great Horwood, and plumped for Richard Lowndes.[12]

John Gibbs (1692–1752) was a cordwainer and also kept the Windmill Inn which he left to his second wife Keziah and then his only son Stephen.[13] The first reference to the inn by name is from the 1709 manor court, and John must have bought it as a going

---

[9] WMC 22 October 1733, see www.winslow-history.org.uk/winslow_court1733.shtm.
[10] HALS, 205AW8.
[11] CBS, BAS 375/22/41/7.
[12] CBS, D/MH 40/2
[13] HALS, 191AW8.

concern.[14] He was a regular juror, but is otherwise difficult to differentiate from several nephews with the same name.

Stephen Gibbs (1696–1767) was a shopkeeper according to his will,[15] but is also described more specifically as a grocer or tallow-chandler. He married Jane Mayne in 1720. His shop was at 2A High Street, and seems to have belonged to his brother-in-law Richard Mayne, maltster, until 1747.[16] He also owned a cottage in Western Lane and some land: 7½ acres of freehold at the time of enclosure. He was a juror from 1726, and bailiff in 1734.[17]

The brothers' dates show that the newspaper story was rather exaggerated. The last time they could all have rung the bells together was 1741, the year that Robert Gibbs III died, and if they had been doing it for 40 years Stephen would have started bellringing when he was five.

The remarkable thing about the Gibbs brothers is not their campanological achievement but the fact that six brothers were able to stay in their place of birth, take on different occupations, raise families (each of them had at least one son) and die in reasonable prosperity where they were born, without any of them apparently marrying an heiress. This was all possible because Winslow at the time was a place of economic opportunities. Their father did not concentrate his resources on one son, as someone with his own land might have done, but provided them all with capital to develop their own businesses, most of which were passed down to the next generation.

The family continued to dominate bellringing through William's sons. The story became confused because some of the various versions thought that the first generation started ringing in 1747, which is more likely to be when the second generation started to form the majority of the bellringers. According to Arthur Clear, quoting a manuscript about the church choir:[18]

---

[14] WMC 9 May 1709, see www.winslow-history.org.uk/winslow_court1709.shtm.

[15] HALS, 191AW13 and 205AW9.

[16] WMC 27 October 1747, see www.winslow-history.org.uk/winslow_court1747.shtm

[17] WMC 12 April 1734, see www.winslow-history.org.uk/winslow_court1734.shtm

[18] Clear, *King's Village*, 86.

'The following are the names of the last six brothers, ringers, who annually supped at Mr. Lowndes' (the squire of the parish) on the first night of the New Year,—Thomas Gibbs, farmer; Robert Gibbs, malster; Stephen Gibbs, butcher; William Gibbs, glover; Richard Gibbs, currier; and John Gibbs, malster.'

John is presumably the churchwarden of 1777 whose name is still on one of the bells. These were the six sons of the first William, born between 1719 and 1739. If the family continuity really lasted for seventy years as was claimed, it is most likely to have been from about 1710 to 1780.

Because of the proliferation of people with the same name, it is not clear when some of the second generation died. They were all alive when their father made his will in 1765. William clearly followed his father's policy: five of his six sons were set up in new trades.

William Lowndes' descendants

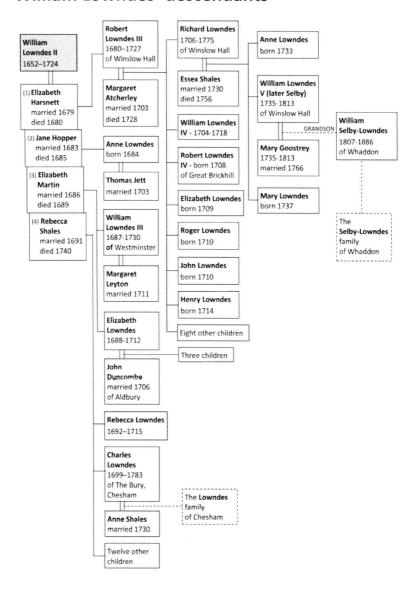

William Lowndes II
1652–1724

(1) **Elizabeth Harsnett**
married 1679
died 1680

(2) **Jane Hopper**
married 1683
died 1685

(3) **Elizabeth Martin**
married 1686
died 1689

(4) **Rebecca Shales**
married 1691
died 1740

Robert Lowndes III
1680–1727
of Winslow Hall

Margaret Atcherley
married 1703
died 1728

Anne Lowndes
born 1684

Thomas Jett
married 1703

William Lowndes III
1687-1730
of Westminster

Margaret Leyton
married 1711

Elizabeth Lowndes
1688-1712

John Duncombe
married 1706
of Aldbury

Rebecca Lowndes
1692–1715

Charles Lowndes
1699–1783
of The Bury, Chesham

Anne Shales
married 1730

Twelve other children

Richard Lowndes
1706-1775
of Winslow Hall

Essex Shales
married 1730
died 1756

William Lowndes IV - 1704-1718

Robert Lowndes IV - born 1708
of Great Brickhill

Elizabeth Lowndes
born 1709

Roger Lowndes
born 1710

John Lowndes
born 1710

Henry Lowndes
born 1714

Eight other children

Three children

Anne Lowndes
born 1733

William Lowndes V (later Selby)
1735-1813
of Winslow Hall

Mary Goostrey
1735-1813
married 1766

Mary Lowndes
born 1737

GRANDSON

William Selby-Lowndes
1807-1886
of Whaddon

The Selby-Lowndes family of Whaddon

The **Lowndes** family of Chesham

Chapter 6:
Squires of Winslow

The *Oxford English Dictionary* defines a squire as 'a country gentleman or landed proprietor, *esp.* one who is the principal landowner in a village or district'.

'Squire' was an informal term which came into common use in the eighteenth century for landowners who lived on their estates. When Robert Lowndes' son was baptised at Winslow in 1708, Robert was designated 'squire' in the parish register, and that was how the Lowndeses were now seen. Before Robert, Winslow had never had a resident squire, only an absentee lord of the manor, but now a member of the Lowndes family lived in the middle of the town.

Squires expected the obedience and loyalty of their tenants and had some moral obligations towards them such as gifts to the poor at Christmas and support for local institutions. How this worked in practice in eighteenth-century Winslow is largely unclear but, as will be seen, the economic and moral authority of the Lowndes family became firmly entrenched.

Robert Lowndes

Robert and Margaret Lowndes were married in London in 1703, and their first two children were born at the house of her uncle Richard Hill near St James' Palace.[1] Hill's housekeeper approved of Robert when she wrote to her employer in 1704: 'Mr. Lowndes is a very good agreeable man and makes a choyce husband and has a very fine child'.[2] By the time the third child was born in 1706 Robert had his own London house in Dover Street, but this

---

[1] CBS, D/LO/6/18/1: family records kept by William Lowndes and copied by his son Henry.
[2] Shropshire Archives, X112/1/1/1/1694, Susan Ferris to Richard Hill, 15 December 1704.

William Lowndes' trustees

THE 1703 MARRIAGE SETTLEMENT

In June 1703 William Lowndes passed the manor of Winslow to his eldest son Robert as part of his marriage settlement.

Robert received Winslow Hall, nearly 600 acres of land, the rights to income from the market and the tithes of the manor. William added a further 286 acres in 1716.

But Robert received only a life interest: the income, not the capital. The hall, land and manorial rights were legally 'entailed'. In other words they were to be held in trust for Robert's son Richard and his successors.

To fulfil the settlement William appointed four trustees:

- **Richard Martin** – brother of William's third wife, Elizabeth Martin, who had died in 1689.
- **Charles Shales** – London goldsmith and brother of William's fourth wife Rebecca.
- **William Gyles III** – Winslow draper and son of William's early business partner.
- **Peter Lowndes II** – Winslow yeoman and William's second cousin.

WILLIAM LOWNDES WILL, 1724

When William Lowndes died in January 1724, his will repeated the entail of the Winslow estate to Robert's son Richard, while leaving other Buckinghamshire estates for William's other sons and money settlements for his daughters. He appointed three executors:

- **Charles Shales** – London goldsmith and brother of Rebecca, now William's widow.
- **Richard Hill** – diplomat, William's long-time friend and uncle of his son Robert's wife Margaret.
- **John Duncombe** – widower of William's daughter Elizabeth, who had died in 1712.

These men would work to fulfil William's intentions in the years after his death.

did not last long: their other thirteen children, including four pairs of twins, were born in Winslow.

Until about 1708 Winslow Hall was therefore occupied for only part of the year at most. Unlike his father, Robert did not grow up in Winslow and cannot have had much personal knowledge of his new tenants and neighbours, even those to whom he was related. Whatever statement William Lowndes was making to Winslow by building his new house, Robert was part of it, but his own feelings are unknown. Some aspects of Robert's life are fairly well documented, but he remains a figure very much in his father's shadow.

Robert did establish friendly relations with the Verneys of Claydon House, and the first Viscount Fermanagh, Sir John Verney, was godfather to one of Robert's children.[3] A letter to Lady Fermanagh is one of the rare occasions when Robert speaks in his own voice:[4]

'Robert Wyat the bearer being inform'd your Ladyship has parted with your butcher, has solicited mee to recommend him to your service. I beg your Ladyship's pardon for the presumption which I would not venture upon, but that I have had long experience of the man's honesty and of the goodness of the meate he provides. My wife (who has help'd me to a couple of boyes this morning) joynes her service with mine to your Ladyship and the rest of your good family.'

At Christmas 1714 'Winslow' was among the guests at Claydon House, and 'the Loundeses' are mentioned as dinner guests on other occasions.[5] There had never before been anyone in Winslow whom the Verneys would have invited to their home.

William Lowndes wrote in his notebook for 1709 that he was allowing Robert £200 a year, but the money was being used to pay off £710 which William had lent him 'toward payment of his debts'.[6] Financial problems dogged Robert for the rest of his life,

---

[3] *Verney Letters*, 1.287.
[4] *Verney Letters*, 1.284 (1 November 1710).
[5] *Verney Letters*, 2.22, 60, 83.
[6] CBS, D/X/1435.

and he found great difficulty managing within the generous terms of his marriage settlement – by which he received the income from 600 acres of land, the manor, the market and tithes of Winslow.

'It seems possible that … William senior found his eldest son Robert rather a trial,' writes Jennifer Moss.[7]

When William made his will in 1721, he released Robert from the balance of debt still due to him. He also left Robert the use of 'all my books, medals, peices of ancient coins and mathematical instruments.' But only for his lifetime; afterwards they were to go with 'the said capitall messuage which I built at Winslow', which had been entailed in the marriage settlement so that Robert had only a life interest.[8]

Robert had to sign a receipt for these in March 1724 when William died: 'I promise to lay them all up safe at Winslow, for use of my son Richard and his successors'.[9]

According to William's Winslow accounts for the year up to December 1723, he paid more than £200 to build a new tithe barn for Robert's benefit.[10] This replaced the structure next to Parson's Close which had been built for St Albans Abbey. Today it has become two private houses. William also paid £11 for timber and lead 'towards the new passage', which sounds like a structural alteration to Winslow Hall, and £30 to pay the debts of 'RL': £20 to the Winslow lawyer John Markham, and, more mysteriously, £10 to 'Mrs Gibs in part of a debt from RL'.

Most of the information about Robert concerns his financial problems. The records have survived because they were kept by his wife's Shropshire relatives, who helped him out and continued to take a close interest in his children after his death.

In 1720 Robert handed over £1,300 to his father and Richard Hill in trust for the benefit of his children.[11] The money was to be used for their education, maintenance and marriage portions. The

---

[7] Moss, *Ways and Means*, 77.
[8] TNA, PROB 11/595/393 (William Lowndes' will, page 8).
[9] Shropshire Archives, X112/1/1/4/2128.
[10] CBS, D/LO/6/9/1.
[11] Shropshire Archives, X112/1/1/4/2091–93.

Eton College Register records a student named 'Lound' in 1718,[12] and two of Robert's sons went to Eton. Richard, born 1706 and another Robert, born 1708.[13] This fund was still in William's hands when he died in 1724. Hill noted that the trust was cancelled that year after he had paid some of Robert's debts.

A new trust for £1,000 'for ye use of Mr. Lowndes and his children' was created, the other £300 having been used for Robert's 'pressing occasions'.[14] It seems that most of the money had been used up by February 1726, and Hill wanted to cancel the trust again.[15] He had £245 in his hands in February 1725, of which £70 had been paid out for Robert's eldest surviving son, Richard, who had recently matriculated at Worcester College, Oxford, with the remaining £175 to be used for his younger brother Robert.

A letter written in 1726 by their uncle William[16] to Richard Hill, who was also acting as one of William Lowndes' executors, says that Robert's children 'stand most in need of regular and prompt payments'.[17] This time the whole bill was £70, including £10 'for a suit of clothes and some linnen for my nephew Robert in May last ordered by his father but I am afraid unlikely to be paid by him', about which the tailor had travelled from Oxford, either to Winslow or London.

There are some letters and bills from Frances Peers, who ran a school at Oxford, to another of Robert's brothers, Charles Lowndes at the Treasury, concerning the education of some of Robert's children.[18] Charles (1699–1783) followed in his father's footsteps at the Treasury, becoming Secretary 1765–67. He also inherited his father's property at The Bury in Chesham.[19] He was left with the main responsibility for sorting out the financial mess

---

[12] Richard Arthur Austen-Leigh, *The Eton College Register 1698-1752* (Eton: Ballantyne, 1927), 217.

[13] This is Robert Lowndes IV, born in 1708 – see William Lowndes descendants' family tree on page 152.

[14] Shropshire Archives, X112/1/1/4/2119.

[15] Shropshire Archives, X112/1/1/4/2134.

[16] This is William Lowndes III, born in 1687 – see the family tree on page 152.

[17] Shropshire Archives, X112/1/1/4/2133.

[18] Shropshire Archives, X112/1/1/4/2096–99, 2108, 2117.

[19] Moss, *Ways and Means*, 91.

left by his brother Robert, and continued to be consulted by his nephew Richard. It is also thanks to him that so many Lowndes records have been preserved, as those which descended to Robert and Richard's branch of the family were taken to Whaddon Hall in the nineteenth century and largely lost.

Mrs Peers wrote about 'Master Harry', who seems to have started with her in 1722 at the age of eight – this is Robert's son Henry, born in 1714. His sister Elizabeth, born in 1709 and now thirteen, was being taught to write from July 1722 onwards. Mrs Peers told Charles ominously:

> 'Sir if you make any objections against any of ye bills be pleased to enquire of Mr. Lowndes of Winslow who will satisfie you, he having had all these bills once and some of them twice.'

Three of the Lowndes children were at the school in the second half of 1724: Harry needed new shirts and Roger had to be bled.[20] And three were still being educated at Oxford by Mrs Peers and 'Mr Bowlder' in February 1725.[21]

On 1 March 1721 Robert had also signed an indenture handing over the manor of Winslow and all his copyhold land, as well as some other north Buckinghamshire property, to his brother-in-law John Duncombe, the widower of his half-sister Elizabeth, in exchange for an income of £400 a year for himself, his wife and younger children.[22] The four eldest sons were excepted;[23] but presumably other measures were taken for their support as they were too young to be earning their own living, and the rents and manorial income at Winslow should have been well over £400.

Duncombe (1679–1746) was a Hertfordshire landowner and one of Robert's father's executors. He remained closely involved in Lowndes affairs.

---

[20] Shropshire Archives, X112/1/1/4/2121. Presumably the third was John, although he apparently attended New College School later.

[21] Shropshire Archives, X112/1/1/4/2124.

[22] Shropshire Archives, X112/1/1/4/2094.

[23] These were Richard, born 1706, Robert, born 1708, John and Roger, born 1710 – see the family tree on page 152.

This arrangement was also revoked in 1724, when his father's death exacerbated Robert's financial problems – at least to the extent that no-one else was likely to come to his rescue.

In 1726 Robert brought a case in Chancery against Francis Ligo, attorney of Aylesbury, which shows that his finances were in confusion and had been for some time.[24] The case involved Robert's debt to Ligo of £50 from 1718 'for prosecuting and defending several actions' (presumably for debt), Robert 'not then being furnished with money which he could conveniently spare'. In 1724 a sheriff's bailiff entered his house at Winslow and kept possession of his goods and chattels for several weeks. Robert agreed to pay Ligo another £50 and to satisfy the bailiff's fees and charges in order to get rid of him. Ligo acknowledged receipt of £50 through John Markham, Robert's new attorney. According to Ligo's answer, he had originally paid the Winslow lawyer Peter Goldsworth £30 on Robert's behalf 'in satisfaction of an execution' (presumably for debt), which Goldsworth had issued against him. In 1724 Ligo had a writ issued against Robert which Thomas Turnham, the county sheriff's bailiff and a regular visitor at Winslow Hall, 'executed very tenderly' because Robert was a gentleman and neighbour.

A dispute over tradesmen's bills had already involved Robert in another Chancery case which he brought in 1725.[25] The agreed facts were that Robert contracted a debt (amount unspecified but less than £40) to a vintner of Westminster in 1720 or earlier, and another for £28 to a fishmonger of Temple Bar. After trying unsuccessfully to get Robert to pay, the creditors ordered a London attorney named John Stafford to bring an action against him. The exact details of what followed were disputed, but the debt spiralled through interest and costs. Robert claimed to have paid at least £100 but had not kept notes or receipts.

He asked Stafford to visit him at Winslow, 'his journey being near a hundred miles theither & back againe', but although he was grateful that Stafford went himself 'rather then putt an officer in

---

[24] TNA, C11/1207/9.
[25] TNA, C11/1194/3.

possession', he did not produce any money. At a meeting on 24 June 1724 Robert agreed he owed £232. An 'execution' was ordered and at Stafford's instigation the sheriff had Robert's household goods, corn, hay, horses and cattle inventoried.

Stafford said that Robert then wrote to him asking that the goods should not be sold, and asked to meet him at Wendover. Stafford arrived there on 22 December, met Robert on the 24th and refused to grant him further time for payment, but no money was offered. He had to stay a week because there was no coach over Christmas. Robert gave him a note for £21 and paid a guinea for his accommodation at Wendover, but did not produce the ten guineas which Stafford asked for his expenses.

This was the point at which Robert brought the case in Chancery against Stafford and the other creditors. There was a hearing on 8 March 1727 at which a judge was appointed to look into the accounts and make an adjudication on how much was owed. The process was halted by Robert's death in August, and his son Richard had to petition on 14 November for it to be revived.[26] Whatever the exact truth – and Robert's various claims of ignorance and of being deceived do not sound very plausible – and whatever the outcome – of which there appears to be no record – Robert was clearly in serious financial difficulties in the 1720s. He was borrowing money to pay other debts, and interest and costs were adding substantially to the principal.

Robert did at least accept his responsibility for the chancel of the parish church. According to Reverend John Croft, who was already vicar in 1703 when Robert became lord of the manor, he 'set up a handsom wainscot, having the Creed, Decalogue & Lord's Prayer curiously wrot with gold upon black'.[27]

Robert died unexpectedly when he fell down dead after dismounting from his horse, and he was buried at Winslow on 3 September 1727. His wife Margaret was buried only seven months later on 23 April 1728. Under the terms of the marriage settlement Winslow Hall passed to their eldest surviving son

---

[26] TNA, C11/371/46.
[27] BL, Add.Ms. 5840 f.202r. This did not survive the restoration of the 1880s.

Richard, Robert did not leave a will; as his property had all been entailed by his father, there may not have been much point.

There is a revealing comment in a letter from Margaret's half-brother Thomas Hill (originally Harwood) to his father Thomas Harwood, who was Margaret's stepfather:[28]

> 'I just now receive an account of the death of Mr Lowndes of Winslow, which a son of his here in town sends me notice of. He was a too good natured a man, and no enimy but to himself and family who I am afraid fared the worse thro' his easy temper which lay him open to every idle designing fellow.'

This was between a paragraph about Richard Hill's will and one about fruit trees. Thomas also wrote to his father about Margaret's death the following year:[29]

> 'And now I am to acquaint you that I first received by post a letter from a physition at Winslow with the case of poor sister Lowndes to carry to Dr Friend here and soon after that, before his prescription could reach there to do her any good, I received by a messenger the melancoly news that she dyed on Thursday about three in the afternoon which was suddener than they imagined though it was not expected she could recover.'

This seems a rather matter-of-fact way to write when, apparently, sending news to their mother of her daughter's death.

The inventory of Winslow Hall, 1727

The inventory taken after Robert's death, probably by the agents for his creditors, gives a clear impression of how the house was used at the time.[30] The total contents were valued at £1,332, of which £201 was related to the coach house and farmyard.

There are few other Winslow inventories for this period with which to compare it, but the farmer John Deverell had goods worth £45 in 1730 and the innkeeper Thomas Hazzard had an

---

[28] Shropshire Archives, X112/12/7/63, 31 August 1727.
[29] Shropshire Archives, X112/12/7/65, Thomas Hill, London, to Thomas Harwood at Tern Hall, 20 April 1728.
[30] TNA, PROB 3/26/181

inventory of £167 in 1737.[31] William Harding of Aylesbury, a rich yeoman farmer who founded a charity, had a personal estate valued at £1,128 in 1719, but most of that was livestock and money owed to him.[32] The contents of Winslow Hall were more valuable than those of Montague Drake at Shardeloes, Amersham, in 1698, which had come to just under £700,[33] and similar to those of Robert Dormer at Dorton House in 1694: £1,066.[34]

Robert's clothes and ready money were valued at only £20, against Dormer's at £50. Drake's clothing alone was itemised and valued at £53. Robert, although poorly dressed, was living in a style expected of a gentleman in a purpose-built house (rather than an improved farmhouse) despite his financial troubles. The higher aristocracy were at a different level altogether: the first Duke of Montague had goods worth £8,279 at Ditton in 1709.[35]

The inventory shows how the house was actually used and how Robert and Margaret lived. Its original plan (*see Figure 13*) was reconstructed by the Wren Society in 1940 from an examination of the house, though without access to the inventory so individual rooms are not named on the plan.

On the second floor, where the inventory starts, the 'Green Room' and 'Yellow Room' were furnished as functioning bedrooms, although their fireplaces were apparently not used. There was a stove grate in the 'Gallery', most likely the largest room at the front of the hall, but the other contents indicate that the room was used only for storage. Servants' rooms in the attic behind the pediment, lit only by the circular windows in the pediments and with no fireplaces, are not included at all.[36]

These three rooms are followed by the 'Fore' and 'Back Stair Heads', suggesting that the appraisers then moved down to the

---

[31] HALS, A25/4714 and HALS, A25/4717.

[32] Hugh Hanley, *Apprenticing in a Market Town* (Chichester: Phillimore, 2005), 43.

[33] Michael Reed (editor), *Buckinghamshire Probate Inventories 1661–1714* (BRS volume 24, 1988), no.140 = TNA, PROB 5/932.

[34] *Bucks Probate Inventories* no.133 = TNA, PROB 4/2573.

[35] Tessa Murdoch (editor), *Noble Households. Eighteenth-Century Inventories of Great English Houses* (Cambridge: John Adamson, 2006), 79–84.

[36] Eland, 'Building of Winslow Hall', 408, 410; Smith, 'Winslow Hall', 244

first floor. However they then list five principal rooms, whereas the plan shows only four. It therefore seems likely that the 'Nursery' with attached closet was actually on the second floor. With more furniture listed in the inventory this would have been the larger rear-facing principal room, while the Green and Yellow Rooms were the smallest principal room and one of the closets.

The principal rooms on the first floor are 'Mrs Lowndes' Room' and the 'Blue Cloth', 'Plaid' and 'Pearl-Coloured' Rooms, evidently named after the drapery of the beds. It is uncertain which room was which on the plan. Mrs Lowndes' Room was furnished for daytime use with a tea-table and board, writing desk and seven chairs. There were three tapestry hangings, a gun and sword, and a repeating clock. The weapons might indicate that the room had been Mr and Mrs Lowndes' before Robert's death. Her closet was used as a dressing room, and the corner cupboard probably contained the plate, which is listed separately.

The Blue Cloth Room also had numerous chairs and two writing desks, with a card table in the dressing room. The contents of this room were more valuable than those of any other on this floor. If it is correctly identified as the south-west room it now has an eighteenth-century overmantel painting in the style of Salvatore Rosa[37] but the inventory mentions only a 'family picture'.

The Plaid Room had six chairs and a card table, and a crimson velvet easy chair. The contents of this room were more valuable than those of Mrs Lowndes' Room. 'Scotch plaid' decorated the bed long before George IV and Sir Walter Scott popularised it, but presumably it had not yet acquired the Jacobite associations it gained as a result of the Jacobite Rebellion of 1745–46.

After the Plaid Room, a capacious wardrobe is listed, whose contents included a field bed and a feather bed, a couch and six chairs, an India cabinet, 'two carved frames with painted stone slabbs', sixteen curtains and an umbrella.

The Pearl-Coloured Room had six chairs as well as a bed, but its dressing room was evidently used for storage with part of two

---

[37] Pevsner and Williamson, *Buckinghamshire*, 756.

bedsteads and five old broken sconces among other things. Perhaps it had previously been used by Robert before his death. The main staircase, on the east side of the building, had eighteen India pictures, which probably means pictures on what was called 'India paper' rather than pictures of India.

The north-east room on the plan now contains four painted panels which occupy most of the internal walls: two large ones east and west and two smaller ones either side of the fireplace which were evidently made-to-measure for the available spaces. Pevsner describes them as:

> 'wall paintings of Giorgionesque ideal landscape in heavy and elaborate ornamental surrounds including caryatids, strap-work and grotesques. The surrounds in the manner of the de Critz are rather old-fashioned in so metropolitan-looking a house.'[38]

In the 1959 Listing[39] they are 'painted canvases in the manner of Daniel Marot[40] with pastoral scenes in elaborate surrounds of swags, scrolls, herms and mask heads.' According to Smith they were probably painted specially in London, and depict garden or pastoral scenes whose meaning is unclear.[41]

If the paintings were in the house in 1727, they must have been regarded as fixtures because they were not listed. The inventory recorded hangings in all the first-floor rooms, which would be superfluous if the walls were covered with paintings. There is also nothing in the building accounts about decorative interior paintings.[42] It therefore seems more likely that they were only added to the house later, probably by Richard Lowndes.

The principal rooms on the ground floor, which were the only ones recorded with working fires, were the 'Little Parlour', 'Great Hall', 'Great Parlour' and 'Back Parlour'. The Wren Society plan assumed that there was no passage between the main front and rear entrances, but that each opened directly into one of the

---

[38] Pevsner and Williamson, Buckinghamshire, 756.
[39] https://britishlistedbuildings.co.uk/101279357-winslow-hall-winslow
[40] Marot was in England 1694–98.
[41] Smith, 'Winslow Hall', 243.
[42] Smith, 'Winslow Hall', 240.

principal rooms, and this is confirmed by the inventory.[43] The four closets on the plan must be the rooms described in the inventory as two 'Studies', 'Buffet Room' and 'Sideboard Room'.[44] None of the principal rooms had contents valued as highly as those of the Blue Cloth and Plaid Rooms, although the library, valued separately at £110, must have been in one of them as no room was designated as a Library. The ground-floor rooms had probably suffered most from the depredations of the bailiffs.

The Little Parlour contained 'seven fine pictures', four tables and ten cane chairs. The Great Hall must have been the dining room: there was a 'phaneer'd [veneered] table', a cedar table and eight cane chairs. The Great Parlour seems to be what would later be called a withdrawing room: there was a settee and eight stools, a large tea-table and two card tables. The Back Parlour had seven pictures, including four family ones, a tea-table and another table, and eight chairs.

The two Studies contained little, but probably housed the library. There was a writing desk but 'three pair of dog couples, one pruning knife, one powder flaske' indicate where Robert Lowndes' interests lay.

The Buffet Room may have housed the china, valued separately at £30, but otherwise the contents were limited although there was a coffee mill. The glassware was kept in the Sideboard Room, but was given a low value, and the contents included 'one reel and lines, one dog collar'.

The appraisers moved via the 'Fore Passage', where bottles were stored, to the 'Dairy'. The 'Lower Kitchen' and 'Lower Servants Hall' must be in the basement of the main house. According to Pevsner, the south side was used for the Servants' Hall,[45] but the servants cannot have used this room for dining in 1727 because the inventory shows there was nothing there to sit on. Eland points out that there is a fireplace seven feet wide in one

---

[43] A cross-passage is shown in Eland's plan, but with some expression of doubt (Eland, 'Building of Winslow Hall', 408).

[44] The Wren Society plan does not show a separate closet for the north-east room, but that must be a mistake.

[45] Pevsner and Williamson, *Buckinghamshire*, 756.

of the larger rooms, presumably for the Lower Kitchen[46] – though the Wren Society plan shows such a fireplace in both rooms.

The appraisers then went via the 'Back Stair Case' and 'Passage' to the 'Brewhouse', 'Old Laundry with a room over it and a chamber', 'Washhouse', various chambers and storerooms, to the 'Servants Hall' (this one did have a table and forms), 'Kitchen' and 'Bakehouse'. Some if not all of these would have been in the 'pavilions', shown on the painting of the Hall soon after completion[47] but not included on the Wren Society plan.

There were four cellars, including separate ones for strong beer, wine (though in the inventory it contains only beer) and small beer; these were probably the four small rooms in the basement.

The garden was equipped for recreational use, with two painted seats, two benches, and thirteen chairs, and for some productivity with four cucumber frames and 216 flower pots. It also had three beehives, but the total contents of the garden were only valued at £21. One entry covers the yard, barn, stable and coach house, whose contents in total were valued at £201. There were six coach mares and one horse, a chariot and a chaise. Three cows supplied the dairy, but there was also some pig-breeding: a boar, three sows and thirteen pigs. A 'water engine' was presumably for firefighting and must have been available to the whole town.

Richard Lowndes

Richard Lowndes was born in London on 16 September 1706. He was Robert and Margaret's second son but his older brother William died in 1718 at the age of 14. Richard was named after his great-uncle and godfather Richard Hill.[48] He and his younger brother Robert were at Eton together until 1724. There is a detailed bill for £74 from Mrs Isabella Snape, with whom they boarded, for six months up to April 1724.[49] It survives because she

---

[46] Eland, 'Building of Winslow Hall', 410.
[47] Smith, 'Winslow Hall', 233.
[48] CBS, D/LO/6/18/1.
[49] Shropshire Archives, X112/1/1/4/2114.

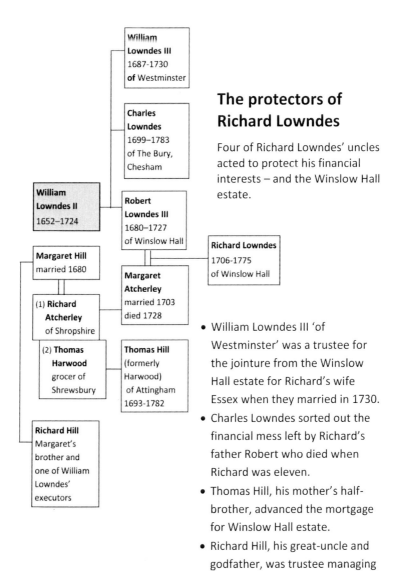

The protectors of Richard Lowndes

Four of Richard Lowndes' uncles acted to protect his financial interests – and the Winslow Hall estate.

- William Lowndes III 'of Westminster' was a trustee for the jointure from the Winslow Hall estate for Richard's wife Essex when they married in 1730.
- Charles Lowndes sorted out the financial mess left by Richard's father Robert who died when Richard was eleven.
- Thomas Hill, his mother's half-brother, advanced the mortgage for Winslow Hall estate.
- Richard Hill, his great-uncle and godfather, was trustee managing his father Robert's debts and executor of his grandfather William Lowndes' will.

had to send it to their uncles after their father failed to pay. There are two items for mending the windows, and one for mending their bed, which they must have shared, but they each had a study. Their coach home in December cost 14s.

The tutor at Eton was paid eight guineas, the master four guineas, and the writing master £1 2s. Books came to £5 9s and 'barber for shaving and 2 wiggs' £5 4s. They had copies of *Paradise Lost and Regained*, and a 'Homer'.[50] There were also some individual bills for 1723–24. One from a bookseller included two Books of Common Prayer, Pope, Horace, 'Johnsons Phaedrus fables' and 'Bucanans poems'.[51] They also had fourteen pairs of shoes in a little over six months (as well as one pair of boots and spurs), and there was an apothecary's bill for 7s which included a purge and a 'composing draught'.[52]

They do not seem to have been inconvenienced much by their father's financial troubles at this stage but Richard's affairs came to be entirely managed by his uncles: Richard Hill and Thomas Hill on his mother's side of the family and Charles and William Lowndes on his father's.[53]

Richard matriculated at Worcester College, Oxford, in 1724 aged 17.[54] He did not graduate, but was much later given a doctorate in 1756, presumably in return for services in Parliament. His tutor at Worcester College was Roger Bourchier, a fellow and benefactor to the college who had to work hard to get Richard's bills paid by various uncles.[55] Tuition was relatively cheap at a guinea a quarter and the bills were mainly for living expenses, including £1 11s for the tailor and £1 8s for the barber. The first bill included £17 for the mercer and tailor and £13 for the milliner, which must have been to get Richard suitably dressed when he started. He also had to provide his own chamber pot and basin. £2 9s was spent on books in one term, giving an idea of what Richard

---

[50] Shropshire Archives, X112/1/1/4/2113.
[51] Shropshire Archives, X112/1/1/4/2107.
[52] Shropshire Archives, X112/1/1/4/2105–06
[53] See the Lowndes and Hill family connections on page 165.
[54] *Oxford University Alumni 1715–1886*, 877.
[55] Shropshire Archives, X112/1/1/4/2125, 2129, 2134.

was studying; the Septuagint and Longinus' *On the Sublime,* so he was studying Greek, and Euclid's *Elements.*

Richard achieved the age of twenty-one in September 1727, the same month that his father was buried, so he must have found himself immediately sorting out Robert's tangled affairs. He inherited the lawsuit against John Stafford about money which Robert owed.[56] He would have had the help of his Lowndes uncles and his mother's relatives in Shropshire, who seem to have brought up some of his younger sisters after their mother Margaret died in 1728.[57]

Under the terms of his parents' marriage settlement and his grandfather's will, all of the Lowndes property at Winslow came to Richard and his heirs male. The administration of the will left Richard with ongoing litigation. In 1729 he brought a case in Chancery against the executors and his own uncles and (nominally) his brothers for non-payment of legacies.[58] Nearly thirty years later in 1756 he was still pursuing his grandfather's estate, claiming that the executors of the last original executor, John Duncombe, had failed to sell the property in London and to realise other assets which should have been invested for the benefit of his father, himself and his son William.[59]

Richard went through a procedure of common recovery in 1728 with the help of the lawyer John Markham.[60] This was to break the entail in William Lowndes' will, only four years after his death, and enabled Richard to mortgage his estate to his Shropshire relatives for £6,000.

The discharge of this mortgage, which took more than fifty years, is recorded in documents preserved by both Charles Lowndes of Chesham, who was Richard's uncle and trustee, and Thomas Hill (originally Harwood) of Attingham (1693–1782), his

---

[56] TNA, C11/371/46 (1727).
[57] There are some letters to Richard Lowndes from his sisters in Shrewsbury (BL, Add.Ms. 37069 ff.222–29).
[58] TNA, C11/1021/16.
[59] TNA, C 11/1121/7. One of John Duncombe's executors was his brother-in-law William Lowndes III, who was Richard's uncle – see the family tree on page 152.
[60] CBS, D97/104/1/19, 3 June 1728.

Interconnections of the Lowndes and Shales families across three generations

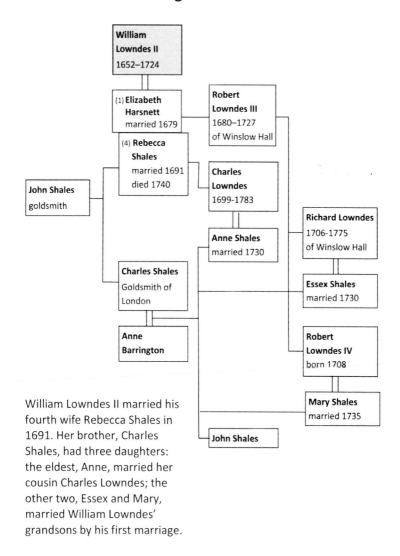

William Lowndes II married his fourth wife Rebecca Shales in 1691. Her brother, Charles Shales, had three daughters: the eldest, Anne, married her cousin Charles Lowndes; the other two, Essex and Mary, married William Lowndes' grandsons by his first marriage.

mother's half-brother and the mortgagee. The money to do this eventually came from the marriage settlement of Richard's son William in 1766, but the principal was not paid off until between 1778 and 1780.[61]

The other solution to Richard's cash-flow problems was an advantageous marriage. A financial settlement for the marriage of Richard Lowndes and Essex Shales was drawn up on 15 June 1730.[62] She was the daughter of Charles Shales of London, goldsmith to the king and banker, who was the brother of Richard's step-grandmother: William Lowndes' last wife Rebecca. Essex Shales' own mother had been Anne Barrington, sister and heir of Sir Charles Barrington of Barrington Hall in Essex and granddaughter of Robert Rich, third Earl of Warwick.[63]

Essex had been left £500 by Sir Charles and £1,000 by his sister Mary. Her father made this up to a marriage portion of £4,000, and she inherited more when he died in 1734. Her brother John and Richard's uncle William (William Lowndes III of Westminster) acted as trustees for her jointure from the Lowndes estate, which consisted of a house at North Crawley and other property there and at Chicheley, Astwood and Newport Pagnell.

Richard paid his grandfather's executors £2,300 to clear unpaid legacies chargeable on the property. Some other property at Weston Turville, Bierton and Stoke Mandeville was set aside to raise portions totalling £4,000 for any younger children of the marriage. The wedding took place at St Paul's Cathedral on 25 June 1730.

Essex's sister Anne Shales married Richard's uncle Charles Lowndes at St Giles Cripplegate on 8 October 1730. Another sister, Mary Shales, married Richard's brother Robert Lowndes at the church of St Benet Paul's Wharf in 1735, when he was said to be of the Inner Temple. She had received a portion of £4,000 in

---

[61] CBS, D/LO/6/2/8/13 and 15 (receipts signed by Thomas Hill dated 15 January and 11 March 1778); Shropshire Archives, X112/12/6/1/Box 93 no.40, and CBS, D/LO/6/2/8/26 (receipts dated 23 February 1780).

[62] CBS, D/LO/2/11–15.

[63] The Barrington estate eventually came to the Lowndes family but not until the 1830s.

1734 under her father's will,[64] so presumably it was her money which enabled him to live for a time at Water Hall, the former home of the historian Browne Willis in Bletchley, and to own property at Bragenham, between Soulbury and Little Brickhill, which he left to Richard's daughters.[65]

As well as Winslow Hall Richard maintained a town house in London, and all his three children were baptised in London: Anne in 1733, William in 1735 and Mary in 1737. He is recorded as having his London residence in Winchester Street (1749), George Street (1750), Craven Street (1752–55) and Pall Mall (1757–69).[66] Letters to him in the 1750s were directed to the Cocoa Club, Pall Mall. Essex died in 1756 and he did not remarry.

Richard Lowndes served as sheriff of Buckinghamshire in 1738, the first time anyone from Winslow had held this office which was shared among the county gentry. It was particularly significant at election time, and could not be held by a sitting MP, but the radical journalist and politician John Wilkes, who was sheriff in 1754, treated it as the beginning of a political career,[67] and apparently Richard did so before him.

He played a significant role in county life, attending Quarter Sessions in his capacity as a JP,[68] and the Buckinghamshire assizes in the summer.[69] He was a commissioner for the Buckingham-to-Wendover Turnpike under the new Act of 1744 which formalised the route through Winslow.[70] He had his portrait painted by Thomas Gainsborough, probably at Bath in 1759.[71]

Richard Lowndes was also the first man from Winslow to

[64] TNA, PROB 11/667/259.
[65] TNA, PROB 11/1194/281.
[66] As recorded in *The English Registry* for the relevant years.
[67] H A Hanley, *The Buckinghamshire Sheriffs* (Bucks Record Office, 1992), 15-16.
[68] CBS, Q/SM/2, Q/SM/3.
[69] *Verney Letters*, 2.205, John Millward to Lord Fermanagh, Claydon, 23 July 1740; 2.210, Lord Fermanagh to Earl Verney, Claydon, 17 July 1744; Francis Griffin Stokes (editor), *The Blecheley Diary of the Rev. William Cole M.A. F.S.A. 1765–67* (London: Constable, 1931), 70 (July 1766).
[70] *Verney Letters*, 2.247, Lord Fermanagh to Earl Verney, Claydon, 10 June 1744.
[71] Sotheby's, www.sothebys.com/en/auctions/ecatalogue/2010/old-master-and-british-paintings-l10035/lot.181.html [accessed 24 January 2020].

become MP for Buckinghamshire. His first attempt was unsuccessful: he stood as a lone Tory candidate against two Whigs in the 1734 election, despite having told people that he would not contest it.[72] His opponents were the sitting MPs Sir William Stanhope and Sir Thomas Lee.[73] He lost heavily, getting 1,314 votes compared to 2,414 for Stanhope and 1,763 for Lee. However this was a repeat of the result in 1727 when Richard's Tory predecessor had also lost to two Whigs.

Analysis shows that the 1734 votes were not just cast on party lines.[74] There were few voters from Winslow because of the lack of freehold property, but some people qualified through owning property elsewhere. All eleven voted for Lowndes: nine were plumpers and two, both Baptists, also voted for Stanhope. Lowndes himself voted for Lee; evidently it was not gentlemanly to vote for oneself. Three voters from Granborough and two from Little Horwood voted for Stanhope and Lowndes. Six from Little Horwood and four from Granborough plumped for Lowndes. Granborough and the Winslow Baptists had voted entirely Whig earlier in the century.

It would presumably have been possible for Lowndes to create a large number of freeholders in Winslow, but he did not do so. There were considerable variations between villages, but in general Lowndes was well supported in the surrounding area. He also received strong backing from Chesham, thanks to his relatives there, the family of his uncle Charles Lowndes, but not elsewhere in south Buckinghamshire.

This was not enough for Richard Lowndes to win a seat in parliament, but he made a strong enough impression for the Whigs and Tories to nominate one candidate each in 1741, when he was returned unopposed with the Whig Richard Grenville. He was then returned with Stanhope in 1747, 1754 and 1761, and with Earl Verney in 1768. Clear saw a copy of his election address from

---

[72] CBS, D-LE/A/2/5/d, Sir Thomas Lee, 16 Apr 1734; D-LE/A/3/1/d, William Gore to Sir Thomas Lee, 7 May 1734.

[73] *History of Parliament*, www.historyofparliamentonline.org/volume/1715-1754/constituencies/buckinghamshire [accessed 23 January 2020].

[74] CBS, D/MH 40/2 is the handwritten record of each vote as it was cast.

1754, and described it as 'a pattern of brevity, and no one can complain of its politics':[75] He quoted Lowndes as saying:

> 'Being encouraged by the freeholders in general to offer myself as a candidate at the ensuing election for this county, I humbly presume to ask the favour of your votes and interest, which will be esteemed the greatest honour.'

Lowndes seems to have attended the House of Commons regularly without doing anything memorable, but he no doubt used his position to promote the agricultural enclosure of Shipton in 1745. Apart from moving some private bills, he is only known to have spoken once, on 9 January 1770.[76] He has been described with faint praise as 'a hard-working knight of the shire'.[77] Having acquired the seat, he benefitted from the convention that sitting county members were not challenged, and from the partitioning of Buckinghamshire between one member each from north and south and between a Tory and a Whig.[78]

The uncontested elections were not necessarily a formality, however. In a letter written to a relative on 4 July 1747 his uncle John Duncombe comments: 'We are very busy in getting cozen Richard Lowndes elected for our county, he being opposed by Mr Grenville'.[79] Richard did not stand in 1775, making a late withdrawal to avoid a contest with the Grenvilles,[80] although perhaps his health was an issue too because he died the following year.

Richard Lowndes was not popular with the Verneys of Claydon House, no doubt partly because he was a Tory and they were now Whigs. He was said to be talking 'very freely' in 1743 about the promotion of the then second Viscount Fermanagh, Ralph Verney, to become the first Earl Verney, 'but they say t'is a

---

[75] Clear, *King's Village*, 82.

[76] *History of Parliament*, www.historyofparliamentonline.org/volume/1754-1790/member/lowndes-richard-1707-75 [accessed 23 January 2020].

[77] Paul Langford, 'Property and 'virtual representation' in eighteenth-century England', *Historical Journal* 31 (1988), 83–115, 103.

[78] Langford, 'Property and virtual representation', 89–90.

[79] CBS, D/LO/6/7/3.

[80] *History of Parliament*, www.historyofparliamentonline.org/volume/1754-1790/constituencies/buckinghamshire [accessed 23 January 2020].

method with him to diminish if he can other people, in order to aggrandize himself.'[81] In August 1745, a man who 'pull'd up a new dead hedge at East Claydon Field' was taken before him as the nearest magistrate, and the fourth Viscount Fermanagh, another Ralph, commented that:[82]

> 'Lowndes told em the hedges were put up without an Act of Parliament … & justices had nothing to do with such unwarrantable proceedings, & therefore he discharged him. L has not been here since I was in the country. Winslow law is always against Claydon, and I wonder L is not ashamed to fly so often in the face of justice, for he always looses his point at the end … L has given all the encouragement possible to set people at work [throwing down fences].'

When news reached Buckinghamshire in December 1745 that Charles Edward Stuart and the Jacobites had reached Derby, and were wrongly reported to be at Northampton, Fermanagh wrote that 'Lowndes pack'd up his plate & his family were to have removed to Wotton yesterday as a more private place,' where the Grenvilles took them in a perceived emergency. But, he added, 'I hear Mr. Greenville was to set out for London not caring to stay.'[83]

In June 1746, John Millward, the Claydon steward, met Lowndes and his sisters at Addington:[84]

> 'He was very liberal with his tongue about Claydon, & said that the Grandborough & Swanborn people had lost their ancient spirit, for formerly they would not suffer any [roads] to be stopt up. And the Oxon road lay through the middle of East Claydon Field, to his knowledge and much more to the same purpose. He then abus'd Pelham & the Grenvilles.'

This letter was docketed by Earl Verney 'Lowndes's spight'.

Reverend William Cole of Bletchley knew Richard's brother Robert Lowndes well, and they sometimes dined together. He

[81] *Verney Letters*, 2.208, Lord Fermanagh to Earl Verney, Claydon, 15 September 1743.
[82] *Verney Letters*, 2.210–11, Lord Fermanagh to Earl Verney, Claydon, 7 August 1745.
[83] *Verney Letters*, 2.200, Lord Fermanagh to Earl Verney, Claydon, 8 December 1745.
[84] *Verney Letters*, 2.255, Lord Fermanagh to Earl Verney, Claydon, 3 June 1746. Henry Pelham was Prime Minister 1743–54.

described Richard, whom he knew rather less well, as:[85]

> 'a very worthy man, and his family estates not very great, seeing he has represented this county in parliament, so many years … When I first came into the county, Messrs Lowndes, with Mr Thos Willis, were of the highest order of Tories … Mr Willis, I suppose, died in that opinion, but both the Messrs Lowndes have since then been veering with the stream …'

He noted that Robert, although 'bred to the law', avoided practising it and concentrated on riding, for which he had more talent. He kept a pack of hare hounds, and often hunted with Mr Selby of Wavendon. Cole's comment about the change of Richard's political alignment agrees with the assessment of him in the *History of Parliament* that he aligned himself with the administration from 1769, with both the Whig Duke of Grafton and Tory Lord North.[86]

Richard was executor of both Thomas Willis, the son of Browne Willis of Whaddon, who died in 1756, and of his son Thomas who died in 1762.[87] After Browne Willis himself died in 1760, Richard was guardian to his heir John Willis (later John Fleming, 1749–1802). This left Richard managing property around Whaddon and Bletchley. Cole implied that he was not very assiduous in protecting John Willis' interests as he was expecting opposition at the election in 1767 and did not want to upset tenant farmers with votes.[88] Mrs Willis, the widow of the elder Thomas, said 'she was sure Mr Ric: Lowndes was not a little vexed at their accession of fortune', referring to an inheritance which had come to her son, as a condition of which he changed his name to Fleming.[89] She told Cole that 'Mr Lowndes had just sent her an arrear [payment due] which she ought to have had 10 years ago'.[90]

---

[85] *Blecheley Diary*, lvi–lvii.
[86] *History of Parliament*, www.historyofparliamentonline.org/volume/1754-1790/member/lowndes-richard-1707-75 [accessed 23 January 2020].
[87] TNA, PROB 11/824/157, PROB 11/882/411.
[88] *Blecheley Diary*, 84–85.
[89] *Blecheley Diary*, 179–80, 30 January 1767.
[90] *Blecheley Diary*, 181, 1 February 1767.

Richard Lowndes made over his Winslow estate to his only son William at the time of William's marriage in 1766. He still owned the property in North Crawley that had been intended for his wife's jointure, which he left to William, and he had acquired property at Swanbourne which he ordered in his will to be sold to pay legacies of £1,200 each to his two daughters Anne and Mary, who remained unmarried.[91] After William's marriage Richard went to live with them at Hillesden. He died on 6 October 1775.

William Lowndes

Richard's only son William Lowndes V was baptised at St Martin-in-the-Fields in London on 31 March 1735. His childhood is unrecorded, thanks partly to his father not being in financial trouble but more to the loss of most of the family documents later at Whaddon Hall. He did not attend Eton or Oxford like his father. In 1756 he recovered from smallpox.[92]

His marriage in January 1766 to Mary, daughter of Thomas Goostrey of Missenden Abbey, meant he took over his father's estate in Winslow and set in motion the agricultural enclosure of Winslow. According to Mary's father's will she had a marriage portion of £10,000.[93] This presumably included the £6,000 which was raised in 1778–80 by the sale of Goostrey's estate at Ickleford in Hertfordshire, and which was used to pay off the mortgage on the Lowndes property.

William's main interest was the Buckinghamshire Militia. He was a deputy lieutenant for Buckinghamshire from 1759 to 1774 and again from 1795. In 1759 he was Captain of a company drawn from Cottesloe Hundred, and is recorded as Major in 1765 and Lieutenant-Colonel in 1774.[94] His other interest was hunting, which was what he had in common with Thomas James Selby, the owner of Whaddon Hall – who made him his heir, much to the surprise of other hunting acquaintances.

---

[91] TNA, PROB 11/1013/211.
[92] BL, Add.Ms. 37069 ff.224–25, Sarah Lowndes to Richard Lowndes.
[93] TNA, PROB 11/1134/211.
[94] CBS, L/P/1.

One of them, the Earl of Jersey, wrote:[95]

> 'Mr Selby you hear is dead, & being always, I believe, a very strange man, has shewn himself so by his will, and cruelly so, for he has left Whaddon Chace & his estate to Maj. Lowndes, "if his heir at law cannot be found". Did you ever hear any thing so hard, it is leaving him a law suit or nothing at all.'

Selby's will refers to Lowndes as Major in the Militia, and leaves him the estate under the terms which Jersey quoted, but the immediate beneficiaries were Selby's cousin Temperance Bedford and his 'very dear' Elizabeth Hone.[96] William is not mentioned in the long list of legatees, and in view of a history of rivalry and litigation between his ancestors and Selby's,[97] and the desire of his great-grandfather William Lowndes to buy Whaddon Chase, it is possible that the will was intended to be a poisoned chalice.

In fact William did eventually make good his claim to Whaddon. He was appointed receiver of the estate and kept accounts for it from 1775; in the first year it produced income of about £2,500.[98] In 1780, his father-in-law wrote to his uncle Charles Lowndes: 'Mr Lowndes has at last succeeded, by having this day obtained, on a trial at bar, a verdict for the Selby estate.'[99] This led to his descendants making their main home at Whaddon and changing their name to Selby-Lowndes, but that is beyond the scope of this book.

Whatever Winslow's lord of the manor in 1770 was really like, he has left the impression of an archetypal hunting, shooting and fishing squire.

---

[95] BL, Add.Ms. 75773, Earl of Jersey to Countess Spencer, 20 December 1772.

[96] TNA, PROB 11/983/330.

[97] TNA, C11/1919/6, C11/1403/25: James Selby v William and Robert Lowndes, 1718, re Shucklow.

[98] TNA C 101/558: William Lowndes' accounts for Selby estate.

[99] CBS, D/LO/6/2/27, 22 April 1780.

The Hogson family tree

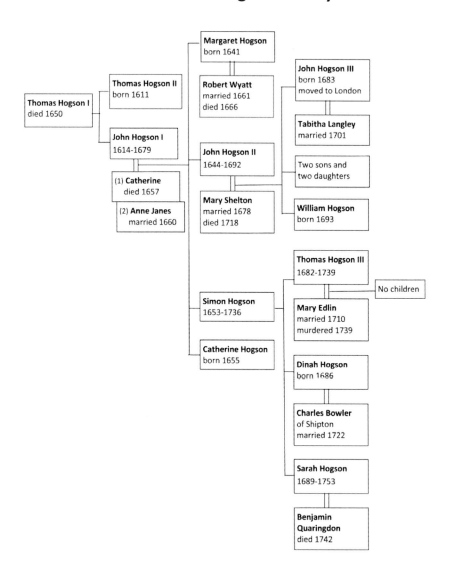

Winslow families
6: **The Hogson Family**

The Hogson (or Hogston or Hoggeston) family first appears in Winslow records in the fourteenth century.[1] In 1556 Robert Hoggeston held a cottage and 38¾ acres in Winslow and Shipton. In 1610 Thomas Hogson held a messuage, a cottage and 40 acres, and he or a son of the same name appears in lists of taxpayers up to 1641.[2]

In 1645 Thomas, who died in 1650, made a surrender to his younger son **John Hogson** (1614–79) of 15½ acres and the house in which John already lived.[3] It is not clear what happened to the elder son, another Thomas, but the whole family property ended up in John's hands. John, who was described as yeoman or husbandman,[4] was married twice. His second wife Anne, a widow, was previously married to John Janes of Biggin Farm. He had a substantial mixed farm: his inventory when he died includes livestock worth £80 and crops worth £80, but his household goods were only valued at £11. He left bequests to his daughters: £30 to one who was unmarried, £1 a year to another who was a widow with £5 for her son to be apprenticed. He left his land intact as one holding which went to his eldest son, also named John.[5]

John Hogson II (1644–92) inherited eight acres of freehold land at Tuckey Mead which at the end of his life he ordered to be sold by his executors to pay debts and legacies.[6] William Lowndes bought it for £150. The rest of the land had been entailed to his son, another John, so could not be sold or mortgaged.

---

[1] The surname is represented in Winslow now, but apparently not from a continuous line.
[2] CBS, WF538/44.
[3] WMC 29 April 1645, see www.winslow-history.org.uk/winslow_court1645.shtm.
[4] HALS, 115AW10, A25/2723.
[5] CBS, D/LO/4/3 page 12: William Lowndes' notebook.
[6] HALS 10AR57 (will), A25/4395 (inventory).

When he died his younger sons, including one with whom his wife was pregnant at the time, were given cash bequests totalling £45, and the household goods went to his daughters. His inventory suggests that the farm was less successful than at his father's death thirteen years earlier: livestock valued at £39, crops at £52, with an additional £15 'for the yeares profit of forty three ackers of land'. Domestic living standards had not risen much: the household goods were valued at £12.

John Hogson III (born in 1683) was only nine when his father died. He married Tabitha Langley in London on 21 April 1701, when they were both said to be of Stepney. They had a son baptised in 1703 at Winslow, where the following year John was a juror at the manor court. But, assuming it is the same people, they had a daughter baptised at Ivinghoe in 1708.

In 1705 they mortgaged 33 acres to Richard Bigg for £150.[7] The entail created by John's grandfather had now been fulfilled so there was no impediment to doing this. In 1709 the mortgage was transferred to William Lowndes II. It now included the whole 40 acres and the house, occupied by John's mother Mary, who died in 1718.[8] At this point John owed £231 including interest.

He stopped attending the manor court after this, and when he eventually sold to William Lowndes in 1717 the land was in the occupation of William Glenister. It appears that the original mortgage had been to raise funds to set John up in business, perhaps in London, and the full sale took place when he decided he would not be coming back to Winslow.

The first John Hogson had a younger son, **Simon Hogson** (1653–1736), who served as constable in Winslow (1682, 1693, 1704), hayward or field overseer (1685, 1698, 1710, 1714), churchwarden (1687, 1697, 1711), assessor (1718) and was a regular juror at the manor court from 1701, sometimes as foreman. He often witnessed wills and appraised the deceased's property, and is also found as a trustee of property arrangements. In other words, he was the sort of unpaid public servant on whom the

---

[7] WMC 25 May 1705, see www.winslow-history.org.uk/winslow_court1705.shtm.
[8] WMC 30 September 1709, see www.winslow-history.org.uk/winslow_court1709.shtm.

manorial system depended before professional lawyers took over. He was his brother John Hogson II's executor, with no financial recompense.

Unlike the younger sons of many farming families, he does not seem to have had any provision made for him apart from a horse and a bullock left to him in his father's will and a debt of £10 written off, although he would have had the reversion of the property if his brother had left no male heirs. In 1681 he lived in part of a house belonging to the Miller family.[9] He must have been a farmer by 1701 because he was fined for pasturing his sheep incorrectly, and he was described as a yeoman in 1723.[10]

From 1709 Simon Hogson is mentioned as the occupier of some of William Lowndes' land. They were close contemporaries (their baptisms were less than five months apart) and perhaps friends from childhood. The concentration of land in Lowndes' hands gave Simon the opportunity to become a tenant farmer, possibly on a larger scale than the 40 acres left to his brother, but he had no property to leave to his own son except 'a messuage or messuages' acquired in 1702 and already entailed.[11] So Simon did not leave a will.

Simon's only son was **Thomas Hogson III** (1682–1739). He also had two daughters, one of whom married Charles Bowler of Shipton, while the other's husband was a carpenter. Thomas achieved notoriety in 1739 by killing his wife. He appears to have died in gaol after an attempt at suicide, but was able to leave a valid will and did own some property.[12]

He left £1 to a neighbour, and £5 each to a nephew and niece if there was any money left. He apparently had no surviving children. His brother-in-law Benjamin Quaringdon, the main beneficiary, referred to Thomas as a yeoman when he made his own will in 1742.[13]

---

[9] WMC 11 October 1681, see www.winslow-history.org.uk/winslow_court1681.shtm.

[10] WMC 4 October 1701, see www.winslow-history.org.uk/winslow_court1701.shtm; and 25 October 1723, see www.winslow-history.org.uk/winslow_court1723.shtm.

[11] WMC 22 April 1702, see www.winslow-history.org.uk/winslow_court1702.shtm.

[12] TNA, PROB 11/707/218. For a full account see page 275 below.

[13] HALS, 180AW15.

Thomas's property consisted of two messuages, sometimes divided into three, inherited from his father.[14] William Hogson 'cozen and heir att law to Thomas Hogson late of Winslowe yeoman deceased' tried to sell them at a manor court in 1742, but this must have been invalidated.[15]

The Hogsons show that elder sons did not wait to marry until they came into their inheritance. Most fathers left some younger children under age when they died, and that was a strong incentive to make a will, but arrangements were disrupted if a father died while all his children were young. The Hogsons' policy of strict primogeniture over two generations was no more successful in preserving the family farm than other people's generous provisions for younger children. There were no Hogsons in the 1798 Posse Comitatus or the 1841 Census.

---

[14] It was in Sheep Street on the site of the house now called Yew Tree Cottage.
[15] WMC 29 March 1742, see www.winslow-history.org.uk/winslow_court1741.shtm.

Chapter 7:
A town of professions

In the Hearth Tax return of 1662/3,[1] the members of Winslow's population whose occupation is known from other sources consisted of farmers, shopkeepers (draper, mercer, grocer), innkeepers and tradesmen (butcher, baker, shoemaker, blacksmith, tailor, barber, carrier, miller). The only people in professions were the vicar and a doctor. In 1798, 135 years later, the Posse Comitatus, which is the first list of inhabitants with their occupations, lists two attorneys, two clergymen, three surgeons, an officer of excise and two schoolmasters.[2] A similar change took place in Buckingham over a comparable period.[3]

The rise of a professional class, providing services to Winslow and surrounding villages, including the Claydon estate, was one of the main social changes in Winslow during the period 1640–1770, and will be illustrated by case-studies of the best-documented individuals.

Education

The nearest grammar school was the Royal Latin School at Buckingham. Winslow's equivalent with a university-educated master, Henry Stubbings' Academy, did not start until 1799, but various other forms of education were available. There are several references to schoolmasters who must have taught pupils in their own houses. Clear gives the text of an application to the Bishop of London and Archdeacon of St Albans for Richard Ginger of

---

[1] TNA, E179/80/352, see www.winslow-history.org.uk/winslow_hearth_tax2.shtm
[2] Ian Beckett (editor), *The Buckinghamshire Posse Comitatus 1798* (Aylesbury: Buckinghamshire Records Society 1985), which will be frequently referred to throughout Chapters 7-10 as 'the 1798 listing'.
[3] John Broad, 'The changing face of employment in Buckingham, 1618–1798', *Records of Buckinghamshire* 34 (1992), 46–60.

Winslow to be given 'licence to teach schoole in the parrish of Winslow' which seems to date to 1681.[4] Ginger wrote most Winslow wills in the late seventeenth century. In 1690, Joseph Dandridge is recorded as a schoolmaster and surgeon.[5]

Joseph Rogers, a currier, whose will was proved in 1723,[6] left £600 to be invested in land, from which the income would be used by trustees for 'the educateing and instructing of such a number of poor peoples children belonging to the said parish of Winslowe in learning as they the trustees shall find the same will answer'. He was buried at Beachampton, and was probably inspired by William Elmer's school there which had been set up under a will proved in 1653.[7]

The Rogers Bequest established Winslow's charity school. Land to support the school was purchased in Great Kimble and is still owned by the Rogers Trust. The first trustees included four clergymen from neighbouring parishes, and the school was intended to be Anglican. Regulations laid down in 1727 required the children to be taught reading, writing, basic arithmetic and the church catechism, and they were to be 'brought to church every Lord's day and prayer days'. This was functional education for children who would otherwise not have received any schooling.

Joseph Gurney was the first master of the Rogers School. He was already living in Winslow by 1715, so probably established his own school before Rogers' bequest. Unlike the Beachampton bequest, Rogers did not leave money for a building, so the school was established in Gurney's house, now 1–3 Bell Walk. His fire insurance policy of 1725 refers to him as schoolmaster.[8]

Gurney died in 1727, and the regulations must have been intended for his successor. His will suggests that he was considerably in debt, and he expected his more valuable

---

[4] Clear, *King's Village*, 99.
[5] HALS, ASA 7/37, visitation of the Archdeacon of St Albans.
[6] TNA, PROB 11/590/325. Rogers' occupation has been incorrectly transcribed in various places (including the probate register) as furrier and carrier, but the will of Francis Armborough (1713) clearly refer to him as a currier (HALS, 10AR240).
[7] *VCH* Buckinghamshire, 2.218.
[8] LMA, Sun Insurance, 11936/15/415/23796.

possessions such as a clock and silver cup to be sold, but he left his wife his books and mathematical instruments.[9]

The immediate fate of the school is not known, but it probably continued on the same premises. 'Richard Reddall of Winslow, schoolmaster' appears in the manor court records for 1752.[10] It seems that Reverend John Rawbone, who was curate from 1749 and later vicar, ran the school himself for a time, and his nephew Thomas became master in 1775 on his death.[11] Thomas Rawbone continued to run both the charity school and a private one from the same premises until he died, when 'a neat cottage residence; comprising parlour and sitting room, with large school room' was advertised to be let.[12]

In her will of 1784, Susanna Bigg left a legacy of £20 to Joseph Hunt of Winslow, schoolmaster.[13] Hunt, grandson of a glazier, drew up many wills between 1758 and 1790. They were shorter and less hypothetical than those drawn up by professional lawyers. The process involved emerges from a statement attached to the will of William Holland of Granborough.[14] This says that Hunt 'visited him two or three times in his last sickness', and on 14 May 1764:

'was sent for to the house of the said deceased … when [Holland] informed [him] that he had mind to settle his affairs. And thereupon [Hunt] did from the deceaseds own mouth and dictating take down the instructions hereunto annexed … and then read the said instructions over audibly and distinctly to the said deceased [who] did then declare his approbation thereof and then desired [Hunt] to make his will from the said instructions.'

Holland was buried on 18 May, so must have made his will on the day he died or the day before, apparently not having made one

---

[9] HALS, 165AW13.
[10] WMC 30 October 1752, see www.winslow-history.org.uk/winslow_court1752.shtm.
[11] Charity Commissioners' report, 1833; text at www.winslow-history.org.uk/winslow_school.shtm#rogers.
[12] *Northampton Mercury*, 27 February 1836.
[13] HALS, 220AW2.
[14] HALS, 202AW10.

before. Hunt lived in Horn Street, but there is no information about what sort of school he ran.

Another form of professional education was apprenticeship to a lawyer, for which records exist from 1710. Peter Goldsworth took an apprentice in 1711 and Nicholas Merwin took eight apprentices between 1716 and 1745, of whom one was from Winslow and two from Little Horwood.[15] Probably some boys from Winslow were apprenticed to lawyers elsewhere.

Several Winslow men (apart from the Lowndes family) went to university, usually leading to a career in the church, but they were very few in number due to the lack of gentry families:[16]

Thomas Stephens, son of Thomas of Winslow, matriculated at Pembroke College, Oxford, in 1637 aged 17 (though he had actually been baptised in 1623). He graduated BA in 1640 and possibly MA 1642–43. He also later received a Cambridge MA in 1664. Thomas his father, whose surname was usually written Stevens, was a yeoman of Shipton and died in 1641, leaving goods worth £116, making him one of the wealthiest people in Winslow.[17]

In 1651, when Thomas junior attended the manor court in person, he was styled gentleman and took over from his deceased mother the mortgage of 8 acres of land belonging to Peter Fige the younger.[18] He was recorded as the mortgagee of another 20 acres belonging to Fige in 1653 when he attended the manor court.[19] After that he disappears from Winslow records.[20]

Richard Purchase of Brasenose College, Oxford (MA 1698), is recorded as the son of Richard of Winslow; his father's occupation is unknown. He was baptised in 1673 and ordained as perpetual curate of North Marston in 1698. He died in 1742 aged

---

[15] TNA, Board of Stamps: Apprenticeship Books, Series IR 1.

[16] Information from *Alumni Oxonienses* and *Alumni Cantabrigienses*.

[17] HALS, 83AW12, A25/3501.

[18] WMC 22 Oct 1651, see www.winslow-history.org.uk/winslow_court1651.shtm. He is probably the Thomas Stevens who married Elizabeth Lea at Swanbourne in 1649.

[19] CBS, BAS 376/22/3.

[20] There were several other men with the same name, notably one in Granborough at the same time.

71 according to his memorial in North Marston church, and was succeeded by his nephew Purchase Denchfield (1715–74), who was also vicar of Little Horwood 1740–75.

Alexander Markham was baptised at Winslow in 1716, son of the lawyer John Markham. He attended Lincoln College, Oxford (MA 1739), and became vicar of East Claydon. He was buried at Winslow in 1767. His own son John went to Brasenose and Worcester Colleges.

John Rawbone (1743–1825) was the son of William and Sarah of 8–10 Horn Street. He was nephew of the John Rawbone who became first curate then vicar of Winslow in 1765, and cousin of a third John Rawbone, schoolmaster, of Aylesbury whose will was proved in 1808,[21] and of the Winslow schoolmaster Thomas Rawbone (1751–1836).[22] His father may have been master of the Rogers School but that is unsubstantiated. He matriculated in 1761 at Magdalen Hall, Oxford, was chaplain of Magdalen College 1769–1821, and became a Doctor of Divinity in 1804. He became vicar of Cheddar in Somerset, then of Buckland in Berkshire, where he died.

Medicine

William Stewart of Winslow, practitioner in physic, was licensed by the Bishop of London in 1663.[23] He had a letter stating that he had been in practice for about twelve years, and was seven years with William Reynolds at Great Shelford in Cambridgeshire. This was signed by the vicar, Samuel Dix, and many others. 'William Stenward', probably the same man, had a son baptised at Winslow in 1658.

Dr Thomas Croft: In the 1690s there are references to Dr Thomas Croft or Crofts, probably a relative of the vicar John Croft. He was paid £2 for 'for his paines & for physick' during the

---

[21] TNA, PROB 11/1476/62.

[22] Will of Reverend John Rawbone of Winslow quoted in the 1775 court book (the original has not been traced); it mentions his nephew Thomas son of Thomas; CBS, D82/1 p.204

[23] J Harvey Bloom and R Rutson James, *Medical Practitioners in the Diocese of London 1529–1725* (Cambridge, 1935), 70.

illness of Anthony Deely in 1691.[24] In 1693 his son John was apprenticed as an apothecary in London. He lived in a house which William Lowndes bought, and appears to have left Winslow soon after 1696, although Lowndes was still repairing 'Crofts house' in 1700.[25]

However the profession of medicine in Winslow during our period was largely the preserve of one family. In 1664 John Bletchley, apothecary, bought a property which appears to be 8 High Street. He had married Emma Low at Great Linford in 1657; she was a widow whose first husband came from the family which owned the manor of Clifton Reynes near Olney. John Bletchley died at Winslow in 1670 leaving goods worth £28.[26]

John and Emma Greene: Bletchley's widow Emma then married John Greene, described as a grocer in the administration of his stepson's goods in 1675,[27] but he had a licence to practise surgery in 1690 and Emma applied for a licence to practise midwifery.[28] The court roll calls him chirurgeon when he and Emma bought the Little Angel in the Market Square.[29] They also acquired another property in the High Street.[30] Their daughter, also Emma Greene, married Joseph Turner in Granborough in 1699.

Joseph and Emma Turner: Joseph was described as a chirurgeon and may already have worked for his father-in-law. In 1700 Emma's parents gave them the reversion of a messuage which they already occupied.[31] Later that year Joseph and Emma took over her parents' practice because her father John Greene had run away after fathering an illegitimate child.[32]

Joseph Turner became a regular juror at the manor court and often witnessed wills, many of which were made by people in

[24] HALS, A25/4408: accounts of Margaret Deely, 1693.

[25] Folger Shakespeare Library, W.a.146.

[26] HALS, A25/3825, 106AW27.

[27] HALS, 111AW30.

[28] HALS, ASA 7/37.

[29] WMC 2 May 1693, see www.winslow-history.org.uk/winslow_court1693.shtm.

[30] Probably at the 1697 or 1699 court for which records do not survive.

[31] WMC 16 April 1700, see www.winslow-history.org.uk/winslow_court1700.shtm.

[32] BQS, 18 July 1700.

their final illness. He and Emma had thirteen children. Two of their sons were apprenticed in London: Joseph as a vintner in 1718 and William as an apothecary in 1730.[33] Joseph benefited substantially under the will made in 1720 by John Markham, yeoman of Little Horwood (not the lawyer of the same name), who left him a large holding of land after his widow's death.[34]

Part of this inheritance, as well as the Little Angel messuage in the Market Square, was used in a marriage settlement recorded in 1725 at the manor court between John Turner, the son of Joseph and Emma, and Jane Bigg, whose contribution to the settlement was a half-share of The Bell.[35] In 1741 Joseph mortgaged to John Turner, presumably his son, a newly built house in the occupation of John or his assigns (now 1 Church Street). Joseph died in 1743, and Emma in 1754.

The Turner family: John Turner was Joseph and Emma's eldest child, born in 1700. He married Jane Bigg at Quainton in 1724. The house at 1 Church Street was probably built as their matrimonial home. She was the daughter and co-heiress of Benjamin Bigg, postmaster of Yardley Gobion and son of Stephen Bigg the Winslow postal entrepreneur. When she died in 1733, John retained a life interest in her share of The Bell, although they did not have any surviving children. He began to serve as a juror at the manor court in 1725.

John was first described as surgeon in his own right in 1730, when the lawyer Nicholas Merwin mortgaged some property to him for £100.[36] His eldest son by his second wife Catherine was baptised in 1735 and apprenticed to his father in 1753. In 1760 John Turner was one of the 'principal inhabitants' who subscribed to a notice that Winslow was free of smallpox.[37]

John seems to have been considerably more prosperous than his father Joseph, probably due to a combination of an advantageous first marriage (nothing is known about the

---

[33] www.winslow-history.org.uk/seventeenthc.shtm#apprenticeship.

[34] HALS, 160AW16.

[35] WMC 5 April 1725, see www.winslow-history.org.uk/winslow_court1725.shtm.

[36] WMC 23 Oct 1730, see www.winslow-history.org.uk/winslow_court1730.shtm.

[37] *Oxford Journal*, 16 Aug 1760.

background of his second wife) and greater professional rewards. In the 1740s the Verneys were impressed by a Dr Turland of Addington, but the surname Turland does not occur in the Addington parish registers, and the Verneys, who did not normally use local doctors for themselves, may simply have been confused about Turner.[38]

In John Turner's will, made in 1764 and proved in 1767,[39] he left to his son, the second John Turner, the house in which he lived and the house adjoining it which his son occupied, though his son was not to receive it until after the death of his mother, Catherine. His son's house is now 16 High Street, formerly the home of Nicholas Merwin the lawyer. According to Catherine's will the rooms included the 'best room' and 'best parlour', and the contents extended to two sea pictures and a silver coffee pot.

He also owned the Royal Oak (14 High Street), the property in the Market Square where his parents had lived, the Peacock alehouse in Great Trinity Lane, London, and land in Winslow and Little Horwood. These were to be sold for the benefit of his other four children: Thomas Harris Turner, a cabinet-maker in London; William Turner; Catherine the wife of William Parker, a brewer in London; and Mary Turner. Their mother Catherine made her will in 1773, after the death of their eldest son, the second John Turner,[40] who had worked with his father. His widow Elizabeth then went into partnership with John Tookey until their son Joseph Turner was old enough to carry on the practice, retiring in 1818.

The Turner family dominated the upper end of the medical market, at least until another doctor, Thomas Prentice, established himself in the 1760s. The two practices were united later in the century when Prentice's daughter married the Turners' partner John Tookey.

There were other medical practitioners, including Mary Gyles. wife of William Gyles II.[41] Joseph Dandridge described himself as

[38] *Verney Letters*, 2.185, 212.
[39] TNA, PROB 11/929/4.
[40] TNA, PROB 11/988/88.
[41] See the Gyles family on pages 84-94.

schoolmaster and surgeon at the Archdeacon's visitation in 1690 and barber-chirurgeon at the manor court of 1693, although he had previously been excise-man or gauger and referred to as gentleman, as well as writing wills.[42]

His son, another Joseph Dandridge, was apprenticed in London in 1679 at the age of eleven and became a merchant taylor in 1686. He was a silk pattern designer and drawer in Moorfields. He described himself as freeman of the City of London and merchant taylor when he made his will in 1737.[43] His claim to fame was as an entomologist; he is 'the great forgotten figure of English entomology' according to one writer. He was a founder of the Society of Aurelians (butterfly collectors), and drew insects and collected drawings.[44] He bought up land in Winslow and Shipton in 1692, and retained his connections with Winslow at least until the death of his uncle William Elliott in 1710, under whose will he inherited another 40 acres of land, after which he rapidly sold all his property in Winslow to William Lowndes.

Apart from the doctors, there was usually an apothecary selling medicines, starting with Emma Greene's previous husband John Bletchley. His business was probably taken over by Charles Harris, who died in 1676.[45] His inventory records 'elecutuarys, conserves, species, syrups' and other stock worth £16. His debts came to more than his assets and were mostly to local people, but he owed £5 to 'a drugster of London'.

The third in this short-lived sequence is James West, who died in 1687 with a shop whose unitemised contents were valued at £45.[46] Another apothecary, Thomas Kenwrick, married a Winslow woman in 1691 but moved to Leighton Buzzard and then London.[47] The will of John Roberson, made in 1702, refers to 'the

[42] www.winslow-history.org.uk/winslow_families-dandridge.shtm.
[43] TNA, PROB 11/752/81 (proved 1747).
[44] Ray Desmond, *Dictionary of British and Irish Botanists and Horticulturists* (London: Natural History Museum, 1994), 192; D E Allen, 'Joseph Dandridge and the first Aurelian Society', *Entomologist's Record* 78 (1966), 89–94.
[45] HALS, 112AW28.
[46] HALS, A25/4293.
[47] www.winslow-history.org.uk/winslow_will_kenwrick1701.shtm.

shop now in the occupation of Mr Foard apothecary',[48] and Mr Ford was still in business in 1707 when he was paid 2s for 'physick' for Philip Bailey.[49]

The Hobbs family: Bailey's widow also had to pay 5s 2d to 'Mr Hobbs for physick', and this is the first evidence for the Hobbs family, who established themselves as Winslow's apothecaries in the eighteenth century. In 1706 Matthew Hobbs acquired part of what is now 17 Market Square, and that was the Hobbs family's shop for the rest of the period.[50] His son William Hobbs continued the business but later lived at 5 Horn Street. He married Anne Glenister, from an established Winslow family, but their children, including a son Matthew who was also an apothecary, predeceased them. William prospered enough to call himself a gentleman when he made his will, proved in 1771, and he had acquired a substantial amount of property.[51] He left to his servant Sarah Batterson 'all my drugs, bottles, gallipots, weights, scales, nests of drawers, counters, shelves and all and every other the goods wares and merchandizes which shall be in or about my apothecary's shop', and she was probably running the business by that time as William was in his seventies when he died.

Lawyers

The rise of professional lawyers in Winslow was assisted by the work which came to them from the Lowndes and Verney families. William Lowndes II was his own lawyer for many purposes but needed a local man at times, and as we have seen his son Robert was gradually overwhelmed by a series of legal problems. The Verneys made little use of Winslow for most purposes but were glad of the legal services of 'old Merwin'.

Nicholas Merwin (1668–1751) was deputy steward of the manor under William Lowndes, and held the manor courts from 1697. He later became steward, and this was the first time a local lawyer had held the office. He was replaced in the 1720s by John

---

[48] HALS, 140AW138.
[49] HALS, A25/4588.
[50] WMC 21 June 1706, see www.winslow-history.org.uk/winslow_court1706.shtm.
[51] TNA, PROB 11/964/109.

Markham, who was appointed by Robert Lowndes. In the 1740s the stewardship passed to the Duncombe family, who did not live in Winslow but were descendants of Robert Lowndes' half-sister Elizabeth.

Nicholas Merwin came from Iver in south Buckinghamshire where his father appears to have kept a baker's shop, although he called himself a yeoman.[52] Merwin arrived in Winslow around 1690, but was sometimes referred to as being of Thavie's Inn, one of the Inns of the Chancery Court in London.

Merwin became involved in a legal dispute in 1692 following the death of the linen draper Thomas Bishop whose will he had drawn up.[53] He said he was aged 24 and had known Bishop for a year before his death. He married Bishop's widow Elizabeth[54] on the day after she got probate of her husband's will. She died in 1738, and no doubt contributed to Merwin's prosperity.

He worked for the Verneys from at least 1702. In 1710, Lord Fermanagh told his son: 'Merwin's studdy broak open at Winsloe, and he robb'd of between 60 and 80 pounds'.[55] Merwin witnessed Robert Lowndes' marriage settlement in 1703 (see his signature in *Figure 11*). He was also steward of the manor of Whaddon.

Merwin's unmarried sister Hannah invested in property in Winslow, and his nephew Henry Langley was briefly a lawyer in Winslow, presumably working with him, and married Jane Gyles.[56] Merwin branched out into amateur farming, and in the 1720s became embroiled in a dispute with James Edmunds, vicar of Winslow and rector of Newton Longville, over tithes and the parsonage house there, which Merwin had acquired when a previous rector fled to Antigua to escape his debts.[57]

---

[52] TNA, E112/620/87: dispute between Nicholas Merwin the father and Francis Price, 1694.
[53] TNA, E112/619/54; E134/4WandM/Mich41.
[54] She was born Elizabeth Seaton – see the Seaton family on pages 206–218.
[55] *Verney Letters*, 1.118, 286.
[56] www.winslow-history.org.uk/winslow_will_merwin1725.shtml. See also the Gyles family on pages 84–94.
[57] TNA, C11/1205/11, summarised at www.winslow-history.org.uk/winslow_will_merwin1751.shtml.

Merwin's remarkable longevity created problems, although he still got some business from the Verneys in the 1740s.[58] John Millward, Claydon steward, wrote to Lord Fermanagh in 1740:[59]

> 'Old Nick Merwin is married and they say two biters are bit. The old man is got allmost superannuated and has but little business and has got low. This wife has some money as will help a little; he is very hard of hearing, tho' he stood very tight to our cause, which was one of his best performances.'

His second wife Susanna must have been much younger, as she outlived him by 24 years. His death was reported in the national press:[60]

> 'A few days since died, greatly advanced in years, of the gout in his stomach, at his house in Winslow in Buckinghamshire, Nicholas Merwin Esq., formerly one of the Commissioners of Bankrupts, Associate upon the Norfolk Circuit, and in Commission of the Peace.'

His will mentions property in Great Horwood, Wingrave and Houghton Regis as well as Winslow, so he had probably invested the profits of his business wisely when it was doing well.

John Markham (1683–1746) started attending manor courts and witnessing wills in Winslow in 1701, initially alongside Merwin, to whom he was probably apprenticed. They do not appear to have been in partnership later. He became William Lowndes' agent in Winslow at the end of Lowndes' life,[61] and lawyer and steward for Robert Lowndes. He also acted for Joseph Lowndes, one of William's younger sons, who had property at Barton Hartshorn.[62] Markham's will mentions property at St Albans[63] and his son Alexander studied at Oxford.

A younger son, Robert Markham, born in 1722, was apparently less satisfactory. His father left him an annuity of £60, a lump sum

[58] *Verney Letters*, 2.202, 205.
[59] *Verney Letters*, 2.207, 26 Aug 1740.
[60] *General Advertiser*, 20 Aug 1751.
[61] CBS, D/LO/6/9/1: accounts 1722–23.
[62] CBS, D/LO/6/2/4/27-42.
[63] TNA, PROB 11/747/420.

of £50 and £450 to be paid to him when he was 30, but he would lose all this except the £50 'in case my said son Robert shall marry Hannah Hazard daughter of Hannah Hazard of Winslowe aforesaid alehousekeeper or any other daughter of the said Hannah Hazard the elder'. The Markhams appear to have lived next door to the Hazards, who kept the Royal Oak (then at 14 High Street). Robert was also to receive his father's law books 'in case he will apply himself to any branch of my business', but it seems that he did not, or at least there is no further trace of him in Winslow.

Peter Goldsworth (1672?–1748) was another Winslow attorney active at the same time. He came from a family of lawyers in Aylesbury, first took part in the manor court in 1696, and married a Winslow woman around 1700 (her father was a glazier). He and Merwin both witnessed a will in 1701 but do not appear to have worked together after that, and Goldsworth took an apprentice of his own in 1711. He sometimes acted as deputy steward of the manor.

He was closely involved with the affairs of Benjamin Dudley, a draper who died in 1742: his daughter Rebecca married Benjamin's son William at Gayhurst in 1730 (one of their children was named Goldsworth Dudley), and his son married Benjamin's granddaughter.

Goldsworth died in 1748. One son who would have continued the family business died before him, and another is not mentioned after 1752. Goldsworth appears to have been a man of rather lower social status than Merwin and Markham, but his will suggests an estate of at least £1,500.[64] He left annuities to his horsekeeper and his barber.

Winslow was well served by these three lawyers until the 1740s, when Markham and Goldsworth died and Merwin was struggling.

Ferdinando Southam attempted to fill the gap. He came from Croughton, on the border of Northamptonshire with Buckinghamshire, and inherited property in that area from his

---

[64] TNA, PROB 11/764/236.

great-uncle Ferdinando Gough in 1727.[65] He was in Winslow by 1741 when he drew up Grace Aldridge's will. Between 1757 and 1760 he was the only person in Winslow apart from Richard Lowndes to pay tax on silver plate, and he also kept a chaise.[66] He was deputy steward of the manor in 1759–60.

However he overreached himself and in 1761 he was described as 'Ferdinando Southam of Winslow scrivener and chapman a bankrupt' rather than 'gentleman' as previously.[67] His debts included £102 to a man from Swanbourne, and his Winslow property was sold on behalf of his creditors. He seems to have been relatively unscathed, as he was able to remain in his house and still drew up a will in 1764. He died in 1768, after which his 'neat well built messuage with balcony in front pleasantly situated in the Market Place' (now 21–23 Market Square) was put up for sale again.[68]

James Burnham (1733–1803), who came from another family of attorneys in Aylesbury, was Southam's clerk.[69] He styled himself gentleman by 1758 while still working with Southam,[70] and in 1761 he and his father were agents in the sale of Southam's property.[71] He stayed in Winslow after his employer's bankruptcy, but did not become a prominent figure until the 1770s, eventually holding the posts of clerk to the Turnpike Trust and coroner for Buckinghamshire.

Samuel Yeates (1723–77) was another new arrival who came to the attention of the Verneys as a possible attorney to do business for them in 1746: 'young Yates who is come to Winslow'.[72] Yeates probably originated from Padbury, which is where he was buried. He drew up the will of John Cox in 1749 but

---

[65] Bartons' History Group, http://documents.bartonshistorygroup.org.uk/Wills/Gough.pdf [accessed 16 Dec 2018].
[66] TNA, T47/3–5.
[67] Indenture recited at WMC 15 February 1762, see www.winslow-history.org.uk/winslow_court1762.shtm.
[68] *Northampton Mercury*, 11 September 1769.
[69] He witnessed John Gibbs' will as Southam's clerk in 1752: HALS, 191AW8.
[70] HALS, ASA 27/1/116.
[71] *Oxford Journal*, 14 November 1761.
[72] *Verney Letters*, 2.211.

appears to have left most of the will-writing business in Winslow to the schoolmaster Joseph Hunt from about 1760.[73] By 1762 he had replaced Southam as the only owner of a private chaise in Winslow, and he acquired at least some of the Lowndes family business as he witnessed Richard Lowndes' will and did work for his son William in relation to Whaddon Chase in 1775.[74] He also acted for the turnpike trustees when they applied for an amendment to their Act of Parliament in 1766.

Yeates made his own will in 1777 shortly before he died, leaving an annuity of £10 'unto my wicked son Thomas Yeates' to begin when Thomas was 25, and £20 'unto my faithful maid servant Elizabeth Eden'.[75] The wicked son and the faithful servant married each other the following year.

Clergy

During the period 1640–1770, every vicar of Winslow died in office, a rare achievement in a period of so much religious controversy. The advowson was retained by the Crown, and the living was normally presented to Oxford graduates with no previous local connections. The dates in the list below are when they held office.[76]

Robert Mainwaring (1597–1648) was Winslow's longest-serving vicar. He came from Shropshire, and was about 27 when he arrived in Winslow. He married into the Edmunds family and his first wife and Peter Fige's wife were sisters.[77] He kept close control of his flock at least to the extent of making nearly all their wills. His inventory shows that he farmed the glebe land himself.[78] His goods were valued at £131 at his death, a modest sum after so long in office, but he had probably already set his son Robert up as a farmer in Granborough, where his descendants remained for several generations. The books in his study were valued at £20.

---

[73] HALS, 186AW5.

[74] TNA C 101/558: William Lowndes' accounts for the Selby estate.

[75] TNA, PROB 11/1039/199.

[76] Some of the information below is from *Alumni Oxonienses*.

[77] For the Fige family see pages 26-30.

[78] HALS, A25/3573.

John Bishop (1648–52): There is some doubt about his first name because a note in the parish register concerning his marriage at Steeple Claydon in 1649 calls him Thomas, and that is also the name given in the record of his institution as vicar on 14 April 1648.[79] According to Clear: 'In 1650 he was returned to be a constant preacher, and the vicarage worth thirty pounds per annum'.[80] He may have been connected with the wealthy draper Matthew Bishop who arrived around the same time.[81] He must have been a Parliamentarian because in 1652 there was an order to pay his widow £25 from the Committee of Plundered Ministers.

John Pownall (1652–63) survived the Great Ejection of 1662 when clergy of doubtful loyalty to the new Anglican regime were purged, so he either conformed to the Book of Common Prayer or took advantage of Winslow's peripheral position in terms of ecclesiastical authority. He took down the nuncupative will[82] of Richard Dingley in 1658, so must have been in attendance at one parishioner's deathbed at least.[83] He did not draw up wills otherwise but regularly granted probate on behalf of the Archdeacon.

Rebecca Gerard, daughter of Peter Fige the elder, left him 40s in her will of 1662.[84] He had a number of children baptised at Winslow between 1652 and 1661, and was presumably the grandfather of Pownall Short, who was active in the early eighteenth century. He appears to have been an MA. He was buried on 7 September 1663.

Samuel Dix (1663–81) was appointed in December 1663. He was previously rector of Horsenden, where he had replaced an ejected minister in 1650. He was also vicar of West Wycombe 1658–67 and curate of Hillesden 1666–70. He was a BA of Lincoln College, Oxford, in 1648, MA in 1650, and fellow of

---

[79] Clergy of the Church of England Database, Record ID: 73860 [accessed 27 January 2020].

[80] Clear, *King's Village*, 54.

[81] Matthew Bishop had a brother called John but there is no reference to his being a clergyman (TNA, E112/619/54).

[82] A will that is given orally.

[83] HALS, 9AR29.

[84] TNA, PROB 11/312/30.

Oriel College until 1657. He made grants of probate like his predecessor, and sometimes acted as appraiser for inventories. He was apparently on good terms with the Gyles family of Baptists, according to evidence given in 1677 when Mary Gyles sent for a witness to come to Dix's house. His inventory, taken in January 1682, came to only £49, which included pigs, bees and harvested crops but less than £3 worth of books.[85]

John Jones (1682–84) was appointed in March 1682, and died in October 1684. He was an MA but there are several Oxford graduates with the same name from the right period. There is no other information about his brief time in office.

John Croft (1684–1716) was appointed in November 1684, and was also vicar of Granborough from 1693. He is probably the John Croft, son of Edward of Tredington in Warwickshire, who matriculated at St Mary Hall, Oxford, in 1668 at the age of sixteen, and graduated MA from New College in 1675. According to a letter he wrote to Browne Willis, he then went on a tour which took him as far as Cyprus.[86] He had children baptised at Winslow between 1685 and 1696, one of whom married a tallow-chandler and another was apprenticed as an ironmonger.

Croft was vicar when the Winslow Baptists went from being a persecuted sect to a significant force, and he clearly resented this. His letter to Browne Willis suggests equal hostility to Catholics, and he claimed to believe that the population of Granborough was descended from the bastards of monks at Biggin.

He was also vicar during William Lowndes' takeover of Winslow. There is no evidence of what relationship the two men had, if any, except that in 1703 he had to witness the Baptist William Gyles III's sealing of Robert Lowndes' marriage settlement (his signature is in *Figure 11*). During his term of office, he regularly granted probate and took oaths of administration. He took Stephen Bigg to the manor court for encroaching on the south-east corner of the churchyard.[87]

---

[85] HALS, A25/4104.
[86] BL, Add.Ms. 5840 f.199v: letter copied by Reverend William Cole.
[87] WMC 25 April 1698, see www.winslow-history.org.uk/winslow_court1698.shtm.

Egerton Cutler (1716–20) is described in the nineteenth-century lists of vicars as 'formerly a sea chaplain'. He was born in 1678, son of Sir Thomas Cutler of Lechlade in Gloucestershire, and attended Queen's College, Oxford. He was chaplain to the Duke of Marlborough in Flanders, and became vicar of Elmsted, Kent, in 1708, leaving there to come to Winslow. He was married twice,[88] and had a son baptised at Winslow in 1719. He died intestate in 1720 and his wife renounced administration of his estate.[89] Administration was instead granted to his creditors, led by Winslow bricklayer Joseph Bigg. He was not buried in Winslow.

James Edmunds (1720–65) was one of Winslow's longest-serving vicars, but a litigious one. He came from a gentry family in Salisbury, and went to Oxford. He was aged 24 when he came to Winslow.[90] At the 1725 manor court it was found that his summer-house was partly built on land belonging to Robert Lowndes.[91] He also became rector of Newton Longville in 1727, and appears to have gone to live there in the 1730s, when the practice of granting probate at Winslow stopped and everyone had to travel to St Albans again. He tried to extend the payment of tithe milk to Shipton in 1730,[92] and brought a case against the lawyer Nicholas Merwin about the parsonage house in Newton Longville and payment of tithe milk in Winslow.[93]

In 1737 he tried (for unknown reasons) to prove that Winslow belonged to the diocese of Lincoln, not London. Richard Lowndes wrote to Browne Willis of Whaddon Hall about it, and Willis replied that it was 'never till now disputed by a person in many more instances out of his senses; & now contended for nothing but litigiousness sake.'[94] He added: 'if a stop is not put & remedy had

---

[88] *Burke's Genealogical and Heraldic History of the Commoners of Great Britain* (1838), 4.689.

[89] HALS, 157AW28.

[90] He signed the parish register of burials on 4 April 1720, although his installation has been recorded as taking place in 1726.

[91] WMC 5 April 1725, see www.winslow-history.org.uk/winslow_court1725.shtm.

[92] Clear, *King's Village*, 52–53. The dispute became irrelevant after tithes in Shipton were eliminated by enclosure.

[93] TNA, C11/1205/11 (1727). The tithe milk issue went back to 1723.

[94] BL, Add.Ms. 37069 f.219.

bad will it be for all lovers of our church in your most neglected parish under such a pastor'.

In 1722 Edmunds voted in the Buckinghamshire election along with the Baptists for an independent Whig candidate rather than those endorsed by Robert Lowndes, which no doubt contributed to his unpopularity with the local gentry, but in the 1734 election he plumped for Richard Lowndes.[95]

John Rawbone (1765–75) was already curate of Winslow by 1751 when he signed an inventory and he became vicar of Granborough in 1756.[96] He was born at Drayton in Oxfordshire, and was MA of Magdalen Hall, Oxford, and chaplain to the Earl of Shaftesbury.[97] He reinstated the practice of granting probate locally in the 1750s. He was vicar at the time of the enclosure of Winslow but there is no evidence for his role in the process. His nephew Thomas Rawbone was appointed master of the Rogers School on John's death in 1775, which suggests that John had been acting as schoolmaster himself until then.[98]

Postmasters and blacksmiths

Stephen Bigg (1647–1704) came from a family of blacksmiths, a trade which had been carried on without much profit by his father Christopher, who died in 1664, and older brother Nicholas, who died in 1683. Christopher's goods were valued at £39 and Nicholas' goods were valued at £38,[99] and Nicholas' estate was taken over by his London creditors.

Stephen was evidently a man of a different calibre, and came to the attention of the Duke of Buckingham, for whom he produced ironwork at Cliveden in 1677–78.[100] He was among the Duke's creditors who were still trying to get paid in 1695,[101] so this was

---

[95] www.winslow-history.org.uk/seventeenthc-poll-books.shtm.
[96] He witnessed the will of Peter Goldsworth in 1748 so was probably curate by then (TNA, PROB 11/764/236).
[97] *Westminster Journal*, 25 May 1765.
[98] www.winslow-history.org.uk/winslow_school.shtm.
[99] HALS, A25/3694, A25/4117.
[100] TNA, C7/240/94.
[101] TNA, C 6/418/50.

probably not very remunerative but it may have got him other aristocratic commissions. A recent dictionary of wrought iron smiths treats him as the same Stephen Bigg who made a wrought iron screen and gates for the Earl of Kent at Wrest Park in Bedfordshire between 1694 and 1702, for which he was paid £545 in all.[102] He did extensive work at Winslow Hall in 1700–03.[103]

In the 1690s, Stephen and his son Richard (circa 1669–1740) embarked on a new business venture as postmasters. The source of the capital they must have needed for this is unknown. William Lowndes is a possibility, but there is no evidence. The Duke of Buckingham had not been in a position to provide it, but his trustee John Wildman was governor of the Post Office in 1689–91 and must have known Bigg from Cliveden. The Post Office was closely controlled by the Treasury and information about the Biggs' activities comes mainly from Treasury records in which William Lowndes features prominently.[104]

From 1693 the Biggs were 'farmers' of part of the London to Holyhead post route from Edgware via Banbury and Warwick to Chester – in other words private contractors who ran the service for a fixed payment and kept any profit. They initially paid £300 for this contract, rising to £900 in 1694.[105] By 1700 their franchise also extended to Norwich.

Granting large concessions to farmers was a new development at this time, and the Biggs had one of the largest. Winslow was a post town in 1702,[106] presumably because of the Biggs' activities, even though it was not on a main road at the time.

---

[102] Edward Saunders, 'Biographical dictionary of English wrought iron smiths of the seventeenth and eighteenth centuries', *Walpole Society* 67 (2005), 237–384, 266. Saunders assumed that he was a Londoner because the Earl's agent was paid 'for going to London to bargain with the smith about the great gates'.

[103] Wren Society, *Seventeenth Volume*, 72. Another Stephen Bigg was active as a bricklayer.

[104] Duncan Campbell-Smith, *Masters of the Post: The Authorized History of the Royal Mail* (London: Penguin, 2011), 61–65. Campbell-Smith thought the Biggs were brothers.

[105] Michael Brooks, 'Postal services in Amersham', https://amershammuseum.org/history/research/trades-industries/postal-services-in-amersham/ [accessed 20 January 2020].

[106] CBS, D192/25/32: where there is an anonymous description of Winslow.

The 'farming' system encouraged the contractors to overbid. The Biggs had another three-year contract from 1697 at £950 for the first year and £1,000 for each of the other two years, being:

'obliged by their contract to accompt to the General Post Office for the port of all letters coming from beyond sea or from Scotland to London for towns within their farm and they have represented that they did not apprehend the consequence of this when they took the farm and if obliged thereto shall be unavoidably ruined.'[107]

It was decided to exonerate them from this additional expense because:

'the King receives more from the farm than was ever made of said branch and farther that the said farmers have been careful and industrious in the management thereof to the great satisfaction of the country.'

Nevertheless they were making enough profit to expand their activities to Lancashire: in 1700 Stephen Bigg was given a contract for Liverpool, Preston, Lancaster and Manchester.[108] The rent was to be £2,526 a year for three years, plus a third of the profits after the first year. Stephen was said to have 'behaved himself with great diligence, satisfaction to the people and encouragement to the revenue'.[109] This new venture, in which Stephen was associated with another of his sons, Benjamin (1673–1707), does not seem to have paid either, and it was cancelled in 1701, perhaps because of competition to Chester from the 'cross-post', routes between provincial towns .[110]

Stephen described himself as postmaster when he made his will in 1703.[111] He does not seem to have been made wealthy by his business activities: he left his wife £50 and an annuity of £11, while Richard received £20 and £200 was to be divided between his grandchildren, with the residue to Benjamin. He had, however,

---

[107] *Calendar of Treasury Books, vol.14, 1698–1699*, 241–42 (16 January 1699).

[108] *Calendar of Treasury Books, vol.15, 1699–1700*, 371 (7 June 1700).

[109] *Calendar of Treasury Books, vol.15*, 396 (1 July 1700).

[110] Herbert Joyce, *The History of the Post Office* (London: Bentley, 1893), 61; *Calendar of Treasury Books, voume 16, 1700–1701*, 279 (4 June 1701).

[111] TNA, PROB 11/476/425.

invested in property in Winslow which had already been settled on Richard, Benjamin and their sister Jane when they got married.[112]

As well as his other activities, Stephen was involved in agricultural farming. He paid William Lowndes £22 rent for land in 1702, and £17 for 'the price of the malting, gatehouse and the stable with little houses adjoyning at Holloways Farm', which suggests that he demolished these buildings which were now redundant.[113] Benjamin was living at Winslow at the time of his father's will but was postmaster at Yardley Gobion when he made his own will in 1707.[114] He was still farming 'by-letters in Chester Road' then at £160 a year.[115] 'By-letters' were those delivered to places not on a main postal route.

In 1705 Richard, in partnership with Richard Dixon of Bourne in Lincolnshire, was awarded a contract to run the postal service in Lincolnshire. He retained his father's contract for the service from London to Edgware, Watford, Hemel Hempstead, Berkhamsted, Marlow, Chesham, Amersham, Wendover, Buckingham, Banbury and Warwick.[116] He paid the Post Office £1,100 a year until 1708, then £1,180. The contract ended in 1712 due to reorganisation of the system under the Post Office Act of 1711, and he was then employed directly by the Post Office instead.[117] In 1712–13 he received a salary of £821 along with 10 per cent of the revenue. By 1715 he was described as 'clerk of the road' on a salary only. He then became 'riding surveyor', one of the senior inspectors of postmasters.[118]

By then Richard Bigg was one of the biggest landowners in Winslow, with a messuage and 80 acres, which he mortgaged

---

[112] WMC 2 August 1697, see www.winslow-history.org.uk/winslow_court1697.shtm (Richard); 26 October 1696, www.winslow-history.org.uk/winslow_court1696.shtm (Benjamin); 1 October 1703, www.winslow-history.org.uk/winslow_court1703.shtm (Jane).

[113] Folger Shakespeare Library, W.a.147 f.67. The holding must have been substantial, as Simon Hogson was paying £24 a year for 60 acres at the same time.

[114] TNA, PROB 11/506/243.

[115] *Calendar of Treasury Books, Volume 22, 1708*, cccxcvi.

[116] *Calendar of Treasury Books, Volume 21, 1706–1707*, cccx.

[117] Campbell-Smith, *Masters of the Post*, 66.

[118] *Historical Register*, 8 June 1721.

between 1729 and 1732 and then used as security in 1736 for his postal activities.[119] He also had property at Weston Turville through his marriage. He was referred to as 'late manager of the Hungerford Branch of the Post Office', which covered an area that included Berkshire, Oxfordshire and part of Buckinghamshire, and as 'greatly indebted to the Crown' when he died. His son had to redeem the land in Winslow in order to sell it. Richard called himself gentleman in his will of 1739.[120] According to the will of his daughter Susanna (1701–84), the last of the Biggs in Winslow, his grandson Robert Bigg also worked for the Post Office.[121]

After the Biggs left Winslow there is little evidence for how the postal service worked, but by 1743 sub-contracting was being used for local deliveries. Lord Fermanagh wrote from Claydon House:[122]

'The Post [meaning the postman] is grown very insolent and takes it into his head not to call here but when he pleases; and on Thursday last our letters did not go. He said it was out of his way to call from Bicester to Winslow and he coud not. T'woud be proper for to write to the Post Master General with complaints of the Winslow Post, either to remove him, or at least threaten him if he does it any more, unless you thought it better to call at the Post Office and speak about it, for unless some case is taken we shall loose the benefit of the post … Morris is the postmaster's name at Winslow but he letts the post to Windmill who behaves so ill.'

By 1756, Winslow, now on the turnpike, was a post town on the route from London through Berkhamsted and Banbury to Shrewsbury and Chester, within a greatly expanded Post Office network.[123]

---

[119] Reported at the manor courts in October 1742 and June 1749, see www.winslow-history.org.uk/winslow_court1742.shtm and www.winslow-history.org.uk/winslow_court1749.shtm.
[120] TNA, PROB 11/703/442.
[121] HALS, 220AW2.
[122] *Verney Letters*, 2.209, Lord Fermanagh to Earl Verney, Claydon, 25 September 1743. Windmill could be William Winman or Windmill who kept The Swan at Winslow 1753–65.
[123] Campbell-Smith, *Masters of the Post*, Map E.

The Seaton family tree

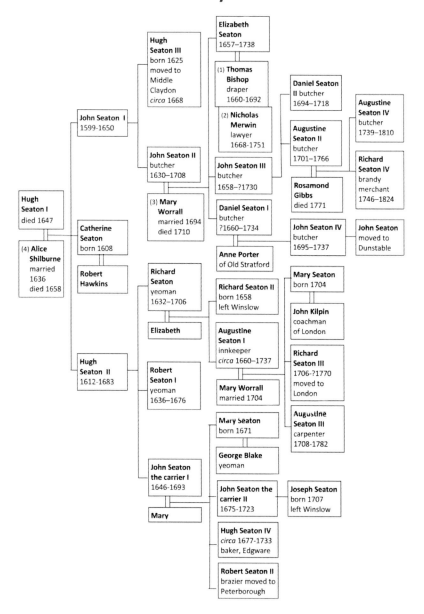

Hugh Seaton I died 1647

(4) Alice Shilburne married 1636 died 1658

Catherine Seaton born 1608

Robert Hawkins

Hugh Seaton II 1612-1683

John Seaton I 1599-1650

Hugh Seaton III born 1625 moved to Middle Claydon *circa* 1668

John Seaton II butcher 1630–1708

(3) Mary Worrall married 1694 died 1710

Richard Seaton yeoman 1632–1706

Elizabeth

Robert Seaton I yeoman 1636–1676

John Seaton the carrier I 1646-1693

Mary

Elizabeth Seaton 1657–1738

(1) Thomas Bishop draper 1660-1692

(2) Nicholas Merwin lawyer 1668-1751

John Seaton III butcher 1658–?1730

Daniel Seaton I butcher ?1660–1734

Anne Porter of Old Stratford

Richard Seaton II born 1658 left Winslow

Augustine Seaton I innkeeper *circa* 1660–1737

Mary Worrall married 1704

Mary Seaton born 1671

George Blake yeoman

John Seaton the carrier II 1675-1723

Hugh Seaton IV *circa* 1677-1733 baker, Edgware

Robert Seaton II brazier moved to Peterborough

Daniel Seaton II butcher 1694–1718

Augustine Seaton II butcher 1701–1766

Rosamond Gibbs died 1771

John Seaton IV butcher 1695–1737

Mary Seaton born 1704

John Kilpin coachman of London

Richard Seaton III 1706-?1770 moved to London

Augustine Seaton III carpenter 1708-1782

Joseph Seaton born 1707 left Winslow

Augustine Seaton IV butcher 1739–1810

Richard Seaton IV brandy merchant 1746–1824

John Seaton moved to Dunstable

Winslow families
7: **The Seaton Family**

The Seatons provide a case study of the variety of strategies used by a family to preserve property, and ultimately a study in downward social mobility. Few members of the family made wills, so most of the information derives from the court rolls and is therefore incomplete.[1]

The Seatons of Winslow were numerous in the seventeenth and eighteenth centuries, but the 1798 Posse Comitatus lists only four male Seatons: a victualler, a butcher and two labourers. Two families totalling twelve individuals were among the recipients of free food and drink at Queen Victoria's coronation, and there were sixteen Seatons in the 1851 Census. But by 1911 there were none. The surname did not die out until the late nineteenth century but its social status changed considerably. In the rest of this complicated section the family members have been given numbers to help link them to the family tree.

The story of the family begins with the patriarchal figure of **Hugh Seaton I** who died in 1647. He seems to have been married four times and had at least ten children. He appears in Winslow records (the parish registers) in 1590 at the time of his first marriage. Apart from farming activities, he kept an inn, probably The Bell. He gave away or entailed all his property before his death so there is no statement of his full holding. In 1647 he gave 7½ acres to his son Hugh II and a shop to his grandson Hugh III.[2] This was probably a near-deathbed surrender as he also paid heriot and was buried three weeks after the date of the manor court.

---

[1] For details, see www.winslow-history.org.uk/winslow_families.shtm. The prevalence of the Seaton surname, with a limited number of first names, means that some misidentifications are possible, particularly among the Johns.

[2] WMC 19 October 1647, see www.winslow-history.org.uk/winslow_court1647.shtm.

John Seaton I (1599–1650), elder surviving son of Hugh I, is recorded in 1638 as being the occupier of 50 acres belonging to the Fige family.[3] He had at least six children but most died young. His elder surviving son **Hugh Seaton III**, born in 1625, inherited a shop from his grandfather but seems to have disposed of his property in Winslow and gone to live at Middle Claydon.[4] This branch of the family was therefore continued in Winslow by the younger son John II.

Hugh Seaton II (1612–1683) acquired a house and 24 acres in his father's occupation from Peter Jackson in 1638, and then gave half the house and some of the land to his stepmother Alice for her life.[5] Hugh II was the younger surviving son, and presumably this arrangement was financed by his father. It is likely that his elder brother John I received a similar settlement in a year for which the court rolls do not survive.

One of Hugh I's daughters, Catherine, who was born in 1608, was married at Winslow to Robert Hawkins, probably of Little Horwood, in 1633. Hawkins received 8 acres from his brother-in-law Hugh II in 1647, which must also have been part of a marriage settlement.

Hugh II sold 4 acres in 1649, then regularly appears in the court rolls mortgaging parts of his remaining holding.[6] This does not necessarily mean financial difficulties, as the money may have been required for investment rather than expenditure, and in fact the size of Hugh's holding increased to at least 36 acres. He also leased a malt-mill, and rented a close of pasture at Middle Claydon.[7] He divided his property between his sons before his death: he gave a messuage and 20 acres to Richard his eldest son (Richard Seaton I), a messuage and 9 acres to Robert his second son (Robert Seaton I), who was already living in the messuage, and 6 acres to his third son John (John Seaton the Carrier I).[8]

[3] WMC 12 September 1638, see www.winslow-history.org.uk/winslow_court1638.shtm.
[4] WMC 16 March 1668, see www.winslow-history.org.uk/winslow_court1668.shtm.
[5] WMC 12 September 1638, see www.winslow-history.org.uk/winslow_court1638.shtm.
[6] WMC 24 October 1649, see www.winslow-history.org.uk/winslow_court1648.shtm.
[7] TNA, E134/1653-54/Hil1: dispute over tithes at Middle Claydon, 1654.
[8] WMC 19 May 1671, see www.winslow-history.org.uk/winslow_court1671.shtm.

All the sons were married, and the settlement was probably motivated by John's marriage as his father granted a new house for him, giving him 'the western end of a barn', other outbuildings and part of the yard 'extending from the principal post of the barn by the bank to the window of the mill-house'. The property given to Robert and John had already been mortgaged. In the 1662/3 Hearth Tax return Hugh had one hearth and Richard had three, suggesting that a larger house had already been divided up.

John Seaton II (1630–1708), son of John I, was a prominent figure in Winslow, serving as constable and churchwarden. He is referred to as a butcher from 1698, partly to differentiate him from other John Seatons. His descendants continued as butchers, but he also owned considerable property, at least 34 acres and three messuages. He was involved in the property market with small-scale sales and purchases, and probably had a substantial inheritance from his father. He also rented land in Addington: at least 42 acres on which he fattened cows and sheep.[9]

He made a will, but in fact had already distributed most of his property among his children, so its purpose was to leave small legacies to his daughters and grandchildren.[10] He had been married three times, and his third marriage, to Mary Worrall in 1694, had involved an agreement giving her an annuity of £7 instead of dower. In 1687 he gave two messuages, neither in his own occupation, to his eldest son John III, and 20 acres to John III and his wife Rebecca, evidently on the occasion of their marriage.[11] In 1692 he gave 11 acres to his second son Daniel (Daniel Seaton I) and his wife Anne, who were married at Wolverton around the same time.[12]

He made a final settlement on 27 April 1708, made his will on 19 July and was buried on 8 August.[13] The arrangement in April concerned the messuage in which he lived, a piece of meadow of 2½ acres, and unspecified other lands. The property all went to

---

[9] TNA, E112/364/79: dispute over tithes at Addington, 1669.

[10] TNA, PROB 11/506/307.

[11] WMC 1 May 1687, see www.winslow-history.org.uk/winslow_court1687.shtm.

[12] WMC 20 April 1692, see www.winslow-history.org.uk/winslow_court1692.shtm.

[13] www.winslow-history.org.uk/winslow_court1708.shtm.

Daniel for his life with an entail to his son John (John Seaton IV), and Daniel's other children were to receive £5 each when Daniel died. This might suggest that John II did not have much confidence in Daniel, but he made him sole executor of his will. John was able to sign his own name, like his cousin John the Carrier I but unlike his other cousins Richard I and Robert I.

Despite the precautions taken by his father in the agreement in 1694, Daniel took his stepmother Mary to court after his father's death.[14] He complained that she had been using his father's goods for the benefit of herself and her own children from her first marriage, to the value of £500, while she said that she had used only her children's money which was held in trust, probably by their uncle. It emerges from the evidence that Mary gave her daughter Mary Worrall a marriage portion of £50 when she married Augustine Seaton I, and that her son Thomas Worrall was apprenticed to his stepfather as a butcher. Thomas was later in business as a butcher on his own account, presumably not in cooperation with his Seaton stepbrothers.

Richard Seaton I (1632–1706), eldest son of Hugh II, served as constable and churchwarden. In 1684, he followed the usual family practice of settling property on his eldest son Richard (Richard Seaton II) when he got married.[15] At the 1691 court there was a procedure of common recovery so that they could sell some of the land to William Lowndes, the first occasion on which the Seaton family took advantage of this new means of turning inherited property into cash. They received £70 according to Lowndes' records.[16] Richard held some freehold property, not necessarily in Winslow, as he was able to vote in the Buckinghamshire election in 1701. Like William Gyles and unlike the other three Winslow voters, he voted for the two Whig candidates.[17]

Richard made a will on 5 April 1706 and was buried on 9 April. His two sons received a shilling each, a sign that they were

[14] TNA, E112/780/79.

[15] WMC 11 April 1684, see www.winslow-history.org.uk/winslow_court1684.shtm.

[16] WMC 15 April 1691, see www.winslow-history.org.uk/winslow_court1691.shtm.

[17] www.winslow-history.org.uk/seventeenthc-poll-books.shtm.

already provided for, and he left everything to his widow Elizabeth. An inventory taken a few days later amounted to £79, consisting almost entirely of livestock (four horses, two cows and a sow) and crops, which was no doubt why he was described as yeoman despite his limited land holding. He was also called a yeoman when reported for trading as a badger (a trader, often in corn) without licence in 1698. If he was dealing in corn that would explain why he had wheat, beans and oats in April 1706 valued at nearly £19 and more than £8 of debts due to him. The house in the inventory matches the three-hearth house in which Richard was living in 1662/3: it had a hall, parlour and kitchen, each with a room above it, as well as a milkhouse, drink house, oatmeal house and mill house; the last must have been his father's malt mill but it only contained a quarter of beans.

Robert Seaton I (1636–76), Richard's brother, was also described as a yeoman. His goods at his death were valued at £42 and show that he was mainly a sheep farmer.[18] He made a will in order to appoint trustees for his only son Robert, who inherited everything and must have been very young.[19] The son was brought up at Gawcott and gradually sold his property in Winslow, so his will made in 1746 refers only to property in Gawcott.[20]

Richard and Robert's brother **John the Carrier I** (1641–93) had to find a new business opportunity in order to make a living. It is possible that he took over the carrier's business of John Meakes, who died in 1687. That was the year in which John was first described as a carrier in the court rolls, to differentiate him from other adult John Seatons.[21] John was able to expand his land to 24 acres, which he divided equally between his three sons, two of whom were under age when he died. The house and the carrier's business went to the eldest, John the Carrier II. He made his will on 12 August 1693 and was buried on 23 August. The property

---

[18] HALS, A25/3986.
[19] HALS, 112AW18.
[20] CBS, MsWillsPec 62/4/15. His sons did have the typically Seaton names of Richard, John and Daniel.
[21] WMC 1 May 1687, using the Latin *vehicularius*;
see www.winslow-history.org.uk/winslow_court1687.shtm.

arrangements were all made by will, after he had gone through the procedure of surrendering his copyhold property 'to the use of his will' through two neighbours who came to his sickbed.[22]

The eldest of Hugh I's great-grandchildren discussed here was **Elizabeth Seaton** (1657–1738), daughter of John II, and she was one of the few Seaton women to stay in Winslow after marriage. Her first husband was the draper Thomas Bishop (1660–92), who left her his copyhold property for her life, as they had no children.[23] He had a personal estate valued at £1,619, mainly in stock.[24] His will immediately involved Elizabeth in litigation in which she had the aid of Nicholas Merwin (1668–1751), the lawyer who had recently established himself in Winslow.[25] The day after probate was granted, Elizabeth married Merwin. This second marriage was also childless, but gave her status as the wife of one of Winslow's most important inhabitants.

Elizabeth's brother **John Seaton III** (1658–?1730)[26] received a substantial marriage settlement from their father John II: two messuages and 20 acres. He and his brother Daniel I continued the butcher's business. John III mortgaged or sold much of his property. He had eight children according to his father's will of 1708, and more later. He must have intended to make a will, because he surrendered his copyhold property to the use of his will, but no record of one survives.

His sons continued as butchers: **Daniel Seaton II** (1694–1718) made a will despite dying so young at the age of 24.[27] **Augustine Seaton II** (1702–65) carried on the business due to his elder brother's early death. He also expanded it, and by the time he made his will in 1765 his eldest son Robert was established at Bovingdon in Hertfordshire.[28] The Winslow branch was continued

---

[22] HALS, 130AW17; WMC 11 Oct 1693,
see www.winslow-history.org.uk/winslow_court1693.shtm.

[23] TNA, PROB 11/411/146.

[24] TNA, PROB 4/8317.

[25] TNA, E134/4WandM/Mich41.

[26] The parish registers record a number of burials of John Seatons without specifying which one, and in the case of John III there is no surviving manor court record.

[27] HALS, 155AW15 (nuncupative will).

[28] HALS, 204AW8.

by a second son **Augustine Seaton IV** (1739–1810), who inherited the house where his father lived at 24 Horn Street. This ceased to be a butcher's shop in 1810. Another son, **Richard Seaton IV** (1746–1824) apparently left Winslow in his youth and returned in about 1787 as a wealthy man, initially styling himself a brandy merchant – he ran the Punch House in the Market Square – and eventually as gentleman.[29] He was able to leave £1,600 between his two daughters when he made his will in 1821.

Daniel Seaton I (*circa* 1660–?1734), whom we have already seen as the second son of John Seaton II, took over his father's house, but the property he received from his father was entailed to his eldest son John IV. Daniel, like his brother John III, gradually turned most of his inheritance into cash by mortgages and small sales with his son's agreement. He must have rented land outside Winslow too, because by 1710 he owed £50 to Viscount Fermanagh of Claydon House, with his brother-in-law Nicholas Merwin as guarantor.[30] In 1719 he and his son mortgaged the cottage in which they lived, probably reduced from the status of a messuage because no land was attached, for £82.[31]

John Seaton IV (1695–1737) must have continued the butcher's business with his first cousins. His will mentions a son and two daughters.[32] The latter received £5 each, an indication of the family's reduced circumstances. He left to his wife Elizabeth and then his son John 'the revertion expectant upon the decease of Ann Seaton my mother' of a cottage. Elizabeth kept the cottage without formally being admitted at the manor court until 1754 although she mortgaged it for £50 and was running an alehouse called the Butcher's Arms there in the 1750s. An inventory valued her possessions at £24. She did not prove the will, and tried to leave the cottage to her sister and niece, leading them into a dispute with her son John, who had become a victualler at Dunstable.[33]

---

[29] www.winslow-history.org.uk/winslow_will_seaton1824.shtm.

[30] WMC 18 October 1710, see www.winslow-history.org.uk/winslow_court1710.shtm.

[31] WMC 16 October 1719, see www.winslow-history.org.uk/winslow_court1719.shtm.

[32] HALS, 196AW11.

[33] HALS, 196AW10 (Elizabeth's will); 196AW10 (inventory); ASA 27/1/115–122 (dispute).

Richard Seaton II, born in 1658, was the eldest son of the yeoman Richard I and inherited his parents' house with some land, but he left Winslow and in 1712 transferred the house, now in the occupation of two tenants, to his brother.

Augustine Seaton I (*circa* 1660–1737),[34] who received the transfer from his brother, was usually referred to as a victualler or brewer, and kept The Bell although he did not own it. He did not need the land he inherited and sold it off, partly to William Lowndes. His wife Mary Worrall was the stepdaughter of John Seaton II. Their children included **Mary Seaton**, born in 1704, who married John Kilpin of London, a coachman, when she was at least 38, a connection probably made through her father keeping The Bell. She inherited The Bull from her childless maternal uncle Thomas Worrall.[35]

Richard Seaton III (1706–*circa* 1770) was apprenticed as a blacksmith in London in 1724, and was later referred to as a ticket-porter (unloader of ships) of Queenhithe, a wharf on the Thames.[36] He owned two messuages in Horn Street which passed to his brother **Augustine Seaton III** (1708–1782), a carpenter, who already lived in one of them.

John the Carrier I's daughter **Mary**, born in 1671, married George Blake, a substantial farmer originally from Murcott in Oxfordshire, who had 34 acres of land and a house at Winslow and land at Thornton. Some of her children were beneficiaries of their Seaton uncles.

Her brother **John Seaton the Carrier II** (1675–1723) was described at different times as a carrier and yeoman. He called himself a carrier when he made his will in 1719, but was involved in farming in a serious way. His first marriage in 1697 was to Catherine Wyatt of Shipton who had inherited a messuage and 22 acres. John seems to have been the only male Seaton to make such an advantageous match, but Catherine died in 1701 leaving no children. The property should have gone to her two sisters, but

---

[34] WMC 21 April 1712, see www.winslow-history.org.uk/winslow_court1712.shtm.

[35] WMC 23 February 1749, see www.winslow-history.org.uk/winslow_court1749.shtm.

[36] CBS, D82/1 p.113.

John came to an arrangement: he bought the house from them and was able to keep the land for his life.[37] He also had the house and 8 acres in Winslow provided by his father, and he bought another house in Horn Street in 1701.

In 1704 John made a marriage settlement with his second wife, Elizabeth Rogers of Hardwick.[38] Then he sold to William Lowndes the house in Shipton, now described as a toft (a plot of land which no longer had a house standing on it), with an adjacent close and a pew in Winslow church. No doubt this pew was the real object of Lowndes' purchase,[39] to provide his son Robert with the status in church due to a lord of the manor.

In 1708 John mortgaged the 8 acres in Winslow to his brother-in-law George Blake.[40] He was also involved in a substantial farming operation at Steeple Claydon, since in 1714–15 he had to use his property as security for a rent of £140 a year.[41] He made his will in 1719 at the time of his third marriage, ordering his trustees to sell his property to pay his debts and to pay £60 to his third wife Mary instead of dower. His children were too young to continue the carrier's business, if it was still functioning.[42]

Hugh Seaton IV (*circa* 1677–1733) turned the 8 acres received from his father, John Seaton the Carrier I, into cash, first by mortgage and then sale.[43] By 1701 he had become a baker, yet another trade for a younger son. Somewhere between 1716 and 1721 he moved to Edgware in Middlesex, which is where he died. He had six children alive when his brother Robert made his will in 1739, and had at least five others who died young.

Robert Seaton II (1686–1743), the youngest son of John Seaton the Carrier I, moved further away than any other traceable member of the family, but retained strong links with Winslow. In 1714 he entered into a marriage settlement with his wife Elizabeth

---

[37] WMC 23 April 1701, see www.winslow-history.org.uk/winslow_court1701.shtm.
[38] WMC 26 April 1704, see www.winslow-history.org.uk/winslow_court1704.shtm.
[39] WMC 25 May 1705, see www.winslow-history.org.uk/winslow_court1705.shtm.
[40] WMC 13 October 1708, see www.winslow-history.org.uk/winslow_court1708.shtm.
[41] WMC 30 September 1715, see www.winslow-history.org.uk/winslow_court1715.shtm.
[42] TNA, PROB 11/590/327.
[43] WMC 21 April 1712, see www.winslow-history.org.uk/winslow_court1712.shtm.

and her father William Watts, an ironmonger of Stony Stratford.[44] She seems to have been the granddaughter of John Watts, ironmonger of Winslow.

Robert was a brazier by trade, and moved to Peterborough where he bought 36 acres of fenland at Farcet Fen. He acquired the messuage and 8 acres of his brother John the Carrier II in Winslow, where he had 6½ acres of his own. His land at Winslow was occupied by his nephew John Blake. He must have prospered because he left almost £1,000 in legacies.[45] His siblings' numerous children benefited under his will, which shows great care for them despite the geographical distance.

His widow Elizabeth retained a life interest in all the Winslow property, which means that as she lived until 1772 she was the only Seaton who held land in Winslow at the time of enclosure in 1767.[46] The reversion would have gone to John the Carrier II's son **Joseph Seaton**, born in 1707, but he sold it to Nicholas Merwin.[47] It is not known what happened to him but he did not live in Winslow.

The most consistent feature of the Seaton family over five generations was their desire to mitigate the effects of primogeniture. They were remarkably successful in producing male heirs, and if they had allowed the normal rules of intestate inheritance to take effect Daniel II would have been heir to enough property to make him a substantial yeoman farmer by Winslow standards. Instead property settlements were made in each generation and each branch of the family, usually at the time of marriage, which provided for younger sons, though not usually for daughters.

The Seatons who made wills usually did so shortly before they died and for specific reasons. Children received their inheritance when they married, rather than postponing marriage until they inherited. This eventually meant that by 1770, the end of the

[44] Recited at WMC 20 April 1715,
    see www.winslow-history.org.uk/winslow_court1715.shtm.
[45] www.winslow-history.org.uk/winslow_will_seaton1743.shtm.
[46] The Enclosure Award incorrectly gives her name as Anne.
[47] WMC 23 November 1748, see www.winslow-history.org.uk/winslow_court1748.shtm.

period covered in this book, the only land still in the family belonged to a Seaton who lived in Peterborough.

The Seatons' other strategies included:

- Diversification into different trades.

This was done successfully by the branch who became butchers, who were still trading in the early nineteenth century. Other trades practised by members of the family included baker, carrier, innkeeper and carpenter, none of which lasted for more than two generations. The Gibbs family[48] used the same strategy much more successfully.

- Turning property into cash.

Land which was insufficient to provide a living could still be mortgaged or sold, and the money brought into the Winslow economy by William Lowndes helped some of the Seatons to make better deals than would otherwise have been possible.

- Marriage.

Only one male Seaton, John the Carrier II, is known to have married an heiress, although it is possible that some other brides brought with them property outside Winslow. John's marriage made no difference to the family's long-term prospects because of his wife's early death. At least two female Seatons made marriages which elevated their social and economic status considerably.

- Migration.

The wealthiest Seaton of the period, Robert II, made his money at Peterborough not Winslow. He retained a close interest in his Winslow relatives, probably because he was childless himself. Several other members of the family are known to have been apprenticed in London. Hugh IV moved to Edgware, presumably for economic reasons. Other younger sons who have left no trace after their baptism no doubt went away for work, and most daughters whose marriages can be traced married away from Winslow.

---

[48] For the Gibbs family see pages 144-149.

However the unusual feature of the Seatons was how many of them stayed in Winslow, something which can be directly attributed to the family trait of providing for younger sons.

Chapter 8:
Shopkeepers, craftsmen and inns

Winslow was a commercial centre for the surrounding villages, with a weekly market and annual fair. The fair on 10 August (St Laurence's Day) was established by the market charter of 1235. Another was being held on Holy Thursday (Ascension Day) by the early eighteenth century, according to Browne Willis though apparently this began after 1673, when William Gyles knew of only one fair. Two more fairs were added later, on 20 March and 22 September.[1] These were for cattle, and in 1857 land was still advertised as 'particularly desirable as a lair for droves and cattle at the various fairs'.[2]

There were fairs for hiring servants on the Thursdays before and after Old Michaelmas Day, 10 October. Employment arranged at Winslow fair is mentioned in Quarter Sessions records.[3]

There are records beginning in 1711 of stamp duty paid on apprentices' indentures.[4] Occupations where apprenticeships are recorded at Winslow include baker, barber, blacksmith, butcher, carpenter, collar-maker, cooper, cordwainer, currier, draper, glazier and plumber, glover, grocer, ironmonger, joiner, mason, peruke-maker, tailor, tallow-chandler, tanner, wheelwright and whitesmith. Apprenticeships were also used for attorneys and surgeons.

---

[1] BL, Add.Ms. 5840 f.176; Society of Gentlemen, *England Displayed* (London, 1769), 280; directory of circa 1795 transcribed at www.winslow-history.org.uk/winslow_directory_1798.shtm.

[2] *Bucks Herald*, 21 February 1857. In fact the number of fairs increased in the nineteenth century.

[3] BQS, 16 January 1746 (CBS, Q/SM/3). The 1780 edition of *Owen's New Book of Fairs* (page 5) lists all of these except the one after Old Michaelmas which was added in 1792. Only the first two fairs are in the 1777 edition.

[4] www.winslow-history.org.uk/seventeenthc-apprentices.shtm.

This is a fairly comprehensive list of trades available in Winslow. The only obvious omissions are apothecary, brickmaker, carrier, gardener[5], innkeeper and maltster. Individual examples of clockmaker, cutler, miller and weaver are also known in the period, and the people who claimed losses in a fire of 1748 included a basket-maker and a shovel-maker.[6] Examples of some of these ways of making a living are discussed in this chapter.

The apprentices tended, where their fathers' occupations are recorded, to come from the same background as their masters, with their fathers in other trades. In some cases the apprentice was from the master's family, but there are also examples where the family business was passed on to an heir who had apparently not been formally apprenticed.

Employers described as chapman, milliner and mantua-maker took female apprentices. Women's occupations were otherwise not recorded in official documents, where they were labelled only as wife, widow or spinster, so it is rarely possible to identify a woman who was working for herself, like the draper Grace Aldridge (née Gyles), or for someone else.

There was a significant growth of retail premises nationally between 1640 and 1770, aided by more people earning wages and having money to spend, and by improvements in the distribution of goods.[7] Selling from a shop rather than a market stall avoided the payment of tolls.[8]

The shop with a bow-fronted glass window was a development of the later eighteenth century,[9] though inventories provide little information about how shops in Winslow were actually laid out. Benjamin Leach the grocer and Henry Stutsbury the ironmonger both had sets of drawers and two counters, which were probably

---

[5] It is unclear if this term is used for someone who ran a market garden or looked after other people's gardens, or both.

[6] BQS, July 1748 (CBS, Q/SM/3).

[7] HALS, A25/1233, A25/2129.

[7] Hoh-cheung and Lorna H Mui, *Shops and Shopkeeping in Eighteenth-century England* (London: Routledge, 1989), 150.

[8] Walsh, 'Stalls, bulks, shops', 44.

[9] Helen Berry, 'Polite consumption: Shopping in eighteenth century England', *Transactions of the RHS* 12 (2002), 375–94, 383.

standard features, while the draper Matthew Clarke provided a table and two chairs, presumably for his customers.[10]

The baker William Short had scales and weights on his counter, and their accuracy was overseen by the manor court.[11] There are a number of references to 'the chamber over the shop', indicating that the shop was an integral part of the building rather than a lean-to addition, and Short's appears to have been next to his dining room. Shop doors and unglazed windows would have been left open as far as possible.

There was nowhere in Winslow before the nineteenth century that specialised in high-value goods such as books, china or jewellery, although Benjamin Keach's book[12] could be bought at the market, perhaps from a chapman who sold a variety of products, and the draper Grace Aldridge sold gold rings, presumably as wedding rings.

Shopkeepers were expected to provide credit to customers:[13] Aldridge and the ironmonger Henry Stutsbury each had money owing from around forty people when they died. The inventories do not show how old the debts were or whether credit was limited. In the seventeenth century, shopping for most goods was expected to involve bargaining, at least when the customer came in person rather than sending a servant, but Quaker shopkeepers were known for their refusal to haggle and perhaps that extended to Baptists.[14] Fixed prices gradually became more common.

In the 1660s some Winslow shopkeepers produced trade tokens which could be used instead of halfpennies and farthings, because there was a shortage of small change in the official currency.[15] These tokens gave the trader's name and place, and sometimes the year, with a design which the trader must have chosen from a

---

[10] HALS, A25/4452, 191AW5; TNA, PROB 3/30/24.

[11] HALS, A25/4541 (1703).

[12] For Benjamin Keach and his book see Chapter 4, pages 97–102.

[13] Berry, 'Polite consumption', 388.

[14] Berry, 'Polite consumption', 390–91; Mui and Mui, *Shops and Shopkeeping*, 223.

[15] J O Manton and E Hollis, *Buckinghamshire Trade Tokens Issued in the Seventeenth Century* (BAS, 1933). Recently discovered examples can be found through the Portable Antiquities Scheme, https://finds.org.uk/.

catalogue. Matthew Bishop, draper, had three boars' heads pierced by arrows. John Crawley and John Dimmock had a hand holding a chopper over a leaf, presumably indicating that they sold tobacco. John Forrest had a shield depicting the bakers' arms and Daniel Sayer had the grocers' arms. Thomas Smallbones and William Gyles (*see Figure 9*) had hats.

The tokens of John Watts (*see Figure 16*) and Thomas Godwin had the legend 'his halfe penny'. Some included initials of husband and wife: WMG for William and Mary Gyles, JKW for John and Katherine Watts. The use of trade tokens was abolished in 1672, after which they lost any value, which is why they are frequent archaeological finds.

Figure 16: John Watts halfpenny.

Drapers

The stock of Silvester Stutsbury, draper, was valued at £167 in 1629, and he also had £32 in 'good debts' and £105 in cash.[16] Some of the stock came from London. When Silvester had presented the accounts of the estate of his father Richard four years earlier in 1625, there were debts of £105 to eight different London traders for 'wares'.[17] Richard had probably taken over the business of his father, Gilbert Stutsbury, described as a mercer when he made his will in 1595.[18] Silvester Widmere, mercer of

---

[16] HALS, A25/3025.
[17] HALS, A25/2862.
[18] HALS, 35AW23. Gilbert's inventory does not include any stock in trade.

Marlow, had draper's and mercer's stock of £185 in 1663,[19] which suggests that the Stutsburys were well stocked for their time.

Richard and Silvester seem to have established their business on a scale not previously seen in Winslow, presumably travelling to London to buy goods. Silvester left only a young daughter when he died, and his widow inherited the stock. She remarried, but there is no indication whether she and her second husband carried on the business, and it is likely that it was sold to the Gyles family.

William Gyles the Baptist[20] was certainly established as a draper by the 1660s, and his house in the north-west corner of the Market Square had been in the family since at least the 1590s, but it is not known when a draper's business began there. Today it is the site occupied by the Bank. William clearly prospered and two of his sons and a number of his grandchildren were involved. The business may have later been split between woollen and linen drapers and passed down through various members of the family.

There is an extremely detailed inventory of his granddaughter Grace Aldridge's goods after she died in 1741.[21] She sold black and scarlet broadcloth valued up to 10s a yard, printed and striped lindsey at 7d or 10d a yard, cotton gowns, leather bodices, men's and women's hose, ribbon, children's shrouds, whalebone and lace. Her stock and debts from customers amounted to about £600. Her two sons had moved away and did not take over from her.

The Gyles family did not have a monopoly in the drapery business. Nathaniel Hazlewood, who lived in part of The Angel, was a woollen draper when he made his will in 1688.[22] He came from a family of drapers in Kettering, but they seem not to have continued the business in Winslow after he died.

Philip Egerton, son of the rector of Adstock, was a mercer in the same premises circa 1706–11, after which there was a change of use.[23]

---

[19] *Bucks Probate Inventories* no.15.
[20] For the Gyles family see pages 84-94.
[21] TNA, PROB 3/41/72.
[22] TNA, PROB 11/395/417.
[23] WMC 15 October 1707, see www.winslow-history.org.uk/winslow_court1707.shtml.

Matthew Bishop came to Winslow around 1650. He was probably connected to the vicar of the same surname who arrived in 1648. He produced his own trade tokens and was a prosperous draper when he died in 1689.[24] He had stock worth over £800 and debts, cash and bonds of £395. The business was still on the same scale when his son Thomas died in 1692.[25] He had expanded into selling tobacco and pipes. For comparison Alexander Ethersey, draper of Buckingham, had stock worth about £500 in 1706.[26]

William Shelton the younger was a linen draper when he made his will in 1727.[27] His stock was left to his widow but she died before his will was proved. His son-in-law James Budd was a lace-buyer, but there were no more drapers in the family.

Matthew Clarke, a widower, died in 1731 leaving draper's stock worth nearly £400, good debts of £92 and bad debts of £232.[28] It is likely that he took over the Hazlewood/Egerton or Bishop stock, but there is no direct evidence for this. Thomas Aldridge, his business rival, was one of the appraisers. His stock appears to have been similar in content to the Aldridges'; it was not a matter of one shop aiming at wealthier customers than the other.

His son George continued the business at 4 High Street, but in his will made in 1757 he ordered all his estate to be sold.[29] His nephew and main beneficiary Matthew Eyre, also calling himself a draper, died soon afterwards, and the business seems to have ended with him.[30]

The demise of the various draper families, apparently for demographic rather than business reasons, led to the rise of the Dudleys, who were Winslow's leading drapers well into the nineteenth century, when they branched out, also becoming land

---

24 HALS, A25/4300.
25 TNA, PROB 11/411/146 (will), PROB 4/8317 (inventory). Much of the latter is illegible but the total estate came to £1,619.
26 *Bucks Probate Inventories* no.150.
27 TNA, PROB 11/631/13.
28 TNA, PROB 3/30/24.
29 HALS, 195AW6.
30 HALS, 197AW6.

agents and auctioneers. The first Dudley to call himself a draper was Benjamin, who made his will in 1739.[31] He was constable of Winslow in 1692 and 1702, overseer of the poor in 1707, and a regular manor court juror from 1701. He must have been in business by 1707 when the newly widowed Sarah Goodier bought ribbon from him.[32] He was described as a woollen draper in 1720 when he joined in a legal action to try to recover debts, and he was a mercer and draper with goods worth £700 in 1724, living in one of the church houses from at least 1714.[33] He was therefore virtually next door to the Gyles family, and he owed money to Elizabeth, widow of William Gyles IV, in 1718.[34] He left the goods to his son William, who died in 1796. In 1781 his grandson Joseph had stock worth £500.[35]

Being a draper in Winslow was capital-intensive: it required heavy investment in stock that must have had a slow turnover. Drapers carried an extensive list of small debtors. Nevertheless it was profitable and attractive, as there were always at least three different drapers' businesses in Winslow from the late seventeenth century and drapers seem to have been the wealthiest shopkeepers. Whatever their respective business merits, the Dudleys outlasted their rivals because of long lives and a continuous male line, so that three of the five drapers listed in 1798 were Dudleys.

Drapers provided customers in Winslow, at least by the 1730s–40s, with a wide choice and a range of colours: scarlet, brown, yellow, green, blue-grey, striped, flowered, checked. They sold material which originated as far away as Persia and India. Their regular customers would not have included the gentry except when there was a Lowndes in residence: Richard Lowndes owed Grace Aldridge 4s 2d. Judging from her inventory, the most expensive fabrics were not available in Winslow.[36]

---

[31] HALS, 179 AW2.

[32] HALS, A25/4588.

[33] TNA, C11/2721/45; LMA, Sun Insurance, 11936/18/239/33684.

[34] TNA, PROB 11/565/38.

[35] LMA, Sun Insurance, 11936/293/446141.

[36] As listed by Berry, 'Polite consumption', 388: Italian silks, brocades, tissues, English embossed velvet.

The clientele therefore ranged from doctors and lawyers to the Winslow poor.

Drapers may also have provided tailoring services, and it is likely that Benjamin Keach worked for William Gyles in the 1660s. Clarke did not have any ready-made clothes in his inventory, and Aldridge only had a few smocks and petticoats, but a large range of hose (stockings), so clothing was normally made to measure. Five tailors were listed in the Posse Comitatus in 1798,[37] and there were probably more men over sixty wno were too old to be listed. Several women were also in business as milliners by the end of the century.

There is no indication whether the tailors worked for themselves or for the drapers, and they probably did both. Joseph Eyre, a tailor who died in 1750, was the brother-in-law of George Clarke the draper. Spufford found that woollen clothing was usually made by tailors even if customers bought linen and cotton to make up themselves.[38]

Ironmongers

Winslow usually supported one ironmonger at a time. This was another trade which required heavy capital investment. The first was John Watts, who lived in Winslow from at least 1642, had a shop at 6 High Street and eventually another at Leighton Buzzard probably run by a son. He produced his own trade tokens in the 1660s (*see Figure 16*).

After his death in 1692, his goods in the shop, warehouse, back chamber and back houses were valued at £169, and he also had £50 in debts and cash, and £28 in bad debts.[39] His stock included rakes, forks, shovels, whips, besoms, scuttles and ropes. He had a quantity of iron, so must have made at least some of his own goods, for which he presumably employed a smith.

---

[37] Beckett, *Posse Comitatus 1798*.

[38] Margaret Spufford, *The Great Reclothing of Rural England* (London: Hambledon, 1984), 104, 123.

[39] HALS, A25/4378.

Thomas Watts (1660–1725) succeeded his father John. It appears that by 1725 the business was run by his nephew and residuary legatee Peter Stutsbury, who was to be allowed to occupy the premises rent-free for two years and in fact seems to have acquired them outright in 1727.[40]

Peter left the business to his own nephew Henry Stutsbury when he died in 1741. On Henry's death in 1750 an extremely detailed inventory was taken.[41] The stock was valued at about £170, with £75 in debts paid and 45 unpaid debts. The building fetched only £30 after the mortgage was paid off. Henry could supply sieves, whiting, pitchforks, beehives, sickles, pattens, yokes, scouring paper, mole traps, wire cages, sheep bells, nails, saws and augers. He had a large quantity of old iron and seems to have fallen into the ironmonger's trap of ever-expanding stock and diminishing turnover.

Figure 17: A clock by John Deverell of Winslow.

---

[40] TNA, PROB 11/604/340.
[41] HALS, 191 AW5.

The business was bought by John Deverell, who initially borrowed £200 from John Watts, ironmonger of Stony Stratford and the nephew of Thomas.[42] Deverell inherited an estate in Swanbourne and his wife inherited one in Granborough, so he should have been a wealthy man. There are a number of surviving longcase clocks bearing his name (*see Figure 17*), so he must have expanded the business and become Winslow's first clockmaker, presumably employing someone to do the work. He left legacies of £1,000 to his children when he made his will in 1758.[43]

John's widow Avis carried on the business until their son Josiah came of age, but mortgaged the premises for £200 in 1769.[44] Josiah's insurance policy in 1777 calls him ironmonger, grocer and chandler.[45] He had stock worth £450, and the premises included a candlehouse, a woodhouse and a salthouse. There was an enforced sale in 1778 for the benefit of his creditors.[46] The business continued as an ironmonger's for a few years but then became Hawley's grocers.

Ironmongers, like drapers, had to carry a lot of slow-moving stock and provide their customers with extended credit. Apart from John Watts no-one seems to have found the business in Winslow very profitable.

Grocers and tallow-chandlers

The first people who were in effect grocers in Winslow were William Davies, chapman (inventory 1588), and Hugh Stutsbury (inventory 1610), who stocked groceries, haberdashery and cloth.[47] Davies dealt primarily in textiles, like most chapmen of the time whether they had a shop or were purely itinerant.[48] Stutsbury's inventory included saffron, mace, licorice, aniseed, turmeric and arsenic.

---

[42] CBS, D82/1 p.74.

[43] TNA, PROB 11/840/378.

[44] CBS, D82/1 p.79.

[45] LMA, Sun Insurance 11936/263/392643.

[46] *Northampton Mercury*, 3 August 1778.

[47] HALS, A25/1233, A25/2129.

[48] Spufford, *The Great Reclothing*, 61–62, 75–76, 173-77, studied him in some detail.

During the seventeenth century shops became more specialised, although it may have taken the rising consumption of sugar and tobacco to make a grocery business viable.[49] When Mary Seaton spent money on 'necessaryes as soap starch sugar and such like' some time before 1709 she probably bought them all from a grocer.[50]

Tobacco had previously been stocked by drapers, but spices were always an important part of the grocer's stock. The spread of tea in Winslow is difficult to trace because of the scarcity of eighteenth-century inventories: they certainly drank tea at Winslow Hall, and the schoolmaster Joseph Gurney and draper Matthew Clarke owned tea-tables in 1727 and 1731 respectively.[51] Margaret Deverell of Swanbourne, who died in 1719, was supposed to have wasted her money on sugar and gingerbread, but there is no reference to her buying tea, and it is thought to have come into widespread use in rural areas only after about 1750.[52] Martha Burch in 1731 is the first person outside Winslow Hall who is known to have drunk coffee: she had silver and copper coffee pots in 1731.[53]

The grocer Benjamin Leach had a shop containing goods worth £5 in 1669.[54] The 1697 inventory of his son Benjamin also refers to the shop, but only records 'two setts of drawers two counters and a morter and pestell', not his stock.[55] He had £53 outstanding in money owed to him. Benjamin senior, like most Winslow retailers in the seventeenth century, was also a working farmer with growing crops and livestock including 61 sheep. His son gradually sold off all his land, and the only relic of farming in his inventory when he died was two old carts.

Another Hugh Stutsbury, grocer, had £9 worth of 'ware' in his shop in 1682 and also 'hempe and working geare for the trade'

---

[49] Mui and Mui, *Shops and Shopkeeping*, 48, 158.

[50] TNA, E112/780/79: Daniel Seaton v Mary Seaton.

[51] HALS, 165 AW13; TNA, PROB 3/30/24.

[52] TNA, C11/661/32: Milward v Deverell, 1719–20.

[53] TNA, PROB 11/647/15.

[54] HALS, A25/3839.

[55] HALS, A25/4452.

and £5 owed to him.[56] His inventory only came to £26 in all, and he had a two-room house apart from the shop. Hemp was normally used in Winslow for rope or 'hempen sheets', and a grocer would not normally require 'working geare', so Stutsbury apparently had another trade too.

The Baptist grocer Samuel Norman, son-in-law of William Gyles, was a wealthy man who left legacies of £1,700. He was the son of a grocer from Steeple Claydon, and owner of substantial property in various places, so it is not clear how much of his wealth came from the profits of the grocery trade. He built a large warehouse for his stock on land next to the Baptist meeting-house. His will, made in 1728, does not mention his business at all.[57] His son, following the Gyles tradition, became a draper in Henley-on-Thames.

Francis Collins, whose wife was a Gyles, had a grocer's shop in the former Gyles premises on the Market Square, but his will, made in 1770, also says nothing about the business, which was probably run by his servant and main beneficiary Elizabeth Newborn.[58]

Other people described themselves as tallow-chandlers, that is makers of candles: two of these were Richard Gardner, who made his will in 1677, and William Deverell, who made his will in 1711.[59] John Snow, tallow-chandler, who was married to the daughter of John Croft the vicar, took apprentices in 1715 and 1719. One of them, Richard West, was recorded as a tallow-chandler in his own right in 1752. Thomas Foster, prominent Baptist and husband of Sarah Gyles, called himself a tallow-chandler in his will of 1745, and had a business in part of the former Angel which belonged to his uncle.[60] His insurance policy in 1725 included a 'tobacco house'.[61] In 1757, 'British Blue for washing and bleaching linens' was available from Mrs Sarah

[56] HALS, A25/4114.
[57] TNA, PROB 11/674/417.
[58] TNA, PROB 11/965/112.
[59] TNA, PROB 11/356/252; HALS 148AW4.
[60] TNA, PROB 11/744/323.
[61] LMA, Sun Insurance, 11936/18/507/35323.

Foster.[62] George Foster, tallow-chandler and grocer in the 1750s–70s, was their son.

In practice the trades of grocer and tallow-chandler often overlapped, and by the late eighteenth century they were usually combined. Josiah Deverell was also described as a soap-boiler – soap was another product based on tallow.[63] Goldsworth Dudley, grocer and tallow-chandler at 1 Horn Street, left his stock to his wife in 1779,[64] and the shop remained a grocer's with many changes of ownership until the 1970s.

Robert Gibbs was established as a grocer and tallow-chandler in part of the former Angel by 1780, when he mortgaged it, but later went bankrupt. His father Stephen had also been recorded as a tallow-chandler in 1747. Grocers were not listed separately in the 1798 Posse Comitatus, but accounted for at least three of the nine shopkeepers listed there.[65]

Collar-makers

Philip Goodier, maker of horse-collars, died in 1707, leaving goods worth £29 and another £8 in money owing to him, most of which his widow successfully collected.[66] He lived in a two-room house with added buttery and shop. He and his wife Sarah slept in the upper room but shared it with most of his stock, including saddle fittings, which he also made, a new collar and leather in various forms. Most of his wealth, such as it was, lay in 'ninety hides with other leather'.

Sarah, his widow, kept detailed accounts which show some of the issues facing a tradesman's wife when he died with no-one to carry on his business, as well as recording the normal costs arising from a death. First she paid three women to lay him out, and the next day she had to pay for a shroud and coffin, bread and cake for the funeral, vicar's charges, ringing the bell and digging the grave. The funeral cost £2. She also had the bills for Philip's illness:

---

[62] *Oxford Journal*, 19 March 1757.
[63] *Northampton Mercury*, 3 August 1778.
[64] TNA, PROB 11/1057/279.
[65] Beckett, *Posse Comitatus 1798*.
[66] HALS, A25/4588.

physic from two apothecaries, and a woman who washed him.

She had to clear an extensive list of small debts to traders who had provided, among other things, straw, faggots, a fat pig, turnips, a new bedstead and a ladder. There were also bills for food including 8s 1d to Philip Budd the butcher. Other people turned up with claims: she paid Goody Fuller 5s 6d which Philip had borrowed from her. She owed Richard Gibbs 5s for going to Stourbridge Fair, near Cambridge, before Philip died. Ten different people charged for ale, which shows that people did not usually pay cash in the alehouses.

Then there were the expenses of going to St Albans twice to take out letters of administration (£1 8s for horses and a man) and the Archdeacon's charges and other legal expenses (£4 9s 8d).

She had to pay her husband's suppliers for horse hide, and wadmal to line collars. She owed Joseph Gyles 8s for a skin which belonged to him and had been stolen from the shop, and some other people 24s 8d for stolen buck-skins. Philip must have traded in skins as well as using them in his business, and Thomas Goodier, presumably his brother or son, was described as a fellmonger in 1705.

Another collar-maker, Philip Bailey, made his will in 1720.[67] His two sons seem to have continued the business, which was originally in The Walk, and one of his grandsons was a collar-maker at Berkhamsted.[68] John Swannell, collar-maker, regularly took apprentices from 1747, while William Mayne, saddler and collar-maker, took an apprentice in 1763.[69] There were two collar-makers in Winslow in the 1798 listing; their descendants were later referred to as saddlers and harness-makers.

Butchers

People of limited resources such as the Goodiers were still eating plenty of meat in the early eighteenth century: Sarah's accounts

---

[67] HALS, 158AW3.

[68] www.winslow-history.org.uk/winslow_will_bailey1766.shtm.

[69] www.winslow-history.org.uk/seventeenthc-apprentices.shtm.

include a total payment of 12s to three different suppliers. Butchers traded in goods with a rapid turnover, and unlike drapers did not need to keep a range of products in different colours or sizes. The north-west part of the Market Square was known as Butchers' Row in 1677, and that must have been where they did most of their selling. According to Thomas Eddyn's evidence in the 1673–77 court case over market stalls,[70] between 1664 and 1668 William Gyles used to set up between two and eleven stalls for butchers, and paid the bailiff £8.

A butcher's shop was more likely to be the place where he slaughtered and prepared his meat, not a retail space. Thirteen butchers in Winslow were listed in 1798, with ten different surnames. Wills and manor court transactions did not normally deal with business assets, and it is therefore difficult to know how the various butchers' businesses were passed on inside or outside families. Some butchers were also farmers, while others had slaughterhouses in the middle of the town. Setting up as a butcher would not necessarily have required much capital, and stock apart from bacon, which was more likely to be produced at home, had a rapid turnover even if customers expected credit.

This was also not a trade which one person could easily monopolise, so there was a profusion of fairly small-scale traders and this lasted until the twentieth century. The most successful butchers, at least in terms of acquiring land, were the Budds,[71] and the longest-lasting family business was that of the Seatons.[72]

William Wyatt, who died in 1658, was a butcher on a substantial scale, and had apparently handed over his business to his son Henry before he made his will.[73] He left legacies of £210 and a property called The Cock in Leighton Buzzard.

There is an inventory for Henry Wyatt (1616–70), totalling £130.[74] He lived in a substantial house with hall, parlour, little parlour, kitchen, cellar, five upper rooms, shop and buttery. Any

---

[70] TNA, E112/354/118. See also Chapter 1 for details of the market.
[71] For the Budd family see pages 246–250.
[72] For the Seaton family see pages 206-218.
[73] TNA, PROB/11/281/503.
[74] Bucks Probate Inventories no.36.

meat he had in stock was not valued, but he must have had land at Ashby St Legers in Northamptonshire, where he owned 90 sheep with 73 lambs valued at £49 and various other livestock including a bull.

In 1664 Henry was involved in a business venture with Robert Lowndes which ended up in Chancery; Wyatt had been sent to Cheshire with £40 capital provided by Lowndes to buy sheep, which he sold at a profit according to Robert or at a loss in his own version, presumably after he had driven them south.[75]

Henry also owned the Rose and Crown, which he had mortgaged.[76]

One of Henry Wyatt's sons was apprenticed as a butcher in London, and another, John, gained advantage from marrying William Lowndes' sister.[77] Robert Wyatt seems to have been Henry's youngest son and to have continued the butcher's business in Winslow.[78] His will, made in 1717, shows that he owned land which was distributed among his relatives, and his widow Dinah was provided for, but they had no children and there were no arrangements recorded for continuing his business.

William Wyatt of Shipton (1631–96) seems to have been another son of the first William Wyatt. He was described as a butcher in his will and a grazier in his inventory,[79] and the two occupations overlapped naturally: a farmer who fattened livestock might decide to slaughter them too, or a butcher might acquire land to do his own fattening as John Seaton II did.[80] William was a prosperous man with goods worth £377. He is the first man in Winslow known to have owned a clock, valued at £1. His house had a hall, parlour, kitchen, buttery and five chambers including a cheese chamber and a men's chamber. His inventory was the same as that of any other substantial yeoman except that he had £150 in the house in cash and £38 in 'money owing for cowes & horses &

[75] TNA, C7/215/77.
[76] WMC 19 October 1663, see www.winslow-history.org.uk/winslow_court1663.shtm
[77] See the Lowndes family tree on page 52.
[78] TNA, PROB 11/559/71.
[79] HALS, 10AR79, A25/4448.
[80] TNA, E112/364/79: Dispute over tithes at Addington.

other sold things'. He was probably a livestock dealer as well, but it seems unlikely that he would have operated as a retail butcher.

John Burrell was a butcher who had 18 acres of land which he did not farm himself, and his only son William became a dairyman at Hogshaw. He was fairly prosperous when he died in 1753: he left £200 to his unmarried daughter, and £70 to his grandchildren by his other daughter, who presumably had already had a financial settlement. The business was in William's hands 1743–62, when he took apprentices. He rented a messuage and slaughterhouse in Sheep Street from Richard West,[81] and owned Angel Close, convenient nearby for keeping animals before slaughter. After he died the close was sold to Augustine Seaton IV, another butcher.[82]

The Gibbs family[83] became involved in butchering as well as nearly every other trade. William Gibbs was a butcher in 1709. Stephen Gibbs, butcher, was taking apprentices from 1759. He had become a victualler by 1768 when his slaughterhouse behind 5 Market Square was occupied by John Swannell and Matthew Clarke.[84] Many other butchers are mentioned and they covered a wide economic range from significant property owners to short-lived businesses in rented premises.

Smiths

Winslow's most successful smith was clearly Stephen Bigg, who did work for the Duke of Buckingham at Cliveden and also became a postmaster. The basic blacksmith's business appears to have been continued by his brother Nicholas,[85] and his nephew, another Stephen Bigg (*circa* 1665–1756), whose only child Anne married a baker.

The Biggs were probably responsible for creating a blacksmith's shop at 3 High Street, between the north side of the Market Square and the churchyard. It was occupied by tenants

---

[81] WMC 31 Oct 1760, see www.winslow-history.org.uk/winslow_court1760.shtm.

[82] CBS, D82/1 p.289.

[83] For the Gibbs family see pages 144-149.

[84] CBS, D82/1 p.42.

[85] He is not described as a smith but his inventory when he died in 1683 (HALS A25/3694) valued iron and working tools in the shop at £13.

until the blacksmith George Cross acquired ownership in 1796.[86]

Christopher Bigg, who made his will in 1775, described himself as a yeoman although he was labelled blacksmith at the manor court in 1780 and left to his nephew William Jackman, blacksmith, who had been apprenticed to him in 1767, a messuage with blacksmith's shop on the south side of Sheep Street.[87] The Jackmans later established themselves as blacksmiths all over north Buckinghamshire.

Evidence for other smiths in the period is limited, but the Biggs did not have a monopoly and there were five blacksmiths and a brazier (a worker in brass) in the 1798 listing. Thomas Bett was identified as a smith or blacksmith at the 1685 and 1696 manor courts.[88] An 'old-accustomed blacksmith's-shop' advertised to let in 1794 later became part of 5 Horn Street.[89]

It appears that working as a blacksmith did not lead to significant prosperity for anyone except the Biggs. It did not require a lot of capital, and a workshop could be attached to an existing house if necessary, but the financial rewards of shoeing horses and doing basic ironwork were limited.

Zacharias Hamms, who died in 1698, was a cutler, with a large-scale operation at Brackley, Thame and Bicester as well as Winslow.[90] His extensive stock, worth £142, included not only cutlery but thimbles, looking glasses and spectacles. Nearly all of it proved to be on credit, and his goods were apparently sold off, so it seems that he had not been able to establish a viable business. Thomas Short was described as a brazier in 1708; his father was a baker, so it was not a family business.

Charles King, whitesmith (they worked in softer metals such as tin and pewter), took an apprentice in 1769, but became a specialised clock and watchmaker by the end of the century, a

---

[86] CBS, D82/1 p.388.

[87] HALS, 216AW2.

[88] WMC 1 May 1685, see www.winslow-history.org.uk/winslow_court1685.shtm; WMC 26 October 1696, see www.winslow-history.org.uk/winslow_court1696.shtm

[89] *Northampton Mercury*, 25 October 1794.

[90] TNA, PROB 11/449/182 (will), PROB 4/15794 (inventory and executrix's accounts).

trade continued by his son.[91] Thomas Capp, whitesmith, occupied part of the future Brook Hall, 9 Sheep Street in 1769.[92] William Firth was described as brazier in a 1775 insurance policy.[93] Thomas King called himself brazier and cutter in 1786, and later moved to Bicester.[94]

The limited evidence for anyone doing metalwork in Winslow may partly result from the work being done by the employees of ironmongers and other shopkeepers. The ironmonger Henry Hughes appears frequently in the Winslow Hall accounts, and the first person from Winslow to make clocks was John Deverell, who was an ironmonger (*see Figure 17*). Henry Stutsbury, another ironmonger, had 31½ lbs of horseshoes in stock in 1750.

Bakers

Three bakers were listed in 1798, and there were four at the time of Queen Victoria's coronation in 1838.[95] A few houses are referred to as having their own bakehouse or oven, but it is unlikely that many inhabitants had the facility to bake their own bread or could have spared the fuel required.

Bakers were traditionally governed by the assize of ale and bread, which was occasionally enforced as a means of controlling prices. This was eventually done by the Quarter Sessions rather than the manor court. Twenty-two people were referred to the Quarter Sessions in Michaelmas 1681 for breaking the assize, but it is unclear how many of those were bakers, and some people dealt in both ale and bread.

The manor court continued to monitor weights and measures used by bakers and other traders, for example in 1740 eleven people were reported because their weights were too light or were not produced at all.[96]

---

[91] HALS, 14AR80: will made in 1809.
[92] CBS, D82/1 p.44.
[93] LMA, Sun Insurance, 11936/240/357362. He lived in one of the church houses in the Market Square.
[94] LMA, Royal Insurance, 7253/11/99433.
[95] CBS, D/X/1495.
[96] WMC 10 October 1740, see www.winslow-history.org.uk/winslow_court1740.shtm.

Innkeepers could also be bakers. Henry Pym of The Bell was reprimanded for selling bread on Sundays in 1636, and his will mentioned his 'cake print'.[97] Nicholas Mitchell of The Bull had a bakehouse in 1665.[98] Henry Burley, from a Buckingham family of bakers, bought The Bull in 1776 and equipped it with 'a large bakehouse and oven capable of baking 12 bushels of bread, with flour lofts over the same'.[99]

There must have been a regular and reliable trade in bread, boosted by charitable distributions from endowments and at funerals. The churchwardens also paid for bread for individuals or families. Three bakers catered for the funeral of Anthony Godwin in 1706: William Short provided biscuit (£2 10s) while Thomas Cox (£1 15s 6d) and John Longbridge (£5) provided dole bread.[100] Perhaps it was the custom to divide the business between various tradesmen, as was the policy in 1838.

The baker John Malens, who died in 1661, had an estate valued at £171, but that included £108 'in money and debts whereof some part is desperate'.[101] Evidently bakers were expected to supply extensive credit. He had 'thirteen sacks and eight quarter of wheat and rye some part ground' and 'in the bakehouse and bredshop two kneadinge troffes one dresser board one bushall one pecke with other small measures, weights, scales, peeles, shelves and bred'. The value of his bakery stock and equipment was £21, so it was not a capital-intensive trade for someone who could take over an existing bakehouse or build a new one, but most baking businesses only lasted one or two generations.

William Short was a prominent figure in Winslow, serving as overseer and churchwarden. His inventory when he died in 1703 came to £149 but that included £65 in debts owing to him.[102] He had 149 lbs of salt in stock, but the value of that and his scales, weights and counter 'in the new shopp' came to less than £2. No

[97] HALS, 9AR80.
[98] HALS, A25/3728.
[99] *Bucks Chronicle*, 14 September 1822. The bakehouse was still being advertised in 1840.
[100] TNA, C5/238/22.
[101] HALS, A25/3631.
[102] HALS, A25/4541.

reference was made to bread-making equipment, but he had already handed over to his son a messuage in the Market Square (part of number 17) with 'kitching' lately erected, so that was probably where the bread was made. William junior sold it in 1711 and it passed to another baker, John Longbridge, who continued baking there until he died in 1739, after which his son sold it.

A younger branch of the yeoman Blake family was established as bakers by 1748, when the will of Thomas Blake specified that £5 of bread bequeathed to the poor was to be baked by his son Robert.[103] Robert was succeeded by his son John, and their bakery was at 10 Horn Street, which remained in the same use until the late twentieth century, although it passed through a number of different families.

Shoemakers and cordwainers

These two terms seem to have been used interchangeably: shoemaker was more common in the seventeenth century and

Figure 18: The bakery at 10 Horn Street run by the Blake father and son.

---

[103] HALS, 200AW2.

cordwainer in the eighteenth. Sixteen cordwainers were listed in 1798, with eleven different surnames.[104] Charles Bowler was not listed as he was over sixty, but he was also a substantial property-owner with at least seven houses and some land in Winslow and other property at Weedon.[105] He died in 1802. His father Charles, also a cordwainer, had had the remains of what was originally a substantial landholding but this had gradually been sold to the Lowndes estate.[106] He had died in 1735.

The Bowlers' prosperity came from inheritance and investment rather than any money they made as cordwainers, and it seems likely that they had employees to do the work. Thomas, the son of the younger Charles, described himself as gentleman when he made his will in 1836.[107]

John Stutsbury (1591–1643) called himself a shoemaker when he made his will.[108] He was prosperous enough to leave £170 in legacies to his younger children. Perhaps he had been helped by Sunday trading, to which he confessed in 1636.[109] His eldest son and heir Andrew was responsible for paying his siblings' legacies, and he was able to claim possession of Bell Close after satisfying all the payments.[110] John and Andrew were clearly farmers as well as shoemakers, and Andrew also had a malthouse.

Andrew's inventory was valued at £87 in 1679, including £18 in bad debts.[111] He left his eldest son John (aged nineteen) 'all workeing tooles & implements that belonge to my trade', and he had in the shop and cutting house £7 worth of 'leather shooes, working tools, hampers and other small things'.

John married Elizabeth Bletchley, an apothecary's daughter. His brother Hugh (1653–82) became a grocer, but the youngest brother Christopher (1660–98) was another shoemaker. His

[104] Beckett, Posse Comitatus 1798.
[105] www.winslow-history.org.uk/winslow_will_bowler1798.shtm
[106] HALS, 172AW1.
[107] TNA, PROB 11/1867/349.
[108] HALS, 89AW11.
[109] HALS, ASA7/31 f.3.
[110] WMC 22 October 1666, see www.winslow-history.org.uk/winslow_court1666.shtm.
[111] HALS, 115AW17.

inventory was valued at £69, including £29 of good debts and 10s of bad ones, but he owed £29 himself.[112] He married the daughter of John Watts the ironmonger, and their children do not appear to have continued making shoes.

Andrew Stutsbury's brother Peter (1629–81) was also a cordwainer, and rather more prosperous than Andrew since his inventory was valued at £145.[113] This was apparently due to farming rather than shoemaking, as 'leather and shooes and workeing geare' in the shop were only worth £3. Peter left no children, and it was Andrew's offspring who benefited from small legacies.

The Stutsburys were shoemakers for at least three generations, but they made money mainly from farming and malting. Shoemakers did not need much capital, but had to provide credit, with each debt for a pair of new shoes being relatively large.

Nicholas Brinsall (1577–1662) was another shoemaker with wider interests. His estate was worth somewhere between £43 according to his inventory (though this reading is uncertain) and the £2,000 that his granddaughter claimed.[114] He had certainly given up shoemaking by the time he died, having outlived all his sons, and his will consists mainly of a list of small debts owed to him, usually for a few pounds. As well as moneylending he provided a will-writing service. One of the overseers of his will was his friend Andrew Stutsbury.

In the seventeenth century shoemakers tended to be among the wealthier people in Winslow, and to combine their trade with farming or moneylending. In some cases they probably had employees. This was the tradition continued by the Bowlers in the eighteenth century, and also by John Gibbs, who described himself as cordwainer and victualler when he made his will in 1752.[115] He left £550 in legacies, and also kept The Windmill Inn which his widow continued after his death.

---

[112] HALS, A25/4484.
[113] HALS, A25/4095.
[114] TNA, PROB/11/309/231.
[115] HALS, 191AW8.

There is also evidence for people whose livelihood resulted mainly or entirely from shoemaking. Robert Grainger seems to have arrived in Winslow when he got married in 1682. When he made his will he had one son to whom he left £12 which could be 'imployed in setting him to a trade', but by the time he died in 1703 he had two more sons.[116] Robert, the eldest, took an apprentice in 1716 but died in 1718. John (1694–1748) was also a cordwainer in Winslow, and took apprentices in 1721–36. He left legacies of £75 between his six children, and although his son Robert was also a cordwainer, the messuage which he occupied was to be sold. Another son, Thomas, was a cordwainer at Long Marston in Hertfordshire.[117]

John's younger brother William Grainger (1701–49) apparently worked with him, and was unmarried so left most of his property to John's children, but his will does not mention tools or stock.[118] The male line of the family had died out in Winslow by 1754. John Toe was a cordwainer with a separate business who took apprentices in 1718–20. It was probably his son John who married John Grainger's daughter Elizabeth. John Toe's apprentice in 1720 was William Bunce. Bunce started having children in 1739, took his son John Bunce as apprentice in 1762, and three Bunces were cordwainers in the 1798 listing.

Apprenticeship records show six other cordwainers operating in the 1730s–60s, some of them taking apprentices at six or seven-year intervals. The apprentices were usually the sons of other Winslow tradesmen, but the cordwainers did not have enough property to make wills.

Inns

Most buildings in and around the Market Square were used for drinking establishments at some point, taking advantage of the influx of trade on market and fair days, but not many people made their living solely from running an inn. The certificate of

---

[116] HALS, 140AW13.
[117] HALS, 185AW7.
[118] HALS, 191AW2.

alehouses of 1577 lists five innholders, a vintner and six alehouse-keepers.[119] The first list of alehouse recognizances, sureties provided for the good conduct of the houses, contains 25 named premises in 1753, of which seven were officially run by women. In practice, the history of the Lowndes family at The Angel[120] shows that a wife might have the main responsibility for running the inn while her husband farmed or carried out another trade.

The Bell, thanks to its prominent situation facing the Market Square, was always one of the principal inns. There may have been rivalry with The Angel, which faced it across Sheep Street but ceased trading in the early eighteenth century. The Bell belonged to Henry Pym who died in 1666, after which ownership passed to his two granddaughters and their descendants, meaning that the business was run by tenants until the early nineteenth century. It was the venue of prestigious events such as a 'floral feast' in 1730 with a prize of a guinea for the best carnations.[121]

A fire insurance policy from the same year shows that the premises included the main house, a warehouse, brewhouse, six

Figure 19: The Bell in about 1909. It was refronted in the early nineteenth century and the gatehouse on the left probably gives some idea of its previous appearance.

---

[119] CBS, D/X 423.
[120] For the Lowndes family see pages 52–60.
[121] *Northampton Mercury*, 27 July 1730.

stables, barn, gatehouse and separate house and stable.[122]

The Bull belonged to the Mitchell family. When Nicholas Mitchell died in 1665 his inventory recorded a parlour, hall, kitchen, four upstairs rooms, cellar, buttery, milkhouse, bakehouse, boulting house (for preparing flour), and shop.[123] It would have looked like a conventional farmhouse with additional premises for baking, not a purpose-built inn. It was rebuilt after a fire in 1748, probably as a slightly smaller building (*see Figure 8*).

Mitchell was a bachelor and it was his sister Frances who ran the inn and kept house for him while he attended to the business of 'bakeing malting or … husbandry'. She looked after him when he had a stroke.[124] This led to a lawsuit between their brother Robert Mitchell, a weaver in London, and Frances' husband Thomas Wilmot, a tailor who allegedly inveigled his way into the family after Nicholas was taken ill.

The Old Crown (*see Figure 3*) is a late-medieval building which is identified as an inn called The Crown in the manor court roll for 1520.[125] The 'Old' part of the name is first recorded in 1753. It still has stone fireplaces on two floors which appear to date from the first installation of a central chimney in the Tudor period. During the seventeenth century, when it belonged to the Gyles family, the northern part was separated off and an entrance to the rear from the Market Square was closed off after access was created from Horn Street. The northern part was later another inn called the Punch House.

There is an inventory from 1708 for Charles King, innholder at The Crown, who was the Gyles' tenant.[126] His goods, valued at £70, included ale and barrels (£15) and cider and brandy (10s). He must have offered sleeping accommodation as he had thirteen beds: three feather, six flock, three straw and one trundle.

The diversion of the turnpike through Winslow, which

---

[122] LMA, Sun Insurance, 11936/32/206/53099.
[123] HALS, A25/3728.
[124] TNA, C8/182/185: Mitchell v Wilmot, 1671.
[125] www.winslow-history.org.uk/winslow_crown.shtml.
[126] HALS, A25/4600.

probably began in the 1720s substantially increased the passing trade.[127] This would have been to the advantage of The Bell, but when advertisements for the Buckingham stage-coach to London started to appear in the 1760s, the calling point in Winslow was the Three Pigeons.[128] This was at 22 High Street until 1775, when a fire started in Thomas Footman's brewhouse and caused considerable damage on the east side of the High Street.[129]

This seems to have led Footman to take his sign across the road to an inn previously called The Swan (now 27–29 High Street) which belonged to John Gibbs.[130] The building as it now stands has a cart entrance and courtyard, to give it the appearance of a coaching inn, but Winslow was too close to Buckingham and Aylesbury to become more than a halt on the stage-coach route.

A different sort of establishment is listed in 1753 as the Duke of Cumberland, a name which cannot be earlier than the defeat of the Jacobites in 1746. Its original name is unknown but it was kept by Mary Turnham, who in 1724 was indicted 'to answer for harbouring vagrants and selling ale and beer without licence' and absconded, leaving her son as surety.[131] In 1753 the landlord was Thomas Tattam, a currier, and it had the alternative name of the Currier's Arms. It disappears from the alehouse recognizances after 1759, when it was called the Duke William.

Tattam died in 1768 but someone who might have been his wife was buried in 1756, which would explain why the business ceased. What is left of the building is now 2 Horn Street, but most was demolished in 1902.

Most inns and alehouses in Winslow tended to be short-term businesses which rose and fell according to family circumstances. In some cases – the Swan, the Royal Oak, the Three Pigeons – the name and presumably a painted sign moved from one building to another.

---

[127] Gulland, *Toll Roads*, 101.
[128] *Jackson's Oxford Journal*, 31 October 1767.
[129] *Jackson's Oxford Journal*, 26 August 1775.
[130] Footman was the tenant of The Swan in Gibbs' 1777 fire insurance policy (LMA, Sun Insurance, 11936/256/382479).
[131] BQS, 16 January 1724.

The Budd family tree

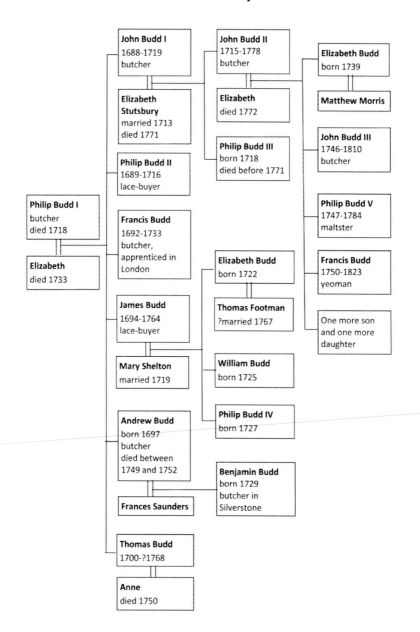

Winslow families
8: The Budd Family

Philip Budd seems to have arrived in Winslow in the 1680s, perhaps when he got married. He lived on the west side of the High Street, north of what is now Vicarage Road, an area which has been completely rebuilt at least twice. In his will when he died in 1718 he left 6 acres to three surviving younger sons after his wife Elizabeth's death.[1] One of them, Francis, was apprenticed to a butcher in London.

Philip assumed that his eldest son John would take over his house as he left him 'my furnice, my biggest meash fatt and my barrell which I had of Mrs. Paxton to continue as standards to the house wherein I now dwell'. He must have regarded the assets of his butcher's business as more important than the land.

A son who died before his father, also named Philip, was a lace-buyer, the first one recorded in Winslow. Although aged only 26 when he died in 1716 he was prosperous enough to leave in his will five acres of land and cash legacies of £72.[2] Another son, James, was also a lace-buyer and was omitted from his father's will, but had already received 2½ acres of land from his parents.[3]

John Budd I, the eldest son, married Elizabeth Stutsbury in 1713. They lived at 36–40 High Street. He died in 1718 shortly after his father. His own eldest son **John Budd II** (1715–78) was aged three when his father died[4] and was admitted to the reversion of his grandfather's house, which he would receive on the death of his grandmother Elizabeth.[5]

---

[1] HALS, 155AW7.
[2] HALS, 154AW7.
[3] WMC 14 October 1717, see www.winslow-history.org.uk/winslow_court1717.shtm.
[4] HALS, 156 AW8.
[5] WMC 13 Oct 1718, see www.winslow-history.org.uk/winslow_court1718.shtm.

John I left his marital home to his younger son **Philip Budd II**, born in 1718, to be his after the death or remarriage of his mother Elizabeth. She subsequently married William Ray of Aylesbury, yeoman, and when her death was reported at the 1771 manor court John II was her only surviving son, so Philip II must have died before her.[6] The family butcher's business was continued by John I's younger brother **Andrew Budd,** at least until his son John II was ready to take over. Andrew benefited under the will of his father-in-law Benjamin Saunders, a baker, so did not make further demands on Budd family property.[7]

John Budd II was established as a butcher by 1742, when he started taking apprentices. He held four acres of land in his own hands in the list of copyhold tenants made in about 1743.[8] At enclosure 24 years later in 1767 he had 37½ acres. This was an impressive piece of self-advancement in a family which had previously owned little land.

Unlike some of the other families discussed, a father's early death did not have bad financial consequences for the Budds. John II inherited his grandfather's house and three acres that had been his uncle Francis' land when his grandmother Elizabeth died in 1733.[9] He must also have inherited the acre to which his brother Philip was admitted in 1733, and the house which their father had left to Philip. He had a wife named Elizabeth by 1739, but the marriage has not been traced and it is possible that she brought money with her. She died six years before him in 1772.

In 1752 John II bought 14½ acres from his cousin, Andrew's son **Benjamin Budd**, then a butcher of Silverstone.[10] He must have acquired another 16 acres at a manor court whose records do not survive. He also rented land at Addington, and in his will he left the stock there to his son **Philip Budd V**: 'my breeding mare and all my stock of cows, calves, sheep, lambs, corn, grain, hay and implements of husbandry'. He divided his land between his

---

[6] CBS, D82/1 p.187.

[7] HALS, 182 AW13.

[8] CBS, BAS 375/22/41/7.

[9] There was a procedure of common recovery for the house at the 1742 manor court.

[10] WMC 30 October 1752, see www.winslow-history.org.uk/winslow_court1752.shtml.

four sons and two daughters,[11] leaving the house in which he lived to his eldest son **John Dudd III**, 36–40 High Street to his second son Philip Budd V, and two cottages to his daughter Elizabeth.

John Budd II seems to be unique in eighteenth-century Winslow in providing an example of upward mobility based on agriculture. He still described himself as a butcher when he made his will, and although the butcher's trade was thought of as a fairly lowly one, in Winslow it could clearly be profitable.

In practice he was more of a farmer than most people who described themselves as yeomen. It is not known whether he became a landowner through a successful business or through money provided by his wife. He clearly was not interested in using primogeniture to transmit his status to the next generation, and went to the opposite extreme by providing for all his sons and daughters, although fortuitously nearly all the land came eventually into the hands of his third son Francis.

At least two of Philip Budd I's sons benefited from marriages to Winslow women of the same social group with inheritances. Andrew married Frances Saunders and benefited from her father's will. **James Budd** the lace-buyer (1694–1764) lived initially with his father-in-law William Shelton, a linen draper, and their businesses were presumably connected. Shelton left legacies to his Budd grandchildren when he died in 1729.[12]

James Budd's own will is unusual because, although he had two surviving sons who received a shilling each and had already had £10, he left everything else to his unmarried daughter Elizabeth: a messuage, 10½ acres of land and all his personal estate and stock.[13] It seems likely that Elizabeth worked with him in his business. She was probably the Elizabeth Budd who in 1767 married Thomas Footman of the Three Pigeons and suffered the fire in 1775.[14]

Later generations of the family had diverging fortunes. There

---

[11] TNA, PROB 11/1043/266 (made 1773, proved 1778).
[12] TNA, PROB 11/631/13.
[13] HALS, 202 AW2.
[14] Jackson's Oxford Journal, 25 August 1775.

were apparently four Philip Budds in Winslow in the 1770s, a butcher, a maltster, a dairyman and a labourer.[15] There were seven Budds in the 1798 Posse Comitatus including three butchers, one maltster and three labourers.

In the 1841 Census, after the death of the wealthy Francis Budd whose sons had moved away, there were three adult male Budds who were all labourers.[16] One of these, yet another Philip Budd, was arrested in 1848 for beating his wife Martha and escaped from the lock-up.[17] He was recorded in the 1881 Census as aged 71 and in the workhouse.

---

[15] CBS, D82/1: WMC 25 October 1773, 30 September 1774, 25 October 1777 and 30 March 1779.

[16] www.winslow-history.org.uk/census1841-intro.shtm

[17] *Bucks Herald*, 24 June and 1 July 1848.

Chapter 9:
Poverty, disease and crime

When Winslow celebrated the coronation of Queen Victoria in 1838 about 93 people contributed to a fund from which 174 households of 'the poor' were to be given free food and drink.[1] This provides an idea of the relative proportions of 'haves' and 'have nots' in the early nineteenth century. There are no such comprehensive figures for the seventeenth and eighteenth centuries.

Hearth Tax returns show that 94 households paid the tax in the year 1662/3, and about 80 were exempted in the three years 1670–73.[2] Different definitions of poverty applied in different contexts. In the 1670s tax exemption came from living in a house of no more than £1-a-year rent, not having more than two hearths and not having goods worth more than £10. Only some of the households exempted from the Hearth Tax qualified for poor relief. Circumstances could also change quickly: the loss or incapacity of the main breadwinner would soon use up any accumulated resources, but children might become an economic asset as they grew up and before they left home.

Poor relief

Under the Poor Law of 1601 every parish appointed two overseers of the poor each year, who were responsible for levying a poor rate and using it to provide work for the able-bodied poor, apprenticeships for their children, and relief (also known as 'collection') for those unable to work. In practice they usually provided long-term pensions to the elderly, especially widows,

[1] CBS, D/X/1495.
[2] TNA, E179/80/352, E179/80/362.

Centre year of nine-year average	Nine-year moving average cost of poor relief (to the nearest £)
1683/84	40
1684/85	39
1685/86	39
1686/87	40
1687/88	40
1688/89	41
1689/90	41
1690/91	44
1691/92	46
1692/93	50
1693/94	56
1694/95	62
1695/96	69
1696/97	79
1697/98	87
1698/99	95
1699/1700	98
1700/01	101
1701/02	100
1702/03	99
1703/04	98
1704/05	98
1705/06	94
1706/07	99
1707/08	102
1708/09	104
1709/10	109
1710/11	117
1711/12	124

Table 7: Average poor relief payments in Winslow, taken from the overseers' accounts.

and short-term payments to people affected by illness or temporary unemployment.[7]

In Winslow the poor rate was supplemented, at least up to 1660, by a payment of 4s a month from the lord of the manor out of the tithes.[4] Overseers and churchwardens were chosen from the more prosperous farmers, tradesmen and shopkeepers. It is not known how the choice of overseers was made in Winslow but there is unlikely to have been any competition for the post, and probably there was some sort of rota to prevent people from avoiding it. Overseers had to satisfy both ratepayers who wanted their poor rate kept low and JPs who could demand an explanation for relief being refused.[5]

Overseers' accounts survive in Winslow for 1679–1715, showing the total disbursements for poor relief each year.[6] Until 1693/94 they remained steady at between £30 and £46 a year. For the next two years they were between £62 and £64. From 1696/97 onwards there was a significant increase. Apart from one year, the lowest figure for a single year was £80 in 1705/06 and the highest £155 in 1710/11 and 1714/15. After 1710/11 the annual cost of poor relief did not fall below £110.

Table 7 shows the underlying upward trend through a nine-year moving average taken from the overseers' accounts.

The 1690s were a period of significant economic problems.[7] Part of this resulted from the events of 1688 and the consequent war with France, but a succession of poor harvests also led to high food prices in 1693–99, with a harsh winter in 1709. Winslow, like south-east England in general, began to feel the effects from about 1693. The information for Winslow stops in 1715 but the general step change in the scale of relief was not reversed.[8]

---

[3] Paul Slack, *The English Poor Law 1531–1782* (Basingstoke: Macmillan, 1990), 27.
[4] CBS, D/BASM 84/16.
[5] Slack, *English Poor Law*, 28.
[6] CBS, PR 237/12/1. Full figures at www.winslow-history.org.uk/winslow_charities.shtm. The accounting year began on 25 March.
[7] Brodie Waddell, 'The politics of economic distress in the aftermath of the Glorious Revolution, 1689–1702', *English Historical Review*, 130:541 (2015), 318–51
[8] Professor John Broad, personal communication.

There was an official supplement to the poor rate. Under the Burials in Woollen Act of 1678, which was intended to help the wool trade, the dead could only be buried in woollen garments. Anyone who buried a relative in a more expensive material such as linen was liable to a fine of £5, half of which was distributed to the poor of the parish. The other half went to the informant, so most people informed on themselves. The Winslow overseers kept careful records of these payments which have survived for a few years, providing details about the individual poor.[9]

In 1680 Benjamin Leach paid 50s under the Act for the burial of his wife. This was distributed in sums between 6d and 4s to 29 recipients: the largest sums went to Widow Hogson and Widow Porter and their children, but only six recipients were noted as widows and there were two other women recipients. In 1684 50s from the burial of Susan Grant was distributed to 59 people: the highest amount, 2s 6d, was given to William Worsley and Samuel Wilston. This was the model which was followed afterwards, as *Table 8* shows. The smallest payment each time was 4d or 6d. If 1s per person was a typical weekly sum for poor relief,[10] then the sums distributed might have doubled some people's income for one week only, so they were not a very significant addition.

Date of burial	Number of recipients sharing the 50s distribution	Number of people labelled widow	Largest individual sum distributed
1680	29	6	4s
1684	59	14	2s 6d
1686	47	15	2s 6d
1687	62	18	2s
1688	63	18	2s 6d
1689	55	15	3s

Table 8: Distributions to the poor under the Burials in Woollen Act.

[9] CBS, PR 237/12/1.

[10] Steve Hindle, *On the Parish? The Micro-Politics of Poor Relief in Rural England c.1550–1750* (Oxford: Clarendon, 2004), 275; Slack, *English Poor Law*, 27.

If the number of people benefiting from these distributions was the same as the number of people receiving poor relief in that year, then recipients received on average about 15s a year in 1687 and 16s a year in 1689. As that is well below the rate of 1s a week, it suggests either that a significant number of people only received relief for part of the year or that the distributions arising from burials went to more people than received relief.

The Workhouse

The Poor Relief Act of 1723, sometimes known as Knatchbull's Act, claimed to be motivated by people applying fraudulently for poor relief directly to JPs without going through parish officers.[11] This certainly happened, although there is no reason to think it was fraudulent. In 1712 Frances East petitioned the magistrates at the Quarter Sessions on behalf of herself and her four children because her husband had gone away.[12] He was apparently still missing in 1719 when he failed to appear at the manor court to inherit his mother's property.[13]

One of the solutions offered by the Act was to allow the churchwardens and overseers, with the consent of the majority at a vestry or parish meeting, to acquire a building and take on a contractor to keep and employ the poor there, instead of paying relief for them to live at home. Any poor person who refused to co-operate would not be allowed to receive relief. This was 'the workhouse test'.

The Act confirmed what had been happening generally since the late 1710s,[14] and Winslow already had a workhouse. In 1722 the churchwardens and overseers bought tenements in the occupation of six different people 'at the Townesend of Winslowe near the Cowe Street, the common street west', in order to make a workhouse (the English word is used in the Latin text) to 'place,

---

[11] Text at The Workhouse, www.workhouses.org.uk/poorlaws/1722act.shtml [accessed 29 January 2020].

[12] BQS, 9 October 1712.

[13] WMC 16 October 1719, see www.winslow-history.org.uk/winslow_court1719.shtm.

[14] Hindle, *On the Parish?*, 186.

keep and employ the poor inhabitants of the parish'.[15]

There is no direct information about how this workhouse was run at first, but in 1784 an advert appeared for a contractor to take over the following Easter, and in 1787 a similar advert referred to a newly erected building of seven bays.[16] Winslow workhouse had twenty places according to a parliamentary report of 1776–77.[17] In 1797, there were sixteen inmates (old women, children and one man) working mainly at lace-making, with a contractor who was paid 3s a week each for them, recently increased from 2s.[18]

Matthew Marryott started a workhouse at Olney in 1714 and became an influential figure in their spread.[19] He acted as

Figure 20: The Winslow workhouse was the building on the right, after rebuilding in the 1780s. By the time of this photograph, taken about 1912, it had become Benbow's confectioners, as their sign shows.

---

[15] WMC 26 October 1722, reciting a surrender made on 22 August; see www.winslow-history.org.uk/winslow_court1722.shtm.

[16] *Northampton Mercury,* 5 April 1784, 5 May 1787.

[17] www.workhouses.org.uk/parishes/index.shtml#Parliamentary.

[18] Frederic Morton Eden, *The State of the Poor* (London, 1797), 2.30.

[19] Tim Hitchcock, 'Marryott, Matthew (bap. 1670, d. 1731/2), workhouse promoter and contractor', *ODNB,* www.oxforddnb.com/view/article/66535 [accessed 27 February 2018].

contractor, using a building provided by the parish and employing an assistant for day to day management, while he supplied furniture, clothing and food. Through the Society for the Promotion of Christian Knowledge (SPCK), the main promoters of workhouses, he advised many parishes on establishing their own. The SPCK provided information on workhouse rules and how the houses should be run.[20]

Marryott may have had at least an indirect effect on Winslow's workhouse but he lost influence and contracts from 1726 and received bad publicity, notably in a pamphlet of 1731 titled *The Workhouse Cruelty, Workhouses Turn'd Gaols and Gaolers Executioners*.[21]

An Account of Several Workhouses, published by the SPCK in 1725,[22] apparently with Marryott's involvement, includes Winslow in its list of active workhouses although no details are provided. Buckingham, Aylesbury and Wingrave are also listed. The case-studies illustrate what probably happened at Winslow too, claiming reductions of 50 per cent or more in the poor rate at Olney, Newport Pagnell and Hanslope.[23]

Olney had a master with a salary of £16, and at Newport the salary was £17. At Hanslope the master was expected to be 'some poor man' who lived in the workhouse with his wife, brewed the beer, prepared the food and had a salary of £13 with board and lodging, so he was an employee not a contractor. These salaries were in the same range as the charity schoolmaster at Winslow would have received at the same time.

The Olney workhouse had an average of 30 inmates, 'such as are like to be a continual parish charge', rather than those who were only temporarily in need through sickness, but Hanslope expected to take in people on a temporary basis.

---

[20] Tim Hitchcock, 'Paupers and preachers: The SPCK and the parochial workhouse movement', in Lee Davison and others. (editors), *Stilling the Grumbling Hive* (Stroud: Sutton, 1992), 145–66, 147.

[21] BL, 816.m.9.(78.)

[22] BL, 104.n.54.

[23] *An Account of Several Workhouses*, 74–79.

'It is owing to the erecting of this work-house [Olney], that several hands, which would be either otherwise idle, or ill employ'd in the breaking hedges, and such like acts of dishonesty, are commendably engaged in labours innocent, useful, and advantageous.'

This may refer to the deterrent effect rather than to people who were actually in the workhouse, 'most of them old' according to the writer. Refusal to work was punished by being sent to the house of correction.

Several regulations mention lace, which was presumably the main work of the inmates; at Hanslope children were to be taught lace-making. At Olney anyone refusing to go to the workhouse was 'refus'd the collection he asks', but at Newport 'they are allow'd little or no collection'. At Hanslope, people were sent to the workhouse 'especially if they become noisy, and are not content with some small allowance, as one shilling a week at furthest'.

Workhouses were intended to have a moral impact rather than to make a profit, and although they usually reduced the number of people on poor relief by at least 50 per cent at first, they did not necessarily save money in the long term.[24] The deterrent principle was undermined by magistrates who issued orders for outdoor relief rather than upholding the workhouse test. Most early workhouses were dependent on an initial wave of enthusiasm and soon failed.[25] In practice they tended to become 'houses of refuge for the old and impotent poor'.[26] This seems to have been precisely what happened at Winslow.

Settlement

The Act of Settlement of 1662 provided for newcomers to be removed within 40 days of arrival if they were 'likely to be

---

[24] Hindle, *On the Parish?*, 187–90.

[25] Hitchcock, 'Paupers and preachers', 160; John Broad, 'The parish and the poor in England, 1600–1850', in J Broad and Anton Schuurman (editors), *Wealth and Poverty in European Rural Societies from the Sixteenth to Nineteenth Century* (Turnhout: Brepols, 2014), 199–219, 205.

[26] Lack, *English Poor Law*, 42.

chargeable' to the parish.[27] They did not have to claim poor relief, only to look as if they might do so, most obviously by being pregnant. From 1692 settlement in a parish could be carried by renting property worth £10 a year, paying local rates, or being bound apprentice or hired as a servant for a year.[28] It was also possible to bring a certificate from the home parish acknowledging responsibility, which is what William Billington and his family did when they went from Winslow to Berkhamsted in 1742.[29]

Disputes about when workers were hired and for how long often reached the Quarter Sessions. For example, in 1737 Addington overseers tried to prove that Hugh Miller was Winslow's responsibility and not theirs.[30] Miller said he worked for Thomas Gibbs at Addington for a year from one Michaelmas to the next and 'had his wages' there, which would have given him a settlement at Addington, but Gibbs claimed that Miller worked for him for a month without a contract, went away, and came back after Michaelmas when he was re-employed, so he did not have a year's continuous service.

This illustrates the lengths to which an employer who was presumably also a significant ratepayer might go to in order to avoid creating a potential burden, but the magistrates saw through the attempted dodge and decided against Addington.

Overseers had particular problems with women who had illegitimate children, although the register of baptisms suggests that illegitimacy was unusual at Winslow throughout the period, with rarely more than one occurrence a year. The overseers wanted the fathers to pay rather than let the children become a charge on the poor rate, but proving paternity in a pre-DNA era was not always straightforward. There seems to have been a general presumption of 'guilt' if the woman named the father, but cases often ended up at the Quarter Sessions.

Thomas Pease, gardener, entered into £40 recognizance for the

---

[27] Lack, *English Poor Law*, 36.
[28] Lack, *English Poor Law*, 36.
[29] www.winslow-history.org.uk/seventeenthc-billington.shtm.
[30] BQS, 13 January 1737 (CBS, Q/SM/2).

child of Anne Oliver in 1680, in other words that was the amount which he pledged to pay if he did not pay maintenance for the child.[31] The surgeon John Greene reacted differently in 1700 when he fathered an illegitimate child with Catherine Greene, as the baptismal register confirms: he ran away and the overseers tried to put a charge of 2s a week on the property which passed to his son-in-law.[32] In 1706 two men gave guarantees of £50 each that Catherine would not offend again after she had a second child.[33]

In 1714 one of the overseers of Stony Stratford was accused of suborning a woman of his parish to say that the very respectable Joseph Bigg of Winslow was the father of her child rather than a gamekeeper from Wakefield Lodge, but the overseer was found not guilty so perhaps the suspicion of Bigg remained.[34]

Charity

The extent of Winslow's charitable provision in 1677 was reported to a committee making enquiries for the whole of the county of Buckinghamshire. This had been built up by donations of which some probably went back as far as the fifteenth century:[35]

- Joan Ford's charity, £100 invested in 6½ acres of land producing £5 a year, income to be distributed to the poor by the vicar and churchwardens. Joan was a member of the Wendover family and lived in London. Her will was proved in 1647.[36]
- The church houses, producing £4 a year in rent for the repair of the church.
- A house for two poor widows.
- The sum of £55, which was lent out on mortgage, the interest being distributed on the direction of the various donors.

Browne Willis recorded three charities in 1730 which produced an annual income of £1 10s, and they were probably part of this.[37]

[31] BQS, 22 April 1680.
[32] BQS, 18 July 1700.
[33] BQS, 18 July 1706.
[34] BQS, 14 January 1714.
[35] TNA, C93/36/20.
[36] TNA, PROB 11/200/85.
[37] BL, Add.Ms. 5840 f.177v.

There were a number of additions after 1677. Thomas Bishop's will, proved in 1692, left £30 which was invested in an acre of land, the rent of which was to be distributed among the poor by the vicar and churchwardens.[38] At the manor court in 1714 the two surviving trustees surrendered all the copyhold charitable property to nine new Anglican trustees.

The charity consisted of Ford's 6½ acres, Bishop's acre, the church houses and church headland, and the cottage for two poor widows. After enclosure, the land was consolidated as what is now known as Poor's Piece, in order to produce an income of £4 10s a year to be distributed to people not in the workhouse or receiving poor relief.

William Gyles' will, proved in 1702, left an annuity of 13s, to be paid monthly to trustees for distribution among the Baptist poor, not necessarily from Winslow. Sarah Fyge Egerton's will, proved in 1723, left an annuity of 20s, to be distributed to the poor on 5 March. She also left £5 for distributions of bread to the poor on the first five Sundays after her death.[39] Browne Willis blamed her executor's abuse for the loss of the annuity, but as the will did not specify where the money was to come from it was highly unlikely to last.[40] Only charities funded by the income from property had any chance of permanence.

Mary Bigg's will, proved in 1746, left an annuity of 30s, to be distributed in the month of her death by the vicar, churchwardens and overseers:[41]

> 'equally to six poor persons widowers widows or other poor housekeepers of sober conversation who do not receive collection from the overseers of the poor of the said parish of Winslowe and such as they shall think to be the greatest objects of charity.'

Like most of the charities this was an alternative to parish relief, not a supplement to it, but 5s each would not have

---

[38] TNA, PROB 11/411/146.
[39] TNA, PROB 11/589/278.
[40] BL, Add.Ms. 5840 f.177v; Clear, *King's Village*, 65.
[41] TNA, PROB 11/746/525.

supported the individuals for long. In addition 50s was to be given in bread at Mary's funeral. Her husband, the Joseph Bigg already mentioned, whose will was proved 1741, had a provision for his land to be held by trustees from Winslow and Monks Risborough, which was his birthplace, with the income to be divided between the parishes for apprenticing poor children, but this never came into effect.[42] These are examples of the sort of 'discriminating testamentary charity' noted by Hindle, but they were not typical, and general bequests to the poor remained the norm.[43]

Some people left money for a one-off distribution, although not on the scale of William Lowndes' £20. Alice Seaton (will proved 1658) left 20s to be distributed to the poor by her executors.[44] Frances Wilmot (will proved 1686) left 6d each to the poor widows of Winslow, and her executor had to pay 50s to the poor as she was not buried in woollen.[45] The accounts for the funeral of Anthony Godwin in 1707 include money for 'dole bread'; as he died intestate, this was either an oral instruction or his widow's decision.[46] Jonathan Townsend (1720) left £5 to be spent at his funeral, at least £2 on bread for the poor.[47] John Markham (1746) left £5 to be distributed to 'such poor people of Winslowe aforesaid as do not receive collection of the parish'.[48] Rebecca Hughes (1751) left £3 for bread for the poor to be distributed by her executrix.[49] Thomas Blake (1762) left £5 for a distribution (at his executor's discretion) of bread to be baked by his son.[50]

These bequests were too infrequent to make any significant difference to the budgets of poor households.

Joseph Rogers' establishment of a charity school was of much greater long-term benefit. By the early nineteenth century, if not

---

[42] TNA, PROB 11/709/307.
[43] Hindle, *On the Parish?*, 126.
[44] TNA, PROB 11/275/237.
[45] TNA, PROB 11/383/61.
[46] TNA, C 5/238/22.
[47] TNA, PROB 11/636/49.
[48] TNA, PROB 11/747/420.
[49] HALS, 191AW6.
[50] HALS, 200AW2.

before, the children of the poor who were to be taught there were specifically from families receiving poor relief.[51]

Despite the various additions, Winslow seems to have been rather short of charitable provision compared to, for example, Bledlow, which had charities providing fuel, bread and clothing.[52] Winslow also lacked a paternalistic lord of the manor such as the Verneys at Middle Claydon, who might help the 'deserving poor', as they saw it, at least until the time of Richard Lowndes: the Lowndes family did eventually establish a habit of charitable giving at Christmas but it is not known when it began.

Housing the poor

The court rolls of 1647 record that William Lowndes I and John Robson, presumably the overseers, were each amerced 12d because they 'permitted the cottages of which they were seised to the use of the poor of Winslow, and the chimneys of the same, to be ruinous'.[53] The manor court records show that the overseers sometimes took a property as security against a potential burden on the parish, which may be how these cottages had been acquired.

In 1713 they took John Shelton's house as a pledge that his daughter's expected illegitimate child would not be chargeable, and John Gibbs surrendered the reversion of his father's house, on condition that he would get it back if no child of his family received relief.[54] In 1720, the churchwardens and overseers took over Alice East's cottage after her death in order to let it and for the rent to go to the overseers, but the cottage was allowed to fall into disrepair and in 1762 Alice's son was allowed to repair it.[55]

In 1771, two people who inherited property made an

---

[51] www.winslow-history.org.uk/winslow_school.shtm: Charity Commissioners' report, 1833.

[52] John Broad, 'Parish economies of welfare, 1650–1834', *Historical Journal* 42 (1999), 985–1006, 987.

[53] WMC 19 October 1647, see www.winslow-history.org.uk/winslow_court1647.shtm.

[54] WMC 20 April 1713, see www.winslow-history.org.uk/winslow_court1713.shtm; 1 May 1724, see www.winslow-history.org.uk/winslow_court1724.shtm.

[55] Reported at the 1771 manor court, CBS, D82/1 p.111.

arrangement that they could enjoy it for their lives, but after their deaths it would go to the overseers with the rent being used for the poor.[56] This was a way which developed in the late eighteenth century for people with a house but no income to make provision for themselves, as they would receive a small pension in return.[57]

Hindle notes that parishes could build up a stock of housing for the poor by taking over the property of those who died without heirs, allowing new cottages to be built without four acres of land, and sometimes by building flimsy cottages themselves on waste ground.[58] By one means or another, Winslow acquired 39 cottages which had to be sold after the establishment of the New Poor Law workhouse in 1834.[59]

The poor who did not qualify for housing provided by the parish and who did not inherit houses themselves must have been tenants of the better-off, but large-scale landlordism seems to have been a fairly late development at Winslow. Bridget Yeates in 1842 inherited ten copyhold dwellings from her brother, who had been acquiring them since 1807: they included some he had built himself and some where a house had been subdivided.[60] No-one seems to have had a portfolio like that before 1770.

The will of Robert Eden of Botolph Claydon proved in 1766 mentions five tenanted dwellings in Winslow, including two sub-divisions of an older messuage, probably the most which anyone owned.[61] Three of them were in Tinkers End, which was probably already developing the overcrowded, poor-quality housing for which it became notorious in the nineteenth century.

Shipton contained farmhouses which lost their function in the eighteenth century and were subdivided into labourers' cottages, some of which survived into the twentieth century in poor

[56] CBS, D82/1 pp.113–15.
[57] Broad, 'Parish economies', 986–87.
[58] Hindle, *On the Parish?*, 268; Broad 'The parish and the poor', 215.
[59] *Bucks Herald*, 21 October 1837 (sale advert). The parish officials claimed to have no record of how most of these were acquired (TNA, MH12/512 no.24a, 8 December 1835).
[60] CBS, D/X/872/3.
[61] CBS, D/A/Wf/95/184.

Figure 21: A subdivided former farmhouse in Swanbourne Road, Shipton, which was demolished in the 1930s.

condition (*Figure 20*). Matthew Hobbs' will, recited at the 1749 manor court, left to his daughter Anne a messuage 'now in the severall occupations of Ann Wyatt, [blank] Phillips and William Perkins', which was originally the home of the yeoman Wyatt family.[62] In 1770 a baby named Anne Oviats was killed and her mother badly injured when the roof of their house collapsed on them while they were in bed.[63]

Work

Lace-making came to be associated with poverty in the nineteenth century, but that was not necessarily the case in the eighteenth, although it was practised by paupers among others. There was a weekly lace market at Newport Pagnell, and agriculturalists complained that women in north Buckinghamshire were not available for farm work because lace-making paid too well, and that men were making lace too.[64]

---

[62] WMC 27 October 1749, see www.winslow-history.org.uk/winslow_court1749.shtm.

[63] *Westminster Journal,* 12 July 1770.

[64] Richard W Davis, *Political Change and Continuity 1760–1885* (Newton Abbot: David and Charles, 1972), 16.

Lace-making spread through Bedfordshire and north Buckinghamshire in the seventeenth century, and Newport Pagnell had a lace-man who organised the work by 1685.[65] In 1797 lace-makers were earning 8d or 9d a day, not much less than male farm workers.[66] There is no specific evidence about how important lace-making was for Winslow was in the period 1640–1770. Even in the 1841 Census[67] it was clearly under-reported because the enumerators did not usually list occupations for married women.

William Lowndes' Winslow Hall accounts show the daily or weekly rates he paid his workers. Craftsmen and specialists, few of whom were locals, usually received about 2s 6d a day. Other workers were mostly paid 10d or 1s a day, such as Thomas George who was regularly employed for 'work in the yard' and 'stacking up chips'. He also received 1s per week as a watchman before the house was finished and occupied. This was temporary work which was never available again on the same scale.

The daily rate may have been typical, however: Sarah Goodier paid a man 1s per day to go with her to St Albans to get administration of her husband's estate in 1707.[68] The daily wage rate for an agricultural labourer in north Buckinghamshire has been calculated as 8d in the seventeenth century and 9d or 10d in the 1740s.[69] At Claydon workers were paid 8d in the winter and 10d in the summer.[70] There were always people available for casual work, which must mean that they did not have enough regular employment.

Farm servants aimed to be hired for a year at a time. Agricultural work at busy times, particularly harvest, required additional labour. Other potential employers such as carpenters and masons may also have needed workers for occasional projects

---

[65] Godber, *History of Bedfordshire*, 275; *Bucks Probate Inventories* no.107: Joseph Jones.
[66] Frederic Morton Eden, *The State of the Poor*, 2.29-30.
[67] See www.winslow-history.org.uk/census1841-intro.shtml.
[68] HALS, A25/4588.
[69] *Agrarian Change*, Appendix III: Statistics, Table XXVIII. That makes it less than Essex: labourers at Terling were earning 12d–13d in the seventeenth century (Wrightson and Levine, *Poverty and Piety*, 41).
[70] John Broad, *Transforming English Rural Society* (Cambridge: Cambridge University Press, 2004), 127.

without providing regular employment. The Posse Comitatus of 1798 shows that out of 242 men aged between fifteen and sixty, 26 per cent were labourers and 21 per cent servants and apprentices.[71] Some of these worked for innkeepers and tradesmen, for example there were two male servants at The George in 1841.

In the adjacent villages about 60 per cent fell into these categories, which would have consisted almost entirely of farm workers. Winslow even at the end of the eighteenth century had a minority of men working as labourers and servants, but the proportion was changing and by the 1841 Census it had risen to about 52 per cent.[72]

One occupation available to poor young men was becoming a soldier. In Charles I's reign parishes were sometimes required to provide men to be impressed into the army, which could lead to constables identifying someone they wanted to get rid of rather than the best potential soldiers. The Militia Acts during the Seven Years War (1756–63) led to the introduction of the militia ballot, and wealthy men who were chosen this way could provide a substitute by paying a poor man to take their place.

One man who made soldiering a career in his early life was William Ovitts (1743–1830). He seems to have been apprenticed by the parish of Winslow to a spinner in Aylesbury in 1750.[73] Other details of his life come from a newspaper report written when he was a workhouse inmate allegedly aged 90, but as he died five years later aged 87 the other details may not be entirely reliable either.[74]

He enlisted in 'Elliott's Regiment of Light Dragoons' in 1758 according to the report, or 1759 when the unit was actually formed by Colonel George Augustus Eliott.[75] The report continues:

---

[71] Beckett (editor), *Posse Comitatus*, 210-13.
[72] For the 1841 Census, see www.winslow-history.org.uk/census1841-intro.shtm.
[73] According to an indenture shown in a local history display at Winslow, *Bucks Herald*, 25 November 1905.
[74] *Morning Post*, 21 January 1825.
[75] Project Seven Years War: 15th Light Horse, at https://www.kronoskaf.com/syw/index.php?title=15th_Light_Horse [accessed 25 November 2019].

'In the battle of Freyburgh, which took place near the conclusion of the Seven Years' War, when the then hereditary Prince of Brunswick was attempted to be carried off the field a prisoner, by two French dragoons, and a foot soldier, Ovitts, single handed, galloped after them, killed the three French soldiers, and rescued the Prince. In this gallant exploit he was badly wounded; the Prince took him to his quarters, had him carefully attended until his wounds were healed, gave him a purse of a hundred guineas, and recommended him for promotion: the latter he modestly declined, on account of his education and habits being such as were not suited to any rank above that of a private soldier.'

On the strength of this publicity and Ovitts clearly knowing his place in the social structure, the Duke of Buckingham and Chandos (according to a note in the parish register) rescued him from the workhouse by giving him a pension of 1s a day for the rest of his life. A regimental history also recorded Ovitts' contribution:[76]

'William Ovitts, an Emsdorf soldier of the Fifteenth, who took part in cutting down and dispersing the Hussars that had nearly surrounded the Hereditary Prince of Brunswick at Friedberg, was residing at Winslow in 1827, in the possession of all his faculties, at the age of eighty-six years.'

When peace with France was celebrated rather prematurely in 1814, Ovitts took part as 'a brave old veteran' and was given credit for saving the Duke of Cumberland rather than the prince.[77] It is not known whether this confusion was due to the leading figures of Winslow who organised the celebration or to Ovitts himself. The fact that he was living in the workhouse later might be due to physical incapacity, if he had no family to look after him.

There was some scope for the poor to supplement their income, or at least their diet, but without woodland or a permanent

---

[76] Richard Cannon, *Historical Record of the Fifteenth, Or the King's Regiment of Light Dragoons* (London: Parker, 1841), 31.
[77] *Jackson's Oxford Journal*, 16 July 1814.

common this was more limited in Winslow than in many places. Gardens are undocumented but must have been important to cottagers. There are occasional references at the manor court to the practice of gleaning (or 'leasing' as it was sometimes called), although as an ancient right it did not usually need to be mentioned. Gleaning had to be done carefully because in 1639 nine people were fined the very substantial sum of 10s each for doing it at the wrong time.[78] An order from 1685 limited the right of gleaning beans without charge to 'those who take collection', in other words recipients of parish relief.[79] Enclosure put an end to this tradition.

Disease

Winslow was hit by a serious outbreak of disease in late 1643: between 1 September and 23 December there were 30 burials, three times the usual rate for a whole year. Swanbourne and Granborough were similarly affected but at Granborough the peak mortality was between 17 June and 14 August. The cause is unknown but is likely to have been a disease spread by the movement of troops during the English Civil War.

The Winslow and Swanbourne parish registers do not show any exceptional mortality during the plague which struck London in 1665, but in August Edmund Verney of Claydon could not 'deal with his butcher at Winslow because the butcher's servant Hogson comes from an infected house', and Winslow was one of the places said to have cases of plague in September.[80]

When the parish chest was opened in September 1718, the four men with keys had to meet at Shipton, 'the town of Winslowe being then very much visited with the smallpox'.[81] The number of burials increased substantially that year: 46 compared to 27 the year before and 31 the year after. Half of them were in the period from June to September. Mortality reached a similar level in 1741 with 49 burials and 1742 with 38. In neither year was there an

[78] WMC 24 September 1639, see www.winslow-history.org.uk/winslow_court1639.shtml.
[79] WMC 9 October 1685, see www.winslow-history.org.uk/winslow_court1685.shtml.
[80] *Memoirs of the Verney Family* 4.124–25.
[81] CBS, D/BASM/84/17.

equivalent rise in burials at Swanbourne, so the outbreaks were localised, but Aylesbury suffered badly from smallpox in 1742 when burials increased threefold.[82]

In 1760 an announcement signed by the 'principal inhabitants' that Winslow was free of smallpox appeared in the *Oxford Journal*.[83] For a market town it would have been important to spread the word as far as possible.

Joseph Turner advertised a service of inoculation for smallpox which involved going to stay at a house at North Marston.[84] This is only recorded in 1809 but he took over the house from his predecessor John Tookey and probably the inoculation procedure too. The number of doctors increased during the period covered by this book but it is not known how far they were available to the poor. Mary Gyles[85] provided medical services, probably not for money. The use of traditional cures and folk remedies is not documented at all, but might have been as effective as professional medicine.

Crime and punishment

Throughout 1640–1770 two constables were appointed each year for Winslow and one for Shipton. They were amateurs expected to raise the hue and cry if a crime was reported to them, and to arrest suspects with the help of their neighbours. The constables of Winslow were usually shopkeepers and tradesmen, probably drawn from a slightly wider range of people than the overseers.

It was a thankless task. In 1683 the two constables were fined 10s each for failing to appear at the manor court, and the same happened to the Shipton constable in 1687.[86] The constable of Great Horwood was taken to the Buckinghamshire assizes in 1676 for allowing the escape of two gypsy women accused of stealing a saddle, and Thomas Gibbs of Winslow was brought before the

---

[82] Hanley, *Apprenticing in a Market Town*, 76.
[83] *Jackson's Oxford Journal*, 16 August 1760.
[84] *Northampton Mercury*, 11 March 1809.
[85] See the Gyles family on pages 84-94.
[86] WMC 26 October 1683, see www.winslow-history.org.uk/winslow_court1683.shtm; 1 May 1687, see www.winslow-history.org.uk/winslow_court1687.shtm.

Quarter Sessions in 1713 'for neglecting his duty as constable in not conveying Thomas Tayler to the stocks'.[87] In 1720 the constables and several other men were indicted 'for assaulting Ralph Cook in his dwelling house', presumably an attempted arrest.[88] People such as William Hunt in 1697 were sometimes fined for failing to help the constables or refusing to obey them.[89]

Constables were not only responsible for dealing with crime and collecting taxes: in 1685 they were ordered to repair the public wells in Horn Street and Sheep Street, and in 1697 they reported John Harrison for having a dangerous chimney.[90]

Winslow clearly had a functioning pillory in 1664 when Benjamin Keach was put into it. In 1700 the manor court was told that it was out of repair and the lord of the manor should repair it, which he apparently did because in 1734 John Short was conveyed from Aylesbury gaol to stand in the pillory at Winslow.[91] Pillory Ditch was the road which is now known as Bell Walk, so the pillory must have been located somewhere around where it joins Horn Street, originally part of the Market Square.

In 1716 a woman was sentenced for a theft committed at Great Horwood 'to be whipped in full and open market at Winslow', and that was another regular punishment although more likely to be carried out where the offender was sentenced.[92]

People arrested by a constable were either kept at his house until they could be brought before the magistrates or put in a special lock-up. There is an entry in William Lowndes' accounts for 1703: 'paid for half the cage' £5 14s 2d.[93] This suggests that a new lock-up was built. Presumably Lowndes paid half as lord of the manor and the inhabitants paid the other half. It is possible that it was attached to the Moot Hall in the Market Square, or it could

---

[87] TNA, ASSI 16/4/4; BQS, 16 July 1713.

[88] BQS, 14 January 1720.

[89] BQS, 15 July 1697.

[90] WMC 16 May 1685, see www.winslow-history.org.uk/winslow_court1685.shtm; BQS, 15 July 1697.

[91] WMC 18 October 1700, see www.winslow-history.org.uk/winslow_court1700.shtm; Clear, *King's Village*, 111.

[92] BQS, 12 January 1716.

[93] Folger Shakespeare Library, W.a.147 f.72.

have been to the rear of The Bell.[94] When a new 'cage' was built in 1838 it was in Pillory Ditch and formed part of the fire engine house, but it appears that the previous one was not located there.

The Quarter Sessions are well documented from 1678 onwards, so it is much easier to trace the accusations of offences which were prosecuted there than less serious ones which were dealt with by magistrates locally or more serious ones which went to the Buckinghamshire assizes. Magistrates from all over the county and jurors drawn from male property owners came together four times a year, usually but not always at Aylesbury. This must have been a major social occasion for the Buckinghamshire élite, as well as a time of crisis for the accused, who might have been kept in insanitary conditions in the gaol while awaiting trial.

Prosecutions were usually brought by the aggrieved party, who had to put up a substantial sum of money as recognizance for proceeding. People might take the law into their own hands instead: in 1703 Charles Price of Whitchurch was indicted for stealing from Charles Coates and Mary Jenkins of Winslow, who were indicted for assaulting Price.[95]

Some offences that came before the Quarter Sessions related to Winslow's position as a commercial centre: for example keeping a disorderly alehouse or harbouring vagrants.[96] In 1712 men from Oxford were accused of 'using and exercising unlawful games i.e. cups and balls' and defrauding William Gyles senior and junior.[97] The witness was a victualler, and this sounds like something which would have happened in an inn on a market or fair day.

Joseph Phipps was taken to the Buckinghamshire assizes in 1718 for stealing cash from a shop.[98] In 1662 the grocer Thomas Sear, butcher Robert Scott and Alice Dandridge prosecuted Nicholas Bigg for stealing £4 10s out of Scott's coffer, presumably the takings of his business.[99] It appears that Bigg was able to 'ask for the book', to show that he was literate and entitled

---

[94] Saving, *Glimpses of Past Days*, 19.
[95] BQS, 13 July and 7 August 1703.
[96] BQS, 10 October 1678, 22 April 1680.
[97] BQS, 17 July 1712.
[98] TNA, ASSI 94/377.
[99] TNA, ASSI 16/4/4.

to benefit of clergy, which meant that he was branded on the hand instead of being liable to capital punishment. Bigg is later found in manor court records as a property-owning blacksmith, so this was not the start of a life of crime.

Some cases must involve a back-story which is not recorded. There are many examples of assault by one individual on another, but sometimes more than one person was accused. In 1680 John Greene was fined £1 and Abraham Day senior and junior 5s each for assaulting Thomas Benbow.[100] In 1681 twenty 'poor women', including Benbow's wife, were fined 3s 4d each for rioting and assaulting a man named Thornton at Winslow market.[101]

A strange case was presented to the manor court during the smallpox outbreak, and does not seem to have gone further: while Benjamin Saunders was sick with the disease, two women banged a warming pan all night and poured down water outside his room to stop him sleeping, after which Saunders died.[102]

The same manor court also started a case against Martha Glenister. She was accused of concealing the death of a bastard male child, which under the legislation in force at the time meant a presumption of murder despite the anxiety of overseers to rid their parishes of bastards by other means. An inventory of her goods was taken, showing that she had her own cottage with at least two rooms and she was not destitute as the valuation came to over £9. If the case was taken further she must have been acquitted, as in 1720 she had another child baptised at Whaddon, which led to her being kept in custody at Buckingham for a year.[103]

Deer-stealing became a problem in north Buckinghamshire in the early eighteenth century. Only the very rich owned deer – none in Winslow – and venison could not be sold legally. In 1723 Lord Fermanagh of Claydon (formerly Sir John Verney) decided to sell his deer because of incidents of theft and intimidation, and offered venison to people of Winslow and other villages if they allowed

---

[100] BQS, 22 April 1680.
[101] BQS, 14 July 1681.
[102] WMC 13 October 1718, see www.winslow-history.org.uk/winslow_court1718.shtm.
[103] BQS, 12 January, 20 April, 23 July, 5 October 1721.

the deer through unmolested on the way to their new home.[104]

A gang which raided Doddershall Park for deer in 1724 was led by a man named Glenister. He was Thomas Glenister of Winslow, a 'higler' or small-scale cattle dealer, perhaps Martha's brother if he was the man of that name baptised in 1698. He already had a criminal record, as he had been apprehended in London for turkey-stealing in 1723.[105] He was charged at the Quarter Sessions along with Thomas White of Granborough with being a 'nightwalker' and destroying the vicar of Winslow's trees.

He was ordered to be kept in custody until he found sureties, and then discharged from Aylesbury gaol.[106] The case was duly heard: Glenister and White said they had been drinking at The Bell, where there had been fighting, while witnesses reported hearing whispering and seeing men go into the vicar's orchard during the night. The verdict is not recorded but in 1725 Glenister was at liberty when he was charged with trespassing on Whaddon Chase and threatening a keeper. He was fined one shilling.[107]

In August 1726 a Winslow butcher was found sending venison to London, and Robert Lowndes, who had been involved in having the wagons searched, was attacked one night riding home from Buckingham. The deer-stealers were not brought to justice because north Buckinghamshire landowners had been successfully intimidated, despite the introduction of the Black Act in 1723 imposing the death penalty for poaching offences.[108]

Glenister's only known punishment for potentially capital offences was much less than that of a constable who failed in his duty. At the 1715 manor court another Glenister, John, was fined only 1s for beating up the hayward so that his life was despaired of, which suggests that intimidation was already going on.[109]

The most serious offence in Winslow during the period which has been traced occurred in 1739 and made national news:

---

[104] John Broad, 'Whigs and deer-stealers in other guises: A return to the origins of the Black Act', *Past & Present* 119 (1988), 56–72, 63. Broad's information about North Bucks is mainly based on the Verney papers.

[105] Broad, 'Whigs and deer-stealers', 66.

[106] BQS, 16 July, 8 Oct 1724.

[107] BQS, 7 October 1725.

[108] Broad, 'Whigs and deer-stealers', 64.

[109] WMC 20 April 1715, see www.winslow-history.org.uk/winslow_court1715.shtml.

'A few days since, one Thomas Hogson, a labouring man of Winslow, in the county of Bucks, having some words with his wife, on a sudden catch'd up a small wooden stool, or cricket, and struck her on the head therewith so violently, that she died soon after. And an inquisition being taken before Mr. Burnham, one of the coroners for the said county, the jury found the said Hogson guilty of *Wilful Murder;* and he was the same day committed to Aylesbury Gaol. And on Friday, the 23rd past, the said Hogson cut his own throat through the wind-pipe, but is still living, tho' 'tis thought he cannot continue so many days.'[110]

Hogson came from a long-established farming family[111] and owned property although he described himself in his will as a labourer.[112] His wife was buried on 19 March and he made his will in the gaol on 27 March after his attempted suicide. He was evidently helped by the lawyers Nicholas Merwin, who drew up his will, and Peter Goldsworth, to whom he left 'all such costs charges and expences as he shall have been at in any way relating to me in my unhappy circumstances'. It is not clear what happened afterwards but there is no record of Hogson being tried or hanged so he presumably died of his injuries. His will omits the usual 'being of sound mind' formula but was evidently allowed to stand.

Winslow in the period 1640–1770 had a level of crime and violence which was probably normal for the area and time. When Robert and Richard Lowndes became JPs resident in Winslow,[113] local offences could be dealt with more quickly but it is not known if that made any difference.

In the early nineteenth century Winslow had a professional constable and an Association for the Prosecution of Thieves, but these were later reactions either to an increase in crime or, as John Broad has suggested, a decline of traditional, informal methods of dealing with it.

---

[110] *Ipswich Journal,* 14 April 1739.
[111] For the Hogson family see pages 178-182.
[112] TNA, PROB 11/707/218 (proved 1741).
[113] CBS SessR 46/28 (recognizance of Joseph Meekes of Addington) shows that Robert was a JP in 1713.

The Elliott family tree

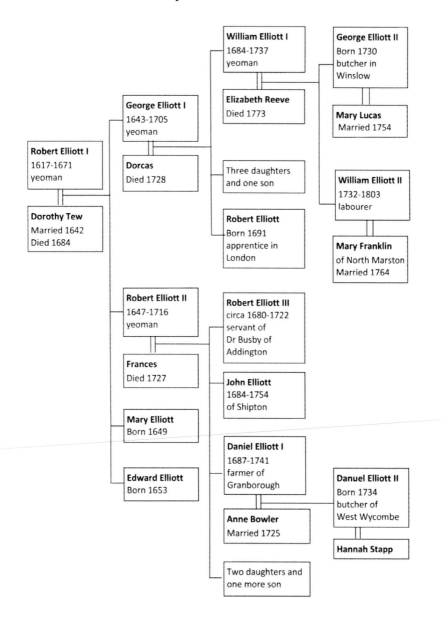

Robert Elliott I
1617-1671
yeoman

Dorothy Tew
Married 1642
Died 1684

George Elliott I
1643-1705
yeoman

Dorcas
Died 1728

William Elliott I
1684-1737
yeoman

Elizabeth Reeve
Died 1773

Three daughters
and one son

Robert Elliott
Born 1691
apprentice in
London

George Elliott II
Born 1730
butcher in
Winslow

Mary Lucas
Married 1754

William Elliott II
1732-1803
labourer

Mary Franklin
of North Marston
Married 1764

Robert Elliott II
1647-1716
yeoman

Frances
Died 1727

Mary Elliott
Born 1649

Edward Elliott
Born 1653

Robert Elliott III
circa 1680-1722
servant of
Dr Busby of
Addington

John Elliott
1684-1754
of Shipton

Daniel Elliott I
1687-1741
farmer of
Granborough

Anne Bowler
Married 1725

Two daughters and
one more son

Danuel Elliott II
Born 1734
butcher of
West Wycombe

Hannah Stapp

Winslow families
9: **The Elliott Family**

The Elliotts held on to their property in Shipton for many generations before experiencing a fairly rapid downturn in their fortunes. They followed rather different strategies from the Seatons,[1] though the two families were alike in producing male heirs in every generation. The Elliotts made wills much more regularly than did the Seatons.[2]

There were Elliotts in Granborough before and after the Black Death in 1348, but their first appearance in Shipton seems to be John Elliott's purchase of a messuage and virgate of land there in 1435.[3]

In 1610 George Elliott held a messuage and two virgates, as well as some other land.[4] There were two other Elliott family branches with land in Shipton who died out in the seventeenth century, so are not discussed here. In both cases their property was acquired by William Lowndes.

Robert Elliott I (1617–71) was the son of George, and was described as a yeoman. He inherited 60 acres of land in Shipton. He married Dorothy Tew in 1642, and lived in a house with two hearths according to the 1662/3 Hearth Tax return.[5] Its layout is shown by his inventory of 1671: it had a hall, parlour with two bedsteads, north parlour and kitchen, but there is no reference to any upstairs rooms.[6] Presumably Robert and Dorothy slept in one bed and any children still living at home slept in the other, with no

---

[1] For the Seaton family see pages 206-218.
[2] For a fuller account, see www.winslow-history.org.uk/winslow_families.shtm. The name is found in many different spellings but one form has been used here for consistency.
[3] *WMCB*, 569.
[4] CBS, WF538/44.
[5] See www.winslow-history.org.uk/winslow_hearth_tax2.shtm.
[6] HALS, 107AW6.

Figure 22: The Elliotts' house, now known as The Pyghtle, photographed in 1934. Rosemary Cottage, to the left, was bought by Daniel Elliott in 1762.

live-in servants. The house was sparsely furnished: four chairs and some joined stools in the hall and nothing else to sit on.

Most of the total value of £83 was in livestock and crops: sheep worth £10 were a major item. In his will, Robert left two cows and calves to Dorothy, and cash legacies totalling £70 to his younger children.[7] George, the eldest son, was executor and main heir, but there had already been a settlement for a second son, Robert, dividing up the 60-acre holding.[8] Dorothy died in 1727.

George Elliott I (1643–1705) was his father Robert's main heir, inheriting a messuage and 44 acres.[9] He did not have children until 1680 and was probably unmarried when his father died. He may have delayed marriage until he came into his inheritance, unlike the practice in the Seaton and Hogson families, with the result that although he lived into his sixties he left under-age children when he died.

---

[7] HALS, 107AW6.

[8] WMC 8 January 1672, see www.winslow-history.org.uk/winslow_court1672.shtm.

[9] WMC 18 October 1672, see www.winslow-history.org.uk/winslow_court1672.shtm.

Presumably he took over the family house, but it was completely redesigned by the time of his death. Today's Grade II listing describes it as a sixteenth-century house, so its basic structure was retained or at least the same materials were reused.[10] Probably George was responsible for replacing the wattle-and-daub walls with brick infill, installing a central fireplace and creating upstairs rooms.

His inventory refers to a hall, kitchen, milkhouse, hall chamber, middle chamber and milkhouse chamber, with a total of five beds: one in the hall and the others in the chambers.[11] There were still only six cane chairs and four joined stools in the hall, and six chairs in the kitchen, but a few more luxurious items are mentioned: a looking glass, pewter dishes and plates. The total value of the inventory was £70, still mainly in livestock and crops including sixty sheep worth £8. Four cows explain the need for a milkhouse.

In his will, George left half his household goods to his wife Dorcas and half to his three daughters, who presumably lived at home; they all married after his death.[12] He also left substantial cash legacies to the daughters and two younger sons, totalling £240 and payable when they were 21. The messuage and land, still 44 acres, went to his eldest son William, but half was to be used as security for the legacies, which could clearly be paid only by selling or mortgaging the land.

George's brother **Robert Elliott II** (1647–1716) benefited from a clear decision by their father to break up the previously intact family holding in order to provide for a second son. The arrangements were made in a deathbed surrender by his father on the same day as he made his will, which is why Robert II is not mentioned in the will. After his mother's death, he was to receive 14 acres and a newly built house (now demolished) which had been added to the north side of the old house, perhaps initially as a dower house for his mother, Dorothy.

---

[10] https://www.britishlistedbuildings.co.uk/101229362-the-pyghtle-winslow.
[11] HALS, A25/4754.
[12] HALS, 143AW2.

This had a precisely defined yard whose boundaries included the street on the west, Thomas Sheffield's house on the north,[13] the open field on the east, an elm tree marked with an R and a pearmain tree. Robert's inventory shows the layout of the new house, at least by the time of his death. It had a kitchen, best room with a bed, chamber over the best room also with a bed, and a chamber over the kitchen containing wood and lumber.[14] Robert's first child baptised at Winslow was actually his third, and was baptised in 1684 a week before his mother Dorothy was buried. It seems that he moved away for a time and returned when he was able to take over his inheritance. He was certainly back in Shipton permanently by 1685 when he was appointed constable.[15]

Although Robert described himself as a yeoman in his will, his inventory only came to £15 when he died in 1716. He had no livestock, only some harvested crops and eight ridges of wheat in the ground (this was in January). He left his wife Frances an annuity of 30s, his household goods, and the use of 'the bedd roome belowe staires'.[16]

Only 8 acres of his original 14 acres of land were left for his eldest son Robert to inherit,[17] and five of those were to be used as security for the legacies to Frances and their younger children. He left the residue of his goods to his second son John, who was his executor, but £20 each to three younger children.

These legacies were, like his brother George's, out of proportion to the size of his estate, but in this case must have been paid without selling the land. His wife Frances died in 1727.

William Elliott I (1684–1737) eldest son of George Elliott I, inherited the messuage and 44 acres in Shipton when he was 21.[18] Since the legacies to his siblings were only due when each of them

---

[13] This appears to be the house now called Rosemary Cottage, visible to the left in Figure 21: https://www.britishlistedbuildings.co.uk/101229301-rosemary-cottage-winslow.

[14] HALS, A25/4675.

[15] WMC 9 October 1685, see www.winslow-history.org.uk/winslow_court1685.shtm.

[16] HALS, 153 AW8.

[17] The sale of the other six acres must have been made at a manor court whose records have not survived.

[18] WMC 25 October 1705, see www.winslow-history.org.uk/winslow_court1705.shtm.

came of age, he did not have to raise the money immediately. He sold an acre of land in 1711, then mortgaged 16½ acres to William Lowndes. This became a sale in 1713, recorded in detail in Lowndes' notebook.[19] Lowndes originally lent £150 which he wrote off, and paid a further £75. These transactions appear to have been calculated precisely to pay the legacies to the siblings.

William's marriage was considerably delayed, presumably because of his financial difficulties. His first child was baptised in 1730, and William died in 1737. There must have been more sales of land because only 8½ acres of the original 44 seem to have been left to his son, and William's will refers to 'my good friend at Winslow to whom I sold part of my lands'.[20] This is very likely to have been the lawyer Nicholas Merwin, since the will orders some money to be invested 'with the advise or approbation of Mr Nicholas Merwin who hath been always assisting to me'.

William apparently continued to farm the land he had sold to Lowndes, as he was paying him rent in 1722, and he still called himself yeoman when he made his will.

There is no inventory for William. His will mentions some goods which were to go to his sons but apart from a large bible they were purely functional, for example hemp and flax sheets, brass kettles, a bell-metal porridge pot. He described these mundane items as 'standards', meaning things to be passed on with the house. There was a bedstead with curtains in the 'best room', but no other indication of whether the layout of the house had changed.

William had £150 invested, presumably the proceeds of the further sale, which was to go to his younger son William (William Elliott II), while the elder son George (George Elliott II) would get the house and remaining land, not mentioned in the will. William clearly realised that his sons could not continue as farmers, because his personal estate was to be used to pay for them to be bound as apprentices. He also left an annuity of £3 to his sister Dorcas Butcher but revoked it in a codicil. If his sons died, the

---

[19] CBS, D/LO/4/3 page 9.
[20] HALS, 181AW4

£150 was to be divided among his siblings and their children, for whom he evidently felt an elder brother's responsibility.

William appointed his brother Robert, who had been apprenticed in London, and his brother-in-law Thomas Reeve as executors and guardians of the two children. His widow Elizabeth was only to receive the interest on the remaining personal estate 'during so long time as she lives sole and unmarried for the duration and education of my said children'. This was a fairly conventional proviso, but the normal practice was at least to make the widow a co-executrix. William thought that Elizabeth might be pregnant when he died, in which case the unborn child would get a share of the £150. He was buried on 18 November 1737.

On 27 April 1739 his widow Elizabeth's daughter by her new husband John Holland, baker, was baptised at Mursley. William's careful provisions were frustrated because the executors refused to act. In 1744, five years later, administration of the estate was finally granted to John Holland, since Elizabeth, as a married woman, could not administer in her own right. Holland died in 1747 and Elizabeth, now 'Widow Holland', returned to Winslow, presumably to the Elliott home. She was buried in 1773.[21]

George Elliott II, William's son born in 1730, was a butcher in Winslow when finally admitted to his inheritance at the manor court in 1752, presumably because he had come of age.[22] He sold it all by 1769 and probably left Winslow after 1773 when his last recorded child was baptised.[23]

William Elliott II, his brother, may not have received the £150 their father left him in view of the problems with the will. In 1764 he was a labourer of North Marston aged 31 when he married Mary Franklin there. They are probably the William and Mary Elliott buried at Winslow in 1803 and 1804 respectively. Seven children were baptised at Winslow between 1767 and 1779. The 1781 and 1786 Land Tax records William as tenant of a cottage in

---

[21] HALS, 181AW4: will and administration bond; see also www.winslow-history.org.uk/winslow_wil_elliott1744.shtm

[22] WMC 30 October 1752, see www.winslow-history.org.uk/winslow_court1752.shtm.

[23] WMC 4 October 1769 (CBS, D82/1) refers to property which he had already sold.

Shipton belonging to the Selby-Lowndes estate, perhaps the one his brother had sold [24]

William's descendants in Winslow were labourers and in some cases paupers. His illegitimate great-grandson George Elliott, born in 1856, was convicted of a minor theft in 1872 and sent to Aylesbury gaol for two months.[25]

Robert Elliott III (*circa* 1680–1722) inherited the junior branch's share of the family property, a messuage and the remaining 8 acres, from his father Robert II in 1716, with five of the 8 acres used as security for his siblings' legacies. He must have been living at Addington as he was servant to Dr Busby, the lord of the manor and rector there.

He was apparently able to pay the legacies before he died, and in his will he left the messuage and land to his mother Frances for her life, then to his brother John, without any incumbrances.[26] He also left £50 to be divided between two other brothers and two sisters, and £30 to 'Elizabeth Betterton my intended wife'. It appears that he had postponed marriage in order to improve his family's finances. Elizabeth married someone else in 1724.

John Elliott (1684–1754), Robert's brother, came into the messuage and 8 acres when their mother Frances died in 1727, and still held them in 1745 at the enclosure of Shipton. He evidently had no children because the property went to his nephew **Daniel Elliott II**, who was born in 1734.

Daniel was described as a butcher after 1759. In 1762 he bought a messuage, today known as Rosemary Cottage (*see Figure 22*).[27] In 1768 he mortgaged the house and land that he had inherited to the lawyer James Burnham for £100.[28] Daniel then mortgaged everything to Burnham for £200, and sold up in 1774,

---

[24] CBS, Q/RPL/5/2.

[25] CBS, Victorian Prisoners, https://www.buckscc.gov.uk/services/culture-and leisure/centre-for-buckinghamshire-studies/online-resources/victorian-prisoners/ [accessed 29 January 2020].

[26] HALS, 161AW11. They were admitted at the manor court in May 1724.

[27] WMC 15 February 1762, see www.winslow-history.org.uk/winslow_court1762.shtm.

[28] CBS, D82/1 p.36.

paying off the mortgage, by which time he was described as a butcher of West Wycombe.[29]

The decline of the Elliotts from yeomen to labourers and paupers was quicker and more extreme than that of the Seatons. After being one of the main farming families in Shipton, by the end of the period they were tenants of the property they had been forced to sell. Owning some real estate, if only a house, helped to keep the Seatons at artisan level, but the Elliotts rapidly fell to the bottom of the Winslow economy once they lost their land.

Apart from Robert Elliott I they did not break up their landholdings to make arrangements for younger children. Instead, by regular use of wills, rather than marriage settlements or deathbed surrenders, they made cash bequests to the younger children, treating sons and daughters more or less equally. These were in several cases too much for the estate to bear, so that mortgages and land sales were used to pay the bequests rather than for investment. This was aided by the willingness of William Lowndes to buy any available land.

The heirs responded by marrying late, with the result that William Elliott I, while not dying particularly early, left young children whose financial interests must have suffered from their mother's remarriage, although their grandfather George's will and their father's friendship with an upwardly-mobile lawyer were bigger problems. The Elliotts did not usually emulate the Seatons in having younger sons apprenticed, and there do not seem to have been any family members who prospered after leaving Winslow, or if they did their money did not come back to Winslow. The decision to create a separate holding for Robert Elliott II (1647–1716) could never have given him a viable farm unless he also had a trade or could rent more land.

The enclosure of Shipton in 1745 did not affect the Elliotts significantly because their holdings were already too small to make a living, thanks to earlier sales, and eventually their entire property belonged to the Selby-Lowndes estate.

---

[29] WMC 1 May 1724, see www.winslow-history.org.uk/winslow_court1724.shtm and www.winslow-history.org.uk/winslow_emclosure_shipton.shtm

Chapter 10:
Farming and Enclosure

The common field system which existed in Winslow in the seventeenth century required detailed regulation. This was overseen by the manor court. The first surviving set of orders is from 1685.[1] They are not comprehensive, and must have been additions to an established set of rules. They continued to be reissued with minor alterations, usually at least every three years.

These reveal some of the main issues: where and in what numbers livestock could graze in the wheat, bean and fallow fields; grazing rights 'upon the common' which in Winslow's case mainly meant the verges of roads; keeping pigs ringed; maintenance of the pound in Horn Street where stray animals were taken.

In 1710 William Eden had twenty sheep impounded for causing damage, and forcibly removed them from the pound.[2] In 1705, problems with drainage had to be addressed: everyone 'shall on eight days notice to them to be given open the furrowes at the end of their plowed lands soe as to let the water out'.[3] Most livestock was kept in a common herd which was moved around as required: it would graze in the fallow field until that was ready to be sown, then move into a field which had been harvested.

Encroachment was a recurring problem. In 1689 fifteen people were fined for encroaching on the common fields, and ordered to lay open their encroachments within a week of harvest.[4] This seems to mean that they had fenced off their strips of land, which also led to the obstruction of roads. Temporary fencing was

---

[1] WMC 9 October 1685, see www.winslow-history.org.uk/winslow_court1685.shtm.

[2] WMC 18 October 1710, see www.winslow-history.org.uk/winslow_court1710.shtm.

[3] WMC 25 October 1705, see www.winslow-history.org.uk/winslow_court1705.shtm.

[4] WMC 5 April 1689, see www.winslow-history.org.uk/winslow_court1689.shtm.

permitted while crops were growing but not otherwise, and people were stopped from putting hedges and ditches around their strips.

The main agricultural offence was overburdening the common, grazing more animals than was permitted according to the size of your landholding. In Shipton 'cow's commons', the right to graze a cow, seem to have become separated from the land which originally went with them, but that did not happen in Winslow.

There was a particular problem with horses. In 1636 there were seven different offenders who pastured their horses illegally, in 1670 seventeen and in 1715 nine.[5] In 1714 people were reported to be pasturing one horse during the day and another at night.[6] The owner of a horse needed to hold ten acres of land in order to have right of pasture for one horse. Lawyers, doctors and carriers needed horses for their work but did not usually have that much land. It seems likely that some people chose to pay the 5s annual penalty, and it explains why others bought up small parcels of enclosed land when they became available.[7]

Keeping a substantial flock of sheep was also difficult in Winslow. In 1667 Peter Lowndes overburdened the common with 40 sheep, and in 1716 William Norman put 80 sheep into the wheat stubble before it was cleared.[8] There was also an issue with people who raised pigs commercially: anyone keeping more than needed for his personal use was to pay 4d per hog or 2d per pig,[9] and they were not to 'bash or break' other people's hedges to get the haws (hawthorn berries) for their pigs. Two drovers were amerced (fined) for pasturing droves of twenty and forty pigs respectively in the common fields.[10]

The manor court records of the seventeenth century show two main changes from the medieval system of intensive arable

---

[5] WMC 27 September 1636, see www.winslow-history.org.uk/winslow_court1636.shtm;
7 October 1670, see www.winslow-history.org.uk/winslow_court1670.shtm;
30 September 1715, see www.winslow-history.org.uk/winslow_court1715.shtm.

[6] WMC 29 March 1714, see www.winslow-history.org.uk/winslow_court1714.shtm.

[7] Saving, *Glimpses of Past Days*, 21.

[8] WMC 21 October 1667, see www.winslow-history.org.uk/winslow_court1667.shtm;
10 October 1716, see www.winslow-history.org.uk/winslow_court1716.shtm.

[9] A 'hog' was a full-grown pig.

[10] WMC 13 October 1708, see www.winslow-history.org.uk/winslow_court1708.shtm.

farming. One was the designation of some land as 'leys', parts of an open field where grass was grown rather than arable crops. The other was the development of some small fenced or hedged closes (not necessarily leys) within the open fields, as well as those adjacent to houses. In 1654 there is a reference to 'the newe close of arrable att Nant Ditch next Mr Edmonds conteyninge twelve ridges'.[11] The creation of such closes was the exception rather than the rule, however, and three or four acres seems to have been the maximum size. In general there was little consolidation of strips in Winslow's open fields: when John Bowler mortgaged 9½ acres in 1760, it was in seven separate pieces of which the biggest was two acres.[12]

The production of butter was of some importance even before enclosure, although it would only have been feasible on a large scale in Shipton where there was a designated Cowpasture on which cattle could graze permanently. Dairying increasingly replaced beef and sheep farming in north Buckinghamshire from the 1670s, initially for cheese and for butter after the mid-eighteenth century.[13] Butter is mentioned in a number of Winslow inventories, usually along with cheese. It had the advantage for the producers of being sold immediately instead of having to mature first, although they had then to wait six months to be paid by the factors in London who took their produce.[14] Waste products from butter production could be fed to pigs.

An area next to the Market Square became known as the Buttermarket in the eighteenth century. Charles March, a butterman of St Clement Danes in London who died in 1746, came originally from Dinton, married a woman from Little Horwood and owned a house in Winslow.[15] The house was occupied by William Gibbs, carrier, and it is likely that he was the Winslow end of a business transporting butter to London. John

---

[11] WMC 18 October 1654, see www.winslow-history.org.uk/winslow_court1654.shtm.

[12] WMC 31 October 1760, see www.winslow-history.org.uk/winslow_court1760.shtm.

[13] Broad, *Transforming English Rural Society*, 223–24.

[14] John Broad, 'Regional perspectives and variations in English dairying, 1650–1850', in R W Hoyle (editor), *People, Landscape and Alternative Agriculture: Essays for Joan Thirsk* (British Agricultural History Society, 2004) , 93–112, 103–08.

[15] TNA, PROB 11/751/155; www.winslow-history.org.uk/winslow_will_march1746.shtm.

Clark was a later occupier, and in 1783 he offered for sale his 'common stage-waggons' equipped with 'a large number of butter flats and cloths', which had been in business for sixty years.[16] The Buckingham and Winslow Butter Waggons which were for sale in 1812 were at least indirectly a successor.[17]

William Dudley of Clare Market, London, butterman, who appears as a mortgagee in 1773, came from the Dudley family of Winslow. Thomas Smith, a butterman from Acton, was killed in an accident to the Buckingham stage-coach near Winslow in 1777.[18] Davis dates the importance for the Vale of Aylesbury of sending butter to London to the beginning of the nineteenth century, but the Winslow evidence suggests that it was much earlier, and predated enclosure by several decades.[19]

Farming under William and Robert Lowndes

William Lowndes bought up land in Winslow from the 1680s to 1720s. He had enough to do without involving himself closely in agriculture, although he tried a little farming of his own on his property at Chesham in 1720,[20] and his son Robert did not have the money to make changes even if he wanted to. By his large-scale land purchases William Lowndes did however turn Winslow and especially Shipton from places where owner-occupier farmers predominated to ones where his tenants farmed most of the land. That means that the land disappears from manorial records and wills, so its use becomes much harder to trace.

Lowndes' own records of rents collected have survived extensively but his descendants' have not. *Table 9* shows rents he was receiving in 1700, although it is not necessarily an exhaustive list.[21] Rent per acre seems to have been very variable but where it can be assessed 6s 8d to 8s was typical. Closes presumably commanded higher rents than scattered strips.

---

[16] *Northampton Mercury*, 10 March 1783.
[17] www.winslow-history.org.uk/winslow_families-ingram.shtm.
[18] Clear, *King's Village*, 67 records his gravestone.
[19] Davis, *Political Change and Continuity*, 19.
[20] CBS, D/LO/6/14/1.
[21] Folger Shakespeare Library, W.a.146.

Tenant	Rent	Lowndes' notes
Thomas Robson	£6	
Benjamin Saunders	£8 10s	
Peter Lowndes	£23 6s 8d	Including £2 10s for Phipps' land, 16s 8d for 5 acres bought of Robert Spooner
John Amborow	£2	
William Townsend	£10 14s 7d	
William Gyles	£5 10s	Rose Close
Robert Gibbs	£220	Manor and rectory
Robert Gibbs	£4 10s	A close called Smalidoles and 3 acres
Thomas Foster and William Firth	£5	
Thomas Deely	£5	
John Seaton	£8 10s	
Henry Hughes	£2 15s	
Robert Wyatt	£2 2s 6d	
John Paradine	£3 10s	
Robert Granger	£2 4s	His tenement now demolished
Thomas Hendly	£9	
Richard Seaton	£8	Norton's land
William Gyles sr	£8	Berry Leys and Bates's Piece
William Edmunds	£13	
Nicholas Merwin	£2 5s	Cowmead Close
Nicholas Pleasted	£6 13s 4d	Half of Tuckey Mead
William Short	£2 5s	
Simon Hogson and Henry Townsend	£24	'They have taken the 60 acres lately holden by Wm Sponer decd & Robt Sponer. They are to pay half a year's rent after their time ends.'
William Perkins	£53 10s	'The farm and parcells'
William Perkins	£2	6 acres late Blake's
John Wyatt, Lowndes' brother-in-law paid no rent.		

Table 9: Rents due to William Lowndes at Michaelmas 1699 or Lady Day 1700.

This land was all transferred to Robert Lowndes in 1703, but William also left details of 'my reall estate per annum' in 1722, recording what he was receiving from property acquired in Winslow since 1703.[22] The income was £204, and the tenants' names are mainly those of old Shipton farming families: Townsend, Henley, Glenister, Elliott. The men who sold him their land continued to farm as his tenants. As he knew some of them personally, he probably allowed them to stay at least for their own lifetimes. Smaller rents were received from people who were not professional farmers, such as the lawyer Peter Goldsworth and the brickmaker Matthew Deely. Simon Hogson,[23] a younger son who did not have land of his own but may have been a personal friend of Lowndes, was able to build up a farm as a tenant.

In 1722 Lowndes was getting a return of around 4 per cent on his investment. His friend Richard Hill wanted to rationalise the farms on the land he acquired in Shropshire, but only did this slowly and with consideration for existing tenants.[24]

Lowndes spent money on the farming infrastructure at Winslow. In 1700 he paid for the scouring of Horwood Brook.[25] He paid a 'moletaker' 8¾d. He could be a reasonably generous landlord: in April 1700 he allowed Robert Gibbs £10 off his rent 'in consideration of a bad crop'.[26] Thomas Clements received 5s compensation for 'a sheep kild'. According to accounts covering a year up to December 1723, there were rent arrears of £63 15s, at least one part of which went back to Michaelmas 1721.[27] The rents were collected by John Markham the lawyer, who received 'poundage' for them.

Lowndes' main expenditure was on the new tithe barn, which cost him £205 and was built for the benefit of his son Robert who received the tithes. He also paid for turning three leys over to

---

[22] CBS, D/LO/4/39/1.

[23] See the Hogson family on pages 178-182.

[24] Clay, 'Landlords', 244.

[25] Folger Shakespeare Library, W.a.146 p.28.

[26] Folger Shakespeare Library, W.a.146 p.37.

[27] CBS, D/LO/6/9/1.

growing furze for fuel, and he grew enough apples for his employees to make cider.

Richard Lowndes

Richard Lowndes was brought up with the expectation that he would inherit a country estate, unlike his father. He had no emotional connections with his tenants, unlike his grandfather. It is therefore to be expected that he would have wanted to improve his estate according to the latest scientific thinking, meaning the conversion of arable to grass and the creation of larger farms with higher rents.[28] The Verneys, when purchasing land during Richard's lifetime, deliberately avoided buying open-field land in Granborough, phased out small farms, and concentrated on permanent pasture and dairying.[29] They enclosed Middle Claydon in the seventeenth century and East Claydon in 1737–43 without needing legislation.

A document has survived headed 'An account of the numbers of acres in the common feilds of Winslow & of the names of the owners & occupyers of the same'.[30] It can be dated to about 1743 from the names of the people, but someone continued to update it later, at least until 1760. The fact that it includes only land suggests strongly that information was being collected about the feasibility of enclosure in Winslow: replacing scattered strips of land with consolidated blocks. It provides the first detailed list of landholders since 1610.

According to the list Richard Lowndes held a total of 627 acres in Winslow, 25 in his own hands and the rest let to tenants. Most of the land had been allocated to four tenant farmers:

- William Gibbs senior[31] had 167 acres according to the original document, which increased to 232½ according to the later annotations, mainly by absorbing 50½ acres previously held by

[28] Allen, *Enclosure and the Yeoman*, 121.
[29] Broad, *Transforming English Rural Society*, 229–39.
[30] CBS, BAS 375/22/41/7; www.winslow-history.org.uk/winslow_enclosure_list-of-tenants.shtm.
[31] See the Gibbs family on pages 144–149.

John Cox. He also farmed the glebe land of 60 acres, 27½ acres belonging to others, and 9 acres of his own.

- John Coles had 143 acres. The annotations show that the tenant changed to John Cobb, and the holding grew to 169 acres.
- William Gibbs junior, nephew of William Gibbs senior,[32] had 83 acres. He also farmed John Burrell's 18 acres.
- John Perkins had 58½ acres. He was descended from the Stevens family.

These people were Lowndes' tenants and the terms under which they held are unknown. They must have paid 'rack-rents' (market rents) but they might have been yearly tenants ('tenants at will') or leaseholders for life or for a number of years.[33] The Gibbs family was well established in Winslow but John Coles and John Cobb were apparently newcomers. It therefore seems that Lowndes brought in only one person at a time to farm his lands, and otherwise used locals.

The two largest holdings were bigger than any that had existed previously, and suggest that the estate was already being run on new economic principles. There were twelve other Lowndes tenants of between one and eighteen acres who were either not farmers (they included a lawyer and a doctor) or rented land to supplement their own holdings.

The total acreage in the original document was 1,404, so Lowndes held 45 per cent of the common fields. The other big holdings were:

- Mr Guy: 100½ acres farmed by Richard West. This would be acquired by Lowndes in 1759 and farmed by William Gibbs senior.[34] Most of it had belonged to the Edmunds family in the early seventeenth century.[35] William Guy's wife's grandfather,

---

[32] He was the son of one of William senior's brothers, Richard or Thomas, but the record does not indicate which – he is not shown on the Gibbs family tree.

[33] William Lowndes let some land at Chesham for twelve years in 1705 (CBS, D/LO/6/1/3), but in other cases for only three years

[34] CBS, BAS 376/22 no.117.

[35] CBS, ST78 is headed 'Terror [terrier] of Esq' Guy's land at Winslow' but actually dates from *circa* 1635. See www.winslow-history.org.uk/winslow_terrier.shtm.

John Townsend of Hinton-in-the-Hedges in Northamptonshire, bought the land in 1654, so it was always in absentee ownership.[36] Buying this land raised Richard Lowndes' ownership to 52 per cent of the common fields of Winslow.

- Mr Blake: 91 acres in his own hands. Most of this was 60 freehold acres which had belonged to the Paxton family in the seventeenth century until they were bought in 1683 along with 40 acres of copyhold land by Thomas Blake of Ambrosden in Oxfordshire. It was now held by his son Thomas (1688–1762), who was an owner-occupier and lived in Winslow at the house in Horn Street later known as Blake House (now Tinkers Corner). He described himself as gentleman when he made his will in 1761, and also had land in Steeple Claydon and Great Horwood.

- Late Richard Bigg's land: 80 acres occupied by William Gibbs junior and George Barrett. It was noted later that 25 acres were sold to John Burrell and 55 acres to Richard Lowndes. Bigg described himself as a gentleman when he made his will in 1739,[37] and his interests were in the Post Office, not farming. This is shown by the fact that his 'heriot', the payment due to the lord of the manor on his death and frequently paid with an object, was recorded at the 1740 manor court as a clock, not a beast.[38] The sale by Bigg's son Robert to Burrell is recorded in 1749, and the sale to Lowndes was in 1760.[39] When added to the Guy purchase, this took Lowndes' share to 56 per cent of the common fields.

- The Gyles family:[40] Daniel Gyles held 56 acres and his niece Jane Worrall (née Jane Gyles) 53 acres, which were all farmed by Richard Gibbs. This was mainly land accumulated by Daniel's father but Daniel and Jane had both added to it. Daniel sold 29 acres to Richard Lowndes in 1759. Jane's nephew

---

[36] WMC 22 June 1654; see www.winslow-history.org.uk/winslow_court1654.shtm.

[37] TNA, PROB 11/703/442.

[38] WMC 10 October 1740, see www.winslow-history.org.uk/winslow_court1740.shtm

[39] WMC 22 June 1749, see www.winslow-history.org.uk/winslow_court1749.shtm; CBS, BAS 376/22/117.

[40] For the Gyles family and a family tree see pages 84-94.

Thomas Aldridge, a silversmith in London, held a further 44 acres, which seem to have been occupied by Richard Cox.[41] Another Gyles family member, described as Mr Norman (William Norman of Henley-on-Thames, the son of Martha Gyles) held 42 acres with six different occupiers. Thomas Foster, Jane Worrall's brother-in-law, had a further 6 acres in his own hands, and William Gyles her cousin had 4 acres occupied by William Windmill.

No-one else had a holding of more than 20 acres. Even without the distorting effects of the Lowndes estate, land ownership in Winslow was very much concentrated in the hands of a small number of people who were mainly absentees and, with the exception of Thomas Blake, did not farm their own land. This is part of a general process of 'acquisition of peasant property by large landowners' during the eighteenth century.[42]

There were, however, 33 other holdings of 19 acres or less, mostly described as being in their owners' own hands. People such as the lawyers Nicholas Merwin and Peter Goldsworth and the apothecary William Hobbs were probably interested in pasture for their horses, not in part-time farming. The total of 33 owners of land is almost identical to the equivalent number in 1610. It was the larger holdings (seventeen in 1610) which had mostly been absorbed by the Lowndes estate.

William Gibbs senior had the biggest agricultural operation in Winslow since the sixteenth century, but when he made his will in 1765 he described himself as husbandman, and both the will and manor court records make him sound like a smallholder because of the little copyhold land he owned.[43] He was 'aged and infirm' by that time apparently in his mid-seventies, and had probably retired. He had six sons who became famous as the bell-ringing brothers.[44] Five of them became tradesmen, not farmers, and despite farming on a large scale William was not in a position to pass the business on to the next generation.

---

[41] The reading of his surname is uncertain.

[42] Allen, *Enclosure and the Yeoman*, 78.

[43] HALS, 205AW8.

[44] See pages 144-149 for the Gibbs family and their family tree.

The Shipton Enclosure

Shipton was surveyed for parliamentary enclosure in 1744–45. By that time Richard Lowndes held 86 per cent of the total 640 acres as well as the great tithes. This contrasts with 1610 when there had been eight separate holdings of 15 acres or more. Four of the nine Winslow residents who paid tax in 1663 lived in Shipton.[45] Modestly-sized owner-occupied farms survived with families which regularly intermarried and witnessed each other's wills.

The change in balance from a hamlet of yeoman farmers to a near monopoly of one owner was due to William Lowndes, who started buying land in Shipton in 1695. Soon after 1700 he had acquired more than half the total acreage in the open fields of Shipton, and continued to expand, buying out the established families.

Two more independent farms in Shipton disappeared in the 1730s. Henry Townsend's death was reported in 1723, when despite earlier sales he still had 50 acres of land.[46] This all came to Richard Lowndes eventually after further deaths and sales. In this case, there had still been a viable farm despite earlier sales, but lack of a male heir in Winslow meant that it already had an absentee owner.

John Wyatt of Shipton was one of William Lowndes' agents in Winslow as well as his tenant. He had children by his first wife, Lowndes' sister Rebecca,[47] and by his second wife Anne. He died intestate in 1720. John must have owned the 18½ acres in Shipton which were sold to Richard Lowndes by his widow and children.[48] His son John became a lawyer, and was deputy steward of the manor in 1740.

The Bowler family had been established in Shipton since 1664, when Charles Bowler of Longwick bought 70 acres.[49] Most of this was sold to William Lowndes in 1698, but Charles Bowler of

---

[45] www.winslow-history.org.uk/winslow_subsidy1663.shtm.

[46] WMC 25 October 1723, see www.winslow-history.org.uk/winslow_court1723.shtm.

[47] See pages 144-149 for the Gibbs family and their family tree.

[48] WMC 22 October 1733, see www.winslow-history.org.uk/winslow_court1733.shtm.

[49] CBS, BAS 376/22/12.

Winslow, cordwainer, grandson of the first Charles, still owned 17 acres when he died in 1735.[50] He left four acres each to four younger children (two sons and two daughters) and an acre of 'furze-ground' to his wife, having already made a settlement on his eldest son. This must have been another four acres, as the five Bowler siblings held 21 acres between them in 1745. They decided to hold the land jointly rather than separating it according to their father's will, and the land called Bowlers Ground was still held in 21 undivided shares in 1802. Charles, the eldest brother, may therefore have been farming on a small scale independently of the Lowndes estate in 1745.

Richard Lowndes probably owned more than 80 per cent of the open fields of Shipton by 1733 and bought more from Anne Wyatt in 1740. The consent of the owners of between 75 and 80 per cent of the land was required for the enclosure process to begin, and the opposition of numerous small proprietors could not prevent it.[51]

There is no evidence that there was any opposition at Shipton, but apparently the enclosure could not be achieved by general agreement as happened in some places.

Richard Lowndes became MP for Buckinghamshire in 1741 after an unsuccessful attempt in 1734. Parliamentary enclosure began in Buckinghamshire with Ashendon in 1738 and Wotton Underwood in 1742, moved by Richard Grenville, the future Earl Temple, who was the other MP for Buckinghamshire.[52] Shipton was the third enclosure in the county, and was not followed by the next, Swanbourne, until 1761. These first three enclosures were all of places where one landowner dominated. Grenville and Lowndes belonged to opposite political groups, but were able to cooperate on matters of self-interest.

On 19 January 1744, a petition for enclosure was presented to the House of Commons, stating that:

---

[50] HALS, 172 AW1.
[51] Allen, *Enclosure and the Yeoman*, 28; M E Turner, 'The cost of parliamentary enclosure in Buckinghamshire', *Agricultural History Review* 21 (1973), 35–46, 35.
[52] Michael Reed, *The Buckinghamshire Landscape* (London: Hodder and Stoughton, 1979), 201.

'the lands of each proprietor lie intermixed and dispersed over the said fields in small parcels; which, by experience, hath been found inconvenient and detrimental to the respective owners and occupiers thereof; and that the said common fields, so long as the same remain open and unenclosed, are, in a great measure, incapable of improvement.'

The Bill moved rapidly through all stages of parliamentary procedure, with some presumably minor amendments by a House of Commons committee. Royal assent was given on 22 March.[53]

The Act provided for the vicar to receive land worth £30 a year in lieu of his small tithes.[54] Such an arrangement was normal in parliamentary enclosures.[55] He was awarded a block of 37 acres south of the road to Swanbourne.

The main requirements for holders of the other new allotments were that they must accept them within six months, and their land must 'be inclosed, hedged, ditched, and fenced out' within eighteen months at their own expense.[56] The costs of passing and executing the Act were to be borne by Richard Lowndes.[57]

The commissioners appointed by the Act were George Southam of Barton Hartshorn gentleman, Thomas Mayne of Oving gentleman, John Anstee of Swanbourne schoolmaster, Edward Elliott of Mursley yeoman and William Parkins of Shipton yeoman. This number of people was usual in early enclosures, although it was later reduced.[58] Southam had some property interests in Winslow and was the brother or uncle of the recently arrived Winslow lawyer Ferdinando Southam. William Parkins was from an old Shipton family. If the commissioners were intended to represent different interests, as was often the

---

[53] *Journal of the House of Lords*, 22 March 1744; www.winslow-history.org.uk/winslow_enclosure_shipton.shtm.

[54] *An Act for Dividing and Inclosing Certain Common Fields in the Hamlet of Shipton, in the Parish of Winslow, in the County of Bucks*, 2.

[55] Allen, *Enclosure and the Yeoman*, 28.

[56] *An Act for Dividing*, 4.

[57] *An Act for Dividing*, 6.

[58] W E Tate, 'Oxfordshire enclosure commissioners, 1737–1856', *Journal of Modern History* 23 (1951), 137–45, 139.

case,[59] Parkins might have acted for the proprietors other than Lowndes.

The survey was completed by 25 March 1745; Charles Bowler the younger was one of the surveyors. The Enclosure Award was dated 29 April 1745. The commissioners reported that the area to be enclosed was 595 acres 1 rood 9 perches. These were statute acres rather than the traditional measurements, hence the different total. Of this they allocated 81 per cent to Richard Lowndes, 6 per cent to the vicar and 13 per cent shared between all the other landowners.

Because the vicar's tithes had been converted to land, Lowndes' proportion of the acreage actually fell slightly from 86 per cent. He received all the Cowpasture, which was about 104 acres, and nearly all of the former Blagrove Field. Other people's allocations largely adjoined the hamlet of Shipton and the existing roads into it, for reasons of access. The commissioners seem to have made some effort to work with existing holdings, with the result that the post-enclosure landscape of Shipton did not contain many straight lines like those created when commissioners elsewhere 'laid their rulers straight across the map'.[60]

It was now possible for Richard Lowndes to reorganise his land in Shipton into blocks, and probably to turn most of it over to pasture and dairy farming, which was the usual intention of early enclosures in this part of England.[61] Several surviving pieces of ridge and furrow indicate a change of use made probably at the time of enclosure. The reorganisation of the Lowndes Shipton estate proved in part to be temporary, because after Winslow was enclosed in 1767 they created two new farms where the Winslow and Shipton field systems joined.

The evidence for Lowndes tenants comes mainly from the surviving Land Tax returns which begin in 1781,[62] and there is no direct information about how their land had been farmed before

---

[59] Tate, 'Oxfordshire enclosure commissioners', 143.
[60] Read, *Buckinghamshire Landscape*, 202, referring to Padbury. There are details and a map at www.winslow-history.org.uk/winslow_enclosure_shipton.shtm.
[61] Allen, *Enclosure and the Yeoman*, 32–34, 110.
[62] CBS, Q/RPL/5/2

then, but the conservative policy of retaining tenants and blocks of land may go back to the 1745 enclosure at Shipton. After 1767 there was no reason why Lowndes property had to be organised according to the traditional division of the Winslow and Shipton field systems, and some of their tenants had land in both, but the Land Tax continued to have a separate Shipton section.

In 1781 the Lowndes land in Shipton was divided between five tenants. By that time the estate had added about 33 acres to its 1745 allocation. If the relative size of the Land Tax payments represents the acreage of the farms, the biggest tenant was Edward Hillyer with about 168 acres.[63] Various notices about sales of contents show that this was primarily a dairy farm.

The farmhouse became known as Red Hall (*see Figure 23*), a name first recorded in 1809.[64] This is a late-eighteenth-century building according to its Grade II listing report and is not shown on the Jefferys map of Buckinghamshire which was surveyed in

Figure 23: Red Hall Farm, formerly part of the Lowndes estate in Shipton

---

[63] A similar method is used for estimating acreage by Allen, *Enclosure and the Yeoman*, 80. The farm sizes should only be treated as rough estimates. The farmhouse and farm buildings would have added to the tax assessment of the land.

[64] *Northampton Mercury*, 25 March 1809.

1766–68.[65] A new access had to be created from the road to Swanbourne. When the Winslow Hall estate was sold in 1897, Red Hall Farm covered 135 acres.[66]

The second largest unit in Shipton was occupied by George Henley in 1781, and the Land Tax suggests it covered about 127 acres.[67] He was probably the George Henley who was buried at Swanbourne in 1792;[68] his relationship to the old Shipton family of the same name is uncertain. Robert Rand was tenant from 1859 and provided the name by which the farm is now known.[69] In 1897 Rands Farm included 174 acres, as by then it had absorbed a smaller farm.[70] Rands Farm was one of the old Shipton farmhouses, the only one which retained its original function. It was adjacent to the road, although realignment since then means that it is now set well back. It is a seventeenth-century timber framed house with an eighteenth-century dairy at the rear, refronted and extended in the mid-nineteenth century.

The immediate effects of enclosure on the rest of Shipton are difficult to see because the court rolls for the next twenty years are only partially preserved. Richard Lowndes was not the only one who turned the land to pasture; when Thomas Bowler sold his share of Bowlers Ground to his brother it was described as 'now laid down with grass seeds'.[71] There were thirteen enclosure allocations to individual owners, some involving more than one piece of land. The largest was 21 acres for the Bowlers, and the smallest was slightly under an acre for Thomas Whiteaves.

There were no immediate sales by people who could not afford the costs of enclosing their allotments, as happened elsewhere. That must be due to the fact that some of the owners had other sources of wealth: Matthew and William Hobbs were

[65] *Buckinghamshire in the 1760s and 1820s* (Aylesbury: BAS, 2000), 4.
[66] See www.winslow-history.org.uk/winslow_winslow_hall_sale.shtm: Winslow Hall Estate Sale Catalogue.
[67] CBS, Q/RPL/5/2: 181 Land Tax Return.
[68] Swnbourne Parish Register, 1792.
[69] CBS, PR 237/5/1: Church Rate Book.
[70] See www.winslow-history.org.uk/winslow_winslow_hall_sale.shtm: Winslow Hall Estate Sale Catalogue.
[71] WMC 26 October 1748, see www.winslow-history.org.uk/winslow_court1748.shtm.

apothecaries, William Guy owned land elsewhere, Richard Bigg worked for the Post Office.

The Lowndes estate gradually absorbed some of the small allotments, starting in 1759. The rest of the land was eventually acquired from the original owners or their successors by various propertied Winslow residents who were mainly interested in using it for grazing. It has been noted that there was a trend for solicitors and other professionals to buy out allottees and retain them as tenants, but that did not happen at Shipton.[72] The doctor John Turner and the lawyer James Burnham bought land in Shipton in the 1770s but did not let it, and those who sold it to them were in any case not farmers themselves.[73]

The Lowndes family was interested in the land in Shipton, but not the houses. William Lowndes V recorded that the house he had bought from John Mayne was demolished. In the nineteenth century Shipton became notorious for bad housing (*see for example Figure 21*). The changed use of old houses was not directly the effect of enclosure, as most independent farmers had already disappeared, but the general trend was for the former owner-occupied farmhouses to come into the hands of people who did not live in them.

The Winslow Enclosure

Richard Lowndes handed Winslow Hall and the manor of Winslow over to his son William Lowndes V at the time of William's marriage in January 1766. The legal procedure to enclose Winslow began within a month, and more effective management of the estate might have been a precondition for his father-in-law Thomas Goostrey to provide his daughter's marriage portion, which enabled the mortgage on the Lowndes estate, taken out nearly 50 years earlier in 1728, to be paid off.

The manor court rolls for the 1760s are poorly preserved but it is clear that the Lowndes family was still acquiring land: a notebook belonging to William records the acquisition of about

---

[72] Turner, 'Parliamentary enclosure and landownership change', 574.
[73] WMC 13 July 1771 and 19 October 1772 (CBS, D82/1).

214 acres between 1757 and 1765.[74] He bought more after the enclosure process had begun.

However it seems unlikely that this was a way of removing opponents: the major vendors had by then either moved away (Daniel and William Gyles, Robert Bigg), never been resident (William and Mary Guy) or belonged to the Lowndes family (Richard's younger brother Robert).

There is in fact no clear evidence of opposition to enclosure at Winslow, and if there was any it was from people without an influential voice. No one went to the House of Commons committee to object.[75] Only the freeholders and copyholders were consulted, of course, not their tenants or employees or people who had traditional rights. As Arthur Young wrote, 'I know of no country where the people [as opposed to the wealthy] are not against enclosures'.[76]

The enclosure of Winslow must have been under consideration from about 1743, but it took another twenty years after Shipton was enclosed, and followed soon after Swanbourne, whose Act passed in 1762. Enclosure was not always a straightforward process even when it got to the stage of a Bill being introduced in Parliament, and a Bill for Quainton was later promoted in 1801 but the parish was not enclosed for another 40 years.[77] However, things proceeded smoothly for Lowndes.

The Winslow Inclosure Bill was presented to the House of Commons for the first time on 14 February 1766 by William Drake of Shardeloes, MP for Amersham[78] It went through all stages and received royal assent on 18 March. It was closely followed by an equivalent bill for Little Horwood using similar wording, presented by Earl Verney of Claydon[79] and receiving royal assent on 11 April.

[74] CBS, BAS 376/22/117.

[75] *Journal of the House of Commons*, 28 February 1766.

[76] Quoted by J A Yelling, *Common Field and Enclosure in England 1450–1850* (London: Macmillan, 1977), 214.

[77] Turner, 'The cost of parliamentary enclosure', 36.

[78] *Journal of the House of Commons*, 14 February 1766.

[79] *Journal of the House of Commons*, 24 February 1766.

The preamble of the Act states that John Rawbone, as vicar, held the small tithes and glebe lands, while William Lowndes had the great tithes and about 840 acres, which would be 60 per cent of the land in the common fields. The Act names Rawbone, Samuel Norman, Thomas Blake, John Budd, William Burrell, William Hobbs, Benjamin Ingram, William Aldridge, John Turner, Stephen Gibbs the elder and Thomas Tattam as the principal other holders of 'unenclosed lands and grounds'.

The commissioners were Reverend John Lord of Drayton Parslow, Francis Burton of Aynho, Thomas Green of Whitchurch, Thomas Taylor of Swanbourne and John Fairbrother of Helmdon. Four of the same men were appointed as commissioners for Little Horwood. A survey was to be made by 1 September. Enclosed land was to be allocated 'as near as conveniently may be to their respective messuages, dwellings or homesteads, or farm houses of their respective tenants, having a due regard to the quality as well as quantity of the land'.

The vicar was to receive land worth £31 6s a year as compensation for the small tithes, as well as an equivalent to the glebe land. His allotments were to be enclosed 'by quickset hedges and ditches, or other proper mounds and fences' at the other proprietors' expense. This was a detail added by the House of Lords in other cases.[80] William Lowndes was to receive land equivalent to the value of the great tithes; no figure was suggested. Copyhold land was to remain subject to the same payment and dues as before, and old quit-rents were to be transferred to the new holdings.

The commissioners could set out public roads which would be 60 feet broad between their ditches, to be maintained at the expense of the inhabitants, but they could not alter the turnpike. The current Furze Lane and Verney Road were created to provide access to new plots, and the original road leading to Addington was blocked off, leaving only Western Lane.[81] A road which

---

[80] W E Tate, *The English Village Community and the Enclosure Movement* (London: Gollancz, 1967), 102.
[81] Terry Foley and Julian Hunt, *The Archive Photographs Series: Winslow* (second edition, Cheltenham: The History Press, 2019), 42.

continued the present Burleys Road to join up with Great Horwood Road and had provided access to the windmill was also superfluous; the windmill had burned down in 1760.[82] Former roads could be included in new allotments, and proprietors could put gates across public roads to keep out sheep and cattle.

There was the usual requirement for the new enclosures to be 'inclosed, hedged, ditched, drained, and fenced' within twelve months at the owners' expense. Anyone who wanted to keep sheep or lambs on their new enclosure during the first five years must 'at their own expence fence their neighbours quicksets' to prevent damage. Proprietors could borrow up to £2 per acre on their land to meet the expenses.

Allotments must be accepted within six months. Anyone wishing to exchange land could do so with the commissioners' consent, regardless of any wills, settlements or other incumbrances which would be transferred to the new property. Four exchanges are recorded in the Enclosure Award,[83] all involving William Lowndes disposing of small pieces of land.

The commissioners would be paid a guinea a day on top of expenses. The costs of the Act, unlike the Shipton Act, were to be borne by all the owners proportionately. There are no surviving accounts for the commissioners' original meetings but they had to attend the Buckinghamshire Quarter Sessions in April 1767 to hear an appeal from Constance Salisbury.[84] For this the five commissioners and their clerk stayed at the White Hart in Aylesbury for two nights, which somehow required eighteen breakfasts. Hay and corn for their six horses came to £1 0s 5d, beer and tobacco 11s 10d, and wine and brandy £2 0s 3d. In total their stay at the inn cost £8 5s, which was paid to the landlord by James Burnham, the lawyer who acted as their clerk.

Enclosure was an expensive business. Tate reproduces an inn bill for £2 11s 11d for some commissioners in Yorkshire and

---

[82] *Imperial Magazine*, 15 February 1760.
[83] www.winslow-history.org.uk/winslow_enclosure_winslow.shtm: Winslow Enclosure Award 1767.
[84] CBS, BAS 375/22/43/8. The appeal was unsuccessful (CBS, Q/SM/5.).

comments that it 'does not seem at all excessive for three skilled men, presumably relaxing after a hard day's work on the moor',[85] but the Winslow bill was for six men who had spent a day at the Quarter Sessions.

The final Award is dated 28 May 1767, fourteen months after the Act was passed. It refers to expenses of £235 for laying the enclosed lands down with grass seed. The expenses of executing the Award were £864 of which William Lowndes' share was £748 and the smallest proprietor's was 8s. Seven other people had to pay more than £20. The charges were between 19s and 22s per acre for the small proprietors. William Lowndes paid slightly over 21s per acre and Thomas Blake well over 23s. The poor were charitably charged only 16s.[86] This was rather expensive for the time but much cheaper than later Buckinghamshire enclosures.[87]

The Award gave William Lowndes 707 acres, including 184 in compensation for the great tithes. This was about 61 per cent of the former open fields, only a small increase in his overall share. The other major landowners had their holdings reduced in proportion, but the statute acre was significantly smaller than the measurement used before so the reduction is not as much as it appears.

Thomas Blake (1715–84) was the only one of these who was a full-time farmer based in Winslow. His land went down from 86 to 47 acres. Enclosure gave him a block of land adjacent to Granborough and Claydon Roads which he was able to farm from his existing house in Horn Street, which already had a large close attached to it. He also owned land in Great Horwood and Granborough according to his will, and left his property jointly to his two daughters. He styled himself a gentleman in his will, but he was more like a yeoman farmer, the last independent one in Winslow.

---

[85] Tate, *The English Village Community*, 211–12, pl.X.
[86] www.winslow-history.org.uk/winslow_enclosure_winslow.shtm: Winslow Enclosure Award 1767.
[87] Turner, 'The cost of parliamentary enclosure', 40–41, gives an average cost in Buckinghjamshire of 78s per acre in the early nineteenth century but only 16.8s for ten enclosures in the 1760s.

Figure 24: Blake House in Horn Street (centre). The land allotted to Thomas Blake was to the right.

Samuel Norman and William Aldridge, who received 29 and 43 acres respectively, were the descendants of the Gyles family, from whom they had inherited their land. William Burrell, who received 27 acres, was the main example in 1767 of a trend which became more significant later: farmers from surrounding villages owning land in Winslow. Some of it had been inherited from his father, a Winslow butcher, and Burrell had apparently moved from Winslow to Hogshaw, presumably as a tenant farmer because his will does not mention any land there.[88]

In 1768 he mortgaged his enclosure allocation to Benjamin Ingram along with his other property.[89] The land in Winslow was put up for sale after Burrell's death in 1776, when it was said to be 'let to an exceeding good tenant, at the rent of forty-five pounds per annum'. It was bought by James Burnham as an investment.[90]

William Hobbs, a Winslow apothecary, received 25 acres. Some of the land held before the enclosure had belonged to his

[88] CBS, D/A/Wf/101/162.
[89] CBS, D82/1 page 34.
[90] *Oxford Journal*, 28 December 1776.

wife Anne. About 1743 it had been partly occupied by William Parkins. Hobbs also owned land in Little Horwood and Shipton and some old closes in Winslow.[91] He mortgaged two of his allotments to Newman Williatt of Great Horwood in 1767 'with the approbation of the commissioners'.[92]

William and Anne had no surviving children and each left their land to cousins when they died in 1771 and 1773 respectively. William's was sold in 1773 to Robert Bigg of the General Post Office, London, when the tenant of both William and Anne's land was Joseph Piddington who is described elsewhere as a yeoman.[93] In the 1781 Land Tax he was William Lowndes' second biggest tenant in Winslow.

Benjamin Ingram (1699?–1778), who was allocated 22 acres, was usually recorded as a victualler and kept the Sow and Pigs. He was recorded earlier as a dealer or chapman, but was also a farmer and entrepreneur. He owned Bell Close and a number of houses in Winslow, and had property in Granborough, Stewkley and Aylesbury. In the list made around 1743 Ingram had only two acres, which he bought in 1742. He also bought six acres from Thomas Aldridge, but his other acquisitions, which were possibly foreclosures on mortgages, are not in surviving court rolls.[94]

Ingram was not a native of Winslow and the source of his money is unknown, but he was probably investing non-agricultural income in property. He bought William Aldridge's land in 1779 which made him the third biggest landowner in Winslow.[95] The land was kept in the ownership of his descendants but was let to various tenants and never formed a farm. It was eventually inherited by a great-grandson in Leicestershire whose agents began trying to sell it in 1813.[96]

Most of the proprietors of smaller pieces of land were people

[91] www.winslow-history.org.uk/winslow_will_hobbs1771b.shtm: The will of William Hobbs.

[92] CBS, D82/1 page 3.

[93] CBS, D82/1 p.166.

[94] WMC 22 October 1744, see www.winslow-history.org.uk/winslow_court1744.shtm.

[95] CBS, D82/1 page 379.

[96] www.winslow-history.org.uk/twentiethc-1813ingramsale.shtm.

whose income came from elsewhere, such as the surgeon's widow Catherine Turner and the grocer Francis Collins. Some were absentees, such as Constance Salisbury of Bloomsbury in London and Elizabeth Seaton of Peterborough.

There were a few people who received allocations of between two and 14 acres for whom the land probably formed part of their livelihood. Robert Parrott, who was left with a holding of almost 10 acres next to Granborough Bridge, was a dairyman of East Claydon. The land would have been a useful acquisition for a farm in an adjacent parish, and the Land Tax always records it as in his own occupation. He left it to his son in his will.[97]

George Maydon was a butcher in Winslow from about 1750. He was allotted about 4½ acres on the north side of Claydon Road. In his will, proved in 1769, he left it to his wife and eldest son, who still had it in his own occupation in the early nineteenth century, presumably as an adjunct of his business.[98]

The people who received the smallest allotments cannot have had any agricultural use for them except as grazing, or to extend an existing close or garden. Robert Crockett, stonemason, and William Firth, brazier, each received less than half an acre. Crockett's was next to his house; his widow sold it to the surgeon Thomas Prentice in 1773 and it eventually became a building plot on the west side of the High Street.[99]

Firth's, on the other side of the street, was also used for building in the early nineteenth century. Robert Gibbs' 16 perches was adjacent to his existing home close, and John Perkins received two acres adjoining his home close in Shipton.[100]

Other than Firth, these people probably accepted a substantial reduction in the quantity of their land in return for having it in a convenient position.

---

[97] CBS, D/A/Wf/115/80.
[98] HALS, 207AW6.
[99] www.winslow-history.org.uk/twentiethc-1806pightle.shtm.
[100] This was known as Chain Furlong Close after enclosure.

The effects of enclosure

Enclosure gave William Lowndes, great-grandson of William Lowndes the Secretary to the Treasury, the whole of the eastern side of Winslow's former open field system, adjoining the already enclosed land of Shipton.

This led to the creation of two new farms, eventually known as Shipton and Magpie Farms, at points where Winslow and Shipton land joined, and some of the newly-enclosed Winslow land was added to existing Shipton farms. The house which became Shipton Farm is timber-framed rather than entirely brick, and seems to have been dismantled in its original location and rebuilt on a new site.[101]

The other main blocks of Lowndes lands were the south-west corner of the parish, which became Tuckey Farm, and the north-west corner, where Dudslow Farm eventually became Redfield. Land Tax returns from 1781 onwards[102] show that there was a gradual process of combining holdings.

The largest tenant in Winslow in 1781 was Thomas Ingram of Tuckey Farm, probably with something approaching 250 acres. By 1786 he had incorporated a farm previously rented by Robert Parrott, adding nearly 40 per cent to his land. Samuel Cole of Tuckey had 301 acres in 1851, and at 315 acres it was the biggest farm in Winslow at the 1897 sale of the Winslow Hall estate. At least some of the Lowndes tenants must have had leases for life because they appear in a list of Quarter Sessions jurors in 1769 for which that was the minimum property qualification.[103]

Enclosure led to a new system of record-keeping by the manor court. From October 1767 all copyhold property transactions were recorded in court books rather than on individual rolls, and a complete sequence survives.[104] It is therefore possible to see how much effect enclosure had on the land market.

---

[101] Foley and Hunt, *Winslow*, 24.
[102] CBS, Q/RPL/5/2.
[103] CBS, JB/1.
[104] CBS, D82/1–10.

In 1767 there were two sales and one mortgage affecting three owners and 30 acres; the purchasers were Newman Williatt of Great Horwood, yeoman, and William Verney of Winslow, glazier, who sold his land in 1774. In 1768 35½ acres were mortgaged by three owners. In the following years there were only transactions affecting small parcels, until people started selling land which they had inherited from the original allottees: Susanna Hawkins sold 9½ acres in 1773 and Susanna Merwin's heir sold 11½ acres to John Bennett of East Claydon, dairyman, in 1775.[105]

In the first ten years of the new system, enclosure does not seem to have had a significant impact on land ownership. The sales which took place were not to other Winslow landholders but either to farmers and landowners from elsewhere or to Winslow traders and professionals.

Benjamin Ingram became mortgagee of some of the land and in 1778, the year of his death, he acquired ownership of William Burrell's 28 acres through non-payment, and his son sold it on to the lawyer James Burnham.[106] Burnham gradually acquired land and houses in Winslow, Shipton and elsewhere, but not directly through enclosure. The 1795 Land Tax record[107] suggests that he was the biggest property owner after the Selby-Lowndes estate and the church.

Reverend William Cole of Bletchley, who knew Richard Lowndes, identified an unintended consequence of the creation of larger tenanted farms. He wrote in his diary on 16 April 1766, probably with Winslow in mind as there were few other local examples:[108]

'The times are so hard, small farms so difficult to be met with, the spirit of inclosing, & accumulating farms together, making it very difficult for young people to marry, as was used; as I know by experience this parish, where several farmers' sons are forced to live at home with their fathers, tho' much wanting

---

[105] WMC 12 October 1767, 25 October 1768, 25 October 1773 and 27 October 1775 – all in CBS, D82/1.
[106] WMC 27 October 1775 and 30 March 1779 – in CBS, D82/1.
[107] CBS, Q/RPL/5/16.
[108] *Blecheley Diary*, 41.

to marry & settle, for want of proper places to settle at, which sufficiently shews the baneful practice of inclosures …'

In the South Midlands area studied by Allen, the average size of a farm in an enclosed parish at the end of the eighteenth century was 122–124 acres. Landlords wanted the higher rents which they could achieve from amalgamating small farms, whether they were enclosed or not, and according to Allen the main effect of enclosure was not so much greater productivity as the redistribution of agricultural income in landlords' favour.[109]

The enclosure of Winslow and Shipton did not entirely remove agriculture to purpose-built farms in the middle of the fields. Tuckey, Shipton and Red Hall Farms were new creations which persisted, and had substantial houses according to the 1897 Winslow Hall estate sale catalogue with three to five bedrooms, cellars, dairies and attics. But Magpie Farm was soon reduced to a labourer's house, and some old centrally-placed farmhouses remained in use: the Blakes' farm, the buildings which became Curtis Farm in Sheep Street, and Rands Farm.[110]

In the 1851 Census there were five other people describing themselves as farmers of 50 acres or more who lived in the middle of Winslow, although their farmyards were probably not attached to their houses. Three of the farms offered for sale in 1897 did not come with farmhouses.[111]

The enclosure of Winslow was the beginning of a widespread trend in north Buckinghamshire. In 1770, Dr Bridle, rector of Hardwick, wrote to Richard Lowndes encouraging him to promote enclosure there, and said:[112]

'… an act is already depending for ye inclosure of Aylesbury Field; a petition for an act to inclose Whitchurch is generally subscribed; another at North Marston is now in agitation; &

---

[109] Allen, *Enclosure and the Yeoman*, 181.
[110] See www.winslow-history.org.uk/winslow_winslow_hall_sale.shtm: Winslow Hall Estate Sale Catalogue.
[111] See www.winslow-history.org.uk/winslow_winslow_hall_sale.shtm: Winslow Hall Estate Sale Catalogue.
[112] BL, Add.Ms. 37069 f.231.

most of ye other fields in ye neighbourhood are already inclos'd ...'

Lowndes' cousin Thomas Lowndes wrote to him in 1771 concerning a meeting held at Newport Pagnell about the enclosure of North Crawley, where he was rector.[113] A possible opponent had said 'that if he was not cursed for not agreeing to the bill while he lived, his son would curse him hereafter'. Thomas believed 'in general it is the small proprietors that are the greatest objectors to inclosing'. Another letter on 8 January 1772 informed Richard that there was a four-fifths majority for enclosure, and it proceeded.[114]

The agriculturist Arthur Young travelled through Winslow soon after enclosure and regarded it as a great success.[115] He found that land had previously been let at 14s per acre but was now at 28s for arable and £2–£3 for grass, with the poor rate at 3s in the pound. He thought this showed why the rest of the Vale of Aylesbury should be enclosed. He believed that rare cases of farmers being unable to pay their rent were due to overworking the land and recommended an eight-course rotation system.

Young's view was optimistic, because a heavy increase in the poor rate followed. Early in the next century it was reported to be 7s in the pound.[116]

Enclosure did not have much direct effect on the structure of land ownership in Winslow, which had already changed in the early eighteenth century. Landless farm workers were hit hardest, as observed by Frederic Morton Eden:[117]

'The rise of the [Poor] Rates is chiefly ascribed to the enclosure of common fields; which, it is said has lessened the number of farms, and, from the conversion of arable into pasture, has much reduced the demand for labourers. An old man of the parish says, that, before the enclosures took place,

---

[113] BL, Add.Ms. 37069 ff.232–233.

[114] BL, Add.Ms. 37069 f.234, Thomas Holt to Lowndes, Newport Pagnell.

[115] Arthur Young, *The Farmer's Tour through the East of England* (1771), 1.25–26.

[116] Rev St John Priest, *A General View of Agriculture in Buckinghamshire* (1813), 400 (appendix by Richard Parkinson).

[117] *The State of the Poor*, 2.30

land did not let for 10s an acre, and that, when he was young, the name of roundsman [someone who had to go round from farm to farm looking for work] was unknown in the parish. It must however be considered, that, now a great part of the labour done in the parish is paid for out of the Poor's Rate, in money given to roundsmen. The rent of land is from a guinea to £2 15s an acre.'[118]

Godber comments: 'The general standard of living was rising, but relatively that of the cottagers was declining.'[119] Winslow had twelve farmhouses and 250 cottages in 1813.[120] It was the abandonment of arable farming which was mainly responsible for the lack of employment.

Eden thought there were only 200 acres of arable land left in Winslow, although the slightly later survey by Reverend St John Priest put it at 300, but this was still only 12 per cent of the land.[121] Priest commented that grain and sheep had decreased, cattle and pigs, for pork and bacon, had increased. In Buckinghamshire as a whole, there was reported to have been a 33 per cent decline in wheat acreage by 1808 due to enclosure.[122] Gleaning was not directly abolished, but its value to the poor was much reduced by the loss of arable.[123]

Enclosure created temporary work with fencing, hedging and erection of new buildings, but it left an over-supply of labour afterwards: 39 men classified as servants and 64 as labourers in Winslow in the 1798 Posse Comitatus.[124] Dairy farming, which now predominated, provided more work for female members of the farmer's family and less for male employees, even if they

---

[118] Rents had not risen much by 1897: some larger farms were not producing much more than a guinea per acre. Yelling, *Common Field and Enclosure*, 227, quotes this passage and notes: 'Whether this ascription was entirely accurate is now impossible to determine.'

[119] Godber, *History of Bedfordshire*, 369.

[120] Priest, *General View*, 386.

[121] Priest, *General View*, 372.

[122] Yelling, *Common Field and Enclosure*, 194–95.

[123] Yelling, *Common Field and Enclosure*, 227.

[124] Beckett (editor) *Buckinghamshire Posse Comitatus*, 210-13.

tended in Buckinghamshire to be the ones who milked the cows.[125]

The extent to which Winslow depended on agriculture had already declined for other reasons and independent farmers were nearly extinct, but enclosure created a landscape of isolated farmhouses and fields made inaccessible by hawthorn hedges which is still recognisable more than 250 years later.

---

[125] Broad, 'English dairying', 106.

Winslow families
10: **The Tomlin and Shaw family**

The Tomlins (or Thomlyns) were one of Winslow's most powerful families in the fifteenth century, producing a vicar and for a time exercising a minor reign of terror over their neighbours.[1] Several Tomlins still owned property in 1556.[2] In 1610 William Tomlin had a messuage and 19 acres in Winslow, and three Tomlins had houses and small holdings of land in Shipton.[3] One member of the family, Walter, was – rather unexpectedly for someone from Winslow – a mariner in London when he died in 1644.[4]

William Tomlin of Shipton (1641–69) was the son of Anthony Tomlin, who died in 1642, and his wife Ellen. William was described as a labourer when his probate inventory was drawn up.[5] His goods were worth £18 including £10 in money, and he lived in a house with three rooms (hall house, hall chamber, chamber) and a barn. He only had one trundle bed to sleep on. He had one ridge of land sown with wheat, and some peas in the barn (this was in December).

In 1708 his only son **Edward Tomlin** (1665–1713), who had been four when his father died, sought admission at the manor court to his father's messuage, acre of land and common for one cow, because of the death of his mother in 1707.[6] He also inherited from his mother 6 acres and two cow's commons.

---

[1] *WMCB*, 754.
[2] David Noy, *Winslow in 1556: The survey of the manor* (Aylesbury: BAS 2013) 52 and 59.
[3] CBS, WF538/44.
[4] TNA, PROB 11/192/250; www.winslow-history.org.uk/winslow_will_tomlyn1645.shtm.
[5] HALS, A25/3851.
[6] WMC 21 April 1708, see www.winslow-history.org.uk/winslow_court1708.shtm.

Edward, a carpenter of Shipton, sold his father's land and another 4 acres in 1708–09.[7] He had married in 1699 and had seven children, including one born after his death. He died in 1713 having made a deathbed surrender of his remaining house and land, which were to be sold for the payment of his debts and raising of his children.

Mary his widow immediately sold the rest of the land to John Wyatt, the purchaser of all the other property, and handed over the house to two trustees for the children's benefit.[8] She probably moved away from Winslow with the children after that because the only later trace of them in the parish registers is the burial of another Edward Tomlin in 1731.

Another **Edward Tomlin, a carrier** died in 1684. His baptism is not recorded at Winslow so his relationship to William and his son Edward is unknown. He left goods worth £35.[9] He owned a cart and two horses for his business, but also some livestock and farming equipment. He made a deathbed surrender of 9 acres of land to his daughter Mary, born in 1655, who immediately mortgaged it.[10]

Edward must already have made similar or better arrangements for his son **Thomas Tomlin** (1650–86), who got only a shilling in his father's will but mortgaged 9 acres in 1682 and at some point became owner of the family home, 8–10 Horn Street (*see Figure 18*) which Edward had bought in 1651.[11] The house had been extended before 1681 to include Thomas' family, but he and his wife Elizabeth had no children.

Edward's part of the house included a hall house, chamber over it, buttery, washhouse, lower chamber, orchard and barns. Edward's widow, Hester, died in 1686 and her inventory came to £7, consisting almost entirely of household goods. The carrier's and farming assets must already have been passed on.[12]

---

[7] WMC 9 May 1709, see www.winslow-history.org.uk/winslow_court1709.shtm.

[8] WMC 30 September 1715, see www.winslow-history.org.uk/winslow_court1715.shtm.

[9] HALS, A25/4198 (inventory), 121AW27 (will).

[10] WMC 17 October 1684, see www.winslow-history.org.uk/winslow_court1684.shtm.

[11] WMC 3 October 1651, see www.winslow-history.org.uk/winslow_court1651.shtm.

[12] HALS, A25/4246.

Thomas died the same year and his widow sold the house. His sister Mary married **Francis Shaw**, apparently also in 1686, who probably took over the carrier's business because he owned a horse when he died in 1687.[13] His assets came to £19. Mary lived as a widow until 1712 when her inventory came to £8.[14] The two inventories give details of the same house, which consisted of lower room and buttery, chamber and garret. This is clearly 6 Horn Street, which Mary's father, Thomas, must have built for her and her husband next door to his own house.

Francis and Mary Shaw had one child, **Sarah Shaw** (1687–1745), who has left an unusual amount of information for an unmarried woman.[15] In 1712 she inherited the house and 6½ acres from her mother.[16] She was able to sign her name to the Oath of Allegiance in 1723.[17] She is usually referred to as spinster, which is a designation of marital status although she could have done paid spinning or lace-making.

Sarah worked for the churchwardens. In 1731 she was paid 8s for looking after a baby, and from 1734 until the accounts written in the parish register end in 1737 she received, as 'Dame Shaw', a variable quarterly payment from them.[18] This was not charity as it was sometimes as much as 19s whereas charitable payments were rarely more than 2s. For three years, and perhaps much longer, she had an income of a little under £2 a year from the church. It appears that she was working when required rather than receiving a regular wage, and probably the churchwardens employed her as a nurse.

She sold an acre of land in 1733, and presumably her other property in years where the court rolls have not survived.[19] Selling land slowly was a means of converting an inheritance into an income for someone who did not have to think about their

---

[13] HALS, A25/4242.

[14] HALS, A25/4655.

[15] Mostly in Winslow Parish Registers.

[16] WMC, 3 October 1712, see www.winslow-history.org.uk/winslow_court1712.shtm

[17] www.winslow-history.org.uk/winslow_oath1723.shtm

[18] www.winslow-history.org.uk/winslow_churchwardens-accounts1724.shtm.

[19] WMC 22 October 1733, see www.winslow-history.org.uk/winslow_court1733.shtm.

children's interests. By 1742 she was recorded as tenant of part of The Bull,[20] so she had sold her house but continued to occupy it, and 6 Horn Street remained in the same ownership as The Bull until the twentieth century. It was clearly not destroyed by the fire which burned down The Bull in 1748.

Sarah's burial was recorded in 1745 with her name written as Sarah Shoe. The last Tomlins in Winslow were among the poorest people for whom there is more evidence than just entries in the parish registers. That was because they had a little property which they gradually converted into cash. Early deaths were mainly responsible for the disappearance of one of Winslow's most notable surnames.

---

[20] WMC 20 October 1742, see www.winslow-history.org.uk/winslow_court1742.shtm.

Chapter 11:
Winslow in 1770

If someone who knew Winslow in 1640 could have returned in 1770, they would not have recognised where they were.

The timber-framed, evenly-sized, thatched houses had been partly replaced by brick and tile buildings. Some were taller than others but all were dwarfed by a huge mansion.

The ridges of the open fields were hidden by hedges, sheep and cattle grazed on formerly arable land, and even the layout of the roads outside the centre was different.

Other changes were less immediately obvious: the descendants of yeoman families had become tenants of the Lowndes estate, the town contained a significant number of professional men, and communications had been much improved by the turnpike.

Many of these changes were part of national trends by which market towns became less agricultural and more urban.[1] A small sign of this was the appointment of a 'scavenger' to keep the streets clean, first mentioned at the 1700 manor court, who helped to get rid of the 28 dunghills reported as creating a nuisance in 1703.[2]

In Winslow some of the changes did not happen until the nineteenth century (street lighting, planned housing development) or were literally superficial (brick fronts on timber-framed houses). Nevertheless, those which took place before 1770 were very significant for a small town, and directly or indirectly linked to what William Lowndes and his money had done.

---

[1] E L Jones and M E Falkus, 'Urban improvement and the English economy in the seventeenth and eighteenth centuries', in Peter Borsay (editor), *The Eighteenth Century Town: A Reader in Urban History* (London: Longman, 1990), 116–58, 119.

[2] WMC 30 March 1703, see www.winslow-history.org.uk/winslow_court1703.shtm.

Population

The population of Winslow was estimated at about 1,100 in *circa* 1730 by Browne Willis[3] and in *circa* 1790 by Frederic Morton Eden,[4] and was actually counted as 1,101 in the first census of 1801.[5] This represents an increase of something like 40 per cent on the likely population in 1640, rather more than the rate of growth nationally. It appears that the population increased significantly and then stabilised, which is most likely to be due to the effect of William Lowndes' money. No similar growth happened again until the railway arrived in 1850.

There is a return of men eligible to serve as jurors from the October 1769 Buckinghamshire Quarter Sessions.[6] They represented the wealthier part of each community, and as copyhold property was no impediment, Winslow produced a substantial number: twenty-four, compared to seventeen for Olney and fourteen for Stony Stratford.

Winslow was now a town with a significant class of prosperous tradesmen. The occupations represented include baker, blacksmith, butcher, carpenter, cordwainer, currier, draper, glazier, glover, grocer, innkeeper, maltster, mason and wheelwright, and there were a number of farmers. Lawyers, doctors and clergy were not included in the return but would have added at least another six. Other trades and occupations known to have been practised around 1770 are apothecary, carrier, clockmaker, collar-maker, cooper, ironmonger, lace-dealer, milliner, postmaster, schoolmaster, tailor and tanner.

Housing

During the eighteenth century, large-scale fires played an important part in altering the appearance of many towns and villages, including Buckingham and Great Horwood. Local authorities tried to stop the use of thatch and to insist on brick and

---

[3] BL, Add.Ms. 5840 f.177v.
[4] *The State of the Poor* (1797), 3.cccliii.
[5] www.winslow-history.org.uk/winslow_census.shtm.
[6] CBS, JB/1.

tile for replacement buildings.[7] Winslow never suffered a devastating fire which led to wholesale rebuilding, and therefore did not acquire anything like a uniform appearance, but there were some small-scale fires which were disastrous enough for the people involved:

- In 1697, six houses in The Walk burned down.[8] The area affected was limited because both 9–11 The Walk and the Baptist meeting-house clearly survived. At least two of the houses were rebuilt by 1698.

- There were two fires in 1748, one on the north side of Horn Street and one at the south-east end of the High Street.[9] Three people reported damage to their buildings in the first and nine in the second, and many more suffered loss of goods.

- In 1775 a fire started behind the Three Pigeons (22 High Street) and spread north, burning down two houses and many outbuildings.[10]

Later alterations make it difficult to see how the rebuilding was done in most cases, but The Bull burned down in the first fire of 1748, and its rebuilt form was not changed substantially afterwards (*see Figure 8*).

The first known fire insurance policies for Winslow are from 1719, and insurance by wealthier residents gradually became more common. Policies from the 1770s differentiate between building styles and show that brick and tile, much preferred by the insurers, was gradually replacing thatch, particularly around the Market Square and Cow Street.[11] The brickmakers who had supplied Winslow Hall early in the century had to find new customers.

Joseph Bigg, who lived at 21–25 Market Square, had a carpenter in 1715 making him a balcony and working on the 'leads' on the roof, which presumably means his house was

---

[7] Jones and Falkus, 'Urban improvement', 120.
[8] www.winslow-history.org.uk/seventeenthc-fire1697.shtm.
[9] www.winslow-history.org.uk/seventeenthc-fire1748.shtm.
[10] *Jackson's Oxford Journal,* 26 August 1775.
[11] Jones and Falkus, 'Urban improvement', 124;
    www.winslow-history.org.uk/winslow_fire_insurance.shtm.

already brick and tile, which is not surprising as he described himself as a bricklayer.[12] However, as the Market Square avoided a major fire, this was a piecemeal process and tended to involve adding a brick façade while retaining the timber frame behind. This was effective enough for a visitor at the end of the eighteenth century to say that the houses were mostly brick.[13]

Few inventories survive after the early eighteenth century. The ones which do exist are for shopkeepers and tradesmen, which represents how the balance of economic power in Winslow had shifted away from farmers, even if it is an accident of survival. There are seven inventories from between 1731 and 1755. Two drapers, one ironmonger and one carpenter had their shop or workshop on the ground floor and lived in two upper storeys, the normal arrangement for purpose-built Winslow shops ever since.

No-one now had a hall. The equivalent room in the house of John Hicks the maltster had become the 'dwelling house', and for

Figure 25: Repairs to the former Plough Inn, Horn Street, in 2007 show how it consists of two timber-framed buildings with brick infill, one thatched and one with a tiled roof providing an extra storey, all rendered and painted when brick became less fashionable.

[12] TNA, E112/931 no.36: Stockley v Bigg (1721).

[13] John Britton et al., *The Beauties of England and Wales* (London, 1801), 1.339.

nearly everyone else the parlour was the principal living room, no longer containing any beds. Only William Stockley, carpenter, had beds in his main living room, described as the chamber over the shop.[14] There was always a separate kitchen, but not in a separate building. Matthew Clarke the draper had a dining room and three bedrooms including a best room.[15] Grace Aldridge had a bedroom with an adjacent closet for her clothes, five other rooms with beds and a garret used for storage.[16] Henry Stutsbury, ironmonger, apparently had a kitchen on the ground floor, and also a back room over the cellar and a little room at the cellar stairhead; in all there were three rooms with beds and 'the room over the shop' served as his parlour.[17]

Thomas Hazzard kept the Royal Oak, so his arrangements were rather different: he had two parlours and three upper rooms.[18]

There was also a significant change in the content of houses, reflecting a broader improvement in material standards of living which is documented in much of rural England.[19] By the mid-eighteenth century people usually had pictures and books. They often had glassware and a clock. They were not restricted to pewter and earthenware: Elizabeth Seaton had some Delft plates,[20] and Henry Stutsbury had a glass dish and stand. Men normally had a 'fowling piece' or other sort of gun; even the spinster Grace Tofield had a gun rod.[21] Furniture had become ornamental as well as functional: William Stockley had a dressing table veneered with ash, a deal table-top painted red and a 'mahogany waiter'.

Entertainment

There is no information about entertainment in Winslow in 1640, but both popular and elite activities around 1770 are documented. Two 'strolling players' were buried in Winslow in

---

[14] HALS, A25/4726 (1755).
[15] TNA, PROB 3/30/24 (1731).
[16] TNA, PROB 3/41/72 (1741).
[17] HALS, 191 AW5 (1750).
[18] HALS, A25/4717 (1737).
[19] Spufford, *The Great Reclothing*, 3.
[20] HALS, 196AW10 (1758).
[21] HALS, A25/4743 (1764).

June 1758, so the town was on their circuit by then, due presumably to the turnpike.[22] William Neal of The Bell, born in 1816, recalled:

> 'Bull-baiting, cock-fighting, and badger-drawing I have witnessed with my own eyes on our Market-square, on Shrove-Tuesday, the great feast day',

so these must have been practised in 1770.[23] According to a description from the end of the century, there was an iron ring set into the Market Square for bull-baiting, and it was 'throwing at cocks' rather than fighting which was the attraction on Shrove Tuesday.[24]

The first reference to a bowling green is from 1801, when James Burnham bequeathed it in his will, but it may already have been functioning in 1770 or soon afterwards as the grocer Francis Collins mentioned a garden on the same site in his will,[25] and bowls was played somewhere in 1796. The original green is now part of the churchyard. Throughout the nineteenth century bowls was a pastime for the professional class and the most prosperous innkeepers and shopkeepers.

The elite pursuit of fox-hunting was established in the area by 1770 and appears to have been the bond between Thomas Selby and William Lowndes V which led Selby to bequeath him the Whaddon estate. It would have been encouraged by enclosure and the consequent prevalence of grassland and hedges. A large estate farmed by tenants who could not object to their landlord's hunting activities was a prerequisite for a successful hunt and exactly what Winslow provided in 1770. Squires 'hunted everything that came to hand', which in Winslow would have been primarily foxes and hares, without any formal divisions between hunting 'countries', and the hunt was also used to pursue poachers and sheep-stealers.[26]

---

[22] Clear, *King's Village*, 73.

[23] *Bucks Herald*, 27 November 1886.

[24] G M Woodward, *Eccentric Excursions* (1796), 90–93.

[25] TNA, PROB 11/965/112.

[26] Raymond Carr, *English Fox Hunting: A History* (London: Weidenfeld and Nicolson, 1976), 57–58.

William Selby-Lowndes (1807–86), William's grandson, is credited with founding the Selby-Lowndes or Whaddon Chase Hunt, but hunting in Buckinghamshire had begun long before that. The Duke of Buckingham established England's first fox hunt, the Bilsdale, in Yorkshire in 1668, and might have started an interest in foxhunting in north Buckinghamshire although he hunted deer in Whaddon Chase.[27] The Althorp hunt in Northamptonshire was pursuing foxes by the 1770s, and the Spencers knew Selby and his Lowndes heir through the hunt; likewise the Quorn and Pytchley.[28] In Oxfordshire John Warde set up his foxhounds in the area which became the Bicester and Warden Hill Hunt in 1778.[29]

Communications

Before the Wendover and Buckingham Turnpike was created in 1721, the main route north from Aylesbury went through East Claydon, not Winslow. In about 1686 a War Office survey found that Winslow had 26 spare beds and 45 standings for horses, about a third of what was available in the much better connected Buckingham and Stony Stratford.[30] The Act creating the turnpike did not specify the route, but it appears that one through Winslow was soon adopted, certainly before 1742 when the continuation Act was passed.[31]

Winslow therefore became roughly the geographical centre, with the result that the turnpike trustees, who included members of the Lowndes family, met at The Bell at least from 1772, and Winslow lawyers served as clerks: Samuel Yeates in the 1760s and 1770s, then James Burnham.[32]

The construction of the turnpike brought the improvement and in some cases realignment of existing roads rather than the creation of new ones, but the fact that the most important route

---

[27] The Bilsdale Hunt, www.bilsdalehunt.co.uk [accessed 30 January 2020].

[28] Carr, *English Fox Hunting*, 52.

[29] Ralph Greaves, *The Bicester and Warden Hill Hunt* (London: Bicester and Warden Hill Hunt, 1948), 7.

[30] TNA, WO 30/50.

[31] Gulland, *Toll Roads*, 101.

[32] Gulland, *Toll Roads*, 100–01.

through Winslow now went north-south, following the High Street, rather than west-east along Horn Street and Sheep Street, was the beginning of a reorientation of the town which became much more significant in the nineteenth century.

As a result of the turnpike, travel to London became much quicker and more frequent. By 1750 there was a wagon to Winslow from the Oxford Arms in Warwick Lane near St Paul's in London on Fridays and a coach from The Bell, also in Warwick Lane, on Thursdays and Saturdays. Winslow had already been served by a London wagon in 1715, which also went to Buckingham and other villages,[33] and in the 1660s a carrier brought wine from London to The Angel, but there was now a passenger service too.

In 1767 the Buckingham Old Stage-Coach advertised a journey to London in one day: it left Buckingham at 4am on Mondays and Fridays, stopping for breakfast at Aylesbury and dinner at Chalfont.[34] The fare for an inside passenger from the Three Pigeons at Winslow was 9s, including 20lbs of luggage. There were also carrier's services between Winslow and London on four days of the week by this time.

Richard Lowndes was the only person in Winslow who kept his own coach, although the lawyers Ferdinando Southam and Samuel Yeates had two-wheeled chaises, so the stage-coach service was the principal method of long-distance travel.[35] Travelling on the turnpike could be hazardous, however. Thomas Ives, his son and a companion were attacked by a robber shortly after leaving Aylesbury on their way home to Winslow, but overcame their assailant and took him back to Aylesbury.[36]

The development of the wagon with four wheels to replace the two-wheeled cart enabled much larger loads to be transported, but only if the roads were good enough.[37] John Meakes the carrier in 1687 had four horses – presumably packhorses – but no cart or

---

[33] *Merchants and Traders Necessary Companion* (1715), 18.
[34] *Jackson's Oxford Journal*, 31 October 1767.
[35] TNA, T47/3-5: duty paid on coaches, 1757–66.
[36] *Whitehall Evening Post*, 25 October 1754.
[37] Gulland, *Toll Roads*, 9.

wagon.[38] Another carrier, Edward Tomlin, had two horses and a cart in 1684.[39] The first reference to a wagon is in the 1706 inventory of Richard Seaton, a yeoman, who also owned two carts.[40] In 1710 another carrier, William Kirby had three horses, a wagon and two carts.[41]

The turnpike allowed the growth of enterprises such as the butter wagons to take agricultural produce to London, although this also led the trustees to complain about low tolls and excessive weights.[42] Winslow later, in 1792, acquired a short-lived weighing engine for checking wagons' loads, commemorated in the name of Chequers (check 'ouse) End.[43] The fact that coal was available in Winslow to a few people, such as the innkeeper Thomas Hazzard in 1737, must also be due to transport by wagon, in that case probably from Bedford, the nearest inland port before the era of canals.[44] In 1798, the Posse Comitatus lists sixteen wagons and 39 carts.[45]

Lowndes-town

Winslow in 1770 was in many ways the town William Lowndes had begun to make it at the start of the century. There is no way of knowing how much of a vision he really had for his birthplace, but he was a believer in promoting his family, he was a strong Anglican and (according to his will) he was an opponent of 'faction' in public life. In all these respects Winslow developed during the eighteenth century in ways which would have gratified him.

Every community develops through its own unique combination of local and national factors, and some changes would have come to Winslow anyway sooner or later, but the fact that it did not shrink into a village or expand into a larger town

---

[38] HALS, A25/4270.
[39] HALS, A25/4198.
[40] HALS, A25/4583.
[41] HALS, A25/4614.
[42] *Journal of the House of Commons*, 13 March 1766.
[43] Gulland, *Toll Roads*, 108.
[44] HALS, A25/4717.
[45] Beckett (editor), *Buckinghamshire Posse Comitatus*, 210-13.

was partly due to Lowndes. It is beyond the scope of this book to compare Winslow to the other small towns of Buckinghamshire, but some changes happened earlier in Winslow – such as enclosure – and others later or not at all – such as systematic planning and rebuilding – because of what Lowndes' descendants did or chose not to do.

Lowndes carefully set up a system of inheritance which his unreliable son could not disrupt, and ownership of the manor and most of his property remained in the hands of his descendants until 1897.

He concentrated land into one estate so that the larger farmers in 1770 were tenants rather than owner-occupiers. It was now possible to become a farmer without inheriting land, but former farming families could also fall rapidly into poverty. Some of the tenant farmers lived outside the town on enclosed farms as a result of enclosure, a change which took place earlier in Winslow than in most of Buckinghamshire because of Richard Lowndes' membership of Parliament.

Few people alive in 1770 could remember what Winslow looked like before Winslow Hall was there. Building the hall had provided a short-term economic boost: temporary employment for many, and in the longer term work for servants and trade for shops. The London craftsmen who helped to build it gave local tradesmen insights into different ways of working.

Winslow Hall was a much smaller house than those built by the Verneys at Claydon and the Temples at Stowe, and the Lowndes family never tried to emulate the Buckinghamshire aristocracy, but it was at the heart of the town instead of being in the middle of extensive parkland. Its visual and psychological effect was therefore different. Its occupants, as JPs and lords of the manor, had legal as well as moral authority over their neighbours rather than over a usually invisible tenantry.

Red brick was a rare sight in Winslow before 1700 but was normal for the best houses by 1770. Most property in Winslow remained copyhold until the late nineteenth century, long after freehold had become the norm elsewhere, at least partly because the seventeenth-century manorial system which the Lowndes family inherited remained satisfactory for most people.

William Lowndes brought substantial money into Winslow which he had accumulated elsewhere. That was not the case with his descendants. Their property in Winslow was their main source of income, and they increased their capital only through marriage. William Lowndes V, his great-grandson, lord of the manor in 1770, did not have any paid employment, although an unexpected inheritance later moved him up to a different level of wealth.

Winslow's economy in 1770 was based on its position as the market town for the surrounding area, with lawyers and doctors who served the neighbouring gentry as well as shopkeepers, tradesmen and farmers. Winslow Fair was a significant place for hiring workers.

The Lowndes family were involved in the building of the turnpike and Winslow's location on its amended route improved connections, particularly with London, providing access to new markets. Meetings of the Turnpike Trust, social activities related to hunting, political and legal business at Winslow Hall, all brought wealthy visitors to Winslow. Economically it was very much a small town rather than a large village, although its legal status remained that of a single manor.

By 1770 the Baptists had declined and the Independents had not yet started, so the Church of England was in a stronger position than it ever had been since 1640, and in John Rawbone it appears to have had an active and resident minister after the long and unpopular reign of his partly absentee predecessor.

Winslow's new status as a conformist and subservient town was satirised by G M Woodward in 1796:[46]

'No people pay greater deference to the will of the *squire* in any part of his Majesty's dominions. The hat that appears rooted to the head during the whole of the day immediately becomes flexible on his approach, and a low bow, almost to the derangement of the spinal bone, takes place on the occasion.

---

[46] Woodward, 'Macklin's Man of the World' in *Eccentric Excursions*, 90–93.

They ask permission at what they call the *great house*, for the most trifling recreation, an instance of which took place on the arrival of a party of players. It seemed the general wish of the town to have them perform, but what was to be done? The squire was from home, and it was impossible any thing could be decided till his return.

'Fortunately he was absent but a few days, and on his arrival was presented with a petition in due form signed by the players, and some of the principal inhabitants. At length after much consideration, and many weighty reasons respecting taking money out of the town, and other *evil tendencies*, a few nights for rational amusement was granted.

'This excess of ridiculous subserviency would admit of no excuse for its folly, only that the present possessor of the *Grande Maison*, and adjacent estates, is a truly respectable character, a worthy man, and what will be admired by many, an *excellent sportsman*. But let the person be possessed of good or bad qualities, it seems a rule in this place to pay adulation to the *higher powers* 'let wha will be meenester.'

This last sentence quotes a character named Sir Pertinax MacSycophant, a devious Scot who has been describing people 'striving to catch a look or a smile fra the great mon' and explains how he did the same for 35 years, whoever was minister.[47]

The whole passage is an exaggeration for comic effect, and there is some evidence of a different attitude among local people. In the 1784 pariamentary election for Buckinghamshire, the first time there had been a contest for 50 years, Winslow had ten electors, but only three of them cast their vote in the same way as William Selby-Lowndes, and two opposed him completely.

Nevertheless in 1770 Winslow had had a resident squire for nearly seventy years.

Woodward also described what Winslow looked and felt like after he was awoken from his night's sleep at The Bell by the noise of a pig-killing:

---

[47] I am grateful to Professor Paul Goring for explaining the quotation.

'The general appearance of the town, from the party-coloured beams, long casements, multiplicity of windows, and balconies, somewhat resembles Pekin in China as printed on ancient bed-curtains. As to the produce of the place, the town and country about is famous for *good pork* and *butter, stale ale* and *intolerable fat bacon*.—

'The inscriptions in the church-yard afford an excellent specimen of their resolution to continue the same set of names from generation to generation. This forms the best part of their characters, as they are much attached to each other, and think nothing on the globe can equal their own precincts, on which account they herd together like a well stocked warren of rabbits!—

'Their morning amusement after the exercise of *pig-killing* is over, is generally a saunter on the market-place, to enquire about the chit-chat of the town, to stare at a *new chimney*, or any other *momentous object*, that may happen to present itself; the afternoon is spent in waiting anxiously for the arrival of the *Banbury coach* from London, in order to look at the *passengers* when they alight at the *Three Pigeons*; and the evening concludes with a game at *bowls*, or *cards*.'

This was of course meant to amuse sophisticated readers, but it was clearly also based on careful observation. A town which had been traumatised by the Civil War and had been the scene of radical preaching and challenges to power was now a well-fed and prosperous place in which nothing much happened.

William Lowndes would probably have approved.

Bibliography

Allen D E, 'Joseph Dandridge and the first Aurelian Society', *Entomologist's Record* 78 (1966), 89–94

Allen, Robert C, *Enclosure and the Yeoman: The Agricultural Development of the South Midlands 1450–1850* (Oxford: Clarendon, 1992)

Austen-Leigh, Richard Arthur, *The Eton College Register 1698-1752* (Eton: Ballantyne, 1927)

Baines, Arnold, 'The signatories of the Orthodox Confession of 1679', *Baptist Quarterly* 17 (1957), 35–42, 74–86, 122–28, 170–78; also published as a booklet (Carey Kingsgate, 1960)

Barley M W, 'Rural building in England', in J Thirsk (editor), *The Agrarian History of England and Wales Volume 2: 1640–1750: Agrarian Change* (Cambridge: Cambridge University Press, 1985), 590–685

Beckett, Ian F W, *Call to Arms: The Story of Bucks' Citizen Soldiers* (Buckingham: Barracuda, 1985)

Beckett, Ian F W (editor), *The Buckinghamshire Posse Comitatus 1798* (Aylesbury: Buckinghamshire Records Society 1985).

Beckett, Ian F W, *Wanton Troopers: Buckinghamshire in the Civil Wars 1640–1660* (Barnsley: Pen and Sword, 2015)

Berry, Helen, 'Polite consumption: Shopping in eighteenth century England', *Transactions of the RHS* 12 (2002), 375–94

Bloom, J Harvey and James, R Rutson, *Medical Practitioners in the Diocese of London 1529–1725* (Cambridge: Cambridge University Press, 1935)

Bonfield, Lloyd, 'Normative rules and property transmission: Reflections on the link between marriage and inheritance in early modern England', in Bonfield L, Smith R M and Wrightson K (editors), *The World We Have Gained* (Oxford: Blackwell, 1986), 155–76

Broad, John, 'Whigs and deer-stealers in other guises: A return to the origins of the Black Act', *Past and Present* 119 (1988), 56–72

Broad, John, 'The changing face of employment in Buckingham, 1618–1798', *Records of Buckinghamshire* 34 (1992), 46–60

Broad, John (editor), *Buckinghamshire Dissent and Parish Life 1669–1712* (Aylesbury: Buckinghamshire Records Society volume 28, 1993)

Broad, John, 'Parish economies of welfare, 1650–1834', *Historical Journal* 42 (1999), 985–1006

Broad, John, *Transforming English Rural Society* (Cambridge: Cambridge University Press, 2004)

Broad, John, 'Regional perspectives and variations in English dairying, 1650–1850', in Hoyle R W (editor), *People, Landscape and Alternative Agriculture: Essays for Joan Thirsk* (British Agricultural History Society, 2004)

Broad, John, 'The parish and the poor in England, 1600–1850', in Broad J and Schuurman, Anton (editors), *Wealth and Poverty in European Rural Societies from the Sixteenth to Nineteenth Century* (Turnhout: Brepols, 2014), 199–219

Buckinghamshire in the 1760s and 1820s (Aylesbury: Buckinghamshire Archaeological Society, 2000)

Buckinghamshire Probate Inventories 1661–1714, edited by Michael Reed (Aylesbury: Buckinghamshire Records Society volume 24, 1988)

Buckinghamshire Gardens Trust, *Winslow Hall* (2015)

Butterfield, Ruth, ' "The royal commission of King Jesus": General Baptist expansion and growth, 1640–1660', *Baptist Quarterly* 35.2 (April 1993), 56–80

Campbell-Smith, Duncan, *Masters of the Post: The Authorized History of the Royal Mail* (London: Penguin, 2011)

Carr, Raymond, *English Fox Hunting: A History* (London: Weidenfeld and Nicolson, 1976)

Clay, Christopher, 'Landlords and estate management in England', in Thirsk J (editor), *The Agrarian History of England and Wales volume 2: 1640–1750: Agrarian Change* (Cambridge: Cambridge University Press, 1985), 119–297

Clear, Arthur, *The King's Village in Demesne* (Winslow, 1894)

Cole, William, *The Blecheley Diary of the Rev. William Cole MA FSA 1765–67*, edited by Francis Griffin Stokes (London: Constable, 1931)

Colvin, Howard *Biographical Dictionary of British Architects* (third edition, London and New Haven: Yale Univerity Press, 1995)

Crosby, Thomas, *The History of the English Baptists* (London, 1739)

Davis, Richard W, *Political Change and Continuity 1760–1885* (Newton Abbot: David and Charles, 1972)

Desmond, Ray, *Dictionary of British and Irish Botanists and Horticulturists* (London: Natural History Museum, 1994)

Dix, Kenneth, *Benjamin Keach and a Monument to Liberty* (Dunstable: Fauconberg, 1985)

Doster, G Reid, 'Discipline and ordination at Berkhamsted General Baptist Church, 1712–1718', *Baptist Quarterly* 27.3 (July 1977), 128–38

Downes K, 'Wren, Sir Christopher (1632–1723), architect, mathematician, and astronomer', *Oxford Dictionary of National Biography,* www.oxforddnb.com/view/article/30019

Eden, Frederic Morton, *The State of the Poor* (London, 1797)

Eland G, 'The building of Winslow Hall', *Records of Buckinghamshire* volume 11 (1926), 406–29

Evenden, Doreen, 'Gender differences in the licensing and practice of female and male surgeons in early modern England', *Medical History* 42 (1998), 194–216

Foley, Terry and Hunt, Julian, *The Archive Photographs Series: Winslow* (second edition, Cheltenham: The History Press, 2019)

Gaunt, Peter *The Cromwellian Gazetteer* (Gloucester: Alan Sutton and The Cromwell Association, 1987)

Gentles, Ian J, 'Skippon, Philip, appointed Lord Skippon under the protectorate (d. 1660)', *Oxford Dictionary of National Biography,*www.oxforddnb.com/view/article/25693

Godber, Joyce, *History of Bedfordshire* (Bedford: Bedfordshire County Council, 1984)

Goose, Nigel and Hinde, Andrew, 'Estimating local population sizes at fixed points in time: Part II–specific sources', *Local Population Studies* 78 (Spring 2007), 74–88

Gough, Richard, *The History of Myddle*, edited by David Hey (Harmondsworth: Penguin, 1981)

Greaves, Richard L, 'Wildman, Sir John (1622/3–1693)', *Oxford Didctionary of National Biography,* www.oxforddnb.com/view/article/29405

Greene, Richard, 'Egerton [née Fyge; other married name Field], Sarah (1670–1723), poet', *Oxford Didctionary of National Biography,* www.oxforddnb.com/view/article/37390

Gulland, Peter, *The Toll Roads of Buckinghamshire 1706–1881* (Aylesbury: Buckinghamshire Archaeological Society, 2017)

Habakkuk, John, 'The land settlement and the restoration of Charles II', *Transactions of the Royal Historical Society*, 28 (1978), 201–22

Hanham A, 'Lowndes, William (1652–1724), Treasury official', *Oxford Dictionary of National Biography,* www.oxforddnb.com/view/article/17099

Hanley H A, *The Buckinghamshire Sheriffs* (Buckinghamshire Record Office, 1992)

Hanley, Hugh, *Apprenticing in a Market Town* (Chichester: Phillimore, 2005)

Hann, Andrewe and Stobart, Jon, 'Sites of consumption: The display of goods in provincial shops in eighteenth-century England', *Cultural and Social History* 2:2 (2005), 165–87

Hanrahan, David C, *Charles II and the Duke of Buckingham* (Stroud: Sutton, 2006)

Harrington, Melanie, 'The earl of Derby and his tenants', *Economic History Review* 64 (2011), 1195–1217

Hill, Christopher, *People and Ideas in 17th-Century England* (Brighton: Harvester, 1986)

Hill, Christopher, *A Tinker and a Poor Man* (London: Norton, 1988)

Hill, Christopher, *The World Turned Upside Down* (London: Penguin, reprinted 1991)

Hindle, Steve, *On the Parish? The Micro-Politics of Poor Relief in Rural England c.1550–1750* (Oxford: Clarendon, 2004)

Hitchcock, Tim, 'Marryott, Matthew (bap. 1670, d. 1731/2), workhouse promoter and contractor', *Oxford Dictionary of National Biography,* www.oxforddnb.com/view/article/66535

Hitchcock, Tim, 'Paupers and preachers: The SPCK and the parochial workhouse movement', in Davison, Lee and others (editors), *Stilling the Grumbling Hive* (Stroud: Sutton, 1992)

Hutton, Ronald, *The Restoration* (Oxford: Oxford University Press, 1995)

Jones E L and Falkus M E, 'Urban improvement and the English economy in the seventeenth and eighteenth centuries', in Borsay, Peter (editor), *The Eighteenth Century Town: A Reader in Urban History* (London: Longman, 1990)

Joyce, Herbert, *The History of the Post Office* (London: Bentley, 1893)

Kelke, W Hastings, 'Creslow Pastures', *Records of Buckinghamshire* volume 1 (1858), 255–67

Kreitzer, Larry J, *William Kiffen and His World (Part 4)* (Oxford: Regent's Park College, 2015)

Langford, Paul, 'Property and 'virtual representation' in eighteenth-century England', *Historical Journal* 31 (1988), 83–115

Lipscomb, George, *History and Antiquities of the County of Buckingham* (London: Robins, 1847)

Livingstone, Natalie, *The Mistresses of Cliveden* (London: Arrow, 2015)

Luke, Sir Samuel, *Journals of Sir Samuel Luke*, edited by Philip L G (three volumes, Oxford: Oxfordshire Record Society, 1947–53)

Luke, Sir Samuel, *The Letter Books of Sir Samuel Luke 1644–45* (Historic Manuscripts Commission JP4, Her Majesty's Stationery Office, 1963)

Lynch, Beth, 'Keach, Benjamin (1640–1704), Particular Baptist minister', *Oxford Dictionary of National Biography,* www.oxforddnb.com/view/article/15202

Manton J O and Hollis E, *Buckinghamshire Trade Tokens Issued in the Seventeenth Century* (Aylesbury: Buckinghamshire Archaeological Society, 1933)

Markham, Sir Frank, *History of Milton Keynes and District* (Luton: White Crescent, 1973)

Marshall, Lynda M, *The Rural Population of Bedfordshire* (Bedfordshire Historical Record Society 16, 1934)

Melton, Frank T, *Sir Robert Clayton and the Origins of English Deposit Banking 1658–1685* (Cambridge: Cambridge University Press, 1986)

Melton, Frank T, 'A rake refinanced: The fortune of George Villiers, Second Duke of Buckingham, 1671-1685', *Huntington Library Quarterly* 51 (1988), 297–318

Minutes of the General Assembly of the General Baptist Churches in England, voume 1: 1654–1728, edited by Whitley W T (London: Baptist Historical Society, 1908)

Moore, John S, *Counting People* (Oxford: Oxbow, 2013)

Moss, Jennifer, *Ways and Means: A study of the life and career of William Lowndes, Secretary to the Treasury and his descendants* (Chesham, 2014)

Mui, Hoh-cheung and Lorna H, *Shops and Shopkeeping in Eighteenth-century England* (London: Routledge, 1989)

Murdoch, Tessa (editor), *Noble Households. Eighteenth-Century Inventories of Great English Houses* (Cambridge: John Adamson, 2006)

Noy, David (editor), *Winslow Manor Court Books 1327–1377 and 1423–1460* (Buckinghamshire Records Society volumes 35 and 36, 2011)

Noy, David, *Winslow in 1556* (Aylesbury: Buckinghamshire Archaeological Society, 2013)

Noy, David, 'Martha Janes (1601–1687), An earl's mistress: from Turville via Winslow and Granborough to the siege of Bolton Castle', *Records of Buckinghamshire* volume 60 (2020)

Peacey J T, 'Holland, Cornelius (1600–1671?)', *Oxford Dictionary of National Biography,* www.oxforddnb.com/view/article/13517

Pevsner, Nicholas and Williamson, Elizabeth, *The Buildings of England: Buckinghamshire* (second edition, London: Penguin, 1994)

Priest, Reverend St John, *A General View of Agriculture in Buckinghamshire* (London, 1813)

Reed, Michael, *The Buckinghamshire Landscape* (London: Hodder and Stoughton, 1979)

Richetti, John, *The Life of Daniel Defoe* (Chichester: Blackwell-Wiley 2005)

Saunders, Edward, 'Biographical dictionary of English wrought iron smiths of the seventeenth and eighteenth centuries', *Walpole Society* volume 67 (2005), 237–384

Saving, Norman, *Glimpses of Past Days: Being a Historical Survey of the Town and Parish of Winslow cum Shipton* (Winslow, 1973)

Slack, Paul, *The English Poor Law 1531–1782* (Basingstoke: Macmillan, 1990)

Smith, Pete, 'Winslow Hall', in Airs M and Tyack G (editors), *The Renaissance Villa in Britain, 1500–1700* (Reading: Spire, 2007), 223–46

South, Raymond, *Royal Castle, Rebel Town: Puritan Windsor in Civil War & Commonwealth* (Buckingham: Barracuda, 1981)

Speck W A, *Stability and Strife: England, 1714–1760* (London: Arnold, 1977)

Spufford, Margaret, *The Great Reclothing of Rural England* (London: Hambledon, 1984)

Tate W E, 'Oxfordshire enclosure commissioners, 1737–1856', *Journal of Modern History* volume 23 (1951), 137–45

Tate W E, *The English Village Community and the Enclosure Movement* (London: Gollancz, 1967)

Taylor, Adam, *The History of the English General Baptists: Part First* (London, 1818)

Thirsk, Joan, 'The sale of delinquents' estates during the Interregnum, and the land settlement at the Restoration' (University of London PhD thesis, 1950)

Thirsk, Joan, 'The sales of Royalist land during the Interregnum', *Economic History Review* n.s.5 (1952), 188–207

Thirsk, Joan, 'The Restoration land settlement', *Journal of Modern History* 26 (1954), 315–28

Tinniswood, Adrian, *His Invention So Fertile: A Life of Christopher Wren* (London: Jonathan Cape, 2001)

Turner M E, 'The cost of parliamentary enclosure in Buckinghamshire', *Agricultural History Review* volume 21 (1973), 35–46

Verney, Frances & Margaret, *Memoirs of the Verney Family* (London: Longman, 1894)

Verney, Margaret Maria, *Verney Letters of the Eighteenth Century* (London: Benn, 1930)

Vigne, Randolph, 'Hill, Richard (1655/6–1727), diplomat and public servant', *Oxford Dictionary of National Biography,* www.oxforddnb.com/view/article/13289

Waddell, Brodie, 'The politics of economic distress in the aftermath of the Glorious Revolution, 1689–1702', *English Historical Review*, 130:541 (2015), 318–51

Walker, Austin, *The Excellent Benjamin Keach* (Dundas: Joshua Press, 2004)

Walsh, Claire, 'Stalls, bulks, shops and long-term change in seventeenth- and eighteenth-century England ', in Furnée J H and Lesger C (editors), *The Language of Consumption* (Basingstoke: Palgrave Macmillan 2014), 37–56

White B R, 'Thomas Crosby, Baptist Historian (I)', *Baptist Quarterly* 21.4 (October 1965), 154–68

Whitley W T (editor), *The Church Books of Ford or Cuddington and Amersham in the County of Bucks* (London: Baptist Historical Society, 1912)

Whyman, Susan, *Sociability and Power in Late Stuart England: The Cultural Worlds of the Verneys, 1660–1720* (Oxford: Clarendon, 1999)

Wilson J (editor), *Buckinghamshire Contributions for Ireland, 1642, and Richard Grenville's Military Accounts, 1642–1645* (Buckinghamshire Records Society volume 21, 1983)

Woodward G M, *Eccentric Excursions* (London, 1796)

Wordie J R, 'The South', in Thirsk J (editor), *The Agrarian History of England and Wales volume 1: 1640–1750: Regional Farming Systems* (Cambridge: Cambridge University Press, 1985), 317–57

Wren Society, *Seventeenth Volume* (Oxford, 1940)

Wrightson, Keith and Levine, David, *Poverty and Piety in an English Village: Terling, 1525–1700* (New York: Academic Press, 1979)

Wrigley E A and Schofield R S, *The Population History of England 1541–1871* (Cambridge: Cambridge University Press, 1989)

Yardley, Bruce, 'Villiers, George, second duke of Buckingham (1628–1687)', *Oxford Dictionary of National Biography*, www.oxforddnb.com/view/article/28294

Yelling J A, *Common Field and Enclosure in England 1450–1850* (London: Macmillan, 1977)

Index

- Places in Buckinghamshire (other than Winslow) have been indexed by parish; other places have been indexed by county.
- Surnames given in brackets are the person's maiden or other married names.
- First names were frequently repeated through the generations and readers should be aware that an entry may represent more than one person of that name. In such cases check the context and, where available, the family section and family tree, to identify individuals.

Buckinghamshire Archaeological Society
OUR RECENT PUBLICATIONS

Pots, Potters and Potteries of Buckinghamshire 1200–1910

MICHAEL FARLEY AND BARBARA HURMAN

Fifty years of archaeological excavations and documentary research across come together in this book, which covers all the county's known potteries and potters – eight centuries of a key industry.

£16.50 including postage. A large-format paperback with 132 pages and 56 illustrations.

The toll roads of Buckinghamshire

PETER GULLAND

The turnpike roads of the 18th and 19th centuries set the pattern for the main road network that we use today. This historical account, with maps and a wealth of detail, makes the past visible on the roads we travel every day today.

£15.50 including postage – A4 paperback, 318 pages.

Winslow in 1556: The survey of the manor

DAVID NOY

A historical panorama of Winslow's people – their properties, their occupations, their families and relationships, their petty crimes and long-term feuds – when the surveyor Thomas Gedge called them to account after the dissolution of St Albans Abbey.

£7.50 including postage – paperback, 160 pages

Order by post

by sending a cheque made out to 'Bucks Archaeological Society' to:
BAS Book Orders, County Museum, Church Street, Aylesbury HP20 2QP

Order our books on-line – see below...

An Illustrated History of Early Buckinghamshire
EDITED BY MIKE FARLEY

This is the history of our county from the Ice Age to the Tudors, drawing on recent discoveries by archaeologists and historians. Its seven specialist authors are all members of the Buckinghamshire Archaeological Society.

£14.50 including postage. A large-format paperback with 135 illustrations and 224 pages.

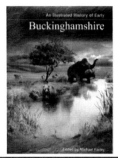

My Dearest Ben…
THEA VAN DAM

An intimate glimpse into the world of Benjamin Disraeli, his family and the women in his life – through their letters. Many books show Disraeli the politician and prime minister, but few reveal his private relationships

£7.00 including postage – paperback, 208 pages

The Chilterns in 1748
BY PEHR KALM, VISITOR FROM FINLAND

The botanist and agricultural economist Pehr Kalm wrote a unique account of life in the Chilterns when on a research mission in 1748. This new edition of Professor Bill Mead's translation is a unique contribution to the area's history.

£8.50 including postage – paperback, 168 pages

Order on-line through the society's website
All our books are available to order on-line, paying by credit card.
Go on-line to https://bas1.org.uk/publications-2 and follow the links.

Buckinghamshire
Archaeological Society

WHY NOT JOIN THE SOCIETY...?

The Society focuses on all aspects of our county's history and works to protect our heritage and historic environment.

So historic buildings and ancient churches, documentary research and the landscapes of the past, local history – as well as archaeology and fieldwork – all are within our remit.

And we're just as concerned about the present as the past: our members were active in assessing the impact that the HS2 high-speed rail line would have on the county's historic buildings and landscapes.

☐ Members receive the annual *Records of Buckinghamshire* free every year, use of the society's Library and winter lectures, summer outings, and the chance to take part in archaeological investigations.

☐ For more details, see the society's website at **www.bas1.org.uk**.

☐ Individual membership, in 2020, is £18 a year, with family membership £22, and junior membership (under 18) £12.

☐ **TO JOIN**, complete the membership form on our website
   or send a cheque to 'Bucks Archaeological Society' to
   BAS, County Museum, Church Street, Aylesbury HP20 2QP

Each year in May society members receive a free copy of that year's *Records of Buckinghamshire*:

Records of Buckinghamshire

New discoveries about the county's extraordinarily rich history and archaeology: from early prehistoric farmers to Romans, Britons, Saxons, Vikings, Normans, medieval lords and peasants ... through to the 20th century all have left marks on our landscape that are visible today.

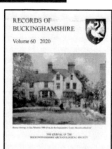

- **To get the latest edition by post,**
   non-members send a cheque for £18.50 to 'Bucks Archaeological Society' to BAS, County Museum, Church Street, Aylesbury HP20 2QP.